Making a Way out of No Way

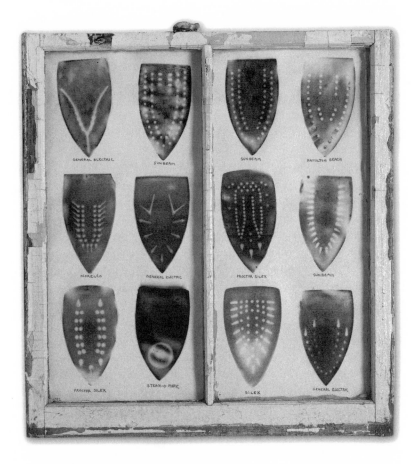

Making a Way out of No Way

AFRICAN AMERICAN WOMEN AND
THE SECOND GREAT MIGRATION

LISA KRISSOFF BOEHM

UNIVERSITY PRESS OF MISSISSIPPI / JACKSON

www.upress.state.ms.us

*Margaret Walker Alexander Series
in African American Studies*

The University Press of Mississippi is a member of
the Association of American University Presses.

Frontispiece (page ii): Cole, Willie, *Domestic I.D. IV.*
1992. Steam iron scorch and pencil on paper, mounted in
recycled wooden window frame, composition (including
frame): 35 x 32 x 1 3/8" (88.9 x 81.3 x 3.5 cm). Publisher:
unpublished. Printer: the artist and The Artist's Studio.
Edition: unique. Acquired through the generosity of
Agnes Gund. Digital Image © The Museum of Modern
Art/Licensed by SCALA / Art Resource, NY.

First printing 2009

∞

Library of Congress Cataloging-in-Publication Data

Boehm, Lisa Krissoff, 1969–
  Making a way out of no way : African American women
and the second great migration / Lisa Krissoff Boehm.
    p. cm. — (Margaret Walker Alexander series in
African American studies)
  Includes bibliographical references and index.
  ISBN 978-1-60473-216-0 (cloth : alk. paper) —
ISBN 978-1-60473-217-7 (pbk. : alk. paper) 1. African
American women—Social conditions—20th century.
2. African American women—History—20th century.
3. African Americans—Migrations—History—20th cen-
tury. 4. Migration, Internal—United States—History—
20th century. 5. Rural-urban migration—United States—
History—20th century. 6. African American women—
Biography. 7. Oral history—United States. I. Title.
  E185.86.B6325 2009
  305.48'896073—dc22   2008033344

British Library Cataloging-in-Publication Data available

For Esther Woods (1913–2005)
and
Madelon Hack Krissoff,
my teachers

Contents

A Note on Style

I wish that all of the women who shared their life stories for this book had had the opportunity to meet. They could have talked together about the Second Great Migration, their attitudes towards work and parenting, and the regional differences between North and South. What a wonderful discussion that would have been! I have in effect lived in this imagined gathering during the years I worked on the manuscript. This book is written in a way that allows the women to come together, at least on the page. When a topic is discussed—for instance, the influence of elders, or treatment by employers—various voices join the conversation, adding personal insights. The reader is a witness to this conversation, just as I am. As with a real-life gathering, the reader does not have to know the complete story of the individual speaking to understand her observation. For readers who would like an occasional reminder of a narrator's life story, I have written biographical sketches, located at the front of the book for easy reference. These sketches provide short descriptions of the lives of the forty women interviewed explicitly for this project. The other voices, drawn from approximately forty additional oral histories located in archival collections, appear intermittently and thus are not included in the biographical sketches section.

I serve as the narrator of the text, bringing the pieces together and adding the historical background necessary for a fuller understanding of the interviews. Throughout the book, the reader will find extended "edited transcripts," or large edited segments in one narrator's voice. These sections are helpful in re-creating the interview experience and in letting a narrator tell her own story in an expanded way. Edited transcripts are used to introduce chapters or book sections. In most cases, the edited transcript on a given subject appears before the historical analysis. This organization was employed with two objectives in mind: 1) the format allows the oral history narrators to speak first, and 2) the format provides readers the chance to explore the nuances and surprises of the oral history transcripts without overt direction.

Transcription has followed this guideline: use the speaker's own grammar, but traditional spelling. There has not been an effort to capture particular dialects (for instance, in dropping the "g" off the end of a verb). At times when a judgment call was needed regarding transcription, I tried to err on the side of honoring what the narrator would have wanted. Statements have been edited for clarity. That said, the best-edited transcripts capture the spoken word, which is far more free-flowing and casual than written text. Transcription is an art form, and a transcription is always a sort of approximation of what was said. Much is attributed to a conversation by body language, voice modulation, nuance, and contextualization.

The questions I asked the narrators have been removed from these edited transcripts. Sentences and paragraphs have at times been reordered so as to make best thematic sense. Words, in most cases, have not been added. In rare cases, statements were trimmed down, with extra words removed, and slightly reworded. While some repetition helps to re-create a true speaking style, too much can prove confusing in written form. For clarification, missing words and references have been placed in the text in brackets.

Certain derogatory terms were left in the narratives, such as racial epithets, as they were used by the narrators to add power to their stories.

I use the women's real names except where pseudonyms are noted.

Biographical Sketches

Mrs. Florence Allison was born in 1926. As a child she lived in Livingston, Alabama. Her parents worked as sharecroppers. Allison married in 1944 and moved to Detroit in 1947. Her husband, a former marine, worked on assembly at Chrysler. Allison had two daughters. She found employment sewing dining room upholstery in a factory, beginning about 1948. She also worked doing alterations at a dry cleaners for approximately twelve years.

Mrs. Annie Davidson Benning was born on June 13, 1911. As a child she lived in Georgia. Later her father moved to Alabama to take a job at the Swift Cotton Mill. Her parents, George and Aidabelle Fannie Davidson, worked as share-croppers. There were ten children in her family. Benning worked at the Belkes Cotton Mill, where she also made nylon during World War II. She worked as a cook and as a nanny. Benning moved to Detroit on September 4, 1948. Her husband worked as a mechanic at a car dealership. After she moved to Detroit, she no longer worked outside the home. Benning raised her four siblings after her mother died.

Mrs. Minnie Chatman was born on March 9, 1916. As a child she lived in DeSoto County, Mississippi. Her parents were Jones and Carrie Richardson. Her father owned a farm, and her mother primarily engaged in housework in her own home. Her parents had ten children. Chatman also lived in Memphis, where she worked in a furniture factory, and in Detroit. She cleaned homes in the Detroit area and also operated her own sewing shop.

Mrs. Lillian Elizabeth Patton Clark was born in 1920 in Flat Lick, Kentucky. Her father was a coal miner, her mother a homemaker; they had seven children. Clark's husband worked for Uniroyal and was a pastor. Clark had two children.

Sharecropper's children, Montgomery, Alabama. Photograph by Arthur Rothstein, February 1937. Library of Congress, Prints and Photographs Division.

The family moved to Michigan in 1943. Clark did not work formally outside the home, but volunteered her efforts on behalf of her husband's congregation (in Ontario, Canada) and in other community efforts.

Mrs. Annie Evelyn Collins was born in 1930. As a child she lived in Admiral County, Alabama. Her parents farmed. She had twelve siblings and even more half-siblings. Collins lived in Covington, Kentucky, in her late teens and moved to Detroit in 1950. She married twice. Collins did day work, served as a housekeeper, cleaned a dentist's office, and worked for the maintenance department at Sears.

Mrs. Ruth Margaret Covington was born in 1930. As a child she lived in Montgomery, Alabama. Her parents were both teachers. Her father also worked as a cook for a doctor and as a minister. He studied Hebrew at a seminary. Her mother worked as an insurance agent for the Atlanta Life Insurance Company. Covington's parents had five children. Covington moved to Detroit in the 1940s, while she was in high school. She married; her husband worked for the DeSoto factory. She had three children, including Zenara Covington, also interviewed for this study. Covington is the sister-in-law of Mattie Bell Fritz. Covington held a wide variety of jobs, including work in a post office and at a VA hospital for thirty years.

Ms. Zenara Covington was born in 1962. The daughter of migrant Ruth Margaret Covington and her husband, she grew up in Lincoln Park, Michigan, and had two siblings. At the time of the interview, Covington was unmarried. She attended the University of Michigan for her undergraduate work, and received a master's degree in speech language pathology from Pennsylvania State University. Covington was a speech language pathologist with the Detroit Medical Center and later at Wayne State University. She opened her own catering business and worked in home health care.

Mrs. Avezinner Dean was born in 1928. As a child she lived in Mississippi. Her father owned his farm, and her mother was a homemaker in her own home. The couple had eleven children. Dean also lived in Alabama, Nashville, and Detroit. She first married in 1946, when she was in the eleventh grade. She later remarried. Dean had several daughters. She worked as a babysitter, a housekeeper, and a hair stylist.

Mrs. Jacqueline Dock (pseudonym) was born in 1932. As a child she lived in Climax, Georgia. Her father worked as a preacher, and her mother labored as a domestic worker, as a hotel maid, and at a hospital. The couple had ten children. Dock moved to Detroit in 1942. She married in 1951 and had two children. Dock worked at a corner store, then found employment as a nurse's aide and a surgical instrument technician. Later she worked as a babysitter.

Mrs. Mattie Bell Fritz was born in 1927. As a child she lived in Montgomery, Alabama. Her father worked in a drugstore. Her mother was a domestic worker, and she later worked at St. Jude Hospital. Fritz was an only child. She graduated from high school, and she married in 1946. Her husband served in the armed forces, then worked for the steel industry. He later worked for Avis Rent a Car. Fritz had three daughters and one son. She worked in private homes, at a children's dress shop, and on the maintenance crew for the UAW offices near Detroit's Belle Isle. Fritz is the sister-in-law of Ruth Margaret Covington and the aunt of Zenara Covington.

Mrs. Sandra Gantt was born in 1938 in Detroit. Her mother was a domestic worker. Her parents divorced when she was two years old. She had two brothers. Gantt graduated from Detroit's Commerce High School, attended Wayne County Community College for accounting, and took classes through the College of Life Long Learning at Wayne State University. She married and divorced, and had one son. As a young girl, Gantt worked as a babysitter. She also graded papers for her teacher. As an adult, she worked as a general clerk for Detroit Edison, an administrator at the Chrysler Financial Corporation, a receptionist at Manpower, a temporary worker at Ameritech, and in the Office of the General Council of Ford Motor Company.

Dr. Dorista "Dotty" Goldsberry was born in Oklahoma in 1933. Her father taught at Langston University. Goldsberry was the first African American woman to be admitted to study at the University of Oklahoma School of Medicine, but she decided not to attend, going instead to medical school at Howard University. She married a fellow doctor and raised four children in Worcester, Massachusetts. Dr. Goldsberry, a psychiatrist, worked at Worcester State Hospital and became executive director of the Worcester Youth Guidance Center. She served on a wide variety of executive boards in the city.

Mrs. Alberta Hardy was born in 1918. As a child she lived in Clarksdale, Mississippi. Her parents owned their farm. Hardy was one of ten children. She married in 1938 and did not have children. She moved to Detroit at the age of twenty-five. Her husband took a job with Great Lakes Steel. Hardy worked in a restaurant and as a housekeeper at a hotel.

Mrs. Bernita Howard (pseudonym) was born in 1916 in Alabama. Her parents owned their farm. She was the only child of her father's second marriage. Her husband worked as a baker for a veterans' hospital. Howard had one child, a boy, who passed away. She moved to Pennsylvania when she was about twenty years old. She later settled in Detroit (approximately 1942 or 1943). Howard labored as a hotel maid and a hospital waitress, and she ultimately opened a bakery with her husband.

Mrs. Beatrice Jackson was born in 1916. As a child she lived in parts of Alabama and Oklahoma. She was one of four children. Jackson lost both of her parents at an early age. She married in 1941, and the couple had two daughters. Her husband worked in a foundry. Jackson was a domestic worker in Tulsa, Oklahoma. She studied elementary education at Langston University. She also worked as a cosmetologist and as an administrator in government offices.

Mrs. Jacquie Lewis Kemp was born in 1962. She lived in various suburbs of Detroit. Both her grandmother and her mother migrated from Kentucky. Her mother worked for Ford, and her father opened his own metal stamping business. Kemp married and had a son; her husband worked as an undertaker. She earned a bachelor's degree and a master's degree (public policy) from the University of Michigan. She had an internship with the Department of Commerce in Lansing and worked at the U.S. General Accounting Office. At the time of the interview, Kemp was serving as the head of her father's business, Lewis Metal Stamping.

Mrs. Fannie Mae Kennedy was born in 1925. As a child she lived in Louisiana and Oklahoma. Her parents were sharecroppers. Kennedy had eight siblings. Her husband served in the U.S. military, and then worked in Detroit. In addition to her work as a mother, Kennedy worked on farms, did day work in Oklahoma and Michigan, took care of an elderly woman in Michigan (home care), and worked for a Detroit restaurant.

Mrs. Thelma Lane was born in 1920. As a child she lived in Montgomery, Alabama. She also lived in Troy, Alabama, Washington, D.C., and Pittsburgh. Lane's parents owned their own farm. Her father also worked as a farrier (shoeing horses). Lane's parents had ten children, seven of whom lived through childhood. She moved to Pittsburgh with her parents in 1922, but as a child she moved back and forth repeatedly between Alabama and Pennsylvania. When she was a young girl, she cleaned nurses' apartments. She graduated from high school in Pittsburgh and earned her bachelor's degree from Alabama State Teachers College. Lane taught school in Alabama and Virginia, and served on the clerical staff of the Department of Defense. She married and had three children. Her husband served in the armed forces and then worked for the federal government, including the Census Bureau.

Mrs. Lottie Lewis (pseudonym) grew up in Dennison, Texas. She moved to Grand Rapids, Michigan, and worked as a housekeeper in the Pantlind Hotel. She married and had several children.

Mrs. Willie Jean Clark Lewis was born in 1941 in Flat Lick, Kentucky. Her mother was a housewife; her father worked on the railroad. At two years old, Lewis moved to Detroit with her parents. She lived in a number of cities in southeastern Michigan. Lewis worked in administration at the Ford Motor

Company. She began at Ford as a secretary and moved on to Human Resources. She graduated from college in 1991.

Mrs. Simone Landry (pseudonym) was born in 1924. As a child she lived in Youngstown, Ohio. Her mother worked at the Christ Mission Settlement. Her father worked in a steel mill until he had a stroke. Her parents had two daughters and two sons. Landry also lived in Detroit, New York City, and Chicago. She married in 1943, and had three daughters. Landry did domestic work and worked in a factory.

Mrs. Jerliene "Creamy" McKinney was born in 1940. As a child she lived in Cullman, Alabama. Her parents were Odie and Ezekiel Caddell; the couple had thirteen children. Ezekiel Caddell worked as a landscaper. McKinney moved to New York in her late teens to live near her sister. The sisters and their families later moved to Framingham and finally to Worcester. McKinney was a domestic worker for families in New York and Massachusetts, and she worked in a restaurant in Queens. She found employment in a coat factory and later a wire factory in Worcester, and she pressed clothes in a laundry. She attended beauty school and became a hairdresser and, after working at a variety of local shops, opened her own shop inside the Plumley Village housing complex in Worcester. She also did hair for a local funeral home. McKinney married twice; her first husband died at thirty-nine. He had worked for General Electric and at the Boston Airport (later known as Logan Airport). McKinney had four children.

Dr. Ogretta McNeil was born in 1932. As a child she lived in Savannah, Georgia. Her parents both attended normal school. In their later years, McNeil's parents worked as cooks. McNeil and her family moved to Washington, D.C., in the 1940s. She took on babysitting and housecleaning jobs to earn money for school. She graduated from Howard University, and in 1956 moved to Worcester to begin working on a Ph.D. in psychology at Clark University. McNeil had two sons with her first husband, who died. She came to Worcester as a widow with young children, and later remarried. McNeil had a long career as a professor at Holy Cross College in Worcester. She was elected to the Worcester School Board and also served on the executive board of the University of Massachusetts system.

Mrs. Anniese Moten was born in 1925 in Mississippi. Her father was a sharecropper; her parents had eight children. Moten married twice, and had no children of her own. She raised her cousin's three sons. She came to Detroit, Michigan, as an adult. She worked as a housekeeper, her primary duties involving child care. For an extended period, Moten served as a live-in nanny for a family in Toledo, Ohio.

Mrs. Gussie Nash was born in 1936. As a child she lived in Arkansas. Her father worked at a flour mill, on the railroad, and as a barber. Her mother was a homemaker, the mother of six children. Nash moved to Grand Rapids to live with an aunt when she was approximately eighteen years old. She had jobs as a domestic worker, a school aide, and a hospital aide. Nash married and had two children; her husband worked as an upholsterer.

Mrs. Alverrine Smith Parker was born in 1936. She lived in Columbus, Mississippi. Her mother worked at a bakery; her father was a bellhop at the Gilmore Hotel and also cleaned at the Merchants and Farmers Bank. Her parents had eight children. Parker also lived in Muskegon Heights, Michigan, in Los Angeles, and in Grand Rapids, Michigan. She moved north about 1944–1945, when her father went to Michigan to work in a foundry. As a child in the South, Parker worked as a babysitter/housecleaner. In Michigan and California, she engaged in factory work and nursing home work, and she drove buses for the Grand Rapids public schools. Parker married in 1960 and had two children.

Professor Barbara Purifoy-Seldon was born in 1943. As a child she lived in Birmingham, Alabama. Her parents had eight children. Her father was a sharecropper in Alabama; in Michigan, he ran a gas station and drove a taxi. Purifoy-Seldon moved to Michigan as a baby and lived in Ecorse, Southfield, and Detroit. She worked as a domestic for only one day. Purifoy-Seldon served in the armed forces. She studied dental hygiene, earned a number of degrees, and became a professor of dental hygiene at the University of Detroit–Mercy. She married in 1988 and had no children.

Mrs. Faith Richmond (pseudonym) was born in 1927. As a child she lived in Durham, North Carolina. Her father was a butcher, her mother a homemaker, and they had four children. Richmond moved to Boston in 1947. Her husband served in the U.S. military and then worked in a factory. Richmond had a wide variety of jobs. She worked at Duke Hospital, was a nanny, worked at GE Goodrich in Massachusetts, served as a teacher's aide, was a social worker for the welfare department, and ultimately opened her own travel business.

Mrs. Lillie Shelby (pseudonym) was born in 1920. As a child she lived in Sunflower County, Mississippi. Shelby never knew her mother. Her father was a field worker and an itinerant peddler. He moved with her to Memphis when she was a child. Later on, Shelby moved to Detroit. She married in 1935 and had eleven children. She did field work and day work, served as a maid in a boardinghouse, and worked in a laundry.

Mrs. Ella Sims grew up in Mississippi and attended high school in Helena, Arkansas. Her father was a sharecropper and a Baptist preacher; her mother was an invalid. The couple had three children. Sims married a young man she met in high school. They had two children, one of whom died at ten months old. When her first husband died of an ear infection, Sims, approximately twenty-two years old, came to Grand Rapids, Michigan, on a trip in March 1946. She decided to stay in Michigan, joining the cleaning staff of the C&O Railroad. She remarried and had more children. Sims worked as a hotel maid and cleaned homes with her mother-in-law. She became an urban agent for an OEO-supported community action group, Kent County Community Action Program. She joined the board of Aquinas College and was hired by Aquinas to run their office of minority affairs. She earned her college degree at Aquinas. Sims served on a wide variety of community boards, including the Grand Rapids Historical Commission and the local branch of the Salvation Army.

Mrs. Inez Crockett Smith was born in 1941. As a child she lived in Houlka, Mississippi, in Chickasaw County. She also lived in Tupelo, Mississippi, Knoxville, Tennessee, Grand Rapids, Michigan, and St. Louis, Missouri. Her father drove a truck for a lumber company. Her mother divorced her father and bought a restaurant in Tupelo. Later, her mother worked in a chicken factory, and ran a juke joint restaurant. Smith's mother went to cosmetology school and also worked occasionally, and under duress, as a domestic. Smith graduated from Lane College in Jackson, Tennessee, with a degree in physical education and secondary education. She later earned a master's degree from Michigan State University. She moved to Grand Rapids in 1965. Smith's husband, who had grown up in Tupelo and had also lived in Cleveland, worked for Steelcase, a major producer of office furniture. Smith raised her children and taught in the Grand Rapids public schools for many years.

Mrs. Addie Smith was born in 1924. She grew up in Claremont and Hickory, North Carolina. Her father was employed as a brick maker; her mother labored as a domestic. Smith left school before graduation to work in a textile mill. In North Carolina, she worked in the field of hospital supply and cleaned homes on the weekend. She moved to Worcester, Massachusetts, to temporarily substitute for another domestic worker in 1960. After the woman died, Smith assumed the job full-time. She later returned to hospital work. Smith married twice and had five children.

Mrs. Mary Smith was born in 1938. As a child she lived in the small town of Sylvester, Georgia. She had ten brothers and sisters. Smith lived in New York, Miami, and Boston, making the move to Boston in 1962. She worked in a wide variety of jobs, including bookbinding, housework, hospital work, keypunching, clerical, and day care. Smith had three children.

Ms. Lois B. Stevens was born in 1902. As a child she lived in Greenville, Alabama. Her grandmother had been a slave, owned by Stevens's grandfather. Her father was a Baptist minister and a schoolteacher. Her mother raised eight children. Stevens moved to Massachusetts when she was in high school. She served in the U.S. Army and as a nanny to a prominent Worcester family.

Mrs. Rebecca Strom was born in 1944. As a child she lived in Alabama. Her parents owned their own farm and had six children. In her late teens, Strom moved to Waban, Massachusetts, to become a live-in nanny for two children. She later worked in factories, and eventually opened a home day care center. Strom married and had two children.

Mrs. Glennette Taylor (pseudonym) was born in 1934. As a child she lived in Lamar County, Alabama. Her mother was a laundress and later performed hospital work. Her father worked for the railroad. Taylor lived in Avery, Mississippi, and Grand Rapids, Michigan. Her husband, who had served in the military, had worked in construction and at an auto plating facility. Taylor worked as a babysitter, a laundry worker, a cosmetologist, and a hospital aide. She raised her own children and a younger cousin.

Mrs. Liddie Hartman Williams was born in 1937. As a child she lived in Rome, Mississippi, in Sunflower County. Williams's mother, Sierra, was a domestic worker. The parents were sharecroppers and had ten children. Williams moved to Chicago at seventeen, after she married. Her husband worked as a tailor, and the couple had four boys and a girl together. Williams's husband also had a son by his first marriage, and Williams considered this child her own. Williams worked as a dishwasher, a seamstress, a technician at a publishing house, and a domestic in a Chicago Gold Coast apartment.

Mrs. Mary White was born in 1910. She grew up in Monroe, Georgia. Her father worked as a laborer and maintained a small farm. He later worked for Michigan Metal and Brass. Her mother sometimes did day work. White had one sister. White had seven children; all but three had died at the time of the interview. She survived two husbands. The first worked at Ford Motor Company, and died at forty-nine of rheumatic fever. White had come to Detroit with her parents in 1923. She labored as a domestic worker, a factory worker, and an assistant in a plumbing and heating company. She attended cosmetology school and opened a salon.

Mrs. Esther Ward Woods was born in 1913. As a child she lived in Cuba, Alabama. Her parents owned their farm. Woods's mother gave birth to thirteen children, eleven of whom survived infancy. Woods lived in East Chicago, Indiana, and Grand Rapids, Michigan. She came to Grand Rapids in 1945 to care for her sister's children. In 1947, she began a long career as a domestic worker. Woods married and divorced. Her ex-husband served time in prison for the murder of a police officer. Woods had no biological children, but helped to raise nieces and nephews.

Mrs. Rosetta "Rosa" Lewis Young was born in approximately 1926. She lived in Abbeville and Holly Springs, Mississippi. Her parents owned a five-acre farm, and her father worked for the railroad. The couple had six children. Young attended Mississippi Industrial College in Holly Springs. She moved to Grand Rapids in 1944, married in 1946, and had six children of her own. She worked in a variety of factories. She also took jobs as a seamstress, doing mending.

Making a Way out of No Way

Esther Woods. Courtesy of Sylvia Krissoff.

Introduction

This book showcases and analyzes recently collected oral histories with forty African American women, most of whom were born in the southern United States in the first part of the twentieth century and then migrated to northern cities in the movement known as the Second Great Migration, 1940–1970. The Second Great Migration brought approximately five million black migrants to northern cities, leaving these cities, and the migrants themselves, forever transformed.[1] The book presents an analysis of the life stories of women migrants, with a focus on their reasons for moving and their thoughts on how work shaped their lives. Although the First and Second Great Migrations have been the subject of a number of wonderful books, the woman migrant herself has rarely been placed in the foreground within these works.[2] Analysis of the oral histories demonstrates how black women forged purposeful lives for themselves despite multifaceted pressures. As Inez Smith said in characterizing her own mother, a talented businesswoman who supported her daughters by the efforts of her hard work, the women featured here "made a way out of no way."

Social historians seek to understand trends in American culture and lived experience. Yet it is difficult for scholars to truly comprehend a trend if the supporting documents have not yet made their way to the archives. Documentation regarding the Second Great Migration has not yet been assiduously collected. Oral histories with black women who were not famous are found in only a limited number of library collections. Thus, to better understand the way in which African American women viewed the migration, I went and asked them, tape recorder in hand. Many black migrants were born in rural parts of the South, while others began their lives in cities. Some transitioned from rural settings to southern cities before making the trek to the North. The North figured centrally in their dreams and hopes, yet the region rarely lived up to expectations.

To understand this migration, a movement in which women predominated, we are well served to consider individual stories. Examination of personal narratives proves particularly weighty when the narrators represent a people and a gender whose documents are underrepresented in the archives. Although millions made the choice to migrate, each individual migrant made the decision to uproot on her own, weighing carefully what she knew of American social structures, pay scales, living conditions, and family concerns. The book asks, why did the migrants come, and what was the migration experience like? What memories do the women retain from their younger years? What did they think of northern cities when they first arrived? What kinds of work did they undertake for pay, and what was the effect of this work on their families?

Due to the limits society placed on African American women, the majority of the respondents in this study worked as domestic laborers during at least a portion of their work lives. My initial interest in the research concerned learning more about migrants who undertook domestic service. Yet the respondents and I usually did not discuss their work experience before our taped session. In our preinterview discussions, I only confirmed that the respondents were migrants or the daughters of migrants. I made this choice because, while highly interested in domestic work, I wanted to understand the broad range of migrant careers. I also sought to interview women who had been domestic workers briefly, and those who had avoided it altogether. Many of these women did not identify as "domestic workers" per se. I understood that American society relegated high numbers of African American women to domestic work in this period, and I knew that simply by interviewing a number of women migrants, I would end up collecting the stories of women who had once worked as household laborers, hotel maids, and personal service workers. In the first part of the twentieth century, the greatest percentage of working African American women performed some type of domestic work. Domestic work, as a field, historically included many different types of labor. Contemporary domestic workers continue to have a wide variety of tasks. The domestic and "personal service" category of the U.S. census encompassed the work of laundress, cook, child care worker, and other domestic roles. As the women workers themselves so often crossed these boundaries in their daily tasks, I have included a broad range of activities under the heading of domestic work. In this study, working as part of a cleaning crew in a public location, such as a hotel or office or on a train, is characterized as a type of domestic labor, as are a wide variety of in-home services.

Unlike most other studies of domestic workers, this one looks both at women who were long-term domestic workers and those who undertook such duties only briefly. The preponderance of academic studies focus only on career domestic workers, while I resisted such limitations. A great many African American women undertook domestic work, and many used the work as a bridge to other fields or as an expedient measure between more desirable careers. As will be demonstrated in the oral histories, domestic work was at times used as an intermittent form of employment by women who achieved middle-class and even upper-middle-class status, as well as by those who remained in the working class. This book examines the women's transition in and out of domestic work, as it served their needs.

Understanding the story of this pivotal migrant generation is a key step in comprehending the experience of female migrants, African American working women, and domestic workers of all ethnic groups. And as black women workers were the nation's earliest and largest group of women who labored outside their own homes, their experiences provide insight into the position of working women in general. The women interviewed for this book were not themselves the first generation of African American women workers following Reconstruction, but their personal understanding of labor was deeply informed by the experiences of their mothers, grandmothers, and other female ancestors.

Of course, for most black women, work did not constitute a "liberating" experience the way it would for the white, middle-class housewives influenced by Betty Friedan's 1963 *The Feminine Mystique*.[3] Black women had no mystique of this nature to overcome—in fact, they urged the larger society to rethink the vicious myths that cast black women into such negative roles as the ever-competent "mammy," the scheming "Jezebel," and the lazy "welfare mother." While many early white feminists considered work a doorway to equality, high numbers of black women yearned for the opportunity to stay home with their children. Friedan assisted in organizing a 2001 conference framed around the global issue of the high demands of the twenty-first-century workplace and the demands' negative effect on quality of life. American black women have known all too much about this issue for far too long. Facing what legal scholar Kimberlé Crenshaw and sociologist Patricia Hill Collins term the "intersectionality" of forms of oppression, black women knew that American society had to change in revolutionary ways before black women, and especially working-class black women, could start to put down the heavy burden carried on their shoulders.[4]

Compellingly, it is because of, rather than despite, the multifaceted hardships faced by black working women that their stories offer a rich set of lessons for all of today's female workers. Even if the workplace was the kitchen in a white home, key trends were established and important lessons were learned. The respondents for this study urged others to glean a better understanding of American work from their experiences. Little prompting was necessary for the narrators to offer general words of wisdom for a spectrum of women workers today.

Aiming for an inclusive look at the industrial North, I have conducted interviews in a number of cities, including Dorchester (an area within Boston), Massachusetts, Worcester, Massachusetts, Chicago, Illinois, Detroit, Michigan, and Grand Rapids, Michigan. The respondents primarily came from rural or small town settings in Alabama, Arkansas, Georgia, Kentucky, Louisiana, Mississippi, North Carolina, Oklahoma, South Carolina, and Texas. Although these settings are diverse, ranging from the upper South to the Southwest, all claim some element of southern culture. All, too, share the tangled historical legacy of prolonged slavery, which persisted in these states until the conclusion of the Civil War. The subject pool includes a few women born in urban, southern locations and a few daughters of migrants. Many migrants settled for a time in other midsized to large cities, both North and South, on their way to their final destinations. The cities the women lived in before their permanent homes (considering here *both* cities of origin and cities of migration), include Chicago (IL), Cleveland (OH), Covington (KY), East Chicago (IN), Greenville (AL), Helena (AR), Knoxville (TN), Los Angeles (CA), Memphis (TN), Miami (FL), Montgomery (AL), Muskegon (MI), Nashville (TN), New York City, Pittsburgh (PA), Savannah (GA), Troy (AL), Tulsa (OK), Tupelo (MS), Tuscaloosa (AL), Washington, D.C., and Youngstown (OH). Thus the relatively small interview sample provides us with insights on a myriad of American sites, both rural and urban, as the women migrants were many degrees more mobile than the general population. This level of familiarity with a high number of regions makes the women's insights about regional differences nuanced and authoritative.

The book also relies on some of the existing collections of oral histories with women in similar situations. These resources included the oral histories of Baylor University's Institute for Oral History and the Texas Collection of the Carroll Library, the oral history collections at the Wayne State University Library for Research in Labor and Urban Affairs, the oral histories of the Grand Rapids Public Library, the Fran Leeper Buss Collections (at both Wayne State and the Arthur and Elizabeth Schlesinger Library at Radcliffe), and the Schlesinger Library study entitled "The Black Women Oral History Project." The Baylor University Institute for Oral History collections, while focusing on Texas women, proved enormously helpful in establishing a fuller picture of black women's lives in the Southwest. Baylor's interviewers asked questions related to my own, and almost all of the women interviewed mentioned relatives who had headed to the North. Related archival research was conducted at the Wayne State library, the Detroit Public Library, and the Bentley Historical Library of the University of Michigan. The notable collections used include the Urban League Papers of both Detroit and Grand Rapids, Michigan, and the papers of Rev. Charles Hill, who was a leftist activist and a champion of women's rights. Substantial grants to fund this research have been awarded by Baylor University's Institute for Oral History, the University of Michigan's Bentley Historical Library, Worcester State College, and the Arthur and Elizabeth Schlesinger Library on the History of Women in America at Harvard University.

Personal Inspirations

Two individuals provided the inspiration for this book. The first is my dear friend Esther Woods (1913–2005). Woods, born in 1913 in Cuba, Alabama, was someone I had known for years. Knowing Esther was a true gift, and my vision of the American past is clearer because of the insights she shared with me. In life there are a few people we end up caring for even more than we have to—a beloved aunt who almost becomes a grandmother through the depth of her interest, a colleague at work who becomes a special friend, a neighbor who becomes a member of the family. My life intersected only tangentially with Esther's at some level, but we both chose to make more of the intersection. The fact that she rejoiced with me at the birth of my brother, celebrated at my wedding, and invited her friends and family to take part in the production of this book means the world to me.

In April 1945, Woods migrated to the "Furniture City," Grand Rapids, Michigan, to care for her sister's children. She then labored for approximately forty years as a domestic worker. She found employment in the homes of a great many of the Jewish families of the city. In some years she worked for a family as a full-time worker; in other years she split her weeks among several families. She cooked, cleaned, watched children, and added her no-nonsense outlook to the households in which she took part. Esther's long-term employers were close friends with my grandparents. My grandmother, Sylvia Krissoff, was also one of the women for whom Woods worked. Woods never worked for my grandmother full-time. Yet the longevity of their arrangement, and the fact that my grandmother was the only working woman for whom Woods labored, imparted a level of solidity to their relationship. As in every such arrangement, tensions swirled. The women were employer and employee—this was clearly not a friendship of social equals—although my grandmother did struggle to break down some of the usual walls.

I do not remember first meeting Esther, for I have known her since I was a child. In addition to her weekly cleaning, she helped my grandmother in the kitchen as a paid assistant during major family dinners, and, in later years, joined the group at many family events as a guest. Although we should not give the family much credit for our "liberal-mindedness" on this point, it should be noted that Esther always sat down to eat with us, even during her working years. Eating with domestic employees remained relatively rare in American households. And in the Krissoff family, all the women present (employees and nonemployees) worked to prepare for and clean up after the dinner. Esther did not serve the meal, nor did she labor at the kitchen sink alone. Why the men sat at the table while the women did the dishes is the subject of yet another book, although I will point out that I vocally questioned this sexist practice at a very early age. "Why doesn't Grandpa get up and help with the dishes?" I would query in a loud voice as my mother, sister, grandmother, Esther, and I would rise to carry the dishes laden with the remains of our dinner back to the kitchen. My mother would shush me. I went on to do graduate work in women's studies and American women's history.

At our yearly Passover celebration, in which the Seder dinner commemorates the freeing of the Jewish people from slavery, it brought particular resonance to the reading of the Haggadah (the prayer book which tells the story of the holiday) when the book was passed into Esther's hands. Then, this beautiful woman would read a portion of the story—a woman whose ancestors had been enslaved more recently than Egyptian times, and in our very own country. She might tell us how Moses asked the Egyptian pharaoh to "let my people go." Or she might explain how the children of Israel were ultimately—after a dramatic chase scene and after surviving the ordeal of forty years in the desert—freed.

Despite the shared history of oppression, and regarding only United States history, things have unarguably gone better for Jewish Americans as a group than for African Americans as a group. The dream of freedom and the growing anti-Semitism of Europe, including the violent pogroms that swept the Jewish shtetls, drove my ancestors out of Eastern Europe and into the boats that took them to the United States and Canada.[5] Families poured their life savings into steamship tickets, and the gamble paid off. While not all of my ancestors could be said to have "made it" monetarily, they experienced immeasurably more comfortable surroundings than their predecessors. They certainly "made it" in terms of acquiring the freedom to worship and to achieve in ways unknown to their families in previous generations. And, of course, my direct ancestors (although not all of their siblings) crossed the ocean at least twenty to thirty years ahead of the Holocaust—a lucky bit of timing.

African Americans, as we well know, do not share this history of choosing to come to America. Instead of having third-class steamship tickets, Esther
Woods's ancestors crossed the ocean from Africa as part of the horrific Middle
Passage, packed into slave ships in which the majority of passengers usually died
before reaching land. Woods's ancestors did not make the journey to America
by choice, nor, as we shall explore here, did Woods or women like her, even generations after slavery, have a great many choices at all. However, these women
did express considerable *agency* in crafting their lives, even though much of society tried to thwart them at every turn. By using the term "agency" here, I recall
usage of the term common to recent social historians writing about slavery. Historians, in these modern works, document the agency of slaves who refused to be
entirely co-opted by the vicious slavery system.[6] The migrants of the Second Great
Migration may be considered truly displaced, due to the failure of the sharecropping system. Historian Peter Gottlieb refers to those who made the First Great
Migration as refugees. Both sets of migrants had few options, but they expressed
as much control as possible over the course of their lives.[7] The admirable ability
to chart one's own course over the turbulent seas of American life was a trait
shared by all the women interviewed for this study. All of them, Woods included,
made the fateful choice to move from primarily rural locations in the southern
United States to primarily urban locations in the northern United States during the Second Great Migration. African American men, women, and children
traveled by train, bus, automobile, and even airplane to what was then the most
accessible, although overly optimistically nicknamed, "promised land."

Esther Woods, like so many African American women, had a special quality that made her an ideal role model for young working women. At Spelman
College in Atlanta, Georgia, scholar Gloria Wade Gayles assigns students in her
Spelman Independent Scholars (SIS) program the tasks of undertaking an oral
history with elder African American women in the Atlanta community and
building a mentor relationship with the women through multiple visits.[8] For
Gayles, "collecting" the oral history goes beyond a single visit. For me, one of
the most important aspects of this book became building a relationship with
Esther. As we chatted over tea in her carefully decorated living room, shared
memories while eating our Thanksgiving pie, or walked through her continually remarkable garden, our relationship began to grow. As my elder, she shared
her viewpoint in order that I could learn from it.

Although I had known Esther Woods all of my life, one particular moment
stands out to me. In early 1999, I visited my maternal grandmother, Florence
Hack, as she was struggling with lymphoma and pneumonia in the final days
of her life. My husband, Chris, and I had driven speedily across the state of

Michigan to her side because she had made it known that she wanted to see our infant son, David, before she passed away. While in the hospital for this dramatic and wrenching event, we also learned that Esther had become ill, and was recuperating in another section of the hospital. We visited Esther in her room. Fresh from our grandmother's side, we were almost overcome with the serious business of hospitals. Esther was not in her final moments, yet she was seriously unwell. However, tucked neatly beneath the white sheet and thin blanket of her hospital bed, she was cheerful and much her usual self. As I left the room, I was filled with a sense of amazement at her power of calm in such uncomfortable surroundings. Although sick, she inquired about our health and our happiness. She smiled a beautiful, warm smile.

The questions that formed in my mind that day about the mindset that would allow for such peace amidst personal illness and the rather bleak setting of the hospital led in part to the commencement of the oral histories on which this book is based. I wanted to better understand the motivations that carried Esther through troubled times and that had fueled her move to the urban North. What thoughts would she share concerning the overall trajectory of her life, the work that sustained her financially, her relationships with family and employers, and the dearth of options for black women? What kind of outlook made it possible to persevere in the face of such obstacles? How did she "make a way out of no way"? Was there an aspect to this ability to keep on despite everything that glossed over the hardships, or did it exist simultaneously with an open evaluation of the racist, classist, and misogynistic American society? And would other women migrants reveal similar lines in their life stories?

Amazingly, I came to find that Esther's trademark tranquility stayed with her through her final days. The clear, handwritten letter she penned from her hospice bed betrays no remorse for an unlived life, nor sadness at the state of being near death. She simply inquired after my health and let me know that she too was "fine." My mother and grandmother, who sat with Esther in her final day, reported that the peacefulness continued into Esther's last moments. My mother reminded her again that this book would be dedicated to her, and Esther smiled.

The second major inspiration for this book is my mother, Madelon Krissoff. In her years as a housewife, she spent her time cleaning and caring for children. Although my mother cleaned her own home and cared for her own children, a task markedly different from that of the domestic workers, she made her high regard for domestic work crystal clear to me. To her, domestic work was not, at its heart, pure drudgery. Indeed it was necessary and important work and could be the source of its own satisfaction. Her attitude coincides with the remarks made by many of the respondents. A number of women found the work satisfying and spoke out against those who critiqued it as unskilled, irrelevant, or mind-numbing drudgery. When my mother, Madelon, left full-time housewifery for medical school and a career in internal and geriatric medicine, she still enjoyed home labor and found it fulfilling in its way.

The words of a popular record happened to make my mother's attitudes clear to me. My favorite toy was an orange and cream plastic record player. It sat squarely in the middle of our partially finished basement, hooked up to an outlet directly above the player in the ceiling. I could spend hours listening to Pete Seeger, Arlo Guthrie, the Beatles's Sgt. Pepper album, or other standards of the day. My favorite album, *Free to Be . . . You and Me*, the folk-pop anthem of most 1970s children of the socially progressive, played nearly every day. From the album, I learned it was all right for boys to cry openly or to love dolls. Girls could pursue a high-powered career or run faster than their boyfriends. Yet even this purported statement of political correctness urged its listeners to disregard domestic work. No one, it decidedly proclaimed, enjoyed work inside the home. "Your mommy hates housework, / Your daddy hates housework, / I hate housework too. / And when you grow up, so will you," guarantees Carol Channing in the 1972 recording. Channing concludes, "Housework is just no fun."⁹

When my mother heard this poem, she expressed in her usual calm yet authoritative way that this was simply, and unequivocally, not true. "Not everyone feels that way," she explained. She herself liked housework, including doing the dishes, and making things clean, and folding our little shirts. She actually asked me to skip over the poem when listening to the record, and I tried to do so when she was within earshot. Although as a child I did not fully understand the politics of gender, I did comprehend that the poem hurt her feelings in a way. And I have come to agree with her attitude towards housework. There are many times that housework is far more appealing than the work of a professor; standing in a sunny window placing dishes in a dishwasher is not inherently distasteful work. I often prefer it to bending over a stack of student papers, or attending yet another college faculty meeting. If housework was inherently awful, my young son would not delight in pushing the dust mop around the kitchen floor, or scrubbing the cupboard doors with an errant piece of paper towel he has located. He smiles as he helps me load the clothes dryer, and once bunched his face up in delighted concentration as we washed marks off a painted wall. It is most likely the low pay and relegation of the work to the women's sphere that encourages our dismissal of the work. Looking down on housework might have just been a last vestige of disdain for all things associated with women and the women's sphere that *Free to Be . . . You and Me*, back in 1972, could not yet overcome. And, as we shall see, working for others, including racist, overtly rude, and sometimes even lecherous employers can make the work distasteful and even dangerous. Performing housework for others also remains vastly different from laboring in one's own home; in the latter instance, home labor is in part a method of caring for oneself. Obviously, the conditions of one's labor matter enormously. Yet in truly listening to the stories presented here, we should note that some of the women in this study found domestic work at least partially satisfying. We need to be able to hear these assertions, and not simply dismiss them out of hand. The contemporary paradigm seemingly only allows us to value work also highly valued by the marketplace. The paradigm may overwhelm our intended empathy with the respondent.

Interview Structure and Methodology

In the face of the brutal hardships of the Jim Crow South and the underhanded form of racism of the twentieth-century northern cities, some might characterize any expression of contentment as a form of false consciousness. Esther Woods's life was irrefutably rough. How could she ever smile, relax, or express moderate happiness? Was Woods's close relationship with some of those for whom she had worked a false relationship? Could it in any way relate to a kidnap victim who begins to identify with her kidnapper, suffering from the so-called "Stockholm syndrome"? Absolutely not, I concluded, after collecting and closely examining hours upon hours of oral histories. While the possibility of false consciousness should be considered, the oral histories in this book quickly dispel such notions. In fact, a sustained discussion of false consciousness belittles the narrators' abilities to judge their own lives. As the whole of the book will demonstrate, the women migrants approached their lives with utmost emotional integrity and open evaluation. The combined weight of the intersecting vectors of oppression weighing on these women would have been impossible *not* to acknowledge. Yet while the pressure made it difficult to breathe, the women refused to have their remaining breath taken from them, or to let it be characterized by unmitigated pain. While all of us might have the tendency to wax nostalgic about our lives when interviewed later in life, the sense of contentment expressed by some of the respondents was not a shallow feeling attributed to forgetfulness, but rather a well-earned peace due to the constancy of their own hard work. In the face of hardship, the women persevered and retained a belief in the goodness of most people. Strong religious commitment and enduring family bonds carried the women through troubled times. Almost no one lives a completely charmed life, and some human beings have faced almost unfathomable obstacles. Pressing forward when it seems impossible and keeping the challenges in perspective is an admirable quality, and one that this work strives to honor.

I was living and working in southeastern Michigan at the time I began this book, and the history of black women seemed a central subject for any historian, white or black, to pursue. In 2000, the majority of Detroit residents were African American. The exploration of African American women's history constituted a logical step for a local historian of urban women. Many have expressed incredulity that I would adopt this research topic—a surprise that I think would not be put as openly were I using strictly archival sources, or were I a black woman pursuing a book on white women's past. In part I am heeding historian Darlene Clark Hine's call for more works of "crossover" history (white or black researchers looking at topics outside of their own race), but primarily I find motivation to study migrants and working women due to my interest in studying the history of urban women and work, and my personal status as a working woman, a former child care worker, and a regional migrant.[10] Yet in conducting oral history, we do need to be exceedingly careful and aware of the power dynamics at work. Many have pointed out the seemingly simple fact that in the oral histories on which this work is based, we find a "white" interviewer interviewing a "black" respondent. (Here racial terms are placed in quotations, as many feel they should always be, because while identity politics weighs heavily on us all in the early twenty-first century, we also know that these are socially constructed rather than true biological categories. For instance, many of the respondents were of both "white" and "black" ancestry. Of course, due to American racial politics, such individuals have found themselves interpreted as "black" Americans.)[11] Certainly many of the interviewees openly commented on the racial difference between us. But only in one interview did this seem an expressly vexing problem, and we had a meaningful interview despite the narrator's initial discomfort upon discovering a white interviewer at her doorstep.

Several mediating factors come into play here. First, the most striking difference between interview subject and interviewer in most cases here was not racial, but age related. In many cases the interviewees were more than fifty years older than I was—in one case, the respondent was close to seventy years older. The interviews often took on the format of an older, more experienced person telling a younger one how the world had functioned in the past and offering insights on the struggles of combining work and daily life. Minnie Chatman of Detroit clearly articulated this role. She saw it as her duty as an elder and a religious woman to speak about the past openly. She announced, "I just enjoy trying to enlighten people and show them a better way."[12]

This age difference was exaggerated by the fact that in more than half of the interviews, students of mine were also present. Audrey Kemp and returning students (of nontraditional age) Patricia Burke and Joan Goss joined me in some of the Massachusetts interviews. All three women also assisted with oral history transcription. Student Elizabeth Cote took part in all of the Detroit-area interviews. I first met Elizabeth Cote at the University of Michigan–Dearborn, when she took my course on American women's history. During her freshman year, she came forward on her own to express interest in the book and ask if she could serve as a research assistant. Her role evolved into one of an official paid consultant and transcriptionist, courtesy of multiple grants extended by Worcester State College. Cote, using my interview guide, conducted interviews on her own as well. Although white, Cote had a deep understanding of Detroit neighborhoods. She grew up in Lincoln Park, just outside of the city proper. Lincoln Park stood immediately adjacent to a Detroit neighborhood that is home to many of the book's respondents. Neighborhood residents Mattie Bell and Andrew Fritz served as Elizabeth's adopted family. The interracial nature of their constructed family belies the easy dismissal of the white interviewer as being too far "outside" the African American world to understand it in any meaningful way. The Fritzes' welcoming attitudes toward the book encouraged many of their relatives, friends, and neighbors to take part and contributed greatly to the success of the work. In almost all cases, interviews grew out of personal connections and through a chain made of women friends, family, or "fictive kin." Once the interview was completed, the oral history narrators' trust in the tenor of the research grew, and the narrators also often introduced me to their friends and family.

As much as possible, I liked to abdicate power to the narrator. It was her story to tell, not mine. I take as one of my guiding principles the statement by historian Luisa Passerini: "To respect memory also means letting it organize the story according to the subject's own order of priorities."[13] I asked few questions and stayed as quiet as possible during the interview. While I had prepared a topical guideline for the interviews, I kept the written guideline in my bag, in order to come as close to replicating a conversation as possible. I did take some handwritten notes during the interviews, although the discussions moved so quickly that these notes were only cursory. I often abandoned note taking altogether, or at least after the conversation warmed. The narrator and I sat close together—at one corner of a dining room table, or on a couch and a facing side chair—and I would make it clear through body language, rapt attention, and responsive comments that everything said was of great interest to me, which of course it was. I found that my techniques and nearly unwavering focus yielded a wealth of information. The interview subjects were very forthcoming, speaking about topics normally considered forbidden. We discussed uncomfortable themes such as the racism of white employers, physical and sexual violence, out-of-wedlock pregnancies, and the white slave owner's sexual relationships with female slaves. In all but one case, the mood of the interview seemed very comfortable.[14] The interviews were set up in advance, and most often took place in a respondent's own home. There was a sense that this was an opportunity to make a statement, to get everything out there that was important to say.

Interestingly, as race is something that African Americans have learned to be incredibly attuned to picking up on, many of the respondents revealed that they did not consider me to be a member of the "mainstream" population. An olive-skinned, black-haired, Jewish woman, I was categorized as a societal "other," or at least somewhat outside of the northern European majority culture, by many narrators. Some of the women knew me or of me though family connections, and in these instances knew that I was a Jew. Some openly commented that they thought of Jews as nonwhite or in some way a distinct race. A few women, both those that knew me quite well and those that did not, listed the races, saying, "Whites, blacks, Jews, and other races." However, the fact that some women considered Jews nonwhite does not de-problematize the racial differences of these interviews. A good number of the narrators worked for Jewish employers. The history of Jewish religious restrictions on the Sabbath day and the fact that the Jewish Sabbath (Saturday) differs from the Christian Sabbath (Sunday) have meant that Jews have turned to non-Jews for labor for centuries, especially for Sabbath workers to fix the meals.[15] The forthcoming manner in which the respondents spoke of Jews—sometimes unfavorably—indicates that the women felt comfortable speaking candidly in the interview.

Educational backgrounds did divide some of the narrators and myself. A few of the respondents had a limited education—a scattering of years of "short session" school in severely shortchanged schoolhouses. Others graduated from high school, and still others completed both high school and college. One of the migrants held a Ph.D., and several had master's degrees. Two women were college professors, and one was a physician. One of the second-generation migrants held a master's degree and was the CEO of the family business. Another woman in the second generation held a master's degree and ran her own catering business. In setting out to interview migrant women, I did not limit the study to the working class. However, a study on migrants in which working-class and lower-middle-class women did not predominate would have been highly irregular. While every gain made by a generation translated into a better future for their children, most migrant families were lucky just to find steady work and secure modest single-family homes. In this case, the matter of class played out simply by chance. I made contacts with migrants, they introduced me to friends and family, and I worked from there.

Mary Catherine Bateson, author of *Composing a Life,* recommends that we look at women's life stories in new ways. Rather than privilege lifelong career focus and goal-oriented behavior, we should celebrate and study the patchwork process by which many of us craft our lives, a technique that is often especially apparent in women's lives. Bateson asks, "At what point does desperate improvisation become significant achievement?"[16] In struggling to establish themselves as agents of their own life direction, the women of *Making a Way out of No Way* ultimately pieced together beautiful lives out of the sometimes tattered scraps supplied to them. Although restricted by the nearly insurmountable boundaries of racism, classism, and misogyny, the migrant women pressed forward with their lives. Defying the odds, most of them considered themselves successful and happy. The migrants maintained great personal dignity in the face of challenges. As Victor Frankl explores in his blockbuster work, *Man's Search for Meaning,* even during unthinkable circumstances some have the strength to control their inner thoughts and outward behavior. As Harold S. Kushner writes in the foreword of the book's 2006 edition, Frankl has demonstrated that "forces beyond your control can take away everything you possess except one thing, your freedom to choose how you will respond to the situation. You cannot control what happens to you in life, but you can always control what you will feel and do about what happens to you."[17]

This book will consider the means by which the women migrants negotiated their way through a tumultuous period in American history. "Choice" may be too broad a term to use in characterizing the women's actions, as it tends to imply a cornucopia brimming with options. Yet it is hard to proceed without the use of this term. In this text, use of the word "choice" will be understood as indicating selections made under severe restrictions.[18] "Agency" is a term which perhaps best characterizes the personal actions undertaken by the migrants. As the oral histories attest, African American women migrants, acting within severe limitations, crafted lives of dignity and meaning for themselves. They made a way out of no way.

Shotgun house, Columbus, Georgia. Library of Congress, American Memory Collection.

CHAPTER ONE

Memories of the Southern Childhood

Examine the foundations of our moment in history. First—dig deep right where you are standing. This is the last time you may find "the old women gathered." This is the last song they may ever sing. I challenge you, historians of tomorrow, to scoop up the baton of their rich heritage and carry it with you as you run.
—ELIZABETH CLARK-LEWIS[1]

Resilience, the capability of a human being to continue on in the face of great adversity, is a word that applies to each and every woman interviewed for this book. Resilience is an often undervalued attribute; resilience is a form of courage, but it requires a continuity of spirit that is not necessarily a component of all types of bravery. A soldier might gather up his personal fortitude, take a deep breath, and run headlong into danger. Resilience entails not only a momentary conviction of spirit, but a continued devotion to persisting in the face of adversity, a commitment to "making a way out of no way." Poetry and speeches speak of bravery, honor, love, friendship, and other laudable human traits with reverence. These traits are even contemplated through song or depicted visually in artworks. Yet resilience is rarely considered at length.

Contemplating resilience proves tricky in the case of African American women migrants. First, we must make note that resilience in no way connotes happiness, or even contentment. The act of resilience simply means carrying on in the face of adversity. One certainly can be resilient and highly aware of the injustices responsible for creating the challenges. In bringing up the migrants' resilience, one might also inadvertently conjure up thoughts of the convoluted "philosophy" that slave owners used to self-placate and that, in a related form, took root in the consciousness of those who employed black maids explicitly for their skin color or perceived racial attributes. Slave owners told themselves that black men and women were especially suited for slavery. Their ancestors in Africa had worked hard under a relentless sun, the theory went, and had bequeathed immunity to hard work and hot temperatures to their bloodlines as well. After the Civil War, and on into the twentieth century, those who strove specifically to employ black maids also often worked from a racist model of difference, and thought black women suited to menial work. The employers used the women's ability to confront the work each day as a way to enrich their racist thinking, believing black women an ideal fit for what was categorized as menial labor. (The job, however, required a host of skills not openly acknowledged by the employers, as will be discussed in chapter five.) As sociologist Judith Rollins has explained, all of the three major sources of power in the twentieth century—capitalist, patriarchal, and racial—come into play in the power structures affecting twentieth-century domestic work. And the mental leap from black domestic to slave can be made with lightning speed. Rollins argues, "The origins of household work are with women; there has been a tradition throughout the millennia for female domestics to be used sexually; housework is manual labor and manual labor is universally denigrated; and until very recent times, there has been an association between domestic servitude and slavery."[2] Employers of black, female household workers easily adopted the attitude that the work especially fit their employees, and added a more negative flavoring to the myth of the "strong black woman."

The key here is to take on the subject of resilience as defined by the women who contributed to this study. Oral history involves careful listening. The women who sat down with me to talk, and the others who contributed their stories to the archives where I studied, all defined themselves as bearing this special type of courage, the courage to persist despite great challenges. One is resilient if one does not let society, even a relentlessly racist, sexist society that greatly favors those who have material wealth over those that do not, define one's person and inner life. The women used a variety of resources, including one or all of the following—personal strength of spirit, excellent parenting, communal networks, knowledge acquired through education, a loving spouse, a closely held belief in God—to try to keep the societal threat at bay. These women kept on.

Esther Woods, born in Cuba, Alabama, in 1913, settled in Grand Rapids in 1945. In this new region, Woods carved out a life of great dignity, even in the face of financial hardship, deep sacrifice to family, and divorce from a violent man. Her life inspired this book. Her story, the first that I knew well, bore many resemblances to the lives of other migrant women. While the stories that follow are of unique individuals, the respondents tended to agree on some fundamental points. For one, they felt their lives bore historical significance. The women were not surprised that their stories were of interest to others, and most shared the belief that much could be learned from their life narratives. In other oral history projects I have undertaken, some of the respondents would ask, "Why choose me?" Doubt about the historical value of personal stories appeared particularly common among female narrators, who were no doubt taught a version of the American past as seen through male eyes. One might guess that this attitude would be enhanced with narrators who were women of color. Evelyn Nakano Glenn, author of *Issei, Nisei, War Bride: Three Generations of Japanese American Women in Domestic Service*, found that her respondents doubted the historical importance of their tales. Glenn writes that if her family and friends had not made personal introductions between herself and the narrators, she believed "that many of the women would have refused to be interviewed. Some might have refused out of modesty; many of the women I interviewed protested that their stories could be of little interest to anyone."[3] Personal introductions also proved important in arranging interviews for this study. Yet, once we met, the respondents of *Making a Way out of No Way* eagerly shared their life narratives, and in fact seemed to have a cache of powerful memories saved up for just such an opportunity. This attitude is a testament both to the positive personal identity these women had and the importance of the growing body of historiography on the American black experience. This historiography, initially fueled by the civil rights movement, was featured in the personal libraries of many of the respondents. These works were highly valued, and the migrants wanted to join the chorus with their own insights. It was time for the stories to be told.

Oral history is the methodology of choice for capturing pieces of the American past that have not been adequately preserved in traditional archival sources. The life stories of African American female migrants have been situated largely beyond the scope of scholarly study because of their absence from the archival depositories.[4] Fewer materials relating to the contributions of African Americans have been collected than one might hope, and documents that relate specifically to the tale of female domestic and personal service workers have almost never been compiled. Leading oral historian Sherna Berger Gluck explained, "Refusing to be rendered historically voiceless any longer, women are creating a new history—using our own voices and experiences. We are challenging the traditional concepts of history, what is 'historically important.' And we are affirming that our everyday lives *are* history."[5] This new idea has gained momentum in recent decades, and there is much work yet to be done. Domestic work sits outside of the purview of American historical collections because it has never been championed as an important aspect of American labor. Labor history as a field largely avoids it; practitioners of women's history and of African American history started their quests to fill historiographical voids by dealing with more "exemplary" subjects, although the pool of works covering a broader range of women's experience grew exponentially in the late twentieth and early twenty-first centuries. Rick Halpern laments the initial oversight, writing, "But although women's labor historians have succeeded in making gender a category of analysis in the field, it is fair to say that oral history has not been an important part of their effort."[6] For historians of urban, laboring women, oral history is a methodology of great, yet largely unexplored, potential.

The female participants of the Second Great Migration, who arrived in northern cities from the South circa 1940–1970, have been particularly underrepresented in our academic texts. Historians continue to devote much of their scholarship to the period of free labor immediately following slavery. The domestic workers of that time period are documented in books such as Tera Hunter's *To 'Joy My Freedom: Southern Black Women's Lives and Labors After the Civil War*. Even general works on domestic workers across race tend to center on an earlier period—books such as David M. Katzman's *Seven Days a Week: Women and Domestic Service in Industrializing America* tell readers of a time in which both black and white women found themselves largely relegated to domestic endeavors. Work on recent immigrants, especially Latina and Asian domestic workers, is changing this trend. Pierrette Hondagneu-Sotelo's brilliant *Doméstica: Immigrant Workers Cleaning and Caring in the Shadows of Affluence* should be considered the new benchmark for works on immigrant domestic work. Susan Tucker's rich collection of oral histories of African American domestic workers and their employees, *Telling Memories Among Southern Women: Domestic Workers and Their Employers in the Segregated South*, demonstrates the power of allowing historical participants to tell their story in their own words. Tucker's work deals strictly with the South. One of the few published academic studies to take on the issue of African American female domestic service in the North is Elizabeth Clark-Lewis's *Living In, Living Out: African American Domestics and the Great Migration*. Clark-Lewis also utilized oral histories in her study and focused her study on the Washington, D.C., working conditions. Clark-Lewis's sample of oral histories covers women born in the rural south between 1882 and 1911. My work is partially a follow-up of Clark-Lewis's because I draw on the life narratives of women who were born more recently and who moved northward in the second phase of the Great Migration. Also of great importance is Gretchen Lemke-Santangelo's *Abiding Courage: African American Migrant Women and the East Bay Community*. Using oral histories, Lemke-Santangelo examines the story of women migrants from the South to San Francisco's East

Bay community during World War II. The work of Kimberley L. Phillips, *AlabamaNorth: African-American Migrants, Community, and Working-Class Activism in Cleveland, 1915–45*, while covering both male and female migrants, uses gender as a category of analysis in a refreshing manner, rather than equating the male experience with that of all migrants. I hope that *Making a Way out of No Way* expands the story told by Clark-Lewis, Lemke-Santangelo, and Phillips by providing an examination that cuts across urban settings. Rather than looking at migrants to only one city, this study looks for similarities in the stories of women who, at the time of the interview, were living in Boston, Chicago, Detroit, Grand Rapids, Washington, D.C., and Worcester.[7]

Historians are beginning to undertake more studies on the theme of women migrants. Joanne Meyerowitz's book, *Women Adrift: Independent Wage Earners in Chicago, 1880–1930*, inspires scholars to explore the history of urban working women. Meyerowitz's work examines women who lived "adrift"—apart from male relatives or employers—choosing to maintain their own dwellings or to live with other women. The book primarily concerns the world of white, young, single women workers who migrated to large cities. While not "adrift" according to Meyerowitz's definition, the largely married African American women of this study also considered the modern industrial city the best setting for financial success.[8] Although perhaps accompanying their husbands to northern cities, the African American women truly demonstrated courage in deciding to leave the region of their birth for the unfamiliar, yet alluring, opportunities of the North.

I grew intrigued by brief mentions of the public protests launched by African American women in northern cities during the World War II period. In an attempt to gain access to higher-paying industrial work, African American women, who were primarily employed in the field of domestic and personal service, took to the streets in an attempt to make their voices heard. Two labor history surveys, Jacqueline Jones's *Labor of Love, Labor of Sorrow* and Alice Kessler-Harris's *Out to Work*, include references to this activism. Inspired by the great changes of the period, African American urban women, many of whom were migrants, looked for alternative work and an enhanced role in public policy decisions. The workers hoped to use the structural and philosophical changes of the World War II era to push for an economic victory on the home front. These examples of local activism are related to the national "Double V" campaign, a movement fighting for democracy abroad and at home. As the local protests opened few jobs and had little lasting effect on the options of black, female workers, they have not as of yet earned more than a few lines in our academic texts.[9] These protests led me to think about the life histories of African American women migrants and the importance of documenting the story of their work lives with more than fleeting references. I dared not hope to find the protestors themselves (and I did not), but to document the lives of women in similar economic circumstances. If the North did not make the full range of its employment opportunities available to black women, why were they so intent on reaching northern cities? Were the women content with the fact that their male family members might have access to better paying, yet also racially restricted, industrial jobs? Did the fact that domestics earned more in the North than the South make the journey worthwhile? Were the protestors representative of a female population with a highly evolved sense of social justice and an understanding of the deep effects of racial prejudice? The study would posit answers to these questions and more.

This study originated as an examination of the life narratives of African American domestic workers in the largest urban centers of Michigan: Detroit and Grand Rapids. The regional focus expanded as the initial findings came in. Although I am an urban historian, and very committed to the process of local history, the main objectives of the study were not place-dependent. My overarching aim was to combine oral histories with the documentary evidence to clearly present the work life of African American, urban women, and to tell a story which had not been fully considered before.

In many ways migrants of the Second Great Migration, initially motivated by the expanding economy of the World War II era, remain outside the existing historiography of domestic work.[10] The northern and modern focus of this book makes it unique. The women of this later period, while facing prejudices due to race and sex, found themselves with more room to navigate in the labor market than their predecessors in the field. For instance, the option to perform day work, rather than assuming the more personally constricting live-in domestic role, had, by and large, been negotiated by an earlier generation of household workers.

The increased standard of living in the United States following the return to large-scale industrial production in the World War II years and the suburban push of the 1950s and 1960s transformed the nation and heightened all workers' desires—including those of domestics—for a bigger slice of what seemingly could be acquired in the American capitalist economy. Although a significant number of the women of this study remained in domestic work and related fields, their frequent emphasis on personal agency reflects the changing world of employment in the 1940s. *Making a Way out of No Way* carefully examines the line between the elements of life that could be chosen by these women workers and the aspects that remained curtailed by American culture.

Making a Way out of No Way draws on an emerging historical field that historians like John Bodnar refer to as the "history of memory." The history of memory considers the interplay of the past and the present. It asks, how is the present lived reality shaped by memories, both personal and collective, of the past? In what ways are our understandings of the past influenced by present-day concerns? Memory is an increasingly popular area of study within the academic field of history. Other intriguing insights are added to the study of memory by sociologists, other social scientists, and literary scholars. An interdisciplinary approach to the study of memory provides the strongest theoretical framework. The sociologist Barbara Misztal concludes that there is no possibility of self-identity without memory. Our memories make us who we are as individuals. Nor can we build a culture without memory, for we need memory to know ourselves as a community or a nation. In a contemporary world plagued by rampant forgetfulness, acts of remembering are crucial for both small-scale concerns like personal mental health and large-scale concerns like good government. Mistztal writes compellingly, "Remembering is not a remedy for all problems, as certain matters require the generosity of forgetfulness; but open and reflexive public recollection can help make social life less alienated, autocratic, or dogmatic and more meaningful, decent, and creative. In short, memory is of value for democracy when it is conducive to democratic justice."

The methodology of the history of memory pays attention to both the strengths and the problems of memory, working with memory's foibles rather than against them. Historians of memory consider the structures and nuances of a story, rather like literary critics. Oral history is not used simply as a way to relate factual evidence. The act of oral history is in itself an act of commemoration, yet on a very small scale, with a listening audience of one or two. Unfortunately, as the scholars James Fentress and Chris Wickham point out, too often oral history stops at the commemoration phase, and does not venture into analysis of the narrative wording and structure.[11]

This study will deconstruct the oral histories to focus on the ways in which the facts presented, the silences uncovered, and the structures of the narratives speak to the question of agency within these women's lives. The women made the move north based on a personal decision-making process. Each migrant underwent this process, even when millions of others were making similar transitions all around her. And all workers have some degree of agency; even the study of slave labor now speaks of the slave worker as an actor, although an admittedly highly constrained one, in his or her environment. Why not then expand this vision to the discussions of the woman migrant and domestic laborer? Female, black migrants, although in most cases limited by lack of training, racism, and other factors to a few corners of the job market, often exerted control over their regional location, choice of employers, acquiescence or refusal to take on certain tasks, and other factors within their work lives.

This book will also take as a central task the reconceptualization of domestic work as valuable and honorable work. While we have places in our pantheon of revered American ancestors for the hard-working male physical laborer, we have paid little attention to and have rarely bestowed honor on the necessary work done by women in homes, hotels, trains, office buildings, and other places of daily life.[12] Domestic work, essential to human survival, involves the raising of children, the maintenance of homes, the washing of laundry, and the preparation of food. The work ranges, as most work does, from tedious to intensely creative and rewarding, yet American culture often uncritically characterizes domestic work as sheer drudgery. Perhaps because most everyone performs some type of domestic work, many feel qualified to make judgments of it. In this environment, we might accord honor to a host of occupations, many perhaps as routine as household tasks, typically held by men, but we find it difficult to honor women's domestic labors.

The oral histories, however, tell of women who report their work to be at least intermittently engaging and personally satisfying. Stories like that of Anniese Moten, the caretaker of many children in Detroit and Toledo over her lifetime, have not previously been a part of our national memory. Born in 1925 in Mississippi, Moten moved to Detroit with her second husband but had to support herself financially after he left her. Although some might not think highly of her career, Moten expressed pride in her skill with children and contentment with the choices she made in life. She reflected, "Every time I think about how far I have come and how the Lord has brought me, I just get joy, unspeakable joy, thinking about how good God has been to me, you know."[13]

Memories of the Southern Childhood and the Rural Life

Personal strength often comes out of a solid base, and the migrants devoted particular energy to relating the stories of their childhoods. In childhood, the migrants had drawn sustenance from the lessons of their elders. Childhood, as the beginning of life, has been explored by social scientists, especially those who draw at least partially on the works of Sigmund Freud, as highly informative when it comes to understanding a person's mental stability. Even for historians, who often focus more broadly on the group picture than that of the individual, it makes sense to begin at the beginning, and trace a life story from its roots.

In their oral histories, the narrators made much of their early years, and then jumped their focus forward in time to the years when they established households in northern cities. Although many of the migrants also lived in southern cities before heading north, they made only passing references to these settings. Southern cities, in these women's story lines, figured only as utilitarian stopping points on the journey north. Cities generally, whether northern or southern, were not described with the rich detail afforded the rural life. In this attribute, the oral histories collected for this study align with those done by other scholars. Memories of place connect strongly to memories of family.

INEZ SMITH
Grand Rapids, Michigan

Inez Smith and I met in the home of a mutual friend. As we sat in the small, meticulously neat living room, winter sunlight spilled through the large window. Smith, sitting comfortably on the traditionally styled ivory-colored sofa, settled in and opened up about her life story. Here, Smith contemplates her early childhood, including the rural setting that meant a great deal to her. Her very detailed memories testify to the power of these early years on her self-conception. Smith's stepgrandmother played an especially formative role in her development. In time, however, Smith tired of the rural life. She concluded this portion of the interview by saying, "When we left there, I had enough of the experience."

Inez Crockett, that's my maiden name. I was born in Houlka, Mississippi, in 1941. My mother and her family, that's where most of them [were] living. I think they were born there too. I can remember little bits and pieces from Houlka—watching my granddad drive a mule and a wagon. That's what stands out in my mind. I guess I rode on the wagon. I can see a little house—a little shotgun house and I see this little shotgun house with a long porch and this part that is cut down through the house. I could never figure out [what] was the reason for the house being cut down through the center. You had two rooms over on this side, and you had two rooms over on this side, and then it had this long porch. I always loved the long porch.

My mother, when she first got married, she must have been around sixteen. My mother worked on the farm and I guess my dad did too. I don't know a lot about my dad's mother and father. I wasn't reared up around them so I really never got to know a whole lot about them. I just know that my dad, by the time he was sixteen or seventeen, was hired as a log truck driver. He was very ambitious, hardworking, and they hired him at this lumber company and my mother said they had the best jobs in the county. He was the only black they hired. She said when they were eighteen, she had saved $750 to have a house built. Dad's family ended up migrating to Columbus, Ohio, and he drove the trucks there. I did go to see him twice in the past eighteen years. He was very stable-minded but could never just really settle down and make use of his money. That's why he and my mother divorced.

My mother's grandfather owned his land. He was able to buy up land that he came into, I guess before all of the children were grown. He had a second wife and had another crew of children. There is two families of him. He did buy up land and I can remember being in college and I got this check. It must have been about three hundred dollars. Or whatever the amount of money it was after it had been distributed to the living family members. You know, we probably didn't get what the land was worth.

My mother had remarried and I had a little baby sister and we moved. My stepgrandmother and stepgrandfather had this farm and my stepdad was a cook. He never worked the farm. He was the only child, had been in the service most of his life, and he worked at a restaurant there in the city and he was the chief cook. My mother was also a cook. She had bought a restaurant in Tupelo—the first black woman to own a restaurant that had been owned by whites. This restaurant was down in the city of Tupelo. I never would forget that it sat across from the jailhouse and this old white man sold it to my mother. She was the first black woman to own a restaurant in the city of Tupelo. It was known for beef stew. The [previous] owner told her that she would have to keep this beef stew going because this is what everybody likes at lunchtime. I can remember her making her own beef stew. I do remember going and it was a hamburger place, but the whites still came at lunchtime for a bowl of beef stew and she added cornbread to the stew. She said that her husband was going to come in with her and they were going to make the business into something.

We stayed with the stepgrandparents for about three years. My mother and stepdad divorced. It's a time in my life that was a very happy time. Like I said before, it was a whole new world that opened up to me, you know, being in touch with nature. My stepgrandmother was a wonderful cook. She was a master seamstress. She put me into 4-H and I learned so much about the environment and the world around me. I was able to learn what farm life was like. My grandmother farmed and she gardened and I often tell my kids about the beautiful flower garden that she had. She grew asparagus. She taught me how to snip asparagus, once they got so tall [they] was too tough to eat. I became aware of how to plant peanuts and potatoes. I learned what the "truck patch" meant. My granddad planting potatoes in the woods and I would talk about that. I was so amazed when it was time to dig up all of these little peanuts at the bottom of the plant growing in the ground. It was amazing.

My job was the roundup of the calves and the horses. There may have been four or five horses and a couple of mules. The world of farming was just so fascinating to me. I would have to slop and feed the hogs and watch them throw away all of the food from the kitchen table. That's what you feed the hogs and I learned how to feed chickens and gather eggs. I used to wonder why so many fruit trees were around over the little orchard. [I found out it was] because they planted them. They planted peaches. They made everything. They cultivated everything.

My stepgrandmother canned. She worked with the 4-H and her canning in a little house out from the smokehouse. There would be these beautiful jars of peaches. She canned everything they raised—corn, okra, tomatoes. I mentioned that she was a master seamstress. People would come to the house and she used the Sears and Roebuck catalogue. They would point to it and say, "Fanny, I want this suit. I would like this dress." She made all the clothes. She was raising a niece from a sister of hers that died. Faye, her name was Lilly Faye, that's all I remember. She must have been a junior in high school and she had taught this young girl how to sew also. Faye was a master seamstress. She helped my stepgrandmother. Whatever she [was] making—I can remember the coats in the catalogue with the three-piece suits. It was a coat, a shirt, a jacket—sometimes it was four-piece suits. They would bring the material and she would stand them up on this old block and take measurements and she would cut patterns from paper bags and everything would be labeled. She taught me how to sew. The first thing I made was a little apron. It was coming Easter time and we were involved with the church. Children had to learn speeches and participate in the Easter program. She asked me one day, "What kind of dress do you like?" I picked out this pretty little blue dress with a scallop bottom and little pink roses. They bought the roses at the dime store. It was just amazing. This young girl that she raised when she graduated from high school, she went away to a black college. They hired her to stay and teach and she became the economics department head.

Everything that I think about now when it comes to sewing, the experience goes back to them [the stepgrandparents]. Everything I learned about churning milk and making butter and picking fruit, every single experience that I had in life goes back to that short length of time. Looking at my grandmother, she even taught my mother how to do much of that, baking cakes and baking biscuits and just cooking. The grandmother was a fantastic cook.

She was noted in that little town for all of this, because it was just part of her life.

I learned a lot from my mother, and, of course, I learned a lot then. It was my job. She taught me how to set the table. Every Sunday the table was set. I look for these glasses now, these long-stem tea glasses. When I washed dishes I had to make these glasses shine. Every Sunday morning before going to church it was my job to set that table because more than likely she would have the pastor over. All of these people would come back to eat with us on a Sunday afternoon. The food was always prepared Saturday and Saturday night. She and my mother baked and they cooked all day Saturday. My job was to go out in the flower garden and pick a bouquet, because you did not set the table without fresh flowers. My job was to draw fresh water from the well. I can remember just straining so hard trying to get that bucket of water up. Ice tea was a delicacy. We would have ice tea with lemon and mint. Mint came from around the well. She would have a little glass of mint sitting on the table if anyone wanted lemon and mint to go in their tea. When I think about it, everything was just in place at all times with my stepgrandmother.[14]

When black migrants arrived in northern cities, white urbanites and members of the long-settled black community disparaged the newcomers by referring to them as "country people," backward in their ways. Recent scholarship has traced the migration paths of the newcomers, and researchers concluded that the majority either were born in southern cities or spent some time in southern cities before migrating. Scholars have chosen to highlight this familiarity with southern urban centers so as to discount the critiques of migrant culture made during the time of the First and Second Great Migration. And the migrants were far more worldly than their critics assumed. The established whites and blacks that made up the Urban League, the most powerful organization providing assistance to black families at the time of the migrations, considered the migrants somewhat embarrassing and initially unsuited for urban life. However, new quantitative and qualitative studies, some of which will be examined further on in the text, demonstrate that migrants did quite well adjusting to northern cities. They located work, established homes, built networks of friends and family, and gave their time to churches and volunteer organizations.

Yet the migrants never forgot the rural landscape. It remained home. Although the majority of migrants had lived in a southern city at some point in their premigration lives, rural settings remained their center, their spiritual "home." Many migrant children lived on farms during their early years. Families frequently moved between small farms and nearby cities, choosing the setting that served them best economically, or where their children could receive schooling. City families traveled out to family farms on weekends, visiting grandparents, aunts, uncles, and cousins, and attending church.

The migrant women's tales illustrate their strong bond with southern rural life, despite the harsh reality of Jim Crow. Many respondents, in making the journey northward, were also leaving behind a rural life. A number moved directly from the farm to the northern city, and others spent time in a southern city before moving north. The majority of their families had at one point made their living from sharecropping (farming land owned by another for a share of the crop) and tenant farming (farming on rented land for a flat rent fee), although quite a few others owned their farms.[15] A few of the respondents had parents with urban jobs, but even some of these families maintained steady ties with rural relatives.

Reminiscences of southern rural life opened most of the interviews I conducted. And I found this to be the case for other interviewers working with southern-born black women of a similar age. I had, in fact, not expected the level of detail provided. Memories of childhood centered on life on the farm, the crops, the seasonal rotation of chores, and the mother's and father's arduous labors. The memories remained poignant, packed with meaning. The delectable fresh foods of a rural childhood remained etched in the migrants' minds— blackberries eaten immediately after they were picked, hand-crafted canned jams, and the cracklings prepared from a freshly slaughtered hog. Memories of later years spent in Tulsa, or Memphis, Nashville, or Washington, D.C., lacked the specificity and layered meaning of these early offerings. Childhood, even for black children in the pre–civil rights movement Deep South, had a luminous quality unmatched by the adolescent, teenage, or adult years. Even children not raised on farms recalled visits to country cousins with surprising detail. Oral history may be best in drawing out childhood memories, as these memories particularly resonate in our lives. When given freedom to explore various topics in their life history, many chose to dwell on their early years.

The southern farming system developed during the mid-twentieth century had direct connections with slavery. In his book documenting the migration of blacks from Clarksdale, Mississippi, to Chicago, Nicholas Lemann writes:

> Slavery was a political institution that enabled an economic system, the antebellum cotton kingdom. Sharecropping began in the immediate aftermath of the end of slavery, and was the dominant economic institution of the agrarian South for eighty years. The political institution that paralleled sharecropping was segregation; blacks in the South were denied

social equality from Emancipation onward, and, beginning in the 1890s, they were denied the ordinary legal rights of American citizens as well. Segregation strengthened the grip of the sharecropper system by ensuring that most blacks would have no arena of opportunity in life except for the cotton fields.

Sharecropping made it possible for the crops to be planted and harvested, even after Emancipation. While the system provided a means to make a meager living for the freed slaves and their descendents, it tied them to the land in a manner more reminiscent of serfdom than freedom. Sharecroppers typically farmed for a half of the crop yield, and thus were referred to as "halvers." Others had different financial arrangements, either more or less equitable. Some black families asserted relative independence on their farms, while some needed to heed the white landowner's calls for additional labor. The vagaries of sharecropping were made even more difficult to bear with periodic drought, infestations, and finally, the move towards mechanization.

As Lemann documents in *The Promised Land*, the mechanical cotton picker, which made much of the black field labor superfluous, contributed in a significant way to the dawn of the Second Great Migration in 1940.[16] Liddie Williams, originally from the area of Rome, Mississippi, noted in her interview with me that her sharecropping family was displaced by the introduction of the cotton picking machines on their plantation.[17] However, many factors contributed to the drive away from the South in this period, and no one piece of the story should be overemphasized, even the very important cotton picker. As in the story of American immigration, which historians often explain as a series of "pushes" from the home country and a set of "pull" factors to the New World, "push" factors propelled African Americans from the (largely rural) South, while "pull" factors encouraged them to consider settling in northern cities. Both "push" and "pull" factors must be in place for migration to commence. One cannot merely experience dissatisfaction with one's current location; somewhere perceived to be "better" must also exist, and one must have the ability to travel there. Migrants followed the train routes, such as that of the Illinois Central, which brought Mississippi migrants to Chicago. Later migrants traveled on buses, and increasingly, private cars. "Push" factors for southern African Americans included the flawed southern farming system, intermittent physical challenges (drought, infestations), Jim Crow restrictions (including disenfranchisement), and physical threats and violence. "Pull" factors included the higher wages of the North, perceptions regarding increased legal freedoms, and the exciting urban cultural life. Despite the problems of the South, blacks were not pulled to the North in large numbers until the job market yielded more openings. The growth in industrial jobs accompanying the outbreak of World War I launched the First Great Migration, and the need for workers was strengthened by the immigration restrictions of the 1920s. However, the Great Depression slowed migration considerably. The migrants of the Second Great Migration were initially drawn by the labor needs of the World War II economic boom.

As young children, protected by the cocoon of the family, some of the women did not truly comprehend the great poverty that engulfed most southern blacks. Poverty is something better understood by older children and adults; unless one is hungry, scantily clothed, or without a roof over one's head, one can be uninformed about one's own financial status as a child. In the shelter of family, with little knowledge of the intimate lives of other families, one's status in comparison to others cannot be ascertained. Hunger is a marker of poverty, and is obvious even to the very young. Farming families, perennially short on cash, also skimped on clothing. A reduced clothing budget may not have been obvious to very young children, but awareness grew with age. Eventually, children came to feel ashamed. Yet parents' ingenuity gained the children's respect, and many in the community bore up under similar financial pains. Rosa Young remembered, "She [Rosa's mother] used to make us clothes out of, ah, you know, the flour sacks. She'd bleach the letters out of there, and make us slips, underwear, and things like that. She was a good sewer too."[18]

Many of the respondents emphasized that although they had little, their families always provided adequate food. As many of the families were farmers, food might have been something they could offer their children, even in lean years. Rebecca Strom of Boston noted that her family grew all of the food they ate on the farm they owned, including corn, sugarcane, tomatoes, potatoes (white and sweet), and okra.[19] Annie Benning of Detroit remembered that her family's Georgia farm provided them with almost the full range of staple goods. She said, "You made a living and then you got a hog, cows, chickens . . . we didn't buy nothing but a little flour."[20] Rosa Young of Grand Rapids remembered that her family gardens provided a bounty of food. Later in life, she found it irritating to have to shop for food in northern stores. Young remembered, "My mother took care of two gardens, and we had everything. When I go to the store now and pick up something, you have to pay for it. You'd go out in the garden and get anything you want. A little truck farm, you know, corn, peas, peanuts, cabbages, lettuces, just anything you want." Young's mother canned the vegetables and kept the broad array of goods in the cellar.[21] Esther Woods, a domestic worker in Grand Rapids, Michigan, was born in Cuba, Alabama, where her parents farmed their own land. They grew peas, peanuts, sweet potatoes, cotton, and

corn, and raised cattle, pigs, and chickens. Woods detailed: "All in all, I think we
had a pretty good life. With all the stuff that we grew on the farm, and then with
the milk cows—we had plenty of milk and butter all the time, and we had plenty
of chickens—we could have chicken anytime we wanted. All in all, we really had
a good life."[22]

For Maggie Langham Washington, a Texan who migrated to Chicago, her
family's farm held almost a magical appeal. Washington's parents were very
good workers; the family was considered "good livers." Her father raised wa-
termelons so large it took two men to carry them. "And I've seen sweet potatoes," reminisced Washington,"—yams, as some call them—as large as some
people's watermelon. Let's see, and our cotton would grow taller compared to
some other people's cotton. We used to laugh at them as kids. They would grow
this little cotton and we would say, 'Oh, they have to pick that cotton sitting on
a slide.'" The family never purchased cornmeal or syrup, furnishing their own.
They rarely bought wheat flour, trading cornmeal for it with others. The family
made their own lard, and butchered their own animals for sufficient meat to
feed the family. They only turned to the local store for sugar and seasonings.
Neighbors would help each other with butchering and other concerns. Washington mused, "People in those days just came to one another's rescue. That was
one of those things they would do automatically; Jim's going to kill a hog today;
we're going over to Jim's."[23]

In contrast, for Ruth Margaret Covington, born in the South but in the
urban setting of Montgomery, Alabama, true hunger grew familiar. Her parents
worked as schoolteachers, and later, her father labored as a cook for a doctor
and his family. The family did not have access to crops as the farmers did, and
needed to make do. And even with limited food supplies, they shared what little
they had with others. "When we were going through the Depression," Covington
admitted, "we didn't have much to eat, but Daddy would come in and peel an
onion and make some gravy and get some salt pork and get some bread and fry
it on top of the salt pork . . . Everybody was always coming over to eat. Sometimes we had nothing but bread and syrup."[24]

Many of the oral history narrators, while acknowledging hardship, depicted
their childhoods in positive terms. Anniese Moten of Detroit related at the beginning of her interview, "First I just want to say that I was happy, a happy kid
down through life and I didn't realize that I was poor, you know, as poor as I
was."[25] Alverrine Parker of Grand Rapids, Michigan, concurred, saying, "We really didn't know that we were really poor."[26] Addie Smith of Worcester, Massachusetts, lost her father, a brickmaker, when she was only three years old. Smith's
mother placed Smith and her sister with her grandparents, who had fifteen

children, many still young and living at their parents' home in the small town of Claremont, North Carolina. Smith's mother worked as a live-in housekeeper, and could not take Addie with her into the home. Yet Smith offered a fairly positive recollection of her childhood with her grandparents: "We had that two-story house and lots of trees, and plenty of room to run and play. We had a good time—a good life."[27]

While, as children, the respondents had varying senses of the deep racial prejudice running through the nation, they had less understanding than they would in adulthood. Thus the respondents remembered the relative innocence of childhood fondly. The warm memories in no way discount the horrors faced by many black families; indeed they only testify to the ability of black parents to shield their children from some of the region's harsh realities. Relations with white landowners ran the gamut. Some migrants remembered the whites treating their parents with some measure of respect. Others were happy to be left relatively alone, and the farm became a sanctuary in which to retreat from the constant clashes of urban life. For other families, the farm served as the setting for the unrelenting threat of violence, interrupted only by visits of actual violence. Annie Mae Prosper Hunt, in an interview with Ruthe Winegarten, remembered the white landowner in Navasota, Texas, unleashing a torrent of violence upon her family in retaliation for an unwelcome comment made by her stepfather. When her stepfather fled to avoid physical punishment, men beat Hunt's mother, and broke Hunt's arm. Seeking retribution for another perceived slight, the landowner later raped Hunt's sister and kidnapped the sister's husband. He was never seen again.[28]

Like many people, the women migrants felt that as their lives evolved, something valuable was lost. Some attributed part of their nostalgia to a disconnection from the land. Growing up in a rural setting, many of the respondents recalled, had a remarkable wonder about it. Farm families had a close contact with the land and a sense of achievement when the crops came in. Children found freedom in the extended physical space of the countryside and the parental permission to roam free. Rosa Young of Grand Rapids, for instance, revealed cherished memories of the 1930s, when she rode cows and played in the moonlight with her siblings on their farm in Abbeville, Mississippi.[29] Even the women whose flight from the South stemmed, in part, from a refusal to undertake farm work themselves, often remembered the beauty of some aspects of making a living from the land.

Separation from the land proved very difficult for some. Migrant families held on to family farms long after the migration. Some parents explicitly informed their children never to sell the family land. Ruth Weatherly Manning's family held on to their family land in Texas for generations, despite numerous offers to sell. Her son hoped to one day build a home on the family property, expressing a great sentimentality for it.[30] Owning land marked significant achievement. More black families owned property than historians have previously assumed; the sharecropping/tenant farmer situation was common but not ubiquitous. From 1870 to 1890, one quarter of black farmers had acquired their own land. In some families, land had even been purchased by relatives who were former slaves—a stunning achievement in that generation. Some black families purchased the land with monies given them by former owners (some of whom were also relatives) who may have acted out of guilt. Thad Sitton and James H. Conrad bring to light the existence of communities in which many African American families settled together on their own land. Several hundred such communities, often referred to as freedom colonies, existed in Texas alone. Sitton and Conrad write, "This focus on black Southerners as victims, however, must not blind us to their achievements against long odds, such as their acquisition of land and establishment of independent rural communities, 'freedom colonies.' To many ex-slaves, nothing mattered so much as getting their own land, which brought the only true freedom."[31]

During childhood, parents and other elders imparted their teachings. Fathers worked to build a dignified life for their families, with as much self-sufficiency as possible. Mothers played an especially important role in the formation of their daughters' self-perceptions and their abilities to succeed throughout life. The bounty of self-knowledge gleaned from the relationship with their mothers assisted the young women when they had to face the harsh restrictions of the Jim Crow South and, ultimately, undertake the work of making a life for themselves in northern cities.

Minnie Richardson Chatman, born in 1916, spoke at length about the beautiful rural setting of her childhood in DeSoto County, Mississippi. Her father, Jones Richardson, had acquired his own 125-acre farm. Richardson had had just a dime in his pocket after he paid the preacher for his wedding ceremony. Minnie's mother, Carrie Richardson, because of her husband's ability to earn a living for his ten children, devoted most of her efforts to housework. Her role as housewife was important to her husband and made an impression on her daughter. Having a stay-at-home mother declared to the world that the family had comfortable finances. Chatman boasted about her mother, "She was [to] be at home and she was a housewife and a mother for us. Whatever time we came home, she would be there to cook and have food." Despite this assertion, Chatman admitted elsewhere in the interview that her mother did bring in some income. Carrie Richardson baked for people and sold butter and eggs. Chatman stated that "different white people from Memphis would come out and get Momma to bake different things when they come and pay her and get it. She sell them fresh eggs too. She was telling me and showing how money would accumulate if you save and do right." Her mother had five hundred dollars beneath her mattress. Yet these activities do not seem to change Minnie Chatman's definition of her mother as housewife, which only attests to the importance of this characterization for Minnie. Carrie Richardson also provided for the poorer families in her area; when she would kill a hog she would give some of the meat to people in need.

Chatman made a point of stressing the solvency of her family, especially in comparison with the financial problems that plague so many families today. "I never remember standing in line like they do now, in soup lines and things, because my daddy worked and he had a farm," she explained. Jones Richardson felt it very important that his family not have to rely on whites to earn their living. The farm allowed the family to stand alone. Minnie Chatman spoke of this commitment by saying that "as long as he was living and had his health and strength" he would provide amply for his family. Jones Richardson also imparted this outlook on self-sufficiency to his children. Chatman said of him, "He said if I talk with my children and [take care in] the way I bring them up, he said, they will always work, and we'll have. And so he did." The wealth of agricultural plantings recalled lovingly by Chatman thus had a deep symbolic meaning to her and her family. Chatman remembers the harvesting of sweet potatoes, white potatoes, tomatoes, string beans, peas, and peanuts on the family farm. "We had a peanut patch and we would go out and gather them by the loads and put them on the wagon and take them home," she recalled. Jones Richardson's achievements, combined with the hospitality of his wife, created a comfortable place not only for his own family, but for neighbors as well. Chatman continued: "My daddy had a cider mill to grind cider and people would bring [fruit] from different places and grind it up and I don't remember no slave life like a lot of people say they had. On weekends other kids would gather and they was crazy about us and we would play ball, have games. My mother would make homemade ice cream, make cake, and they just loved her."

Carrie Richardson's homemade extras, such as the ice cream and cake mentioned above, in conjunction with her deep personal wisdom, added to the family's sense of largesse. Carrie Richardson admitted that because the family had so many children, certain sacrifices had to be made, but no one would be left behind and everything would be all right. Chatman related, "My mother said, 'It's a lot of y'all, [so] you might not have ten or fifteen outfits to put on, but you've got clothes . . . We are going step by step up the ladder together.'" Jones Richardson even was able to bequeath this farm to his children. Of his impressive one-hundred-twenty-five-acre farm, everyone inherited ten and three-quarters acres upon his passing. Chatman sold her share.[32]

Annie Evelyn Collins of Detroit was born in 1930 in Admiral County, Alabama. When her mother left the father of her twelve children and went back to live on the farm of her youth, Annie became acquainted with all aspects of a successful rural business. Collins's grandfather owned a two-hundred-acre farm, complete with his own sharecroppers, and he built his daughter and her children a home on his extensive land. Collins remembered, "We had goats and sheep and, well, we had just about everything in livestock—cows, horses, and little colts, mules and little mules, we had everything. He had all the fruit trees and all of the nut trees. He had two orchards—an orchard in the town and an orchard in the country." Collins's grandfather operated two stores where he sold his farm goods. Collins milked her grandfather's cows and sheared the sheep. She did not like the work especially, although it made a strong impression on her. She detailed, "We would milk the cows and he took milk to the town every day. We had to milk those cows late evening and early morning. My job was to wash the bottles, sterilize them, and cap them and set them in those crates—wooden crates." Collins also related her memories of goat shearing: "When it was time to shear the goats, I had to hold the goat's feet to keep the goat from kicking. Oh, listen, they was crazy because they didn't like the idea of pinching. When you shear them, sometimes you pinch the skin and they squeal and they was hollering like little babies because it hurt. We had to hold them down so they wouldn't kick."[33]

Avezinner Dean, born in Mississippi in 1928, also lived on an extensive farm owned by her family. Her grandfather had amassed a very large farm, so large that he needed to recruit a sizable labor force to tend to the plantings. Dean's grandfather gave his land to Dean's father and his siblings. Every one of the related families carved out their own individual spaces on the large estate. She recounted, "They grew cattle, cotton, hogs, children [sic], yams. We had a four-hundred-acre farm. My grandfather left it to us. Everybody was living on the farm. Two brothers and one sister lived on the farm. My grandfather had it." Like Collins, Dean remembered the sharecroppers and day laborers working land owned by her family. "My father had sharecroppers and they would go and get truckloads of people and bring them out on the farm and they would pick cotton, chop cotton, and all that," Dean stated.[34] At around ten years of age, Dean began monitoring the yields of the sharecroppers. Dean explained, "I would work on the farm when they would be gathering. They would weigh the cotton and I would tell them how much they made." Despite this relative wealth of land, Dean, of course, was still subject to the cruel injustices of the Jim Crow

South, including a segregated, substandard education. She received her education in a one-room schoolhouse. Dean married when she was in the eleventh
grade (when African American schools in the South typically ended), and she
later pursued a beauty school degree.[35]

Like other African Americans, some of the female migrants in this study
had white ancestors as well as black.[36] This has been a point on which many
have remained silent. Sexual abuse often led to white male slave owners im-
pregnating their female slaves. In rare cases, however, whites acknowledged
their mixed-race family by bequeathing them property. For at least a few of the
respondents of this study, white ancestors played a part in the acquisition of
farmland. Thelma Lane, born in Montgomery, Alabama, in 1920, had a white
great-grandfather who owned a plantation and gave property to Lane's side of
the family. Lane mused, "My great-grandparents owned the land and it was
passed down. Part of the family was free and part was slaves, but I understand
that my grandmother's father was instrumental in buying the land." Lane here
refers simply to one side as "free" and one as "slave," yet her terms also denote
"white" and "nonwhite," in this context. For Lane, both sides are seen as family.
Yet Lane's mother could not bridge the gulf dividing the white side of the family
from those with a mixed legacy. She refused her inheritance, given its prov-
enance. Lane explained, "She would have got it [the land] but she didn't want it.
She had a cousin whose husband went down and paid some taxes owed and he
got it. My mother was not going to have any of that."[37]

In 1932, Dr. Ogretta McNeil was born to a couple who had both attended a
normal school (teachers college) in Atlanta. Life in Savannah, Georgia, was difficult for the family, although they made the best of things by drawing on family
connections and the good will of friends. McNeil's parents placed her with a
family in what was considered a nicer neighborhood than their own in order for
McNeil to attend school there. As a city girl, Ogretta had a sentimentalized picture of her visits to her father's family home in the country, although she disliked
the more odorous aspects. Early on, she thought of her rural family as impov-
erished. Later, however, she learned more about the dire circumstances facing
African Americans as a group and she reexamined her assessment. McNeil revealed, "You get embedded in other people telling you your history and you
kind of in your head think that everybody, including your family and yourself,
are poor and indigent and nobody had anything. But when I really look back
on it, they did okay." McNeil noted that the farmhouse's electric lights indicated
that the home was somewhat well appointed for the time (1930s) and region. She
reminisced, "We would go on a cart with the horses pulling you. But you know
the house was a comfortable house. You would go up there for pig killing and

making the syrup and it was always such a nice time." McNeil, however, objected to walking around much on the farm. She remembered, "I didn't like walking in the outside, because of the chickens. I didn't want to step on the chicken stuff. I was always tiptoeing and they always teased me about being a city girl."[38]

Fannie Mae Kennedy's memories of the southern farming life are more bleak, and in fact more in keeping with the majority of the tales usually heard about African American experiences in the rural South. Her family earned a living from sharecropping, growing cotton, corn, sweet potatoes, peanuts, sugarcane, and sorghum. Due to the amount of work required in tending to her nine children, Kennedy's mother devoted herself to housework at all times, except for cotton picking season, when all available hands were needed to bring in the precious crops. Despite their hard work, at the time of settlement (when the sharecropper's income for the year was tabulated by the landowner), Kennedy's father earned little cash. Kennedy recalled a typical harvest of thirty-six bales of cotton from their sharecropped farm. She remained unsure whether their lack of cash could be attributed to any dishonest bookkeeping on the part of the landowner. Like many sharecroppers, her family purchased goods, often referred to as "furnish," from the plantation store throughout the year on credit, settling up accounts after the cotton came in. This system of purchasing on credit contained considerable danger for the sharecropping families, for the books remained in the possession of the storekeeper/landowner, with little or no assurance of fairness or honesty. Kennedy explained: "Because, see, all the year we got our groceries from this man's plantation, that we lived on, from his store. But we were charged, you know, [for] the groceries. So at the end of the year that's when they call settling up. I know sometimes they say we didn't get nothing because we used it up. I can't explain it much because, like I said, I was a child. As long as I was eating I didn't pay that much attention." Kennedy's last comment points to the likelihood that she did not always have a full stomach. She insisted, "I always had enough to eat, such as it was . . ." These last words, "such as it was," also lead us to believe that some family meals were very spare. Yet at the same time, we see Kennedy's family pride that they made do despite the deep injustices of the system in which they sold their labor.[39]

Anniese Moten's experiences dovetail with Kennedy's. Her family struggled to get by. Her father worked as a sharecropper, but "the man got it all" despite the yield on the crops from year to year. "He [the landowner] would take care of us during the winter months and then when we make the crop, well, see, we had to give it back to him," she explained. Her early home did not have electric lights, and the family cooked on a woodstove. Their new house featured lights, a refrigerator, and an electric range. The landowner built them the new house and supplied the appliances, but the family paid for the home three times over through their yearly crops and labor.[40] Liddie Williams of Chicago has a similar recollection of sharecropping in the area around Rome, Mississippi. Williams said, "My parents had a farm picking cotton. They was sharecropping and at the end of the year, like they say, sometimes you get something and sometimes you didn't, and that's the way it was. Most of the time, that I can remember, they always got something in the end. Some of them [the owners] was honest and some of them was not. I think they was pretty honest. But they [her parents] always got their money at the end of [the] crop at the end of [the] year."[41]

Bernita Howard remembered the family warmth that surrounded her on her Alabama farm. She easily contrasted the security net of living among extended family in Alabama with the uncertainties of relying on fewer family members in the North. Even though she came to Detroit following her sister, she felt lonely in Michigan. Her life in Detroit "was different than it was at home." Howard categorized Detroit as "OK," but her reference to Alabama simply as "home" belies her deeper feelings towards her childhood haunts. She struggled to explain, saying that the difference between the two regions lay in the absence of most of her family of origin. She felt uncomfortable in the North, "mainly because when I was at home [Alabama], I was on the farm and here I was by myself."[42]

Some interview subjects revealed that working the land imparted a deep sense of accomplishment. For Annie Benning, this achievement also demonstrated her capability to take on the work of men, breaking gender boundaries. Benning recalled, "I used to plow. Helped my daddy plow when the bigger boys got grown and left. He didn't think I could do it. I told him, 'Yes, I can. You go and do what you do. You plow it first and let me come behind and put the seeds in with my plow.' I put the seeds in. He made the best crop he ever had since he had me farming." Yet, even with this sense of accomplishment, farming was not for Benning. She asserted, "I didn't like farming because I didn't like them flies and bees and all of them different things. But you got to do what you got to do."[43]

For some migrants, a love of the land, imparted in childhood, persisted throughout life. Lillian Clark, born in Flat Lick, Kentucky, in 1920, became the wife of a minister. She did not have to work outside the home and had the inclination to take part in volunteer efforts. Clark joined the extensive world of African American women's clubs in Detroit. Having had a garden in Kentucky, Clark acquired the skills necessary to become a member of the Gardening Angels group in Michigan. Through Gardening Angels, Clark taught gardening to others.[44] Esther Woods of Grand Rapids, who grew up on a farm, also found gardening a compelling and practical hobby. Even in her late eighties, she planted flowers all around her home and tended a vegetable garden in her backyard. She stated, "I'd rather do that than be sitting in the house like some people, feeling sorry for myself. I'd rather be out doing something. And some of the people just want to know from me all the time if I ever get tired. I say, sure, I get tired. But then that's what I want to do—I like to be, you know, outside."[45] With this urban gardening, the division between urban and rural life was lessened. Professor Barbara Purifoy-Seldon noted that even Detroit had a rural feel when she first arrived in the 1940s. Deacon Road, the home of a number of the book's Detroit-based interviewees, had been a dirt road at the time. And the southern farming families still raised some animals on the small plots of their new urban homes. Purifoy-Seldon related, "I can remember people having in their backyards pigs, hens, chickens. I can even remember my father wringing the neck of something we were going to eat."[46]

Of course, not every migrant remembered the rural aspects of their southern life fondly. Some fled the South in part because they did not want to labor in the fields. For these migrants, both the economic opportunity of the northern cities and the urban life itself proved irresistible. And some migrants who loved the land or remembered the rural life with fond sentiments also reveled in the social opportunities of the city or even preferred the urban lifestyle. Lillie Shelby of Detroit, born in Sunflower County, Mississippi, in 1920, said simply, "I was glad to get back from country life." The work, Shelby noted, was hard and did not spare children from labor. "When you're on the farm you start early," Shelby remarked. She continued, "You were young but you could go out there and take water and pick cotton and stuff like that."[47] Many of the respondents worked the land as children, and some labored for pay in the fields as young adults before their northern transition. Rebecca Strom of Boston noted that she picked both peanuts and pecans for pay in Alabama, beginning this labor at around thirteen or fourteen years old.[48] Ella Sims chopped and picked cotton for pay before heading to Grand Rapids, Michigan. She took pride in her work, boasting, "I was a good cotton picker." Yet, in terms of the formation of her self-image, her work as an Office of Economic Opportunity (OEO) organizer, college minority programs director, and college trustee, figured far more centrally.[49]

The migrants' oral histories offer a nuanced assessment of childhood in the rural South. As blues musician Solomon Burke explains in his song "Detroit City," the South, for all the inherent violence of its societal structure, remained home. Burke sings, "Last night I went to sleep in Detroit City / I dreamed about those cotton fields back home." The lyrics reveal that the young man was busy making a good living in Detroit, but the lush southern fields, his family members, and even the girl he left behind haunt his dreams. Burke laments, "Oh, how I want to go home."[50]

Oral histories, especially those that stray from the interview guide in order to allow the narrator to take the interview in her own direction, often contain surprises. Despite the emphasis made in recent historiography on the migrants' premigration familiarity with urban settings, the women interviewed here, and indeed in other studies as well, devoted considerable space to rural memories. And the memories prove surprising in their vividness and their poignancy, especially after all these years. Despite the inequalities of the South, the region remained home, the place associated with family, early education, and childhood. Clearly childhood offered a time in which the self was secured. Parents, grandparents, and other elders provided excellent models for hard work and steadfast emotional support. Mothers, grandmothers, and aunts taught housewifery skills to young girls, aided occasionally by visiting home extension agents, paid by the state, and clubs like 4-H. While some migrants fled the backbreaking labors associated with agricultural work, and hoped never to perform such work again, others found real satisfaction in the rhythms of farm work. Many women sought to reconnect with the land by establishing urban gardens in their new homes.

Parental guidance, the positive characteristics of the regional distinctiveness of the South, and the powerful institution of the church, explored in chapter two, provided crucial educational and spiritual underpinnings for the young women, who would come to face daunting challenges. Restricted from so much, black men and women took solace in the resources they were left with—the wisdom and warmth of family, the healing doctrine of the church, and the magical, yet capricious, beauty of crops rising up from the earth. Farming was not an occupation for the faint of heart. Patience, foresight, and thriftiness were all necessities in farming. The challenges of farming proved to be a helpful learning experience for women migrants, who would go on to face the feelings of displacement, economic uncertainty, and persistent discrimination in their new northern homes.

Women at a revival meeting, August 1938, Missouri. Library of Congress, Prints and Photographs Division.

CHAPTER TWO

Guiding Influences and the Younger Years

People whose history and future were threatened each day by extinction considered that it was only by divine intervention that they were able to live at all.
—MAYA ANGELOU[1]

The Role of Parents

MINNIE CHATMAN
Detroit, Michigan

My student Elizabeth Cote and I went to meet with Minnie Chatman on a cold October day. Chatman lived in a high-rise, low-income housing project in southwestern Detroit. Cote and I faced startled reactions from the young people relaxing in the building's lobby; obviously few white visitors came to the project. The building manager, sitting behind glass, required that we show identification before heading upstairs in the elevator. Chatman's apartment was extraordinarily well organized, and paneled in a warm, wood tone. She offered us freshly baked and truly delicious corn bread and allowed us to take some home to enjoy later that evening as well. Her generosity was a trait imparted by her mother, Chatman explained. Both her parents had a great impact on Chatman's personal philosophy, but she had a deep relationship with her mother. Even in her late eighties, Chatman conveyed her abiding love for her mother and an appreciation of her mother's teachings. Her mother still had an affect on her daily outlook.

I was born in Mississippi. They called it DeSoto County. March 9. That is the third month and ninth day and the year 1916. I had four brothers and there were six girls. I was the seventh child of the family and my mother and father was named Jones Richardson and Carrie Richardson. They are both deceased. My mother died when she was seventy-nine in '59. My father died in 1984 in the same house. In July of '59 I saw my mother's death. I went to her and I told her. I am the seventh child and they say that I was born with a veil over my face. Things would come to me and the Lord would speak. And when I told her she grabbed me just like that and say, "Girl, how did you see it?"

I left the next day after we had that talk. Maybe I was here [Detroit] four days, and, just like I told it, she went to the doctor and he gave her a full report and say there was nothing wrong. She cooked dinner that day and left it sitting on the stove. When they came back she was lying on the ground. She had got through cooking and turned everything off. It was night and everything was still warm. They got on the phone and told me that I had to turn around. I hadn't unpacked my things. When I got back down there it was cold, you know. It just dawned on me that my mother and I could wear the same size. So I went in her closet in her room and got some cool dresses out. I come out the door with the dress on and my other sisters and brothers had a fit. They didn't want to see me walking around there because I was dressed like her.

I felt she was the best person in the world. She would sit down and talk to us and explain and we could understand. I don't believe that today's young people have the love of their mother like I had. She said, "If you don't understand something, and it is bothering you, talk to me." She would explain it to me to the best of her knowledge, using the education that she had. She was special to me. I remember a lot of times I would fall and hurt my hand and arm. If my mother would just put her hand on it and kiss, it was the best doctoring in the world. And you would stop crying and be smiling because she always had something.

Mama would make tea cakes and she had a round jar with a big top on it. She would keep it full and then they would make butter roll because we had cows and chickens. We didn't have to go out and buy food. She raised hogs and they had cured ham. She had chickens and sometimes we would gather a dozen eggs a day. When people talk about how they didn't have anything, I would say, "I just can't believe this because my mother had white potatoes, sweet potatoes."

When I got married I waited to go on my honeymoon. When I did go I was so lonely. I said to my husband, "I can't hardly make this week without seeing Mama's face."

I don't believe in dirty dishes and things. Mama really sit down and explain it to you. "Why should you throw this down here, you could put it where it go? But if you put it down here, you know it don't go here and you have to move it." When we got dressed and pulled off our clothes and took baths, she say, "Take your dirty clothes and put them in the clothes hamper." You were shown when you come in from school to pull your school clothes off and after you do that you put your books in place and then do your chores. After your chores, then you come in and have your dinner. The next thing, take a bath. Then you would get your studies and then you would go to bed. It was fun to me.

I am proud of them because so many kids didn't have. Mama killed hogs and if her friends and neighbors didn't have no meat, she would give them some meat, give them eggs, and give them butter. Mama would raise cows and it was just fun to me. I never forget where I came from. She say, "Don't ever be selfish, and the Lord will bless you." I have never been hungry a day in my life, and I have never been without a dollar. My mother said, "If you do right, right will follow. And if you [are] honest with yourself, the Lord will bless you," and I know she telling the truth.

She would say, "I am trying to teach you to love and care for people. Don't try to take their way away from them because everyone ain't alike." You know, I am glad she taught me that. I see so many people every day and I really don't believe that a lot of people really know what love is all about. They say they love you and go right out the door and you hear them say something about you. You can't help but flinch or draw up. My mother say, "Everybody ain't alike."

Family members played pivotal roles in guiding younger relatives. As the oral histories here attest, extended family networks enabled migrants to make the perilous journey north. Migrants referred to grandfathers, grandmothers, aunts, siblings, and cousins as teachers and confidants. Yet, as in Chatman's story, the preponderance of memories surrounded the parents' care in imparting practical skills and moral lessons. Migrants remained impressed with the ability of their fathers to persevere in the face of the backbreaking labor of the farm. Minnie Chatman's father provided a solid living for his children; they were not hungry. Stories abounded about fathers who took a stand for the dignity of their children and their wives. Whites felt emboldened to make sexual advances towards blacks. Black fathers, risking extreme physical hardship, if not death, sometimes defied societal restrictions and defended their families, either with strong words or feigned physical threat. For a black man to actually enter into a physical fight on behalf of his family would have been tantamount to assembling the lynching party, although a brave few had to risk this ultimate threat on behalf of their families.

The migrants' reminiscences regarding parenting centered on mothers. The majority of the women interviewees learned how to tend to their families from their mothers. Jacqueline Dock's statement, "Everything I learned was from my mother," finds echoes in many of the oral histories.[2] Lillian Clark, who never worked outside the home for pay as an adult, remembered that her mother taught her "sewing, gardening, canning, everything." Clark, who graduated from high school at the top of her class, continued, "We learned from her. She did everything and we watched."[3] Those who pursued domestic work as a paid job drew on the skill set imparted from their mothers or other female family members in the workplace. Teaching domestic skills to female children constituted a valuable gift. In one sense, it was just necessary. With readily available prepackaged food not yet a reality, and with the ability to hire paid help far from the means of most black families, women needed to be able to cook, launder, care for children, and clean a home. And as the categories of jobs open to black women were few, many women found themselves employed in domestic service or related fields at some point during their lifetimes. Even those who obtained middle-class or upper-class status in their later years had often relied on service jobs during childhood. Mothers concentrated on teaching domestic lessons to their female children; male children primarily had other concerns. They would have wives to serve as homemakers for them. Scholar bell hooks writes of her own southern upbringing in *Bone Black: Memories of Girlhood*, "We don't like the way our brother never has to iron, wash dishes, or take care of babies. We don't like the contempt he seems to feel for us girls as he watches us doing these things, as he sweet-talks us into doing his chores, mopping the floor, putting out the trash."[4]

The training perpetuated black women's role as servants; black women were readied for this role by their mothers or other family members. Acquiescing to the system remained necessary for family survival, but it did partially enable the system. Rural domestic work often would differ from urban domestic work in terms of the technology used, but the same careful attitudes served the women well in both locations. Like Minnie Chatman, Esther Woods remembered her mother's high standards for housekeeping. Even though her parents had thirteen children (eleven of whom outlived childhood) the high standards never wavered. Bed linens were ironed and changed every week. Spray starch was added to the pillowcases to avoid the transmission of hair oil while sleeping. Female children helped with the process of the caring for the bedding and other laundry, but the mother closely supervised. The girls did laundry in large metal washtubs and cleansed on rub boards dipped in the warm water. Clothes, including field clothes, everyday nonfield clothes, and dress clothes, were boiled and rinsed twice. Woods clearly recalled:

> My parents taught us from childhood up to be clean, nice, and neat with everything, and we knew nothing else. And the main thing was we knew we better do it when they said do it—or else, you might get a little spanking. Of course, things wasn't like we have now. It was much different in the country. But we kept things nice and neat. We was taught that, and we had it to do. My mother never wanted you to put bed linens on the bed unless it was ironed. And of course you know, back then, everything was ironed with a press.[5]

Creamy McKinney also related her mother's housework routines in detail. Again, laundry stood out as a major event of any week. McKinney, owner of her own hair salon in Worcester, Massachusetts, numbered the steps involved, saying, "And back then, peoples used to wash their clothes, and put them in a big iron pot outside with a fire under it to boil them. They boil their white clothes, then they would put some of their colored clothes into the hot water, believe it or not. It was really something. My mom made her soap—they called it oxidine, oxidine soap. We would say 'oxen soap.'" McKinney's mother also inspired her daughter's interest in hairdressing. Her mother did neighbors' hair on the weekends, outside on her farm in Alabama. The work made a big impression on young Creamy, who later became a professional hair stylist (see chapter seven).[6]

Liddie Williams of Chicago remembered similar lessons imparted by her mother. Williams's mother worked as a domestic and told her children that she enjoyed the work. Williams stated, "My mom say we couldn't come out of our bedrooms until we made our beds. Every morning I do that. Because she say make your bed before you come out. That sticks with me and I still do it. I make it when I get up. That's the first thing I do every morning. She told me always keep your clothes clean. If you keep your clothes clean, your house is pretty much clean."[7]

For parents who farmed, helpful children were a requirement, especially in big families. Rebecca Strom's parents owned a farm in the area of Cahaba, Alabama. Even as the second youngest of her mother's children, Strom's mother needed her daughter to take on many chores. Strom said, "She [her mother] had one other child after me. I was doing all the diaper changing and bottle feeding. When they were in the fields she would send me home to cook. I would go home and in an hour have dinner ready. That's how she taught me all the things I know about cooking. She would sit there and say, 'Put this in and put that in.' That's how I learned to make cakes, pies, and everything." Strom worked in a private home and in a variety of factories. She later opened her own home day care. "From small, that's how you learned," Strom explained. She continued, "That's how I was able to leave my home and go to work in someone's home and be able to clean, cook, and care for their kids. Otherwise I would not know how to manage."[8]

Some mothers formalized their teaching into structured lessons. The education was something women could pass down to their daughters. Annie Benning shared these memories of her mother's teaching: "I used to stand [on] a box and see her cook and I learned how to cook. She taught me how to cook different things and it just grew up in me." The careful lessons did enable Benning to serve as a paid cook and to prepare delicious meals for her husband. Benning laughed, "I love to cook roast and I love to cook pies and I love to cook cakes. Anything cookable I like to cook it. Still doing it yet."[9]

Addie Smith's mother taught her daughter to cook. Smith, who was a domestic worker in Worcester, Massachusetts, had a myriad of skills. At her job, she kept busy "doing laundry, housecleaning, cooking, which I know how to cook because you know, [I was] brought up in the country, [so] you know how to do [it]. Because your parents make you do all those things, you know." Smith's mother was an excellent cook, with no need to measure her ingredients—she did it all by eye. Smith boasted, "She could make the best cakes and lemon meringue pie—every time I think about lemon meringue pie . . ."[10]

Minnie Chatman's mother also hired an outside tutor, a white seamstress, to teach her daughter a trade. Chatman said, "Well, my mother would sit down and tell me [about sewing]. Then I had a teacher. She was white [and lived] in the country. My mother could sew before I was born, and her mother taught her. So when I was born I just sit down and watched her and I could pick it up. I could make a straight line. Other than that [training], I just kept on sewing." Chatman revealed a passion for the sewing with this comment: "I wanted to sew and help people fix clothes, because a lot of people need clothes. I said you can find a lot of material, like remnants, on sale at different places. I could be able to sew them into something." Later in life, Chatman opened a tailoring shop in Detroit.[11]

Other mothers incorporated their teaching in practical lessons when their children accompanied them to their domestic jobs. Just as the entire family labored on the farm, so too would available children assist a mother or an aunt with their domestic positions. Shirley Ann Watson Graves of Texas worked side by side with her mother sometimes. Graves remembered her mother, Mattie Watson, making just twenty-five dollars a week during Graves's childhood (probably early 1950s) for her full-time labors in a private home. She left the house at six a.m., walking the four or five miles to the job, and returned home at five or five thirty. Often her husband would drink away the majority of the proceeds of this labor in the local bar. Shirley sometimes worked with her mother on Saturday mornings. Watching this dutiful work, Graves learned about the difficulties of women's work and the hardship of separating from children. When a historically destructive tornado ripped through the area in 1953, Mattie was at her job at the time, cleaning the dormitories at Baylor University, and the children were home alone. The children dragged a mattress to a protected hallway, and huddled together. They remained safe even when the windows of their home blew out, spraying glass. When Mattie rushed back home after the storm, the children collapsed in her arms, making a memory they would never forget.[12]

Lois Stevens of Worcester, Massachusetts, utilized her mother's teachings regarding housework during her career as the caretaker of two little girls. Interviewed just after her one hundredth birthday, Stevens was the project's oldest respondent. She was born in Greenville, Alabama, in 1902. Stevens's family history was directly influenced by the legacy of slavery. Her grandmother had been a slave, and her grandfather was a wealthy, white slave owner. Stevens related, "They brought over a group of people from Africa, and there was a woman and her daughter in the crowd, [and] he bought them. The little girl became his mistress, I guess. She had my mother. She died when my mother was three years old." Stevens's mother, the beloved daughter of the slave owner, had been coddled and spoiled by her white father, even to the point of having former slaves to call on for help with her own work as a housewife. The reasoning behind her mother's attitudes concerning housework was highly atypical. In recognition of her own lack of skill, Stevens's mother insisted that her children learn how to properly keep house.

Her mother's insistence on household skills helped Stevens to earn her living—something that was necessary, as she never married. She confided, "No one would have me," and blamed her unmarried state on her stubborn character. Stevens explained, "She [her mother] being an only child and having a very rich father and having kept all of his slaves, they took care of her." Stevens referred to her grandfather's household workers as slaves, even though they would have been freed slaves by the time of her mother's marriage. The term reveals their ongoing, perhaps unquestioned role as servants for the family during Reconstruction and beyond. Promptly after Stevens's mother returned from her honeymoon, her father asked if she wanted someone to come in and help her with the housework. He offered her the help of his former slaves. Steven repeated the tale, handed down as an important family memory: "She said, 'Oh no, I can do it.' She had never washed a teaspoon in her life. [Yet] she said she was determined to be a good housekeeper." Stevens's mother's motto remained her oft-repeated phrase, "You are no good if you can't do things." Stevens's mother did accept help with child care; she had a busy household of eight children. Stevens and her siblings grew up right across the street from her white grandfather's home.[13] Despite the Stevens family's relatively comfortable life, Stevens's mother taught her the skills necessary for her lengthy career as a nanny for a wealthy family in Worcester, Massachusetts.

Alberta Hardy, born in Mississippi in 1918, drew a sharp distinction between her paid domestic labor in a Detroit hotel and the domestic work she performed for her own family on their farm. Although her family chores seem fairly involved, Hardy characterized her work at home as light. She admitted that she preferred working at home "because my mother was there. I wasn't on my own there. I didn't have too much to do, but I did help out [with] the kids and everything, but hard work I didn't. I did the cooking and the washing and the ironing."[14]

For Inez Smith, family teaching regarding paid housework made a lasting impact, but the lessons learned came from her aunts rather than her mother. Smith's mother, who also played a formative role in her thinking, detested cleaning the houses of others. For her aunts, however, domestic work retained a dignity and importance. There was a right way to approach the work, according to these women. But the low pay and low respect the work garnered from white clients bothered Smith greatly. Smith, later a college graduate, undertook domestic work as an adolescent, working alongside her aunts. Smith asserted:

> You had to do everything. And you learned a system. My aunt taught me a system of how to clean. When you got there you started with your cleaning. Get your cleaning done and I mean, you had to clean. My kids get so mad at me. When I clean, I mean, I want it clean. I said, "I have to show you, and I have to pass this on, the way that I learned how to do this." And I am very proud of it. My two aunts took care of me when I was very young, maybe thirteen, fourteen years old. I would go to those houses with them, and you stood back and you looked at the room, you polished everything and you cleaned those floors and you learned how to work fast and get that work done. And it doesn't leave me to this day. Now I am proud of them teaching me that. And the only qualm that I have with it

when I think about the great big houses when you clean them—at the end of the day my aunt was given four dollars. That just gets me sometimes.[15]

Born in 1930, Annie Evelyn Collins had to earn a living at an early age. Collins's mother and father separated around the time of her seventh birthday. Her mother had some support from her family of origin during her difficult years. Collins explained, "She lived on her daddy's place and her daddy had two hundred acres and he built her a new house and that's where we stayed." Upon leaving home at eighteen, Annie took up day work, working alongside her sister, in Covington, Kentucky, for about four months. "One would do the cooking and one to do the cleaning," Collins recalled. "I helped with the light cleaning and then I left that and I come to Detroit." Her older sister taught her how to properly keep house. Collins said that she learned "from home—you had to do it at home. My oldest sister was the one who taught us how to mop and wash because my mother was always on the go, working and stuff. Not working out [domestic work] but working with her father, and the second oldest sister was left to tell us what to do."[16]

For many women, the mother's lessons came in the form of passing on attitudes towards education and hard work. Thelma Lane of Washington, D.C., undertook paid labor in a succession of different fields—working as a maid, a teacher, and finally as a clerical worker for the Department of Defense. Her parents, despite limited education themselves, strove to raise educated children who valued learning. Lane explained, "My mother read and studied. She finished eighth grade. My father, who was the eldest of his group, wasn't able to finish grade school, but he could read and write and could do math better than I could. His parents died very early, so being the eldest, he assumed the role of caretaker." As with Chatman, the teachings of Lane's parents stayed with her into her later years. Even the little things they did to facilitate Lane's access to education had seared into her memory. Lane said of her childhood in Montgomery, Alabama:

My mother and father always said, "If you are going to stay home from school it had better be bad." If you didn't pass the role at school, ten minutes later your parents knew that you weren't in school. The truant officer would call and your parents were fined. In my family, the only reason you stayed home from school was if you were sick, and I mean sick. So I just got up every morning and went to school. My father worked at night and would come in in the morning and he would start breakfast. My mother would get us ready for school. On snowy days when the deep snow went up to the knees, he would make tracks for us to walk [in]. Every child had to [go to] school and we went through grade school and high school.

Lane also commented on her parents' attitudes towards hard labor. They understood that all work had dignity to it, and Lane called on this attitude during her years as a maid. Lane said, "I had really no great qualms about it [domestic work]. My mother always said never be ashamed of whatever you had to do as long as you were earning an honest dollar. She said, 'If you have to scrub the floor, scrub it well.' So that was the basis for us."[17]

Faith Richmond of Boston gained inspiration by watching her mother tend to her family as a single mother. Richmond, born Faith Parsons, came into the world in 1927, just before the Great Depression. Her father, a meat cutter, died at an early age. Initially, Elijah Parsons owned his own store. Richmond related with sadness:

When that closed up, he worked for a Jewish man that owned a store. My mother didn't work at all. In this store, in the back part of the store, they had a cast-iron sink in which they cleaned fish. They kept a big wooden spoon hanging over the sink, and everyone used this spoon. They didn't realize a man that worked there had tuberculosis. My father caught tuberculosis, but he was doing fine. He was in a sanatorium in North Carolina. The same one FDR was in. When he was almost ready to come home, he asked an orderly to go to the store and get him some peanut brittle, he loved that. He was eating the brittle and choked, hemorrhaged, and died.

When he died, the oldest girl, May, was just in first grade. I might have been a year, I am not sure. My sister is the oldest, my brother the second, and then I'm third, my other sister is the fourth. Mother had a hard time.

It seems to me, I remember growing up in a two-family, two-room house. It was like a duplex, and the toilet was on the back porch. It had a kitchen, bedroom, and living room. This is where we lived.

She worked in a tobacco factory. It was hard for her. She then worked for the Batchelders in Durham and she cooked for them. She would bring home food to help out and clothes from the children of the Batchelders. I was the fresh one that bragged over things that I thought were a big deal. Not too many people had turkey for Thanksgiving.

At that time things were really cheap. You could go to the store and get what they used to call veal, but we called it chicken chops, it had a lot of gristle. It looked just like veal. She would get five cents' worth of that and make gravy and rice. She wasn't a good cook, but we enjoyed it. It wasn't like some people who were good cooks. She also always made jelly cakes with jelly in the center.[18]

Dr. Ogretta McNeil, a retired psychology professor from Holy Cross College in Worcester, Massachusetts, journeyed from Savannah, Georgia, to Washington, D.C., as a child. McNeil's mother worked steadfastly to provide financially for her family. Although her mother later expressed ambivalence about McNeil's pursuit of a college degree at Howard, she went to great pains to secure the best possible schooling for Ogretta as a child. When McNeil's father migrated north for work, fleeing the violence of the region, her mother, who remained in Savannah, began working and moved in with McNeil's grandmother. Young McNeil was placed in the home of a family friend across town, perhaps because the public schools were stronger in that neighborhood. McNeil recalled, "I remember that she would try to come and get me on the weekends, but not always be able to do that because sometimes I'd go to church with them." McNeil's family had few funds and even had limited access to food. As urban dwellers, the family did not have the largesse of the fields to fall back on. McNeil still remembered the gift of a special doll for Christmas, secured at great sacrifice by her mother. Arriving in Washington during World War II, both her parents struggled to make ends meet on the limited salaries of the jobs open to African Americans. Despite their years of study at a teachers college, McNeil's parents obtained access only to menial jobs. These jobs resulted in a recognizable contribution to the broader community, especially in the case of McNeil's mother, who worked in the same hospital kitchen for many years. Her mother's job also provided financial stability to the family. The family moved from a rooming house to a better rooming house with kitchen privileges, to a rented house, and ultimately to a house they purchased. McNeil stated:

When she [her mother] went to Washington, she did day work. She worked as a domestic cleaning their house until she got a job at Bethesda as a cook at the hospital. Both she and my father did that. They finally got settled jobs.

He did not stay [at the hospital job]. He then got a job as a short-order cook in restaurants and stuff like that. His work was less stable than my mother's. He had an alcohol problem.

Her whole life history was there at the hospital in the same place, in the same kitchen. She certainly knew the kitchen, because what do you do. You go into the kitchen, you work, you come home, but, you know, people knew her and stuff. She was there all the time. I never really thought about that.

Due to her mother's work hours, McNeil's father had the responsibility for much of her day-to-day care—attention she appreciated. McNeil's parents raised their children rather strictly. They required significant discipline. McNeil, who took a highly unusual career path, does not praise this early training, but rather distances herself from it at some level. McNeil stated, "Your behavior was very much controlled by your family. I participated in doing the wash and the cooking. Of course, I am not any good at that stuff."[19]

Like McNeil, Addie Smith, while growing up in Claremont, North Carolina, had to withstand a separation from her mother while she worked. Smith enjoyed her life at her grandparents' home, but she missed her mother with an intensity that ultimately proved too strong to bear. Smith's mother lived with a wealthy white family and visited her daughter on the weekends. Smith's mother eventually moved into her own place. Smith detailed:

And I went to live with her because my sister was already with her, and she had gotten her a job. So, I went because I was lonely, you know. I missed my mother and my sister. But I also always had lots of my uncles and aunts [on the farm]—I had them to play [with]. But, I missed them, you know, so I just said I'm going to go. I tell you what, I said to my great-grandmother—she was blind. I said to her one day, "I want to go where my mother is." So she said, "Don't say anything. I'll give you the money and you can go right out there and catch the bus."

So she gave me—I think it was about fifty cents, and she gave me money. So I slipped out that Saturday and got on the bus. I didn't even know how to get to my mother or nothing. I just—as I got off the bus and I asked people along the way. My mother got home from work, and [words omitted] I was sitting on the porch. Oh, and she wanted to spank me.[20]

Not everyone cast their mothers as unchallenged heroes. A few of the women resented having to help out so much at home, and some even wondered why their mothers had brought so many children into the world. Alverrine Parker's memories of her mother centered on her pregnancies; Parker, born in 1936, said, "My mother was having a baby every Monday morning." Parker substantially contributed to the upbringing of her many siblings, and thus felt like a grandmother when she had her own two children. Parker's grandmother took in washing for whites in their community of Columbus, Mississippi. She earned a dime for a blouse, and made her own soap. Her father labored as a bellhop and on the cleaning staff of a local bank, and Parker's mother held down a job at a bakery for a time. Parker did the needed work at home. "Washing, and cleaning, scrubbing floors. My aunt always teases us and says that's why our hands look so bad. She says because we had to do so much work. We did a lot of work," Parker admitted. Yet this did not sour her on housework entirely. She still took the time to iron her sheets a little. Parker confided, "I like ironing. I hate to see people with wrinkled clothes on."[21]

Liddie Williams worked as the primary caretaker of a breathtaking apartment overlooking Lake Michigan in Chicago's so-called Gold Coast neighborhood at the time of the interview. Williams, the second oldest of ten children, recalled her mother's lessons in work, saying, "They [had] taken me to the cotton field when I was seven years old. She would have me to get up in a chair and to do the dishes, and I started cooking pretty early because she learned me how to cook. She would put the food out and leave (she would go to the field and stuff) [leaving] me to take care of it. I was very young." Although she acquired usable skills, Williams considered the work load significant. She exclaimed, "I would watch my young brothers and sister and I would pray that my mother would have no more babies. Because in her second marriage, she had three more after her first marriage. Yeah, I was the babysitter—shaking and rocking. Well, that's what learned me to take care of kids."[22]

Avezinner Dean spoke forthrightly about trying to get out of the chore of helping her mother care for her eleven brothers and sisters. Dean admitted, "I would babysit sometimes when she was busy. I stayed home too much from school. My mother was the one that had all of the children." Taking children out of school to attend to chores was not unheard of at this time; families made considerable sacrifices to pull through. Dean's mother had herself come from a large family of ten children, and thus sizable families were well known to her. Yet one-third of Dean's mother's siblings had no children of their own. Living in a large family could discourage marriage and/or child raising in the next generation, for the level of work such families entailed was made plain.[23] A close look at the biographical sketches located at the front of the book illuminates this trend. Women whose families of origin contained many siblings tended to have small families. Compellingly, the opposite also proved to be true. Mothers of large families tended to come from a small group of siblings themselves. Perhaps they yearned for a greater family connection, or even felt compelled to create larger families after migrating far from their families of origin.

Rosa Young of Abbeville and Holly Springs, Mississippi, vividly remembered caring for siblings, even though she was the fourth of six children. Young stated, "I remember, too, helping out with the younger baby, you know." But one day her baby sister fell from the porch. "So," Young began, "my dad wanted to know who did it. None of us wanted to confess to it, see. But he gave all of us a whipping, until he get the right one, he gave all of us a whipping."[24]

The migrants interpreted the no-nonsense parenting style of their parents in different ways. The dictate that things be done right, and done right the first time, stayed with the women through their lifetimes. Their parents' voices still rang in their heads. Yet migrants realized that some of the parenting had been contrary to today's standards. Some felt the old style preferable, while others felt it outdated, or worse. Barbara Purifoy-Seldon of Birmingham, Alabama, and Southfield, Michigan, achieved success as a professor of dental hygiene. She approached her upbringing openly, saying:

> My mother only had one job in her life. Before she got married, she walked a lady's dog. She didn't want anyone to know that she did that. Education was important to her. They raised us like they were raised. They didn't use Dr. Spock. They didn't use any of the psychological things. If you did wrong you got a "wuppin.'" I was still angry today at some [of] the ways that I was raised, because I know there was abuse there.

Purifoy-Seldon, born in 1943, just slightly predated Dr. Spock's initial fame. Spock published his first edition of the highly influential *Baby and Child Care* in 1946. This psychologically influenced child-rearing method, with emphasis on caring for the individual, did start to circulate in Purifoy-Seldon's early years and could have had an effect on her parents' approach to parenting, had they been aware of or amenable to such advice. Purifoy-Seldon did soften her assessment of her parents by warmly recalling the family's great conversations at family dinners and their unequivocal support for education. "Everything they were denied they wanted their children to have. They wanted us to have a good education," she stated.[25]

Many of the migrants lost touch with their fathers due to divorce and harsh economic realities. Lillie Shelby was atypical in having had absolutely no contact with her mother. Shelby, born in Sunflower County, Mississippi, lived in Memphis and Detroit. Her father, a peddler and field worker, raised her on his own. The break with her maternal history is so complete that one wonders if some secret was involved. Shelby mused, "I know nothing about my mother . . . I know that her name was Lucille Smith before he married her. That's as far as I know. I know nothing about none of her people. Never heard of them, never seen them, or nothing. I just knew that my father had three sons, so I know them and I knew his mother."[26]

The Role of the Church

It is impossible to overemphasize the role the church played in the women's lives. Throughout the interviews, the migrants made observations that reflected a Christian upbringing and worldview. Christian values, including caring for the less fortunate, loving neighbors, striving to lead a meaningful life, and bearing up under suffering in order to earn grace from God permeated the thinking of the women. The hope of a heavenly reward for earthly suffering figured centrally in many women's belief systems. The lessons of the church stayed with the women for a lifetime, attesting to the power of their early church schooling. The vast majority maintained connections with church throughout their lives, and many were exceedingly active in their religious communities. The deep connection with religion bridged the migration; the teachings, taking up no physical space whatsoever, were easy to pack up and bring along on the move. Not only did the feelings and attitudes of church cross regional boundaries, but often the actual congregation moved as well. It was not unheard of for whole churches to make the move north about the same time. Certainly many migrants joined northern churches where they had long-standing ties with other congregants.

Carefully monitored African American girls frequented only three places—home, school, and church. Sundays were filled with church services and youth organizations. Baptism, usually undertaken in late childhood, figured as one of the most memorable moments of a young person's life. Religious teachings figured centrally in the women's ability to work through difficult times. Ophelia Mae Mayberry Hall described her life of hard work, saying, "The Lord has been good to us. He had blessed us beyond measures, and to him I am grateful. I haven't had it peaches and cream, but I shouldn't grumble. We should never grumble. And we are looking forward to one day to maybe go on into heaven."[27] Hall's statement echoed many other oral histories. While open-mindedly viewing the tragedies that marked her life—and there were many—Hall trusted God and attributed all of the good in her life to God's blessing.

Many of the migrants' fathers served as leaders in the church, from ministering their own congregations, as Lois Stevens's father did, to itinerant preaching for a variety of communities (many small communities could not maintain a dedicated minister, but rather made do with visiting clergy every other week), to serving as church deacons. Mothers often provided leadership for the Sunday school or other church organizations. Migrant women followed their mothers' examples by volunteering on behalf of their own churches.

Formal church organizational membership began in childhood with youth groups and choir participation, and continued on into the women's later years. Blues legend Koko Taylor, interviewed for *Living Blues* in 1993, said of her youth outside Memphis, "I was raised on gospel, because my dad say everybody in his household had to go to church on Sunday, and we did. So every Sunday I would go to church, and I would sing in this little Baptist Church choir." Ella Sims recalled singing as a very young child while her minister father preached, and she spoke on stage at just eight or nine. Sims looked forward to revivals, for she anticipated the excitement of seeing men and women claim the faith and come forward for baptism. She, like so many at the time, also eagerly anticipated large church picnics, which constituted some of the most important social events of the year. Sims remembered the exact moment of her own commitment— August 11, 1933, at twelve noon. The nine-year-old stepped forward and testi- fied that the spirit had moved her.[28] On reflection, some women doubted their understanding of the true import of the moment, or even the truth of their spiritual awakening. Ophelia Mae Mayberry Hall revealed that when she and her friends all joined the church at the age of nine, "We didn't know really what we were doing, but He opened the door of the church and He says, 'Come as a little child.'"[29] Many attested that their faith grew as they aged. Lillian Gill of Grand Rapids stated straightforwardly, "I have a deep faith."[30] Only a few women candidly admitted that they had moved away from some of the teach- ings of their youth.

For migrants, few of whom would have been welcomed in the social and service clubs run by middle-class and upper-class women of the nonmigrant African American community, church-based clubs provided a valuable social outlet and a chance to broaden in spirit by taking part in philanthropic activi- ties. Migrant women organized groups to build female social networks, feed the sick and less fortunate, assist with church services, and provide a helping hand for the elderly. Church, an institution which typically welcomed a wide variety of the faithful, offered a comfortable port in the storm of late twentieth-century race relations. Creamy McKinney, who characterized her life by saying, "I just go to work and go to church," devoted her time to running the Pastor Aid Soci- ety of the Second Baptist Church of Worcester. As with many migrants, church served as her primary activity in addition to paid employment.[31] Liddie Williams left her own church to join that of her mother and grandmother, First Baptist Congregational of Chicago; Williams had to drive her relatives to church activities anyway, so the move made sense. Williams kept fit doing aerobics at the church. She served on a mission board and as a missionary at her church. Her duties included visits to the sick. She attended church every Sunday and every Monday.[32]

In some cities, churches did break down over financial distinctions, but the distinctions could be a bit more difficult to discern than in the white churches. Domestic servants for wealthy whites often claimed membership in the migrant community elite.[33] Highly paid industrial workers had considerable clout. In the North, the long-settled African American community, those descendents of free blacks, escaped slaves, or pre–Great Migration migrants, sometimes kept to their own churches, while the migrants, adopting a more southern flavor in their worship service, kept to theirs. With the arrival of migrants, a flurry of new churches were formed, sometimes "storefront" churches set up in modest physical spaces, like rented shops.

The harsh lifestyle of the farmer inspired belief in a higher power, often the only form of solace in an unrelenting world. Lois E. Myers and Rebecca Sharpless elucidate, "Rural people knew well the need for God's presence; they saw evidence every day in the rains that did or did not come, the seeds that did or did not sprout, the landlord who could be kind or difficult." The church espouses a survivalist philosophy, Myers and Sharpless explain, placing value in keeping on when American society was weighted heavily against southern black farmers. In the early twentieth century, approximately ninety percent of African Americans had an affiliation with either the Methodist or Baptist denominations. African Americans followed Baptist teachings over Methodist at a rate of two to one, according to Myers and Sharpless.[34]

A few women spoke to me of a heightened sense of awareness they attributed to a religious connection. Esther Woods owned books about the power of angels. Her often-invoked phrase, "Earth has no sorrow Heaven cannot cure," testified to her abiding belief in an afterlife. As recounted in her edited transcript earlier in the chapter, Minnie Chatman said, "They say I was born with a veil over my face and things would come to me and the Lord would speak." She purportedly had premonitions about her mother's death, her husband's death, and even my visit to conduct the oral history. Chatman also had a power to bring people into the church. As a child she encouraged an alcoholic to declare his faith and undergo baptism. Chatman related, "You know, I caught his hand and go over and got down on my knees by the bench where he was and I prayed. He said he never heard a person as young as I was to say a prayer to God about somebody. I said, 'That's what you asked me and that's what I asked the Lord to do for you.'"[35] Ruth Margaret Covington held fast to a similar spiritual belief.

Covington's father died shortly before her daughter was born, and she always believed "all of his spirits were in her and went into her."[36]

During many of her years in Detroit, Anniese Moten attended services at the Holy Tabernacle Church of God and Christ on a daily basis. She mixed her formal religious practice and belief system with an understanding of a spiritual power of her own. Moten's mother ate a large chicken meal while pregnant, and Moten believed this act "marked me with a chicken," bestowing on her a physical mark signifying special powers. When Moten's mother grew ill and lay dying, Moten related that she laid her hands upon her and brought her back to life. Moten laid her hands on her mother often, not ceasing the practice until her mother begged her not to do it again, citing the age of her body and spirit. Moten's mother finally did die, falling in the kitchen at the back of Moten's Detroit home. Yet she still haunted Moten's dreams. Moten admitted, "I have had dreams about her and she said, 'Don't worry about me, you just come on and be with me.' And I just tell her, 'When I get this house straightened up, I coming.' She said, 'Don't worry about that house, you just come on.' Yes, God has been good, I tell you."[37]

Childhood Employment

Farm children learned the value of hard work. Older children bore particular burdens, as they had to take care of the younger children while their parents attended to the fields or other chores. Texan Ruth Weatherly Manning continually lamented that her younger siblings had more opportunity for schooling than she did. Manning detailed, "Lou Ann and me had to do all the work, you know, that was our share in the country. We had to milk the cows and drive them into the pasture. Rowena and Myrtice and Gussie didn't do anything but go to school."[38] Migrant Maggie Langham Washington explained, "I didn't do much farm work when we lived in the country because I had to take care of the smaller children. You see, when I was six years old, I was keeping house like a woman. I had the babies to care for, the food to cook, clothes to wash and iron the hard way." She had to coordinate everything so that it was ready for dinner at twelve o'clock sharp. Her mother would come into the house, breast-feed her youngest child, and return to the field. Yet Washington had warm memories of her younger days, and reminisced, "But that was our happy time. We loved to see night come." The family would gather in their parents' room, roasting pecans and spreading them out on a chair for each child to enjoy. They would also cook small potatoes in the ashes of their parents' bedroom stove.[39]

As children, the majority of the female migrants had to undertake paid work. Sometimes they contributed to the overall family economy; other times they earned money they could keep for themselves. Most of the women labored either as assistants on the family farm or as domestic workers for white neighbors. A few helped out their parents by laboring in family-owned stores or restaurants. Another small group heeded their parents' wishes to stay out of the work force altogether, concentrating on their schoolwork.

Bernita Howard worked exclusively on the family farm in Alabama. Her father restricted female family members from working in the homes of whites. His stance proved typical; many of the project's respondents would report that their husbands felt the same way (see chapter five). Few fathers or husbands had the wherewithal to enforce these desires, however, for economic realities won out. The respondents did not always agree with their father's or husband's restrictions, but followed his wishes if financially possible. The women well understood the importance of the request. Howard expressed, "My dad always said he didn't want his wife to go in a white man's kitchen—so we never worked out." She continued, "My mother never did work out. In fact, my daddy said before he got married he made sure he was able to take care of his wife so she wouldn't have to go out and work, but she did work around the house and she worked on the farm, but that was enough."[40]

Other interviewees spoke of working while young, but insisted the work was limited in scope because of their father's financial stability. Minnie Chatman stressed that her mother did not work outside the home in Mississippi, although she did earn some money on the side selling crops and baked goods. Chatman herself only began working outside of her own home at sixteen, which would be rather late. Chatman asserted, "I picked cotton and I would go and clean up for people and then I would go in and cook. That is the only kind of work that I ever remember doing, because, you know, my father had his own home."[41]

Faith Richmond, growing up in the urban environment of Durham, North Carolina, had access to a wider array of job opportunities than those who lived in small towns and rural settings. She provided added income that proved crucial for her widowed mother. Richmond expressed, "When we would go out we had to pay our way, that's what my mother taught us. That was the rule." But Durham's job market proved highly restrictive. Richmond characterized the region by saying, "Down there jobs were terrible, even in the services it was bad." Richmond's first job, watching a baby, was typical in its restrictiveness. Richmond began working for pay when she was around fourteen to sixteen years of age. Even at this young age, she could not abide by her white employer's work rules and spoke up for herself. As Susan Tucker found in her study of southern black domestics and their employers, white employers were not uniformly wealthy. Even working-class whites in the South hired domestic help. Richmond's employers both labored in a Durham factory. The baby's mother demanded that her black employee keep to the back of the house when she went outside. "She told me never to have anyone visit me there, and no one on the front porch," Richmond revealed. "If I wanted to sit on the porch, even with the child, I was to sit on the back porch." Richmond went on:

> They didn't have anything in the house but a kitchen set, bedroom set, and the baby crib. This guy I was going with drove me to work one morning and we sat in the car talking until it was time for me to go in the house. She didn't say anything about that; maybe she didn't know. The lady that got me the job worked across the street. One day, when I had the baby in the playpen on the front porch, she came over to see how I was doing. I got her a chair so she could sit, and the people next door told the lady that I had company sitting on the front porch. She said how she had told me not to have any company sitting on the front porch. I was to sit on the back porch. I said, "Let me tell you something, give me my money right now." Of course, we had an argument. She gave me my money and I left. I didn't go back.

Richmond's second attempt at domestic work proved similarly disappointing. "That lady walked around the house naked all the time," Richmond complained. "I couldn't take that. This was all the time. I worked there three days or a week. There were children in the house, but that didn't stop her." Here Richmond faced the uncomfortable situation born by all personal service workers—being overly acquainted with the peccadilloes, as well as the more egregious offenses, of one's employer. Richmond did not work in a private home again.

As a young adult in the early 1940s, Richmond landed a job at Duke Hospital, a part of Duke University. She experienced racism at work, and the insults fueled her desire to move to the North. She would, as will be discussed in chapter four, also encounter deep hostilities in Boston. Richmond felt compelled to speak out about white prejudice. She remembered taking a stand against unfair treatment, even at this early age. Her forthrightness as a young adult attests to a changing South, for she certainly would have faced dire repercussions for such attitudes and resulting actions in an earlier era. Richmond described her employment, saying, "I worked at Duke Hospital feeding the fellows that came into the dining room. They were very nasty and insulting. They used to call me some names of a movie star. We would sling food at them, and some of us would spit in it. It was awful. I never could keep my mouth closed. I would curse them out, the supervisor and everybody."[42]

Some young adults formed tight, albeit multifaceted, bonds with their employers. This is another trend explored by Susan Tucker in her study. Tucker writes, "That domestics have been a central factor in southern culture, then, cannot be denied. Their experiences and the memories of them have woven complex bonds between the white and black people of the South. Through the accounts of these bonds, we can begin to reconstruct the past and thereby move toward an analysis of the multiple pictures of the lives of domestic workers."[43] Tucker's observations hold for northern domestic workers as well, although the practice of hiring black servants was not as ubiquitous in the region, where poor whites and immigrants also worked in private homes in high numbers. When human beings mingle their lives together, even as employer and employee, close relationships form. Sometimes the relationships resemble familial ones and involve serious feelings. Yet the paid aspect of the connection remains omnipresent, and must flavor all dealings between employer and domestic worker. The racial difference between employee and employer also affected all of these relationships. Race has been too salient a category in American history for anyone to completely ignore it. At times, generosity on the side of the employer helped to mitigate hard feelings. When an employer went beyond the minimum in providing for the employee, it could be read as a sign of high regard. Avezinner Dean babysat for two boys when she was a teenager (from approximately twelve to seventeen years of age). Her employer set up an account for her at a nearby store. Dean stated, "She bought all of my clothes and I traveled with her. I got to go to many places. She paid for it. She was a schoolteacher. Very nice." When Dean cut the teacher's hair, the teacher gave her a chocolate pie as a tip. Dean, a forthright person, characterized the relationship as one of true fondness. She insisted, "We didn't have all of this trouble that I hear people talking about."[44]

As a child, Gussie Nash worked as a domestic for the Crawford family of Arkansas. Generations of the family carried warm feelings for her. Nash did not encourage the connection, or even regard it highly, as she attributed the affection to guilt. Nash had met the woman she called "Miss Crawford" because her grandmother did Crawford's washing and ironing. Nash became the elderly woman's personal assistant. Like many young women of the early 1950s, she performed duties that in a later era would typically be performed by a home health aide. Nash would work as a hospital aide in adulthood. Between the approximate ages of fourteen and eighteen, she spent each day after school until five o'clock, as well as Saturday mornings, with Crawford. Nash cleaned up the kitchen, mopped the floor, and helped with the cooking, all for fifty cents a day.

She laughed, "It's funny. Now her grandson comes back to Arkansas every so often and he want to know what he can do for you because she did never pay much and he wants to help out."[45]

Jobs came to young women quite easily. Nash's memory of securing her job through an introduction made by her grandmother is typical. As most girls needed added income and the system of racialized domestic work remained so entrenched in the South, young black girls found themselves approached frequently. Glennette Taylor of Lamar County, Alabama, simply went to a store to buy bicycle accessories, and was offered a position by a white family in the store. Having babysat for her family, she was familiar with the work, and she accepted the job of caring for twins, a boy and a girl, after school. She later worked a press in a steam laundry each day after school, beginning in about eighth grade. Taylor said sarcastically of the hot and heavy press, "Oh, yeah, it's fun all right."[46] Like many of her contemporaries, Taylor learned about strenuous labor at a young age.

Creamy McKinney found work at about nine years of age through her father's boss. McKinney, who grew up in Tuscaloosa, Alabama, remembered, "I used to stay with this lady on the weekends. She was quite sick, and she didn't have anybody to help to take care of her. And my father knew the peoples there. They was related to his boss. And I used to go and stay with them on the weekends and help her—clean her, her bed, you know. Do little things for her, serve her food. And, I did—so, I did a lot of that, every weekend I went to live with this lady and take care of her."[47] McKinney's work would be known as "personal attendant" work or at-home nursing in today's economy, and would not be performed by a child. As scholar Lynn May Rivas reports, such work, in the twenty-first century, is often performed by immigrant women, many nonwhite. The work requires providing the illusion that the patient is more independent than their health warrants. Thus the patient finds that social distance or the ability to render the caregiver invisible is helpful. Rivas writes, "Immigrant women are easily cast into roles that require invisibility, because they already belong to a category that is socially invisible."[48] McKinney, as a young black girl in Alabama, may similarly have been socially invisible to her white charge.

For all women working in the homes of others, physical or sexual abuse remained a significant threat (see chapter five). Women were terminated from positions for not acquiescing to the sexual overtures of their male employers. Beatrice Jackson left her home in Calhoun County, Alabama, in 1936 to help her sister and attend college at Langston University, where she would earn a degree in elementary education. While living in Tulsa, Jackson took a position as a domestic to pay her college expenses. She earned just $5.50 a week. Jackson related:

My first job was for an army sergeant from Minnesota. He ran an ad in the local paper and I answered it. My job was to do the cooking and I knew nothing about cooking, so I learned as I went along. He did the shopping.

I learned as needed. I used to teach myself at the sergeant's house. He was a widower, and he kept a fresh flower, a rose, each day for his wife. He had her outfits on the bed always.

In the end he got a little too interested in me. He wanted me to stay Sundays with him and that was my day off. I was very young and didn't know how to turn him off. I told him I was not a call girl, so I terminated the job.[49]

Jackson's job, working for a single man, carried warning signs. But she needed the position, in which she made five dollars and fifty cents a week. She was vulnerable and alone, and her daily presence in the home led her employer to express unwanted familiarity and make sexual advances. Like many women, Jackson had to end her job, and thus, of course, her much-needed paychecks, because of the abhorrent behavior.

Some of the other respondents related to Jackson's lack of knowledge about cooking. Despite training by their mothers or other female relatives in house-work, young girls often had to acquire some of the requisite skills on the job. Even when there was preliminary training, positions frequently required some skills with which workers were unfamiliar. The disjuncture between training and real employment is heightened for the young. Fannie Mae Kennedy re-membered, "When we went to Oklahoma, I started trying to do a little day work and didn't know what I was doing. I remember one time ironing for a lady and [I] dropped the lady's iron and broke it. You know, because by that time, maybe I was sixteen. You know, you know nothing."[50]

During her childhood in Montgomery, Alabama, Ruth Margaret Coving-ton babysat for family and neighbors. Watching children constituted her main work for pay. She also aided her grandmother and great-grandmother with their work as laundresses. Taking in the laundry of white families proved to be a popular way to earn a living in the years before the widespread use of electric washers. Ironing, one of the most ubiquitous components of household labor, became the duty of hired help, due to its difficulty. Artist Willie Cole has ex-pressed his memories of his mother and grandmother's domestic labors through his stunning pieces. Cole often utilizes iron scorches, once only viewed as mis-takes, as a way of declaring, "I WAS HERE. MY WORK MATTERS." In some pieces, Cole has set the scorches in window frames, inverting them and thus rendering them less than immediately recognizable. Cole has also fashioned the scorches into shieldlike clusters, a fitting tribute to these women, and even flowers, a testament to their enduring womanhood. For Cole, the scorch marks also resemble African masks. Cole has also made super-sized sculptures of irons, irons that fill a room. In creating such large irons, Cole reminds us never to forget ironing, and the racial and gendered subjugation that still accompanies the task. For Ruth Margaret Covington, as for other narrators, memories of ironing abounded. Covington detailed the way in which she ironed:

> I used to iron with charcoal [irons]. We made little charcoal fires and you would heat your iron on this stove to get it hot. There was a certain way you had to take it off the fire and put it on your cloth. Always had to have a towel—you could use old sheets. My great-grandmother took in laundry—she lived near the army base and they would bring their things and she would wash them and press them.
>
> You have to be careful with that iron too because you could scorch it because it was so hot. You had to get the temperature gauged. That was a matter of throwing water on the iron. They was heavy and you had to make sure you had enough cloth to wrap around the handle of it so you wouldn't burn yourself. You would use your cleaning cloth to make sure the iron wasn't too hot to iron the clothes and then you have to sprinkle the clothes also so they stayed ironed. You would get the wrinkles out of them—so it took a lot more time.[51]

Ironing formed an important part of Alverrine Parker's childhood income. The teenager earned just twenty-five cents an hour for babysitting, and her employer also demanded that she iron and complete a variety of other domestic chores. Parker resented the low pay and wondered why the white families could not perform their own chores. White girls also took on the work of babysitting, but employers seldom required the array of tasks Parker was assigned. Parker remembered:

> For twenty-five cents an hour I'd work all day, and you had to clean, and mop floors, and wax floors, and polish shoes. And because I polished my shoes, one lady that I used to work [for], she wanted me to polish shoes, and iron clothes. I was there to babysit sometimes at night. It would prevent you from doing a lot of studying to do all that work. Twenty-five cents an hour and they got all their work done.
>
> One night I was ironing a very good dress of hers, and I don't know if the phone rang or something, I left the iron on the dress, and burned a

great big hole in it. She didn't ask me to do too much that required ironing any more.

Parker's act of burning the dress appears accidental, but the consequences proved beneficial. In retrospect, intentionally scorching a dress might not have been a terrible idea. When one faced inordinate demands, indirect actions such as incorrectly performing a task—as the modern common phrase goes, "accidentally on purpose"—could be the only way to gain an employer's attention. Parker remained outspoken regarding the injustice of requiring children to take on so much work. She acknowledged with incredulity whites' seeming inability to care for themselves. She remarked, "It was just that I didn't understand why we had to always be taking care of them. They never did anything, you know, you were always 'yes, ma'am' and 'no, ma'am' and taking care of them."

The racist attitudes of employers cut deeply into the memories of the young women, teaching them early lessons about the meaner aspects of the world. Alverrine Parker never forgot the way in which the woman she worked for would clean the bathroom immediately after she had used it. In an earlier era, white employers would have forbidden their black employees from using the bathroom facilities altogether. But this slight advancement in practice did not mitigate Parker's distaste for her employer's behavior. Clearly this employer still had deep-seated prejudices. At just fourteen, Parker openly mocked her employer, slyly teasing that she must have had the cleanest bathroom around. Parker recalled:

> So I told her, her name was Crago—I said, "Mrs. Crago, you must have the cleanest bathroom in town." She said, "Why?" I said, "Because I clean it before I use it, and you clean it after I use it." She didn't think I knew that she did that. She felt if I used the bathroom, some of my blackness was going to come off, I guess.
>
> And that taught her something, and it taught me something too. Here I was cleaning and keeping her kids and nursing them, and how can people feel that [way] because of color. See, that's what I couldn't understand.[52]

Children also performed other types of work. Jacqueline Dock worked at a neighborhood store, beginning at about eleven years of age.[53] Inez Smith labored for pay in the juke joint owned by her mother and her aunt. The small establishment served fried chicken and fish and offered entertainment. The careful way in which she recounted her memories attested to the joy of working for one's family business, rather than at the behest of a white family. Smith recalled ordering the groceries—five pounds of trout and ten pounds of chicken. She swept and washed the counter. She placed the soda pops in their iced container. Smith detailed, "My aunt would give me a dollar and, you know, it just meant so much to me. She would give it to me in quarters every Sunday morning because I would pay my Sunday school money out of it." Smith continued, "I can remember Orange Crush and Coca-Cola. You would have to get the ice from the ice truck. It would be my job to go on Saturday morning and wait for the iceman to come down through the alley. He sold ice on the back of a truck and I would have the kitchen door open so he could get through the kitchen and put the fifty-pound chunk of ice over this pop container. I would have to take the pop out and sort them out."[54]

Education

As Thelma Lane discusses earlier in the chapter, the emphasis the migrant women's parents placed on acquiring education stood out clearly in the interviews. Families struggled to find the best possible school for their children, keep them in school, and send them to college, if at all possible. Extended families banded together to foster high educational achievement among young family members. If relatives lived near good schools, especially those that offered the advanced grades, they expected to offer housing for children. Typically, rural children attended a one- or two-room schoolhouse in the first years of schooling, and headed to town to board with relatives for the upper grades (perhaps seventh through eleventh). Small communities did not offer middle school and high school educations to black students. A good many of the respondents for this book graduated from high school. High school often ended with graduation exercises at the end of eleventh grade. A blurring existed in the curriculums of high schools and colleges, as many of the black colleges and normal schools (teachers colleges) open to blacks offered high school–type studies right at the college. Segregated southern colleges offered programs in high school curriculum as well as the expected college education, in order to offer high school to those who had been deprived, as well as to provide remedial courses for those going on for their undergraduate studies. A few of the narrators of this study earned vocational degrees, a handful earned bachelor's degrees, and a few even attended graduate school. Many parents considered the acquisition of education a crucial component of the successful life. Although I made no formal tally, the percentage of the migrants' children who pursued bachelor's degrees and beyond was significant.

The ancestors of these migrants had dreamed of acquiring a formal education. State laws often prohibited the teaching of reading and writing to slaves. After the Civil War, the South was slow to offer public education to all of their black residents. Some freedmen gained access to education through the schools funded by the Freedmen's Bureau, but these schools were underfunded and short-lived. Families compensated by opening schools for their children through churches, institutions to which almost all black southerners belonged. Eventually, the church schools received some meager funds from the county governments, and, in many cases, cast-off furniture and books from the white schools. The southern counties segued into offering public schooling for black youth, schooling that even the Supreme Court upheld in *Cummings v. Richmond Board of Higher Education* (1899) could be "separate but unequal." And unequal it was. But the thirst for education continued for southern black families. Harriet Caulfield Smith, interviewed by Thomas Charlton in 1977, spoke of the strong desire for education in her family, a desire that she traced all the way back to her grandmother, born in slavery. This ancestor, Harriet Williams, dramatically recounted stories of emancipation to her granddaughter, with whom she lived. Williams's owner lost ownership of her in a gambling bet, and this loss led to Williams's relocation from Sumter County, Alabama, to a Texas ranch. Williams raised her nine children and kept the family going through the perilous Reconstruction years. Despite the death of her second husband, Harriet Caulfield Smith stated proudly, "She managed to send three of her children through college; and after all her children were grown and she had this little farm paid for, she was able to accomplish her greatest ambition and that was to learn to read and write. Now it was a Baptist college on Sixth Street [in Waco, Texas], right up above old New Hope [Baptist Church], which was known as Central Texas College and my grandmother attended that college." Grandma Williams completed her studies through the fifth grade through the course offerings at Central Texas College.[55]

Rural southern schools for African American children typically met only after the completion of the cotton harvest. The school session started anywhere between mid-October and late November, and then let out in the spring as the planting and hoeing began. The school year was referred to as the "short session." Some schools had a bit longer or shorter school year, depending on local tradition. Students would come in and out of class based on farm demands. Teacher Harriet Caulfield Smith remembered that her school had more students on rainy days.[56] The labor-intensive crops of the black farmers and the razor-thin margin that separated these family farms from utter failure made reliance on child labor a necessity for many families. Some of the schoolteachers in these rudimentary schools had not completed college. Teachers turned over rapidly. A bit more flexibility regarding married teachers existed in black schools than their white counterparts, due to the informality of the system. And many married African American women needed to work outside of the home. White school districts often dismissed married women. The small schools, at times built only of raw, unpainted lumber, had to, as Smith remembered, accommodate additional children when weather and crops permitted. Some young children were needed in the fields, and older children, devoting most of their time to farm work, sometimes attempted to fit in a few more days of schooling to augment their earlier years. Rural schools typically had only one room and one teacher for the entire student body; urban segregated schools offered more space and expanded teaching staff, but the schools' buildings paled in comparison to those of the white schools. Rural schools made do with minimal furniture, and a few did not even have blackboards. Some students studied at church schools, the only option in their communities, and sat in pews to learn their lessons. Books and supplies were those cast off by white school districts. One woman remembered never seeing a whole piece of chalk until she went to a segregated school in the city.[57] Outhouses served as the only restroom facilities in the rural schools. Teachers played the role of custodian, arriving early to start the wood stoves that warmed the room. Children gathered wood during recess, or arrived with a few pieces at the start of each school day. Outdoor games might consist only of simple childhood singing games or ball sports. Students sometimes shared a single ball one classmate had brought from home.

Unfortunately, education did not necessarily translate into increased job opportunity, especially in the migrant generation. A number of the respondents with college degrees labored as domestic workers or in other jobs considered working class or blue collar. Historian James N. Gregory, relying on data from the Integrated Public Use Microdata Series (IPUMS), concludes that "education counted for little in the African American economy. In fact, IPUMS income data exposes a tragic idiosyncrasy in the racialized labor markets of the mid-century North. Despite generations of talk about the value of education, in 1949 (and as late as 1959) a grammar school drop-out African American migrant could earn almost the same income as a high school graduate."[58] Education would not prove to be a reliable route to improved economic status until the generation after migration.

Barbara Purifoy-Seldon overcame an initial fear of school to become a leader in higher education. She confided, "I was really afraid to go to school. I would wet my clothes every day and they couldn't understand why I wet my clothes every day. But the truth was I was afraid. I heard that alligators lived in the toilets." This shaky start would not be an indication of things to come. Purifoy-Seldon stated with pride, "I was the smartest kid in the class. I was. When I graduated from middle school I was the valedictorian." She skipped a grade when she entered Cass Technical High School. Her parents supported her pursuit of a college education after her years in the U.S. Army. Purifoy-Seldon said, "My parents had always told me that I must go to college." She earned a bachelor's degree in 1970 and a master's degree in 1972. At the time of the interview, she held the post of associate professor with tenure at the University of Detroit Mercy School of Dentistry. She elaborated, "I have been teaching for thirty-five years now and I could retire any moment if I wanted to, but I am not ready to retire."[59]

Ella Sims's father also dearly wanted his children to have access to an education. Her father had left home at thirteen, having only completed fifth or sixth grade. Sims attended a large country school. The students were often much older than their functioning grade level due to time lost from the classroom because of farm labor. She recalled, "I can remember almost until I was in the eighth grade, I was always the youngest and the smallest in my class. Because it was nothing for kids to be—when I was eleven and twelve—for kids to be sixteen and seventeen, if they hadn't married." In their later years, Sims's father boarded his children with families in Helena, Arkansas, so they could attend high school there. Helena offered a high school for African American youth. But her parents' support for study ended there. College was not expected for the children in the family. Sims remembered, "If I had had people to motivate me, I would've still been in school." Sims married at seventeen after graduating from high school. She would enter college, as is chronicled in chapter seven, as an adult, with support from her employer.[60]

Sims's placement with relatives for high school studies was typical in the South. Harriet Caulfield Smith described her familial support system in Texas. Smith moved to Waco in 1913, to attend the upper grades and high school. She had appealed to her parents to consult with her urban relatives, her uncle and aunt, about living with their family while she attended school. Smith described, "I had always told them I wanted to be a teacher, so they talked it over with Auntie and Uncle, and they said, 'We will take her and keep her.'" In making this move, she followed the educational career of her older sister, who, Smith said, had "always" lived with her aunt and uncle. The transition Smith made from the country to the city was not without incident; children mocked her quiet country ways and her studious nature. Smith later recalled the searing treatment in a play she wrote in college.[61]

Lois Stevens and her siblings attended an Alabama boarding school that was open to African American children. Before the 1960s and the schools' financial decline, close to one hundred such African American boarding schools existed, primarily in the South. Stevens would have attended her school in the 1910s. Her parents believed in education, and felt special pressures due to Mr. Stevens's community position. Stevens explained, "My father was a minister, so we had to live a certain way. My family would say, if you didn't get an education, then no one would want [to marry] you." Stevens joked that her parents wanted to "get rid" of all of their children by placing them in the school. Stevens left the school quite quickly, attributing the decision to her stubborn nature. She remembered: "My mother said, 'Why did they let you go?' I said, 'The food was garbage, and everything else was not to my liking,' and she asked me, 'Are you going to live your life getting away from everything you don't like?' I said, 'I probably will!' So, one day I was walking down the street and I saw some girls that were joining the army, so I joined too."[62]

Some migrants had to negotiate ways to complete their schooling while making moves across the country. Thelma Lane was born in Montgomery in 1920, but spent most of her childhood in Pittsburgh, where she attended school. When her mother returned to Alabama for health-related reasons, Lane finished high school there. She then went on to Alabama State Teachers College, where she studied English and foreign languages (French and Spanish). Her siblings also attended college. The migration between the North and South did not disrupt their desire to learn and complete their educations.[63] Similarly, Alverrine Parker stayed in high school, despite having moved from Mississippi to Muskegon, Michigan, and then back to Mississippi to live with her grandmother. After one year of college in Michigan, Parker left for a job in California.[64]

Pursuing an education proved difficult for some. Rosa Young attended Mississippi Industrial College in Holly Springs for a year, studying algebra, trigonometry, Italian, and biology. But her studies were interrupted when the family relocated to Grand Rapids. Anniese Moten left school as a small child, after she was run off the road on her morning journey to school. Following the accident, Moten experienced uncontrollable spasms and had to leave her education behind.[65] Alberta Hardy attended school through ninth grade, but described her reading skills as minimal, saying, "I just read enough to get the lesson in school. I never read a lot of books."[66] For some migrants, schooling came to an end due to an early marriage. Fannie Mae Kennedy did not finish high school, running away from her home in Louisiana to get married at eighteen. Most migrant women married young, as marriage served as the key marker of adulthood.

A number of migrants found that the dream of an education could not be realized, and they deeply regretted this loss. Creamy McKinney, the owner of a salon, had worked alongside her sister for a white family, both in New York City and in Framingham, Massachusetts. The family offered to pay for McKinney's education, and encouraged her to pursue a degree in medicine. McKinney, even after years had passed, labeled the relinquishment of this dream her biggest mistake. McKinney said wistfully, "They were just crazy about us. They wanted my whole family. Yeah. That was my biggest mistake—I should've went on to college, and I should be a doctor. And they offered to pay for it." McKinney believed that she would have enjoyed work in the medical field "because I took care of kids and stuff like that."[67]

Ogretta McNeil, who earned a bachelor's degree in psychology from Howard University and a Ph.D. in the same field from Clark University, had parents who supported her desire for education in a general way, but had different overall goals for their daughter. McNeil admitted, "My parents weren't socially alert. They were working hard to try to make ends meet." She related, "You know, I really see that there was a close relationship between my dad and I, mainly because he did the child care for me and, you know, for him, he is the reason I went to college, not my mother. My mother saw my place as you get an education, you do it well, but you do it to get married well. It was not to have a career. You get an education to be a good wife." McNeil felt her pursuit of a graduate degree placed her mother "in a panic state. I don't think she recovered until the day she died. She really felt that somehow she had not done her job adequately and spent her time kind of apologizing to my husband because I wasn't a good wife in a sense because I had this career." McNeil would lie asleep as her husband prepared breakfast, and her sons had spent years in day care—things that were anathema to McNeil's mother. Yet McNeil credited her parents for how she turned out, saying, "I just feel really so blessed because I think they did a good job." McNeil did well in college and achieved renown as a scholar and a community activist in Worcester, Massachusetts. Coming to Worcester to pursue graduate school constituted McNeil's bravest life choice—at home in Washington, D.C., friends and relatives wondered at her sanity. McNeil characterized her journey to Clark University in 1956—she was then a widow with two sons—as a "monumental step. That was like stepping into the middle of [a] hole, a dark hole."[68]

For a significant number of the respondents, vocational school proved to be an important component of securing a fulfilling career. Cosmetology, as we shall discuss in chapter seven, proved to be a popular final career for many migrants. Mary White of Detroit, born in Monroe, Georgia, in 1910, became a beautician, but not without being first dissuaded from a career in business by the racist practices of the human resources department at the company where she interviewed. From White's remarks, it seemed she may not have realized that the excuse offered by the company smacked of racism. Or perhaps she simply did not feel like sharing this assessment. White, who graduated from high school in 1928, simply stated, "I studied shorthand and typing for business. A lot of the girls that graduated with me went down to Michigan Bell and applied for jobs, but were not hired. I finally went and took the hour-long test, but the lady told me they could not hire me because I was left-handed. So, at that time I did domestic work for a dollar or a dollar fifty cents a day." At fifty-five years old, White attended cosmetology school at night. White admitted, "A friend said to me, 'Why at your age are you doing this?' and I said, if it gives me a better life for just a few years, why not? After I worked in this area for a while, I opened my own shop."[69]

The South provided the setting for the migrants' early years, when their parents nurtured their spirits and provided, in most cases, a solid, no-nonsense approach to life that would serve the migrants well as they proceeded on their difficult, cross-country journeys. Mothers and other female relatives imparted an approach to work and diligent attitude that could be applied to many aspects of life. Mothers taught the philosophy of doing things right the first time, and living by a certain standard of irreproachable conduct. Fathers inspired their children with their devotion to providing for their families. Fathers had to defend their families against the reproaches of whites, while remaining vigilant to the unstated limitations of their powers in this bitterly racist society. Parents often urged their children to pursue as much education or training as possible, so that they could provide for their own children, and escape the ravages of racial inequality to the greatest extent.

Religion offered a valuable solace to the migrants, as well as a means to form a social network. Regular attendance at church services and events brought migrants in contact with a solid community. Friends and neighbors assisted one another with a whole host of concerns; the women interviewed here provided vital assistance to others in need, even when at times they were not financially solvent themselves. Although the interviews conducted for this book centered on work and the migration experience, references to religion were made throughout. From their first connection with the church as young children to the assurances the church offered in later years, the church and Christian teachings offered a respite in life and a hope for better things to come in an afterlife.

As female children aged, they took on work for pay. Working-class households of all races relied on the income of children to make ends meet. White employers seeking household employees frequently approached preteen and teenage black girls. Some families were able to shield their children from such intimate contact with whites. Other families felt that the early training would position the women to take other domestic jobs, and many families needed the additional income. Writer and activist Anne Moody recalled securing her first job in Mississippi, sweeping the porch and sidewalks for a white woman, at age nine. Moody's mother "laughed until she cried," because the seventy-five cents and two gallons of milk Moody earned were a vital addition to their household, which failed to subsist on the five dollars a week Moody's mother earned as a domestic. In her second position, Moody earned three dollars a week for easier work. Moody writes, "Now I could pay our way to the movies every Saturday and then give Mama two dollars to buy bread and peanut butter for our lunch."[70]

As young adults and adults, the women migrants would come into increasing contact with the treacherous society beyond their family structure. Outside of the family, African American women faced a compound form of discrimination, made up of racism, misogyny, and prejudice against those in poverty. Negotiating this landscape drew on a base of personal strength often established in childhood.

Child going up the stairs into a "kitchenette" apartment house, Chicago, Illinois. Photograph by Edwin Rosskam, April 1941. Library of Congress, Prints and Photographs Division.

CHAPTER THREE

The Move North

The most urgent, the most disgraceful, the most shameful and the most tragic problem is silence, not bigotry and hatred.
—RABBI JOACHIM PRINZ[1]

The Jim Crow South

ALVERRINE PARKER

Alverrine and I met just three days after Christmas, in the home of a mutual friend in Grand Rapids, Michigan. We sat in the friend's living room, looking out at the cold, gray Michigan day. The home's picture window featured a direct view of my father's elementary school. Parker's memories demonstrate the terror racism could inflict. The Jim Crow system left her with unforgettable incidents that changed her outlook. Parker stressed that the United States was far from achieving racial justice.

I'm Alverrine Parker. I spell my name with two r's. I don't know why, but my dad wanted to make it difficult. I was born in Columbus, Mississippi, March 14, 1936. My father had two jobs—he worked as a bellhop at the Gilmore Hotel, and then he did cleaning at a bank. Merchants and Farmers Bank. My mother did work at one time at a bakery at night to help out with money.

My dad moved to Muskegon Heights, Michigan, to escape prejudice and to try to find a better living for his family. He must've had friends, because they went to work at Lakey Foundry. He didn't really know it was hard, dirty work. My younger sister was born in 1944. And he come back after she was born and had to go back to Michigan, but he came back to Mississippi. And we must've come to Michigan, probably around 1945.

It was hard for me to understand how people judge people because of their color. And it's still hard for me to understand that. Because your blood is red and mine is red, and if something would happen with you, my blood wouldn't turn you black, and yours wouldn't turn me white. So it's God's plan that all people are people, you know, and not to be judged and put down in slavery and all that because of the color of their skin. Something that they could not help. Nobody can control the way they come into the world.

So, it was hard for me to understand that black people had to say "yes, sir, no, sir" and ride on the back of the buses and all like that. I never could understand that. So, my grandmother protected us a lot. We did a lot of walking, to avoid a lot of things. My grandfather must've died when I was around ten or eleven, and I went to school in Muskegon through the sixth grade. And my grandmother wanted us to come back and live, so I went back. I am the only one that graduated school in the South, so I'm happy that I did now. I graduated R. E. Hunt High in Columbus, Mississippi, in 1955.

I worked; I did little jobs for some of the neighbors. We lived in an area where blacks owned everything. They were owners of little restaurants, cafes, barber shops, and shoe shops, all that. So I did some babysitting and I worked to be able to support myself. I lived with my grandmother. Babysitting and cleaning and stuff [for white people], you learn a lot.

One white family that I worked for, he was the principal of a school. He was glad that I was graduating because he said he knew then it was going to be terrible when the schools integrated.

I didn't understand why we always had to be taking care of white people. And they never did anything, you know, you were always "yes, ma'am, no, ma'am" and taking care of them.

I graduated in the top ten from high school. I could make a skirt then in about thirty minutes. With two yards of material, you had a real nice, little pleated skirt. Black teachers taught a lot, because they know what we had to go through. So we learned how to make our clothes. In fact, I made curtains for my grandmother's window. You learn to do a lot. So that's what we did. We learned to sew, and most of my friends, we had jobs after school. Professor Hunt is the man that they named the school after, right across the street from us on Ninth Avenue, in Columbus. There were mostly teachers in that block. Everyone helped everybody. Kids had to obey all older people. But I didn't like how they called our grandparents "auntie" and "uncle" [when we called whites "ma'am" and "sir"].

In the South, you knew exactly where you stood. I could never understand it. We all come here the same way, and we go the same way. See, that's what I can't understand, the prejudice about color and work. See, they try to make black people feel like they're not capable of doing it, and it's not true.

See, that's another thing too, the white man was after the black woman. Because my grandmother used to tell me that they had to send her to Alabama and leave her four children. A couple of white men was after her in Mississippi there. See, they had children by black women, and they didn't treat them fair.

I used to walk downtown to pay her light bill for my grandmother, and there were two white boys that pushed me off the sidewalk and down onto the ground. I was supposed to get off the sidewalk. And they just pushed me down. But I looked and saw a great big lock, a rusty lock in the grass. And I took one and banged one of them so hard, trying to get them off of me. Blood came from them. They ran. But when I got home, my little starched and ironed dress dirty, my grandmother was wondering. I had to leave home that night; she sent me back to Michigan. She was afraid they would come and try to hurt me. Because I think, after that, Emmett Till was killed down there in Mississippi.

Now these were two healthy big boys that she felt would've hurt me. You have a lot of experiences where black people have to fly away by night. I remember she put me on a Greyhound bus. It was during my cycle. And I remember her taking her tablecloth off her table. She tore a piece out of it, and she made a strip for me to sit on, because you couldn't go to the bathrooms and stuff like that to change. That vinyl cloth kept me from soiling my clothes. The further north you came, you could change, you know. We had to sit in the back of the bus. That still rings—I'm sixty-six years old, and that still rings in my mind.[2]

Parker's story illuminates many of the issues facing African American women coming of age in the Jim Crow South. Parker knew Columbus, Mississippi, intimately; even after decades in Michigan, she could still recall particular street names and locations. Yet the city of her birth did not foster solely warm memories of extended family and childhood playmates. Parker also spoke of her southern home as the place her grandmother fled in terror. As the mother of mixed-race children, Parker's grandmother attracted the wrath of white men who feared miscegenation. She may also have been sought after sexually by other white men, who considered her available because of her mixed-race children. Parker's grandmother had to leave her children for a time and take refuge in Alabama.

Parker traveled between the North and the South repeatedly. As a child, she could move more easily between the two regions than her parents or grandparents. Moving necessitated the changing of schools, but family welcomed Parker in both the North and the South. Parker's frequent moves were not unusual for a migrant child. Sending children back and forth helped to build a bridge between family members separated by long distances. Parents could send children back to the South when they themselves might find such transitions challenging. For adults, such relocations would have been possible, although far more difficult. Changing work arrangements entailed considerable planning, and would have meant negotiating new employment or discussing wages anew with former employers.

Adults, particularly adult males, often came north as a result of the violence directed at them by whites in the community. Men transversed the boundaries that separated the white and black worlds of the South with greater frequency than women. Men were more often a visible part of the city streets. Adult African American men and women both worked outside of the home, and individual African American female domestic workers were the most well-known connection to African Americans for many white southerners. Yet women were less likely to tarry away from their homes in public spaces than male contemporaries. Women worked, shopped, and retreated to the safety of the family. Young girls would have been the most protected family members. Parents and grandparents sheltered young girls as close by the family home as possible. Even African American children understood the danger of the southern streets, but as these oral histories attest, African American men faced particular dangers. Their very manhood ignited a virulent racism in some southern whites, who viewed it as a challenge. Black men's quest to keep their families from harm and to provide for them financially consistently butted them up against the walls of racism, antagonizing the whites who worked to maintain the status quo. This racism helped drive them from their home states. Addie Smith's uncle had to leave North Carolina suddenly to avoid a lynching at the hands of whites.[3] Ogretta McNeil remembered her father beginning his migration from Savannah, Georgia, on account of violence. Although just a child at the time, and sheltered from the full details of racist violence, McNeil recalled an incident in which "some black person had gotten beat up or killed or something in the family."[4] Alverrine Parker spoke about her father's desire to flee the psychological violence that had been done to him by the regulations of Jim Crow. A white man Parker's father knew had been nursed right alongside him by his own mother, and, as youngsters, the boys shared a bond known to some as "milk brothers." Yet, later in life, Parker's father had to refer to his former friend as "Mister." Parker stated, "And I think that was part of his reason for wanting to leave there—he wanted to come where he'd be treated like a man, not like a boy. You'd never grow up when you're down there. I think the black man was a threat to the white man, and they tried to keep them down and they did."

Parker is unique among the study respondents in fleeing the South because of a violent incident that involved her personally. Parker's grandmother dared not wait even a day to send her to Michigan; if Parker had remained in Mississippi, the boys who pushed her from the sidewalk might have come looking for her. Yet, as she explained in the narrative, Parker had her menstrual cycle, not an ideal condition for travel in the Jim Crow era. Parker could not use the bathroom on the bus (if the bus was thus equipped), nor could she rely on locating an adequate rest room at the bus stops. Parker's ingenious grandmother rigged her a wrap made of a vinyl tablecloth, as well as a seat cover made of the same material. Thus attired in a serviceable, yet perhaps not discreet fashion, Parker made her way to Muskegon.[5]

Addie Smith's memories of North Carolina also resonated with the theme of violence. Smith summarized, "It's a really bad, serious thing, growing up in the South." She started to witness horrible things at age five or six, when she hid behind hay in the barn or just walked down the street. Like Parker, Smith stood up for herself when she encountered injustice. Smith shuddered about what she had witnessed, saying, "I've seen people walk behind people and just hit them. They don't even know what happened." She explained, "I was brought up in the South—I saw a lot of things that I didn't like, but never in all my life, even as a child, [did] I let anybody walk over me." She admitted, "I think I got it from seeing things, and feeling. I've always felt like, why should this person do this to this person? Nobody taught me that—I just said I wouldn't do it to someone. And I'm not going to take it from anyone—that's the way I felt. I got a lot of spankings for my mouth."

Smith vividly remembered when her grandmother gave her a severe spanking as a punishment for a fight with a little white girl. The grandmother punished Addie to pacify the white family, even though the white girl had begun the fight. The white girl had referred to Smith demeaningly as the "new cow" in the pasture. Smith, refusing to be compared to an animal, bloodied her nose. Smith's grandmother sought to appease the whites and avoid further violence. Smith divulged, "Even though it was wrong and she knew it was wrong, you had to do that to save face. You know, because it's just a lot of things went on in the South, and that [are] still going on in some places, that would shock you. Because there's a lot of little graves in those woods, I'm telling you. And if those barns and all those fields down there in the country could tell the tale—if they could tell the story," she confided, it would be a dark tale, full of bloodshed.[6]

Rosa Young of Holly Springs, Mississippi, recalled having a need to stand up to the injustices of the racist system. Young credited her parents for instilling her with a sense of social justice. Young asserted, "I always said that if any of them [white kids] bothered me, I was going to whip the stew out of them. And I said, I had said, 'Mother, I am not going to work for any of them, either. Let them do their own housework.'" The white residents knew Young's father well, and his status in the community shielded his family from the worst of the racism. Young recalled fighting with a white boy when she attempted to get a soda from a Kresge lunch counter. She also remembered that she and her contemporaries walked to school, as the school district provided no bus for her segregated school. The long walk left Young and her siblings open for harassment by marauding whites. When a man threatened her brother, her father struck out. Young related, "He [her dad] hit him, [and said] if he put his hand on his children, he'd blow him down. He got his shotgun . . ." If her father had not been well respected by the town residents, such actions would have united a lynching party. Young said, "We never did see anything like that [a lynching] in that town where we lived. You know, they could've brought up a bunch of men out there and took him out and killed him or something, you know. So that kind of stuff was going on down below."[7]

Faith Richmond of Boston witnessed a physical altercation between her brother and a white soldier in Durham, North Carolina. The mid-1940s incident, which predated the Rosa Parks–inspired Montgomery bus boycotts, demonstrated another moment in which a bus served as a space for racial antagonism. Undoubtedly, others have stories like Richmond's. One afternoon, while Richmond and her brother rode a bus, a white soldier demanded that another black passenger relinquish his seat. Richmond's brother verbally defended the black passenger, and the soldier hit him. The brother hit back. Richmond explained:

> This was Christmas Eve and the bus was full with black people because it was going over the train tracks. Black folks always lived over the tracks. The soldier got on and he told a fellow up front to get up and let him have his seat. My brother said, "Don't you move." So the soldier said, "I'm talking to this guy." Of course, he didn't say it that way. [Richmond is implying that the soldier used a racial epithet.] My brother said again, "Don't give the seat to him." Well, the guy was scared, so he got up and my brother jumped into the seat before the soldier could sit down. He hauled off and hit my brother, and my brother hit him. Now, the bus stopped right at the courthouse, and my brother was jailed there.

The young adults' uncle Will soon bailed Richmond's brother out of jail. Richmond rejoiced at her brother's stand. "Honey, you talk about someone being happy," Richmond said. "We were happy! My brother stood up for his rights. It didn't matter what we got for Christmas then."

The sheer weight of events fueled Richmond's response to the discrimination that swirled around her; her mother had not taught her children this kind of outspokenness. Richmond recalled that her mother "would cry because I would be cursing someone out." When a landlord swore at her mother, demanding the fifty-cents-a-week rent that she could not spare, Faith and her brother attacked him. Richmond stated, "He was rude to her. I went outside and got me a stick, rocks, and things, and we tore him up. We broke his car windows. He told Mother he was coming back to put her things on the street, but he never came back. He knew we would kill him; we almost did."

Richmond spoke about the desire to leave North Carolina for the North, because she dreamed the North would not feature the same kind of cruel, everyday racism for African Americans. After settling in Boston, she would come to find northern racism to be of a different type than its southern cousin. Yet Richmond pronounced the northern type similarly relentless and hurtful to the human soul. As a young woman, she eagerly anticipated an easier life. Like many migrants, she learned details about the North from migrants visiting the South. Richmond recalled that when she was in high school "this girl would come down to spend the summer and she would tell us how she didn't have to worry about going here and there like we do in Durham. She would tell us there was no prejudice. Oh, that was where I wanted to live. So, when I met my husband and he wanted to come to Boston, I was quite happy about it."[8]

Lynching remained a constant threat for the African Americans whom whites perceived to be violating a law, or even those whom whites perceived to be crossing over the boundaries of segregation. The transgression could be minute, or was often imagined. Vigilante justice remained a key means racists employed to strengthen the divisions between the white and black worlds. It is impossible to pinpoint the exact number of lynchings in the United States. The practice of lynching, a vigilante group's seizure and murder of a person—often involving a formal hanging—was also augmented by other types of violence. Historian Neil McMillen estimates that 3,786 lynchings took place in the United States between 1889 and 1945. Historian James H. Madison writes that between 1880 and 1930, 4,697 people were lynched in the United States, 3,344 of them African American. While both whites and blacks were lynched, the method had particular utility as a means to enforce racial boundaries. Lynchings were summarily meted out for crimes, again often imagined or incorrectly attributed to an innocent party, of a sexual nature. Emmett Till was seen to have transgressed racial boundaries by saying something deemed inappropriate to a white

woman. Till, lynched in Sunflower County, Mississippi, in 1955, became a rally-
ing point for the burgeoning civil rights movement. Yet according to James H.
Madison, the great majority of the victims were not accused of sexual crimes.
In fact, Madison argues, contrary to popular opinion, women made up the largest group of victims. Perhaps most disturbing is the fact that crowds of white
men, women, and children turned out to witness the lynchings. These adults
in effect taught racial intolerance and violence to their offspring, condoning
and even celebrating the ghastly events by their presence. African Americans
making use of public space unfortunately also bore witness to the intentional
murder of members of the community. Those who witnessed a lynching, even
as small children, never forgot the event. Lynchings were more commonplace
in the South than the North (lynchings were 95 percent southern in the 1920s),
but northern vigilante justice was not unheard of. Between 1880 and 1930, 123
people lost their lives to northern lynch mobs, 79 of them in the Midwest.[9]

Ida Mae Mitchell, who migrated to New York City as an adult, lost her
brother Bennie in a lynching in Texas. The story, chronicled in the book *Leavin'
a Testimony: Portraits from Rural Texas* by Patsy Cravens, involved the lynching
of two young boys in 1935. They were blamed for the rape of a white neighbor, whose own brother reportedly admitted to the crime on his deathbed. The
memory of the incident continued to haunt Mitchell many decades later.[10] The
assertion that these incidents are safely "in the past" ought to be reconsidered.
In the early twenty-first century, men and women who had witnessed a lynching or lost a family member to the heinous crime were still alive. The attacks
bequeathed searing memories to the witnesses, who passed on the stories of
terror to subsequent generations.

Carrie Skipwith Mayfield, born in 1903, witnessed the aftermath of a lynching in Waco, Texas. Her memories are of a "spectacle lynching," complete with
"torture, mutilation, and the immolation of the suspect" in front of crowds. The
story she recounted resembles both the lynching of Jesse Washington, convicted
of a rape and murder in an improperly constituted trial in 1916, and a similar
incident involving an attack on Jesse Thomas in 1922. Convicted of murdering
Lucy Fryer on May 8, 1916, Jesse Washington was dragged from the McLennan
County Courthouse by a mob of white men. Men cut off his ear and castrated
him. They hung him and repeatedly lowered him into a fire, right in front of
Waco City Hall. A crowd of ten to fifteen thousand bore witness to the horror.
Unmasked men posed for pictures with the corpse; the pictures, taken by pho-
tographer Fred Gildersleeve, were late sold as postcards.[11]

The second incident took place on May 25, 1922. A white man was murdered
on a highway east of Waco, and his girlfriend raped. The girlfriend described the

assailant as a light-skinned black man with a gold tooth. A deputized white Wacoan thought Jesse Thomas matched the description. The deputy brought Thomas to the woman's house, and she screamed. Her father shot Thomas dead. Thomas's body was dragged down to the center of town, hung in a tree, and set on fire. Mayfield would have been around thirteen at the time of the first incident, and around nineteen at the time of the second. Given the nature of her description, the 1916 lynching may have been the one she was describing, but it remains unclear. As Patricia Bernstein points out, "Black memories of the lynchings of Washington, Thomas, and other victims of mob violence blurred together, eventually becoming one horrible racial catastrophe in the minds of most black Wacoans." On the day of the lynching she witnessed, Mayfield recalled that her father had urged her to take a different route home from school. Always curious, Mayfield defied her father's wishes. She came upon crowds of whites in the city center. Pieces of the young man's body were displayed in shop windows. Mayfield recalled, "We came home and we looked in the windows— and come along and looked in the window: 'What is this?' And some of them says, 'That looks like such-and-such, say, part of a person.' Went up there—go on up to another store and something—see something else. Put two and two together and finally find out that it was a person. Got home, everybody was just up in the air talking about it."[12]

Lillie Shelby spoke of the constancy of southern prejudice; at seemingly every moment, whites interpreted her actions and the actions of her family through a racialized lens. To their white neighbors, Shelby's family members were never simply residents of Sunflower County, Mississippi—they were always black. Shelby explained, "You always knew you were the Negro. You knew you were different. They let you know you were different." Shelby's husband put three quarters in a slot machine and won a twenty-five-dollar jackpot. Shelby recalled, "Well, these whites done never let him forget it. Well, that's the nigger that won all that money. You're 'nigger rich.' You always knew you couldn't forget it. With these young people up here [in Detroit], they don't know a thing about that."[13]

Some of the migrants had a degree of protection from southern white hostilities. Alverrine Parker remembered, in her extended narrative at the beginning of the chapter, how her family would avoid public transportation. Yet her grandmother could not clear the city streets of wayward white youth for her. Annie Evelyn Collins lived ensconced on her grandfather's two-hundred-acre plantation, as much out of harm's way as the family could get her. Collins's grandfather furthered relationships with area whites by offering a free dinner to neighbors, white and black, every year. Collins nonetheless was in a position to compare southern racism with the northern brand; her family could not shield young

Collins completely from the ravages of racism. Like some of the migrants, but not all, Collins judged southern racism as more sinister than northern racism. She stated, "It was worse in the South. There is some segregation still here [Michigan], but it was worse in the South. I really didn't deal with a lot of segregation myself. My grandfather just had two hundred acres and we were just on my grandfather's place all of the time."[14]

Many of the migrants posited that a key difference separated southern and northern racism. In the South, black families had raised children to anticipate racism, and whites expected a rigid protocol to be followed. In the North, blacks anticipated a loosening of racial strictures and did encounter some freedoms—yet they nonetheless were hit with racism. This less-anticipated racism stung sharply. Ruth Margaret Covington provided the opinion that in the South "we knew what we had to do there. You see, you know what you've got to do and you did it and we were blessed to have some good white neighbors right in the back of us. There was an everyday over-the-fence conversation. There was sharing because Momma had fruit trees and gardens. And my grandmother was [a] light complexion woman so therefore there's white blood in our family." Covington expressed a "turn-the-other-cheek" philosophy about reacting to racist incidents. She asserted, "I just tried to show love and concern," when faced with prejudice.[15]

Thelma Lane expressed a contrary view. After careful consideration of the consequences, she would act if provoked. Lane, living in Washington, D.C., at the time of the interview, also had lived in Montgomery and Troy, Alabama, Pittsburgh, and parts of Virginia. Lane put forth her own philosophy, saying, "I was always quick to defend. I had to be told that you don't always act. My mother always said you think twice and act once." Lane characterized Washington, D.C., as the South, although some of its inhabitants wanted to bequeath the national capital the status of northern city. Lane recalled:

> Oh, yeah, they used to have signs up, even in Washington. The department stores weren't too bad, but the signs [reading] "White" or "Negro" bathrooms were the same as in Montgomery.
>
> I was at Virginia State one summer taking a reading workshop and I went downtown and they wanted me to go to the back of the store and I wouldn't buy any of that. I went to buy a hat and I wanted to try it on and they put a stocking cap on me. Those are some of the humiliating things I had to go through. People in Washington, some of them, because it is called the District of Columbia, a lot of them think they are in the North, but they are part of the South. They say, "Oh, down south they do such and such a thing." But just a moment, we are in the South. I said I

wouldn't want to be any further south than I am right now—right here in Washington. There is no difference except that they could ride the bus and sit anywhere they want. I said, "Do you know your geography or your history? Do you know where the dividing line between the North and the South is?" I said, "We are right here in Washington. We are below the Mason-Dixon line. That is up in Maryland."[16]

Ogretta McNeil did characterize life in Washington, D.C., as significantly different from that of Georgia, even though she lived in a largely segregated African American community in D.C. She relished the feeling of Washington, although she balked at the disdain shown for African American students in her integrated D.C. elementary school. McNeil remembered:

Actually, I had a lot of freedom in Washington. I didn't really feel it [segregation] because there were no [negative] encounters, whereas there was a clearer message in the South that nobody had to say anything to you directly because it's in the air. Everybody feels it, everybody responds to it; it's just a part of what you learn without anybody sitting you down and saying, "You can't go here and you can't do this and whatever." You just know your limits. You just know that you are treated differently.[17]

Individual memories illustrate that the real world of the Jim Crow South was more complicated than many imagine. An extensive legal framework of oppression ruled the region, yet blacks and whites had intertwined lives as neighbors and employers and employees. Though interracial social forums were few, blacks and whites interacted in business and shared the same streets. It was impossible for people of different races to live completely separate lives within a single physical community; that impossibility is just one factor demonstrating the ridiculousness of Jim Crow. Sometimes people could overcome legal and social strictures, albeit in a limited way. Gussie Nash of Grand Rapids remembered interacting in a positive fashion with whites during her Arkansas childhood. Nash claimed, "Down there we just mixed with white people. There was no prejudice. Everybody [in my hometown] knew everybody."[18] Here, Nash chooses not to categorize the racialized system of her Arkansas home, where, among other restrictions, many black women found themselves relegated to performing domestic jobs, as "prejudiced." Nash does not find fault with her white neighbors, whom she knew personally, for the system. No doubt Nash considered the highly ordered racist system of the region more powerful than any particular historical actors.

Avezinner Dean's memories of Mississippi included a bit of social mixing between races. Her memories did not entirely coincide with the history of the period as described in today's history books. Or perhaps Dean overplayed the exceptions to racial segregation because she bristled at having her past explained by historical generalizations, when the Mississippi of her memory remained more haphazard. While her world remained mostly black, it was porous around the edges. Dean expressed warm feelings for her white employers. She remembered the mixing of white and black residents at sports facilities, both public and private. Dean mused, "You know, like this integrating and segregating. The white kids come over to our pools. We didn't have no [school] buses to ride when I first started school but after years they had buses [for the black schools]." Dean's brother taught math at an African American school, and received local attention from white educators for his methods. In this case, the black schools had a pedagogical approach that the white school personnel envied. White students and teachers came to take part in his classes. Dean said, "They would come by school and sit in on math class. When they integrated school we didn't understand, being children in our heads, because we never had those problems. We used their gyms and played on all of those things."[19] It is interesting that Dean is not categorizing the segregated school itself here as a "problem."

The Migration

ELLA SIMS
Grand Rapids, Michigan

Ella Sims and I met in her lovely, second-floor apartment in Grand Rapids, Michigan, on a warm summer day. We sat in her living room, overlooking the dense tree canopy and scattered flowers of the apartment grounds. Sims and I had previously gone out to lunch together, along with a mutual friend, Estelle Leven, who wanted us to meet. Leven and Sims had known each other for years, through the variety of volunteer positions both had held. It was Sims's leadership roles at the local Office of Economic Opportunity in the 1960s and in later years as an employee and trustee of Aquinas College, a local Catholic institution, that had garnered her great respect in the city. Sims had been interviewed before; an earlier interview was housed in the Grand Rapids Public Library. Her phone rang repeatedly throughout the interview; family and friends were all eager to speak with her and seek her advice.

Sims explored her motivations for moving to Michigan. Like many migrants,
she came north on a vacation and stayed. She came to Grand Rapids for a short-
term visit to her female cousin and was offered a job. Blue-collar jobs were rela-
tively easy to locate and obtain.

Well, I was born in the South. My parents were sharecroppers—we grew cotton and corn. One of three girls, and I'm the middle girl. My daddy was a Baptist preacher. We moved a heck of a lot. Because they always say the preacher's always moving, and I think that was the truth. But I guess we had a normal childhood. We used to go and sing while my daddy preached. We had a mother that was really [an] invalid. I think she must've had polio, before she met my daddy, before she had any children.

When I went over to Arkansas and went to high school,[20] I married right out of high school in my senior year, when I was seventeen. I met him right there in high school; he was just a grade ahead of me, and I guess that's how come it was so easy to talk me into getting married.

I was married for three years before I got pregnant. I had a baby boy. And my baby lived to be ten months old and died very suddenly one night. Soon after that I got pregnant again. So then my second son was born. And he was born the twenty-eighth day of September, and on Thanksgiving morning my husband woke up sick. So the baby was about two months old. And my husband was just sick five days, and he died.

When we went to bed that night, I woke up the next morning with him calling me, and he said, "Oh, I'm as sick as I could be." Now this is what's strange—from the moment when he said that until he died, he never had another pain. He was just very sick. Something had burst in his ear. We had a very hard time getting a doctor on Thanksgiving, and so I finally got a doctor out to the house, and he didn't tell me much, just to give him some pills. And so then our doctor, who was gone Thanksgiving, was back in town. My husband's uncle went to his house. You know, a little small town, everybody knows everybody. Dr. Miller told the uncle, "Go on, Wes. I'll be all set." [And the uncle said,] "No, I am staying right here until you get up."

I knew there was something very serious by the way the doctor put his tube in my husband's ear, and he wasn't saying anything. The doctor said these words to me, he said, "We're going to see if we can save his life. We're going to take him to the hospital right now, and we are going to start giving him this new drug [penicillin]." Now, after he died, the doctor put on the death certificate "abscess in the brain." And with my children, if somebody says they have an earache, I am scared to death.

I remember saying over and over, "I'm twenty-two years old and my life is over." By March, I was in such terrible shape. My doctor asked me if I had any relatives anywhere so I could just take a vacation. And that's how I came to Michigan. Incidentally, my cousins that had moved to Grand Rapids, Michigan, was the same cousins that I went to live with to go to high school in Arkansas.

I came for vacation. My cousin said, "Oh, why don't you stay for the summer?" I said, "Well, I think I will." She said, "I bet you could get hired at the Pantlind Hotel." And so, I got hired at the Pantlind Hotel. Back then, even if you went to General Motors, you could get hired the same day. I came here in March of 1946. My husband died December 1945. My baby was born September 1945.

And so, when I started working, I had to have a babysitter. A neighbor, she sat keeping the baby for me. And so one day she said to me, she was asking me if everything was okay, and I said, "Well, I don't know." I wasn't getting the check from Social Security then. She said, "They are hiring at the railroad." And she told me how to get out there on the bus. And I went out there and got hired! They hired me on the second-shift job, and they wanted me to come to work that night. And she still kept the baby, because she just stayed two doors from my cousin's. So I could pick the baby up—I didn't get off until eleven at night. I must've maybe worked out there for a year before I got on days. But she was a good friend and she kept the baby. After that I got an apartment away from my cousin, and I also met my future husband. I'd been there a year when I met him.[21]

Existing archival collections feature few stories of the Second Great Migration, and only rarely has the movement been considered from the female viewpoint in oral histories. Of the resources that exist, few could rival the specificity and wrenching emotion of Sims's memories. An examination of the broad array of reasons for African American women's migration expands our understanding of this key American movement. Sims's tale of her difficult southern life, including the frightening details of her first husband's illness, makes her need for a Michigan vacation clear. Her recollection of an almost accidental decision to remain in Grand Rapids bears noticing; so often major life moments "fall into place" as this regional shift does for Sims. Darlene Clark Hine, in her article "Black Migration to the Urban Midwest: The Gender Dimension, 1915–1945," argues that historians must focus much more effort on analyzing the story of the female migrant. She writes:

we need micro-studies into individual life, of neighborhoods, families, churches, and fraternal lodges in various cities. Examination of these themes makes imperative an even deeper penetration into the internal world of Afro-Americans. Perhaps, even more dauntingly, to answer fully these questions requires that the black woman's voice and experience be researched and interpreted with the same intensity and seriousness accorded that of the black man.

Information derived from statistical and demographic data on black midwestern migration and urbanization must be combined with the knowledge drawn from the small, but growing, numbers of oral histories, autobiographies, and biographies of twentieth century migrating women . . . Actually these sources, properly "squeezed and teased," promise to light up that inner world so long shrouded behind a veil of neglect, silence, and stereotype, and will quite likely force a rethinking and rewriting of all of black urban history.[22]

This study, and perhaps especially this section, add a somewhat overlooked element to the history of African American migration: analysis of women's personal reasons for the migration. Certain societal structures, including the economics of southern society, political disfranchisement, the raging, daily insults of a discrimination defended by law, and the threat and reality of violence—a violence for which few whites were ever punished—pushed families from their homes. Simultaneously, the pace of the northern industrial world and the culture of the northern cities pulled individuals to the bus depots, train stations, and highways. However influential such factors were for southern African Americans, every migration began with a very private and personal discussion. Although everyone follows trends, we do not choose to comprehend the great changes in our lives as defined by the grand structures or systems in place in society, but as our very own, very private history. Only the individual truly understands the interplay of factors contributing to the watershed moments in his or her life; oral history proves to be an excellent way of documenting what individuals know about these factors.

Historian Peter Gottlieb argues that frequent movement within the South became a critical means by which African American families negotiated the almost nonnegotiable economic structures there. Blacks had long considered changes in physical location as a reasonable, feasible means by which to better their lives. Migration out of the region followed a long-lived practice of moving within the region. Since the dawn of Reconstruction, African Americans had relocated. Gottlieb focuses on the First Great Migration, which began about the time World War I broke out in Europe. He writes, "Long experience in moving to jobs within their native regions gave southern blacks added traction as they began moving toward new job openings during the war."[23] For Gottlieb, the move north came as a result of a combination of the inequities of the South and the migrants' culture, which at times encouraged migration as a response to difficulties. Just generations ago, any movement whatsoever had been solely at the discretion of the slave owner. For black sharecroppers, moving to another farm brought the hope of a fairer share of the crop yield, a better accounting in the books kept at the plantation commissary, or more humane treatment by area whites. Migration to southern cities brought access to a broader array of jobs and the delights of urban life. And migration northward brought even wider job opportunities, access to the glittering entertainment venues of the cities, and the whispered promise, often unrealized, of a more just society. Unfortunately, the North had its own system of legalized and de facto discrimination and segregation. Recent scholarship has taken to calling this formalized system "northern Jim Crow."[24]

Family ties figured strongly in the moves. Some migrants moved primarily because of the decisions of male family members. In traditionally oriented families, male heads of households often had the most weight in decision making. Yet some husbands did follow their wives to the North. Although almost all the women of this study were part of tight-knit family units, the women consciously structured their economic choices and weighed their options regarding physical location—these women did not "end up" living in the North, but deftly negotiated the narrow labor market open to them as well as their migratory path. Few of the study's respondents claimed to be the very first family member to make the move, however. Almost all followed siblings, cousins, husbands, or other relatives to their intermediate and final destinations. This "chain migration" brought the approximate six and a half million migrants north during the First and Second Great Migrations.

As shown in Ella Sims's history, some of the women came north without male guidance, following a female family member to the northern city. With historical hindsight, this appears to be quite revolutionary behavior. Fitting the definition of "women adrift," the term put forth by historian Joanne Meyerowitz to describe unchaperoned women in the city, the women made history by traveling unfettered by male bonds, but they did not envision their moves as atypical. Meyerowitz's term uses historical language to describe the women's lack of male supervision; she does not imply that these women were literally lost or adrift, and the oral testimony demonstrates that the migrants felt fairly secure traveling and relocating without men. Acting on their own seemed a reasonable solution and, in most instances, perfectly within the bounds of propriety for the era. Sims, for example, surely would have preferred to remain within a household with a male head, but her husband had died. The female-oriented chain migration resembles a female pattern for women immigrants, particularly the women of Ireland. Historians are just now according proper weight to these stories of female migration and immigration. Irish women at times constituted the majority of people flowing out of their struggling homeland. Especially in the case of the Catholic nuns who came to work in the schools and hospitals of the United States, connections with other women motivated the Irish women immigrants. The Catholic sisters came to America in two characteristically different, yet overlapping waves, the first described as 1812–1881 and the second during the late 1860s to the early twentieth century. Historian Suellen Hoy writes, "The recruitment of young women by sisters who had emigrated earlier represents a previously untold form of chain and serial migration that was so prevalent among the millions who left all parts of Europe from the 1840s to 1914."[25]

Florence Allison, born in Livingston, Alabama, in 1926, represents those migrants who moved primarily due to the wishes of their husbands. Her husband, a marine who later worked at the Chrysler assembly plant in Detroit, led the way in this particular choice. Allison explained, "After being in the army he didn't want to be back in the country anymore so he decided to move."[26] Annie Benning, born in Georgia in 1911, came to River Rouge, Michigan, so her husband could work in the auto industry. Her husband's brother had already arrived. Benning remembered, "Well, he had a brother that lived here and his brother wanted him to come here and to work with him in the steel mill but he didn't like working in no mill. He come here and got him a job as a mechanic and that's where he stayed until he passed." Mr. Benning made a comfortable living in a garage of a car dealership. At the time of the interview, Annie Benning lived in a well-appointed brick home with an array of lush plantings outside. The street itself, although bordering less affluent neighborhoods, contained many homes of this kind. The homes testified to a certain level of accomplishment by their owners. Benning continued, "He couldn't get no job working down there [in the South] and he wanted to come where he could make it. It didn't make no difference to me and he come to find him a job. I stayed home about three months and then I come to Michigan." Benning's husband also disliked the way black men were treated in the South. She said, "He did [face discrimination] when he was in the southern states, so that's when he come here, but he didn't have no trouble here." The Bennings proved typical in that the husband got settled in his position and established a living space for the couple before the wife made the move. Such systems also were typical of many immigrant groups coming to America in the early twentieth century. Like many African American men, Annie Benning's husband located a job quickly. Benning characterized her view of Detroit by saying, "It was real nice and you could get jobs. No job was too hard to find here."[27]

The majority of the respondents reported that their husbands had initiated the migration. The women did not express displeasure at the move, but in their patriarchal homes, the husband's plans dominated. Such male leadership is not unusual, even today. Because men still tend to earn higher salaries than their spouses, it proves reasonable for families to favor finding the most lucrative position possible for male workers. It remains highly unusual for families to relocate regionally for a female's job.

In the world of blues music, the oft-repeated tale told by migrant and blues vocalist Koko Taylor represents the sharp distinction between southern and northern pay rates, and the number of hopes and dreams bound up in the decision to migrate. Taylor, interviewed in 1993, recounted her future husband's announcement that he was heading to Chicago in 1953. Taylor refused to be left behind. Robert "Pops" Taylor landed a position at the Wilson Packing Company, a real achievement. Koko found work as a housekeeper for a Wilmette family, where she would earn $5.00 for an eight-hour day. In Tennessee, Taylor had had to care for white families for $1.50 a day, and sometimes just $3.00 a week. The couple was thrilled with their new city, yet they had arrived with very little in their pockets. Taylor said, "We rode from Memphis to Chicago with 35 cents in our pockets and a box of Ritz crackers."[28]

Faith Richmond boarded a train in North Carolina to go and live with her husband's family. Yet her family of origin warned her about the difficulty of living with in-laws. Richmond related, "He brought me up to Boston and [I] had to live with his family. I remember my aunt saying, if you must live with your in-laws, try very hard to get along."[29] Lillian Clark followed her husband to Detroit soon after he secured a job at Uniroyal. Her husband had followed his brother-in-law to Michigan. Clark's husband's joy at arriving in the Midwest has become a favorite family anecdote. Clark related, "When he got off the train, he was so excited he left the bags on the train."[30] Minnie Chatman depicted her migration story as a rather passive part of her life; in keeping with her husband's leadership position in the household, he made most of the decisions for the couple. His position at U.S. Rubber, far better than he could hope for in Mississippi, launched the family's migration. Chatman recalled, "He came first and he was working and then I stayed and later he sent for me." Chatman's husband had no desire to live in the South again. Chatman said, "He was looking around to see if we could find a place because he say we never going back there and he didn't go back there." Chatman remained in Michigan although her husband passed away about a decade after she arrived.[31]

Mattie Bell Fritz moved to the North immediately after she married, motivated by her husband's wishes. Fritz, born in Montgomery, Alabama, in 1927, married Andrew Fritz shortly before he headed off to the army. Fritz admits, "I got married on a Sunday and left [the South] on a Monday. He [Andrew Fritz] is originally from Pittsburgh, but his family was in Alabama so they moved back and then he moved here [Detroit] and he went into the army from here." Her father balked at the sudden wedding and move. At just eighteen and a recent high school graduate, Mattie Bell married in the recreation center near her home. She recalled, "I told my dad, he say, 'But baby, why do you want to get married so early?' I said, 'He swept me off my feet.'" Mattie Bell settled in near her husband's cousins in Ecorse, Michigan, outside of Detroit, and visited the cousins often. She entered into her husband's tight-knit family. She admitted that the family quickly became her own. Fritz stated, "Most everyone thinks that Andrew's family is my family because we all get along. One big family."[32]

Liddie Williams came to Chicago from Mississippi in 1954; she was just seventeen years old. Newly married, Williams accompanied her mother-in-law to the big city; Williams's husband had already relocated. Perhaps because of her young age at the time, she found the migration difficult. She said, "It was pretty hard. My mother was in the South. A couple of years later, she came here." Williams also revealed that her stepfather's behavior contributed to her desire to move north. She intimated, "I had kind of [a] mean stepfather, that's why I wanted to leave, but I hated to leave my mother." Many years earlier, Williams's parents' divorce had come as a direct result of her father's move to Chicago. She explained, "Her and my father, the reason they separated, it wasn't that they didn't get along, he wanted to come to Chicago and she wouldn't come with him. So they separated." Williams's story demonstrates that a wife's relocation was not a foregone conclusion; all married women did not dutifully follow their spouses. The married women also weighed the consequences, and determined if the migration fit their own needs as well as their husband's.

Of the migrants who admitted to misgivings, homesickness for family members played a significant role.[33] Rosa Young, who followed her father to Michigan from Mississippi in 1944 (she was about seventeen), recalled sadness over leaving her small town. Young's father came to Grand Rapids to attend his son's wedding, and found work in a railroad yard during his vacation. Young mused, "I was glad, I guess I was glad to come, but I hated to leave my home, you know, my homeland, Holly Springs, because that was really tough for me, you know."[34]

For some women, male relatives other than husbands decided to move the families north. Ruth Margaret Covington, part of the Fritz/Covington family interviewed for the study, left Alabama because of her brother's wishes. Covington stated simply, "He [brother Andrew Fritz] was the reason we came here. He felt like it would be better for us here than to stay there."[35] Glennette Taylor remembered following both male and female family members to Grand Rapids; they persuaded her to come and she was glad they influenced her. She had been contemplating a move to San Francisco when her family urged her to come to Michigan. In retrospect, she feels that, given her fear of earthquakes, it was best to live in the Midwest. Her aunt, uncle, sister, brother, and cousins all settled in the city before she did. Taylor moved to Grand Rapids from Alabama with her husband; she still delights in the fact that she found a position before he did in their new city.[36]

Esther Woods presented the decision to migrate as her own, but also cited her brother's need for help with his nieces and nephews, who lived with him in Grand Rapids. Woods's sister had entered the state hospital, leaving the children without a parent to care for them. One of the nieces ended up living with Woods for much of her childhood. Woods admitted, "And I came here—frankly that's why I came here—to help him with those kids." Yet this pressing need only provided the catalyst for the move. Woods believed the migration to be her only reasonable option for a solid economic future. Note that her language points to a return to the South constituting more than a visit; her relocation did not occur all at once. "I wouldn't have stayed there," she said bluntly, "because there was nothing there to do. I worked in York, Alabama, which was about eight miles from my home, before I ever left there *the first time*. But it is a small town—wasn't very much work there for me any longer, so I figured it was time for me to move on for something better." Members of Woods's family migrated to many cities, including Los Angeles, Toledo, Detroit, and New York City. Her personal inclination to move was in keeping with the decisions made by the rest of her family, yet she came to her decision over a matter of years and with considerable personal reflection. An extended excerpt from Woods's interview begins chapter five.[37]

A number of the interviewees moved north with their parents when they were children. The personal stories of minors are not often mentioned in the historical literature. As minors, they of course had little or no say in their parents' decision making. Yet the move constituted a major life event, even for those who moved as very young children. The migrants' life narratives still highlight the importance of the migration in the women's self-conception. Stories abound of the journey, their parents' reactions to the move, and their scattered memories of the South. Although they came north as children, the women still saw themselves as southerners. Memories of childhood are often recollections of tales told to the individual by his or her parents, explains sociologist Barbara Misztal.[38] For some migrants, who moved as very small children or even infants, the story relied overtly on such parental tales. Barbara Purifoy-Seldon's explanation of her move highlights the centrality of the migration and the resonance of southern culture in the self-image of a woman who made the migration as a youngster. Purifoy-Seldon came to the North from Birmingham at just five months of age, so she had no personal memories of the transition. Nonetheless, she had plenty to say about the migration. Her story, which contains apocryphal details about the drive itself, demonstrates the power of this story for the whole family:

> I was born April 6, 1943. It was in a little lean-to, because back in those days we didn't go to hospitals to have babies. We had midwives or grandparents and things like that. It was on Seventh Street in Birmingham, Alabama. Right now when I go back to visit there, there is a plant. It is always nice to know that somewhere in the plant was a lean-to house that I was born in. That was April 6, 1943. When I was five months old, which was about September or so, my parents left there and they came to Ecorse, Michigan. They left there because they wanted to get a better job and work in the factory. They heard that you could make—what is it—five dollars, or something like that, a day by coming up here. So this is what they did, okay.
>
> My sister tells me, and I was too young to remember that they drove a car up. They had a little car and she remembers her feet being [through] holes in the bottom of the car—walking along with the car on the roads on the way up here.

Purifoy-Seldon's sister's assertion that the family placed their feet through the holes in the bottom of the car and walked to Michigan is obviously incorrect in terms of its factual content, but presents many aspects to explore. The sister, also young at the time of the move, remembered the unreliable nature of their car, and the difficulty with which the family made their way from Alabama in 1943. Most likely the car did have holes in its floor. She may have heard adults laugh about the difficulty of the trip and the unreliability of the car. They may have even joked that walking would have been easier. Exaggeration showcases the importance of the tale in the family history, and in fact reveals more truths about the emotion of the experience than simply saying, "We drove to the North."

The pull of northern war jobs made the treacherous journey possible. Purifoy-Seldon's father left his factory job and his sharecropped farm to join the bustling "Arsenal of Democracy"—the city of Detroit. Detroit gained this nickname (which called attention to the widespread retooling of Detroit's industries on behalf of the war effort) due to the use of the term by Franklin Delano Roosevelt during one of his popular radio broadcasts, the "fireside chats." Once in the area, Purifoy-Seldon's father worked for a taxi company and opened his own gas station. With just a third-grade education, her father had provided for his family. In Alabama, he had proposed efficiency procedures for the factory in which he worked, and factory management quickly implemented his suggestions. His contribution netted him a new watch, but no additional pay. Purifoy-Seldon credited him for his work ethic, saying, "My father had his own gas station, so we didn't get to see him very much. He had eight children, so he had to work two jobs to just exist—not to have a great life, just to exist. But if you ask me if I were poor, I'd say no."[39]

It is important to highlight the significant minority of the respondents who followed other women to northern cities. These stories add nuances to our understanding the migration process. Bernita Howard, born in 1916, followed a female migration route. About twenty years old, she left Alabama to live with an aunt in Pennsylvania and then, a few years later, followed her sister to Detroit. Howard described the process matter-of-factly, saying, "I had an aunt living there and I went and stayed with her for two years, and then I came to Detroit." Howard's story reveals her role in easing her sister's loneliness during her husband's World War II deployment. We also see her sister's desire to stay with her family of marriage. Howard related, "My sister was in Virginia—her husband was in the service—she came to Detroit. She wanted me to come with her, but she didn't have an apartment. When she got an apartment, I came. She came to Detroit because she had a brother-in-law living here." Howard's sister, then, had undertaken the migration because of the choice of a male in her extended family. Howard cleaned rooms at a Detroit hotel, and then began working as a waitress at the veterans' hospital. She met her husband at the hospital, where he labored as a baker. After they married, her husband solidified Howard's commitment to stay in the North, for he found the region a better place to raise children. Howard explained, "I started a family and my husband didn't want me to go back since we started a family." Howard's father remained in Alabama. Her mother had passed away before Howard left the region.[40]

Annie Evelyn Collins of Detroit also migrated due to female ties. Like Sims and other migrants, Collins meant to come to Michigan for a visit, yet she stayed permanently. She joked a little about the casual beginning of this major life change. Economics greatly influenced her decision. Like Bernita Howard, Collins sought to keep a female relative company. Collins's mother proffered important advice. In the passage below, Collins worked through a degree of incredulity at the way in which small choices end up affecting people's lives in major ways. Her words attest to a degree of ambivalence about the migration. She clearly had not worked through her ideas on the migration fully, and perhaps had not been asked about it for some time. Collins explained at length:

My sister was here and my mother [felt] that she shouldn't be by herself. She had two sisters in Kentucky and one sister in Cincinnati and she [her mother] told me to come to Detroit so this sister wouldn't be here by herself. I come to stay two weeks and then have fifty years. Ain't that terrible. Now, ain't that terrible. Come to spend two weeks and then get fifty-three years. Fifty-three years, now that's terrible, ain't it. No, that's good, I like living here.

Well, coming here you had better ways of living and making money. The houses was different and the money was different and it was different than the South, even though it wasn't all bad living in the South. There is more money in Michigan, you know. I didn't work that much, but I had more chance to work.[41]

Mary Smith also relied on a network of female relatives to help her decide where to live. Smith, born in 1938 in Sylvester (Worth County), Georgia, moved to find better-paying work. Her quest led her on a circuitous journey—to New York City, back to Georgia, back to New York, on to Miami, Florida, back to Georgia, and finally to Boston. Childbearing also played a part in helping Smith choose her location, because she returned to Georgia to give birth to her babies in a familiar location. The children all stayed with her mother in Georgia for most of their lives (see chapter six for more on Smith's children). An aunt and a sister had found work in Miami before she arrived. Smith said of her job hunt, "The jobs were very easy to find. All you do is get the paper and you call, and you go for an interview, and most of the time, you know, they hire you." Smith lived in a female-centered world. Although she mentioned off-handedly that she had married, she raised all of her three children with only her mother's assistance, and seemed to provide the sole economic support for her family. Smith made her way to Boston, where, at the time of the interview, she ran a day care center out of her three-decker home. The three decker, a common housing type in New England, consists of three separate apartments, arranged one per floor. Smith owned the building, and she resided on the top floor, where she also located the day care. Smith came to Boston at her sister's urging. Smith said straightforwardly, "She sent for me and I came here."[42]

Work also led Rebecca Strom from Alabama to Boston. Strom, born in 1944, stood out as the only respondent not to mention another relative blazing the trail north ahead of her. She did not remember how she heard of the option of working in Boston, guessing only that someone she knew had probably made the trip. Strom also remained one of the few respondents, joining Mary Smith, Anniese Moten, and a handful of others, who labored as a live-in domestic. Most domestics had abandoned live-in work for day work by this time. The fight for the right to live out had been undertaken by an earlier generation of domestic workers, such as the Washington, D.C., workers chronicled by historian Elizabeth Clark-Lewis.[43] As with any social practice, however, change came incrementally. Not all employers allowed workers this advantage, and some women did not desire this option. For a very young woman like Strom, rent for an apartment would have proved prohibitive at this stage of her career. Strom stated, "Well, see there was not a lot of work there [in Alabama], and we heard about working for families that would pay for you to come here. So, you would work for them to pay them back, and then you would have your regular money." The systematized approach to migration mentioned here allowed Strom to move without even having to come up with travel fare. Working to pay off travel costs echoes the technique employed by many immigrants from abroad, who had employers advance the cost of their ship fare. Strom's reference to "we" in the above excerpt indicates her understanding of the great flow of migrants she joined by heading to the North. Strom remembered, "They met you at the bus station and you went to their home. That was our home till I met some other people who told me about Freedom House on Crawford Street, and how you got a regular job outside of living in with a family." (Freedom House, a social service agency run by social workers Otto and Muriel Snowden, drew together the white and black residents of its Dorchester neighborhood in Boston.) [44] All of Strom's siblings left Alabama, leaving her parents behind. Strom felt that she would have eventually located work or entered college if she had remained in her home state. Boston brought her alternative work and an alternative future, but relocation to the city was not the only option open to her. By the time she left, in the last decade of the Second Great Migration, the South was, according to her, a region with some economic opportunities. Like Mary Smith, Strom made a living at the time of the interview by operating a home day care.[45]

Migrants could move back and forth between regions, taking jobs in the North for a time, yet returning to family and friends in the South for several years or more. African American migrants undertook this form of "shuttle migration" to a lesser extent than the white, southern migrants detailed in Chad Berry's excellent study, *Southern Migrants, Northern Exiles*. Berry explores the commonplace tactic of moving to the North out of economic necessity, but returning home when possible. The moves might even correlate with the planting season. Berry writes that an official for the Champion Paper and Fiber Company of Ohio noted that "men would routinely leave the mountains after the autumn harvest to work in Hamilton [Ohio] and then return to Kentucky in time to plant a crop in the spring." Most African American migrants did not carry quite the case of "divided heart" that the white migrants did. White migrants considered the South home, but needed the heavier pay packets to be found in northern industry. As we have seen, African American migrants' searing memories of southern Jim Crow restrictions somewhat tempered any warm feelings for their home states. Despite some of the pleasant childhood memories held by the migrants, many believed strongly that the North offered them the possibility of a more just society along with the higher pay.[46]

Yet, as we have seen, the study respondents did report some cases of shuttle migration that mirrored that of the white southern migrants. Not only did Dean move between a number of cities and towns around the United States, but her relocation was motivated by her desire to further her education and career. Avezinner Dean, a domestic worker turned hair stylist born in Mississippi in 1928, moved frequently between South and North. She characterized the moves as fitting her own needs, rather than complying with the wishes of a male family member. Dean related her convoluted path: "I worked in Alabama and had a [beauty] shop. I lived in Alabama and moved to Inkster [Michigan]. I moved back to Alabama and stayed seven years. My big girl was born in Alabama. I went to Nashville and got another diploma. I wanted to bob hair and I didn't know how. Then I moved back to Michigan and married my sweetheart in 1955. I have been here ever since."[47]

Beatrice Jackson moved to Michigan to join her family, and, unusually, her fiancé followed her to their new home. Jackson traveled to Michigan to live near her brother and his family. Years before, she had joined her sister in Tulsa. The sister needed her help because her husband had entered a sanitarium; during Jackson's years in Tulsa, she worked as a domestic and earned a college degree in elementary teaching, which she never utilized directly in her employment. Jackson did not think highly of the Motor City. "The summer of 1941," Jackson said in her low, tired voice, "I went to Detroit and my husband-to-be followed me. My brother was in Detroit. He didn't have a job at that time. His wife didn't have a job. They had two kids—I was disgusted with Detroit."[48]

Jerliene "Creamy" McKinney followed a female family member northward, and also drew her boyfriend along with her. McKinney, born in Alabama in 1940, followed her sister to New York City. Anticipating her move, McKinney's boyfriend (and later husband), Theodosis, moved to the Bronx. McKinney detailed, "My sister moved from Florida to New York because she used to do jobs of living in with peoples, doing housekeeping and stuff like that. So she moved from Florida to New York, and when I got old enough, I kept asking my mom, 'Can I come to stay with her for a while?' So, when I got older, my mom let me come up to New York to stay with her." After about four years, Creamy and Theodosis married, and had four children in New York. "Then the peoples that she was living there with moved here [to Massachusetts]," McKinney explained, "and they wanted my husband and her husband to come to live with them here." Both husbands found jobs at Boston's airport, while Creamy and her sister worked for the family. Eventually McKinney moved her family to Worcester, Massachusetts, and her sister followed.[49]

At just eleven years old, Gussie Nash moved to Grand Rapids, Michigan, from Arkansas. She came because her aunt, the mother of two boys, had always wanted a girl; Nash's mother in effect "loaned" Gussie to the aunt for the year. The arrangement benefited Nash by giving her access to northern schools, as well as providing her with a taste of northern life. Nash did not consider Arkansas rife with racism, and after the year was over, did not express great eagerness to return to Michigan. Yet her mother urged her to return after high school graduation, as the rest of her six siblings (five sisters and a brother) had already resettled in Grand Rapids. Nash mused, "I didn't want to come back [to Grand Rapids] and I was the oldest girl at home still and my mother kept saying that 'you go to Grand Rapids with the rest of them.' I don't want to go, so I stayed there [Arkansas] for a couple of years after I graduated and then come back [to Michigan]. After getting back I worked at Kent Community [health care] and I met my husband and got married and raised two children."[50]

Such an arrangement of child-sharing might strike readers as unusual in today's highly "child-centered" society. Today's emphasis on bonding and the relationship with the biological parents makes such an action almost unfathomable. Yet might not Nash's mother's placement of her daughter with other family members be seen as a rational way to give her a better education and an enduring connection with a northern community in which she might want to make a life? The rationale behind the placement was not out of keeping with the actions of others. Ella Sims, as we have already learned, lived with cousins in Arkansas while attending high school, because there was no high school for black students in her Mississippi community. Alverrine Parker left Michigan for Mississippi during high school to live with her grandmother, a recent widow. The study's respondents would make similar choices for their own children. Children's welfare was valued above everyday connections with biological mothers. Extended family members worked together to raise children. This theme will be further explored in chapter six.

Olivia Watson Mitchell of Burton, Texas, allowed her first child, Linda, to live with the woman who had raised Olivia's husband. In Mitchell's family, kinship was a fairly elastic term. Caring relationships brought people into the family circle, while at the same time questions about biological fathers sometimes confused relationships. As a child, Mitchell had not known the identity of her father, and some of her siblings, born of different fathers, had similar questions. "I didn't know who my daddy was at first," explained Mitchell. "So I ask my mama where was my daddy—I always—never did know my daddy. And she said, 'Oh, yeah. You see him every day.'" A married family friend was indeed her biological father. Mitchell's parents later married. Olivia's husband was raised by a woman named Miss Mary, who wanted desperately to care for Olivia's daughter Linda as her own. Mitchell recalled, "Miss Mary the one that wanted to take Linda away from me. I say, 'No, you not going to take no Linda away from me, because that's my child.'" Yet Mitchell ultimately relented, after boarding with Mary for a while to make sure she would treat Linda well. It appears that Linda lived with Miss Mary on just a temporary basis, for she later returned to Mitchell's narrative. Mitchell's reference to Mary as *Miss* Mary may have indicated that she was a white woman. If so, it would have been more socially difficult for Mitchell to resist Mary's pleas for her child.[51]

June Cross, author of *Secret Daughter: Mixed-Race Daughter and the Mother Who Gave Her Away*, writes poignantly about her placement with her white mother's African American friends. Cross's mother, Norma, left June, a child she had had out of wedlock with African American comedian James "Stump" Cross, at the home of friends Peggy and Paul Bush in Atlantic City when the girl was about six or seven years of age. Cross maintained contact with her mother, eventually staying with her and her husband, the Jewish actor Larry Storch, every summer in Los Angeles, but she would live permanently with her "aunt" and "uncle." Cross's story is complicated by her mother's white race, her unmarried status, and the violent nature of her parents' relationship, yet it is perhaps less unusual than she herself realizes. Part of the motivation for the unofficial adoption lay in the Bushes' childlessness. Like Gussie Nash's aunt, Peggy and Paul Bush yearned to welcome the little girl into their home. Norma hoped to ease the prejudice directed at her as the mother of a mixed-race child, and she may have also felt for her friends in their longing for children. She may have thought it harmful for June to be raised solely by a white mother. Children became a resource to be shared, their upbringing also considered more of a community responsibility than many regard it today. Cross reveals the psychological scars of what she terms a type of abandonment in her memoir; only by producing a documentary film on her life story does she come to terms with her mother's reasoning.[52]

The interviewees who shared their memories for this study add considerably to our understanding of the Second Great Migration. Although many did move north at the behest of their husbands or other male relatives, their stories reveal important facts about the men's roles as family leaders and the women's views of themselves. In the twenty-first century, it remains highly unusual for women to initiate cross-country migrations for their families. My explanation that my own family relocated from Michigan to Massachusetts in 2000 because of my pursuit of a tenure-track teaching position has led to many an incredulous response. Almost everyone outside of academia who has asked about the move has queried, "So, you came here so your husband could take a job?" In the mid-twentieth century, it would have been atypical for families to travel hundreds of miles solely to pursue better-paying work for the females of the family. And as we will examine at length, black women made more money in the North than the South, but they largely remained in domestic positions until the last decades of the twentieth century.

In these rich narratives we learn about women who undertook the trek to the so-called "promised land" as children. Even though they traveled as young people, the migration figured heavily in their self-conception. Migrants like Rosa Young mourned the loss of connection with their beautiful southern homeland. Others understood the physical and psychological dangers of the South and rejoiced at heading to the North, despite that region's own considerable challenges. Some of the young women traveled between the North and the South, strengthening bonds between extended families by joining another household for a while. Most spoke of these moves as an important part of their educational or emotional development.

Stories like that of Creamy McKinney and Beatrice Jackson, however, document that some men did follow their girlfriends and wives northward. McKinney and Jackson, both exceedingly motivated, knew the region would improve their economic security. Their male counterparts refused to be left behind. Other women, including Mary Smith and Rebecca Strom, came north without any male companion at all. Smith would remain the sole breadwinner for her family, and Strom would meet her husband only after settling permanently in Boston. Some women, like Liddie Williams's mother, divorced their husbands rather than follow them to the North.

Viewing the Great Migration through a feminine lens upsets our previous understanding of what was arguably the most historically important movement of people in the United States before the present era. Although millions relocated, the decision to do so stemmed from highly personal life choices. Each family struggled, sometimes for decades, over where to best make a life. And for many families, the decision to head north was never truly conceived of as permanent. In the late twentieth and early twenty-first centuries, hundreds of thousands of African Americans have been migrating to the South. Many are the children and grandchildren of migrants. Migrants themselves have returned to their region of origin. In this period, African American college graduates are more likely to settle in the South than the North after graduation. The vast majority of the new migrants settle in the southern suburbs.[53] The South draws new residents of all races with its job opportunities and sunny weather. Previously, the region had limited appeal due to its warm and humid climates; its boom owes much to the widespread use of air conditioning. Interestingly, many of the African Americans flowing south to follow their dreams envision the move as a "return" rather than a simple migration. The South still figures as an actual or metaphorical homeland for a significant number of African American families.

Three-decker housing, Worcester, Massachusetts. Photograph by Lisa Krissoff Boehm.

CHAPTER FOUR

Encountering the City

The struggle is always there, and it's always uphill.
—BARBARA PURIFOY-SELDON[1]

You knew where you could go in the South. Up here, it had a different face on it, completely different. They worked with you and they stabbed you in the back and talked about you. So it wasn't all that beautiful coming to the North, as long as your skin was black. If it was a different color, it was better.
—FAITH RICHMOND[2]

MARY SMITH

Boston (Dorchester), Massachusetts

Mary Smith and I met through a student I knew well; the student, Aiwa Lewis, was Smith's granddaughter, and majored in urban studies at my college. Aiwa was an outgoing and thoughtful student, a favorite of her professors and classmates. She took an interest in my research, and offered to introduce me to her grandmother. I conducted the interview in part as a training session, with two undergraduates in attendance. Although interviews are usually best done one-on-one, the atmosphere did not seem greatly affected by the students' presence in this particular case. Smith appeared at ease on this Saturday morning, at home in the top floor of her three decker home. Three deckers, the common solution to multifamily housing in New England, are free-standing buildings with one unit per floor. Architectural enthusiasts often malign the three decker; they frequently have little ornament, and the tall, rectangular boxes stand in relentlessly repeating rows in the neighborhoods of Boston, Worcester, and many little towns in between. The three decker was characteristically covered in siding, initially wood and eventually aluminum or synthetic materials. In Chicago, the small, three-story apartment building, the cousin of the three decker, was built in brown brick with minimal decorative detail. The siding of the New England three decker ranged in color from white to vivid aqua, yet the color usually did little to abate the monotony of the housing stylistically. The three decker offered relative privacy for the immigrants and migrants streaming into New England in the late nineteenth and early twentieth centuries. Later on, it became a frequently chosen housing option for African American migrants, and the form still proves popular for immigrants and the working class. The ease of having three families connected to the city's water, waste, and electrical resources at one location, rather than in three separate, single-family homes, helped cities to serve their expanding resident base quickly. Dorchester claimed more than 288,000 residents in 2005. Smith's particular neighborhood, one of the four within Dorchester, was 59.9 percent African American, 21.4 percent white, 5 percent Asian, and small percentages of others in the 2000 census report.[3]

Smith owned the building and allowed some of her family—including Aiwa Lewis and her mother—to board in the floors below her. Like many three deckers, the building showed its age, but it offered a warm home to Smith's family as well as a setting for Smith's at-home day care business. We all sat in Smith's small, windowless living room. Playthings lined the shelves in the dining room, within sight through the open doorway. One could imagine the children at play, although, considering the uncertain gait of young children, the third floor location appeared perilously far from the home's front door and small yard. The small patch of grass, surrounded by a chain-link fence, would offer the only outside respite for the children during the day.

Like her granddaughter, Smith had an aptitude for analyzing the changing city. She noted the evolution of her Dorchester neighborhood from a community of European immigrants to a mostly African American community to a site under pressure from urban renewal and higher real estate prices. As the neighborhood transitioned in the mid-twentieth century, retailers had fled. In recent years, the area's consumer options had begun to expand. More Asian and white residents moved to Dorchester. Smith feared she would be pushed out, as those seeking an easier commute to Boston's central business district bought out her neighbors for staggering sums. During the interview, Smith recalled, apparently with ease, precise dates for the major migrations in and out of Dorchester. Note also Smith's ability to pinpoint dates for changes in her own life—she has a keen understanding of change and an uncanny memory for specific detail.

I was born in Georgia, February 19, 1938. I am one out of ten—I'm the fifth child. My mother, who was married to him, my father, had five girls. And then she divorced. And she had got married again, and she had two boys, and then two girls and a boy, I think, at the end. And I was the fifth child, and I was there with the four older ones, and I was there with the five younger ones.

And out of all of us girls to leave home, I think I was the last to leave home. I stayed home longer than any of them. And first I left and went to New York, and I stayed a year, and then I went back home. I had family in New York, two sisters and aunts and cousins. New York was nice, you know, then at that time, in the '50s. It was nice. When I first went I was eighteen.

I worked at a book-binding. They made all kinds of books and magazines, and stuff like that. And in '56, I came back home for vacation, and then I go back. Then, at the end of '57, I went to Miami, and I stayed there, and I worked for a family that lives on Miami Beach.

I moved to Boston in 1962. My sister again sent for me, and I came here. My sister was in New York, Miami, and then here. She got hitched and sent for me. And I got a job working for Mass General. And I had put in for Mass General and Boston State. Mass General called me first, so I went there. And about a month later, the State called me, so I went to the State. So I worked for Boston State Hospital in Mattapan for about two years. I was a dietary aide, and during the time I went to school for IBM computers. I finished that in 1964, and in 1965 I got a job working at Stop & Shop [grocery] doing keypunching stuff, like.

Then I started working for an agency. They sent me to First National Bank of Boston, I worked there. And then I worked at State Street Bank, doing nothing but payroll. And then I worked at Liberty Mutual, too, for about a year. You know, part time, at nights. And then when I left Liberty Mutual, I went to Shawmut Bank, and I stayed with Shawmut Bank from 1967 until 1970. Then I didn't work part-time no more. I just stayed at Harvard. Because I start working at Harvard in November, in 1966. I was working in accounts receivable. I took an early retirement from Harvard in 1993. Because after being at Harvard twenty-seven years—that's a long time. So, I needed a change. And I started doing day care.

When I first came here, I came through Framingham, it was like at night. And life was nice. And it was really nice, up and down the road, this area. Each corner had a drugstore, and each corner a gas station, fire station, furniture stores, cleaners, bakeries, and supermarket. You really didn't have to go downtown for anything. You just walk right to Blue Hill and you would see the stores. Even if you wanted to go somewhere, you'd just go to Douglas Station, and it was like a little Boston. You could get anything you want there, and it was really nice. And I, you know, rarely went downtown, but then, in the late '60s, '68, early '69, the Jewish people start moving out. I moved here in '68, and then, everybody else was in here was Jewish. They start moving out. By '72 practically all them was gone. I really miss it, because you could walk right to Blue Hill and get clothes, furniture, anything. You just walk right to the avenue, and you got it.

Before, if you needed furniture, you could walk up there to the furniture store. And then pick out what you want, and they'd bring it, you know, the same day. And then if you wanted fresh bread, the bakery were right there, then it's your supermarket. A drugstore—one was on each corner. Drugstores, movie theaters, everything was in walking distance, you really didn't need a car. And you could walk out here at any time of the night or morning. Nobody bothered you. You know, you hadn't be worried about whether somebody going to snatch your bag or hit you in the head.

But everything now's so different. Really it is. I really liked it. I see Blue Hill is coming back, but it's not the same. If they could bring it back like it were, it would be nice, but it's not. I see now it's changing back again, because I see a lot of people that had moved out in the suburbs are moving back. I'd give it another two or three years and there'll be less of us [African Americans] around here because we can't afford the rent. Because they buying the houses up like mad and one bedroom is fifteen hundred dollars. You can't pay that type of money. I mean, really. What you got to buy clothes with? What you going to eat? You can't afford that. I paid sixteen thousand seven hundred dollars for this house. Right now, if I sold this house, I could get over three hundred thousand. And in Roxbury, a lady sold her house for four or six hundred thousand. So, that's telling you right there, if you're going to pay that type of money for that house, that you got money. And you don't need no tenants.

And a lot of the Korean people and the Chinese people, they got money. So they always team together and they pool that money, and they can run you away from here [laughing]. I usually see them in [groups of] three or four, walking up and down looking in the neighborhood, looking at different houses, and they all have briefcases. And when they got them briefcases, they got money. Black-American people, they don't stick together.

If I had waited to come for a few years, I probably never would have left [the South]. I would've just stayed down there, because I got sisters and nephews, and they got beautiful homes in Georgia and Florida. They have them built, and it is really nice. And they got the good jobs.[4]

Mary Smith has watched Dorchester change from her third-floor unit for many decades. She made the area of the city her home before many other African Americans did. By working long hours and climbing the administrative ladder in small steps, she earned enough money to purchase a home and provide for her three children. Technically married, Smith nonetheless had to serve as head of her family. She made no mention of any particular man in her life story, although she offhandedly referred to herself as married. No one shared the mortgage with her, or worked to gather money to send to the children and their grandmother back in Georgia.

Twenty-four-year-old Smith arrived in Boston in 1962, as the Second Great Migration neared an end. The middle child of ten siblings, she never expected life to be easy. She had seen her mother marry twice. Smith had been migrating for years; in the 1950s she had lived in both New York and Miami, along with regular stretches back home in Georgia. As discussed in chapter three, Smith returned home during each pregnancy, in order to give birth with her mother nearby. Due to the dearth of hospitals catering to blacks, African Americans often gave birth at home. The trend lessened over the course of the twentieth century, as hospital access increased. A female network proved very important in childbirth, both for the birth itself and the aftercare necessary for mother and child. Historian Gretchen Lemke-Santangelo notes this phenomenon when she writes, "Most migrant women were born in their mother's or grandmother's homes, with a midwife there to assist their delivery. An expectant mother often returned to her mother's home and stayed until a month or more after giving birth . . . It was customary to keep both mother and child inside and out of daylight for a month and to wrap the new mother's stomach with a cloth to help her abdominal muscles retract."[5] Like many women, Smith had to rely on her mother to care for her three children. Smith's mother was needed as a permanent, rather than temporary, child care solution. Smith negotiated Boston on her own, gaining a hard-won understanding of urban change from the years of closely observing the ebb and flow of people in her neighborhood.

Smith used migration as a tool—by better locating herself in the national job market, she could secure better pay. Although she grew accustomed to changing locations, the city still had an effect on her. She did not get lulled into inattention by her frequent comings and goings, but rather had a heightened awareness of the urban landscape. Smith's review of the social systems of Dorchester critiqued the area's current circumstances. She longed for a successful neighborhood that remained in the hands of African American homeowners. She noted how the bustling storefronts of the early 1960s gave way to a less vibrant economy as the neighborhood grew increasingly African American. As home prices in Boston soared in the early part of the twenty-first century, making it among the most expensive housing markets in the nation, savvy dealmakers looked for untapped real estate markets with access to downtown. White and Asian "urban pioneers" ventured out into heretofore avoided neighborhoods, hoping to make a great deal. Smith had begun to take note of the high number of "for sale" signs on her block. The temptation of the high sale prices proved too much to resist for many, although Smith herself revealed no plans to sell. Noting that some ethnic groups pool resources to invest in real estate projects, she bemoaned what she considered the African Americans' failure to take up similar investment schemes. She hoped to preserve her neighborhood as an African American one.

Smith's detailed memories of her encounters with the city, and her overall analysis of the way in which northern cities work, link her to countless other migrants. In part due to my own prior research on popular perceptions of urban spaces, I encouraged the discussion of such memories in the oral histories. African American authors, in works of both fiction and autobiography, have long taken up the theme of urban encounters. Memories of the very first impression of the city have been a particular favorite of many. Gwendolyn Parker's engaging memoir, *Trespassing: My Sojourn in the Halls of Privilege*, chronicles her journey from North Carolina to New York. For Parker, like the women interviewed for this study, the actual trip from the South to the North becomes a key life moment, a time in which sights, sounds, and personal feelings get emblazoned forever in one's memory. The journey holds an important place as part of the life story, a narrative bridge from the saga of one life to another. The story need not be published, like Parker's, or even often told to others, to have explanatory value. Even if only repeated to oneself, the story impacts one's personal identity.

Parker's prose captures the importance of the journey for her own personal narrative. As a superachiever from an early age, Parker planned to bear witness to the entire drive, to drink in every drop of the changing landscape:

> I wanted to stay awake the whole trip. The back seat of our Lincoln was filled with blankets and pillows and food and boxes, but I was determined not to sink into its comfort and fall asleep. Twilight turned quickly to darkness and we began to pick up far flung stations on the radio. My parents double-checked route numbers and landmarks as one road changed seamlessly into another. Occasionally we passed another lone car, but for long stretches of road we saw only our own headlights, and no matter how hard I fought it, sleep would not be put off any longer. When I finally awoke early the next morning, it was to learn that we had arrived. We turned off a narrow highway and were suddenly in a warren of streets shrouded on both sides by a thick green foliage. This was what I first noticed: the color of the trees, a darker green than the variety of trees in

the South, and the street, cast in deeper shade. There were houses hidden
behind the green, set back a discreet distance from the street. It was as if
they had pulled back just a bit, claiming greater privacy for themselves.
We turned and turned and turned again, and I feared we were lost, until
we climbed a steep hill at the crest of which we came to a stop.[6]

For Parker, the transition from southern to northern life proved rockier
than expected, especially when she attempted to fit into her integrated school.
Yet, ultimately, the North was the site of Parker's economic ascension. Other
migrants fared less well economically. For some, the harsh realities of the North
became apparent quite quickly. Richard Wright, in his lyrical autobiography
Black Boy, demonstrates how migrants' long-cherished dreams for the northern, urban life could be dashed irrevocably upon the initial sight of these cities.
Wright recalls, "My first glimpse of the flat black stretches of Chicago depressed
and dismayed me, mocked all my fantasies. Chicago seemed an unreal city
whose mythical houses were built of slabs of black coal wreathed in palls of gray
smoke, houses whose foundations were sinking slowly into the dank prairie."[7]

The oral histories collected for this book, as well as the supporting documents consulted, reveal the stark realities of northern life. Although migrants
yearned for social equality and unfettered access to good-paying jobs, long veins
of racism ran under the northern soil, just as they had done in the South. For
some, the racism was readily apparent during their initial moments in the city.
For others, the true nature of the North revealed itself with time. The economic
opportunities the North offered still made the journey worthwhile, and many
migrants deemed the northern brand of prejudice preferable to the southern
type. Migrant Lilly Shelby summed up the thoughts of many with her comparison of the North with the South: "It's just a little better but it has a long way to
go."[8] The migrants could hardly even dream of a world where prejudice did not
exist. Racism was so entrenched that its absence was, and perhaps still is, almost
unimaginable.

The ambiguity of the gains made by the move to the North is showcased
in the paintings of Jacob Lawrence. Although he was born in New Jersey, the
Great Migration of his parents and their generation captivated the artist. His
1941 series *The Great Migration*, consisting of sixty panels and completed after a
study of the subject at the Schomberg Collection in Harlem, covers the recoil-
ing of black migrants from the vicious attitudes of the South at the time. In
panel 44, Lawrence depicts a loaf of bread and a slab of meat sitting on a plain
brown table. Under this painting, the inscription reads "Living conditions were

better in the North." Yet Lawrence's works fail to paint a uniformly rosy picture of the North. Although panel 31 reads "After arriving North the Negroes had better housing conditions," viewers soon learn that this was not the entire story. Panel 47 features a family of nine sharing a single bed in a stark room. Lawrence explains, "As well as finding better housing conditions in the North, the migrants found very poor housing conditions in the North. They were forced into overcrowded and dilapidated tenement houses."[9]

For Addie Smith of North Carolina, the initial encounter with the looming red brick factories, winding streets, and reserved Yankee attitudes of Worcester, Massachusetts, shook her. Smith wondered if she had made a mistake in coming north. While she liked the Jewish family she worked for, she had not planned to move north. She came to work temporarily, and found herself staying because of the financial security her new job provided. But she questioned the move. Smith remembered, "I was here about a month and I hated it, and I cried all the time. But I didn't let them know—the folks I was living with. I just didn't like this place—I just can't stand it, you know. The people were so different, you know, but people at work were real nice." Smith improved her new situation by joining John Street Baptist Church. Church membership led to new friendships, and, eventually, a new spouse.[10]

Avezinner Dean numbered as one of the few respondents who decisively cast her native Mississippi as preferable to Michigan in terms of racism. Dean announced, "I have run in[to] the most problems in Michigan than I ever [have] in my life. You know, the difference in Mississippi and Michigan—white people didn't want to be bothered [in the South], and you know it. You know what I am trying to say. They stayed away and had nothing to do with you. They build their homes off from you and stayed away from you. Up here you can be door to door. In Mississippi, this white guy would pull fresh corn out of my garden, and we didn't have no problem." Dean's take on regional difference is compelling, in part because some argue quite the opposite—that in the South blacks and whites mixed on a daily basis, but that in the North "black" and "white" constituted two different worlds. Dean, of course, lived in a Detroit neighborhood that claimed a nearly 90 percent African American population. During my forays there over the years, I never saw a white person on the sidewalk or even in a car passing by, except for an occasional white utility worker. Dean's memories of the South reveal some unclear characterizations. She remembers living near a white man in Mississippi, a man who picked corn from her garden, but then said, "they build their homes off from you."[11]

African American parents taught their children to tread carefully in the white world. The lessons may have been taught during southern childhoods, but their underlying message made sense in northern cities as well. Lois Stevens's father, as a preacher, made sure that his children behaved in public. Good behavior was necessary because both white and black residents of Greenville, Alabama, scrutinized the children of this well-known family. Extra focus came from the family's open ancestral link to one of the city's leading white families. Stevens related, "My father, being a public man, made a little difference for us. You had to walk a straight line while they were looking at you." Stevens did not overstress the differences between white northern and white southern racial attitudes. "It's the same," she characterized. "You do meet different kinds of people [everywhere]." Stevens found that one's own personal outlook had a great bearing on how much racism could penetrate into everyday relations. But her words also revealed a certain resignation to the existence of prejudice. She asserted, "It all depends on yourself. If you take people as they are, and you don't expect too much, you get along." Her words "you don't expect too much" are very important here. Many of the migrants categorized what they found in the North as preferable to southern life, but their expectations were low. Unlike European immigrants, some of whom really expected to find the New York City streets paved with gold, African American migrants had advance warning of northern conditions from friends and relatives. Although some, like Wright, expected to be more pleased upon arrival, no migrant anticipated a total absence of prejudice in his or her new city.[12]

Mundane interactions with white city dwellers became moments that had to be carefully read. In the place of the South's all-too-clear Jim Crow laws, the North presented a tangle of cultural practices and legal restrictions. Racial difference still played out as an important defining element in social interactions, but in unexpected, inconsistent ways. Migrants had to keep vigilant. In their vigilance regarding everyday interactions, women also made note of subtle unfriendly attitudes that could grate deeply. Worcester, Massachusetts, resident Addie Smith commented on the uneasiness in a simple "hello" with a white pedestrian. Smith contrasted northern and southern attitudes, saying:

> Prejudice here is sorta covered up, you know what I mean? It's here, believe me, it's here. I think they're [northerners] a little more subtle with it, but I don't think they're ever gonna eliminate discrimination. Because there's some people just think they're better than others. They got that idea in their head and you can't take it away. And you walk down the street sometimes—I don't know about you—but I walk down the street sometimes and I see people coming, and I say hello or good morning, and people get like "What are you speaking to me for?"[13]

The interviewees' musings often turned to whites' presumption of their own cultural superiority. Historians studying colonial America have uncovered how white colonial employers and slave owners promoted racism among their white workers to discourage them from banding together with nonwhite laborers.[14] In early America and on through the twentieth century, racism kept people apart in a variety of workplaces, ranging from the agricultural fields to the shop floors and even to the corporate boardrooms. In the twenty-first century, racism still manages to keep Americans from uniting, whether it be as a neighborhood, a city, a social class, or even as a nation. The persistence of racist attitudes puzzled the narrators of this study; many used our conversations as a time to seek reasons for this cultural malignancy. Alverrine Parker stated forcefully that the "color of your skin doesn't have anything to do with your mind and your heart, so there's a lot of that in Grand Rapids. There's a lot of prejudice here, yeah. I can't figure it out—and maybe you can tell me, too—why do people think because their skin is white they are supposed to be superior?"[15]

Public education in the North proved problematic at best. Most of the women interviewed for this study had completed their elementary education before the migration, but the subject still came up. The failure of public education in the North to adequately serve African American and other minority students slowed down the upward trajectory of migrant families and their neighbors. Schools segregated due to neighborhood demographics often had substandard facilities. Integrated schools often exposed black students to the unexpurgated prejudices of schoolmates and teachers. Ogretta McNeil, later elected a member of the school board in Worcester, Massachusetts, recalled the antipathy of the Washington, D.C., school system towards black students. McNeil said of her Middle Atlantic school district, "They sort of assume you are retarded and stupid."[16]

Long-time child care worker Anniese Moten vividly recalled her introduction to Toledo, Ohio. She accompanied her employer to the new city, after living for years in Detroit. Moten revealed, "After she [her employer] got married and we moved to Toledo, well, I didn't like Toledo. These peoples over there act like I was an animal or something. When I come out doors they close their doors and go in the house. I says, 'I am going back to Detroit.'" Despite the ominous beginnings, white neighbors eventually warmed to Moten. No doubt they still held prejudice towards African Americans generally, but Moten's skill with children brought her respect as an individual. The white neighbors also tried to convert Moten to Catholicism, a move they may have interpreted as kind, but which she resisted.[17]

Historical Encounters

FAITH RICHMOND
Boston (Dorchester), Massachusetts

Faith and I were introduced by a mutual friend. Richmond lived in a tree-lined neighborhood in Dorchester, a community inside Boston with a significant population of African American families. She was in the general vicinity of interviewee Mary Smith but on a more affluent street. Faith's single-family home featured solid, traditionally styled furniture. Her mantel and dining room were dotted with family photographs. Before the formal interview began, Faith reminisced about important sites in Boston history, including the Charles Street A.M.E. Church of Boston and the Joy Street meetinghouse. By thus mentioning these important African American landmarks, she intertwined her story with the history of African American people as a whole. Although Richmond's story is the story of an individual, by taking part in the project she was making her memories part of the public face of black Boston as well.

The interview took place at Richmond's dining room table. A window facing the sunny backyard brought some light into the very formal room. Occasionally, Richmond would run into the nearby kitchen for a brochure or picture to highlight a memory.

I came to Boston on March 4, 1946. It was terrible, it was so cold and dreary, dirty and snowy. I was born in Durham, North Carolina, tobacco world.

After my father died, my mother didn't want pictures of her wedding on display in our home. Many people told us how pretty she was and how much my father loved her. When they would argue about something, my father would say, "All right, I'll see you later," and go out some place, and when he would come back he would throw his hat in and say, "Is it safe to come back in?" We used to laugh when she would tell us about it. She would tell us how much our father loved us.

Quentin and I were married at my auntie's house. She had a beautiful house. He brought me up to Boston and I had to live with his family. Quentin was from Roanoke, Virginia, but they moved around a lot. His father was a lawyer. He had lived in Baltimore. That's where they caught Quentin. He had been ducking the service. He had to join in Baltimore, Maryland. I met him in Durham. He was in the Marine Corps.

We came by train in 1946; we lived with my mother-in-law. Quentin found an apartment for rent nearby. The owner showed him the apartment, and Quentin said he would be right back with his wife. He came back to get me. As we were coming up the street, the man was sitting in the window. Quentin said, "That's the house." He didn't point or anything. When we got to the door and Quentin rang the bell, the man came to the door and said, "May I help you?" Quentin said, "I'm the man that just left here. I brought my wife to see the house." The man said, "I have never seen you before."

"I just left here fifteen minutes ago. We just live around the corner. You said I could have the apartment."

"No," the man said, "I have never seen you before."

Well, my husband looked Armenian or Jewish, you could take him for either. I was brown looking. Since I have been in the North I have gotten lighter. If I was in the South I'm sure I would be darker. I think that is the reason the man would not rent to us. Oh, I cried, that was so hurtful.[18]

Richmond's experience of being openly discriminated against in the housing market mirrored that of countless African Americans in the mid-to-late twentieth century. Landlords like the one Richmond and her husband, Quentin, encountered could be found in every American city. Real estate agents kept the races apart by refusing to show and sell housing units in historically white neighborhoods to African American clients. Unscrupulous agents fed into white racial fears by instilling panic regarding racial changeover in white neighborhoods bordering urban black belts. These agents aimed to acquire homes at rock-bottom prices and then to sell them off to African American buyers, who often found themselves paying above-market prices. Black families that managed to obtain housing in predominantly white neighborhoods could find themselves fearing for their physical safety, as was notably the case for Dr. Ossian Sweet, his wife, Gladys, and their daughter, Iva, in Detroit in 1925. Sweet, a migrant from Florida who relocated during the First Great Migration, became the national symbol of this housing problem. A mounting white mob circled Sweet's property the evening of the move. Men inside the house fired guns out the windows when rocks were thrown towards the house. One white man, Leon Breiner, was killed, and Sweet and his family and friends faced a protracted trial. The NAACP and famed, albeit aging, attorney Clarence Darrow came to the Sweet family's aid, giving the issue of housing segregation one of its first causes célèbres. After an initial mistrial, Henry Sweet, Ossian's brother, was tried alone for the murder. Upon acquittal, the charges against Ossian Sweet, his wife, and his friends were dropped.[19] Restrictive covenants based around race remained legal until the Supreme Court ruling in *Shelley v. Kraemer* in 1948. The Fair

Housing Act of 1968 toughened national laws regarding equal access to housing. Yet divisions of neighborhoods by race remained far longer than legal statutes openly supported them. In fact, the United States has remained unable to solve the problem of housing segregation.

Urban planner June Manning Thomas clearly delineates the problem, using the case study of Detroit, in her work *Redevelopment and Race: Planning a Finer City in Postwar Detroit.* Thomas explains:

> Thousands of African-American families came to Northern cities during and after World War I and World War II, attracted by work in the area's industrial plants. Discrimination forced them to live in the most deteriorated sections of town. Racial barriers to better housing were lifted only slowly, and Blacks pried open previously White neighborhoods a block at a time. Because Whites refused to accept mixed neighborhoods, the arrival of Black residents led to White exodus and neighborhood instability.[20]

Black families who saved enough to purchase a single-family home considered the act one of the most important achievements of their lives. At the same time, though, the migrants were not overly concerned about the acquisition of material possessions. A sense of "making it" in economic terms did not come in and of itself from home ownership, or the purchase of any other item. Nor was economic achievement judged as the most important marker of success. This was especially the insight of old age. Achieving a good life came from acquiring balance. Being able to support oneself and one's family, and yet having the wherewithal to contribute to the community and pay respects to God—these were the markers of a good life. Psychologist and migrant Ogretta McNeil nicely summarized, "For us, doing okay is not having a big house and a big car. It's paying your bills and being nice to people and sharing and being recognized that God has His place in your life."[21]

In many cases, the migrant's status as a home owner came even more dearly earned, because the security had been achieved by a single breadwinner. Some women migrants became home owners based exclusively on their own salaries. Housing type varied by region. Relegated to particular areas of the city, African Americans often lived in small housing units converted from larger apartments or homes. Segregation made it necessary to rent substandard housing; segregation curtailed choice. In Chicago, many migrants lived first in "kitchenette" apartments, a single room featuring a simple kitchen. Often multiple generations and even extended family would crowd into such accommodations. Those who did purchase homes might have done so by means of "installment contracts," a form of what we might now call "rent to own." Those who took out such contracts could lose all credit for their former payments if they were late on any single payment during the contract period. Thus families who had paid for homes for years could be evicted. Arnold Hirsch, in *Making the Second Ghetto: Race and Housing in Chicago, 1940–1960*, tells of families living in basement units and units illegally separated by highly flammable building materials. Lacking windows and suitable egress, families could perish in house fires. Overcrowding produced such conditions, conditions exacerbated by the high flow of migrants heeding the demand for laborers during World War II. Hirsch writes, "The 1940 vacancy rate for Chicago was only 3.9%. The Metropolitan Housing and Planning Council believed a 5% rate to be the 'danger line' below which a genuine housing shortage existed. By mid-1941, however, the vacancy rate dropped to 1.5% and plummeted even further, to 0.9% by April 1942."[22] In Boston and Worcester, the three-family home, or three decker, prevailed. Mary Smith, whose words begin this chapter, purchased her own three decker, and, like most home owners, considered this the key monetary investment of her life. From the home, she ran her home business, a day care, and gained equity as the real estate market improved her home value over the years.

In Detroit and Grand Rapids, more African Americans lived in single-family homes than in many other cities. The homes available to African Americans were located in highly segregated neighborhoods. These homes were most often small and of poor quality. Neighborhoods were overcrowded. In 1940s Grand Rapids, with the exception of the Henry Street neighborhood, blacks lived in blighted areas of the city. In Detroit, the black population increased about 50 percent between 1940 and 1944, and black neighborhoods faced double the densities of elsewhere in the city.[23] Fire often destroyed homes in the African American neighborhoods of Detroit, as it did in Chicago. Sanitary conditions remained poor, with insufficient trash pickup and a good many homes lacking even rudimentary bathroom facilities. A 1938 report by the Detroit Housing Commission found that in the Eight Mile Neighborhood, only 45.5 percent of homes had at least one bath and one toilet. Thomas Sugrue writes of 1940s Detroit, saying, "Detroit blacks were entrapped in the city's worst housing stock, half of it substandard, most of it overcrowded. They lived in overwhelmingly black neighborhoods, a reflection of the almost total segregation of the city's housing market. Detroit's black population had doubled between 1940 and 1950, but the pool of available housing had grown painfully slowly."[24] An investigator for the Grand Rapids Urban League, quoted in a 1940 report, encountered black residents living in condemned homes, as well as families dwelling in basement apartments and units where the wallpaper hung down in shreds due to extreme dampness.[25]

Native Mississippian Anniese Moten highlighted the story of finally paying off her mortgage. Moten had a rather big home for her neighborhood. She boasted, rightfully so, saying, "I paid for this house doing domestic work. Working in the houses." Over time, Moten had improved the home, adding a fence and a new roof. She regularly sent her cousin's sons to the local bank to pay her mortgage statements. With her limited education, Moten sought out assistance at the bank for help with her billing questions. When the boys came back one day, grinning, to announce that Moten owed no more on the house, she expressed incredulity. Despite health troubles, which normally kept Moten close to home, she headed over to the bank to see for herself. The moment had enormous meaning for Moten, who, despite two marriages, had largely fended for herself financially.[26]

Most migrants did not move directly into single-family homes, but first transitioned through some less-than-desirable housing. Willie Jean Clark Lewis recalled, "What I first remember [of Detroit] is the basement of the house on Joseph Campau, that's what my first memories were of. We didn't stay there that long. We just stayed there until we found a house, and then we moved to the east side of Detroit."[27]

Avezinner Dean remembered the 1955 purchase of her home, a modest ranch-style house from which she later would operate her own beauty parlor.[28] Having bought a home, the migrants, once so apt to change locations, became rooted in place. Alberta Hardy, who was born in Clarksdale, Mississippi, and moved to southwestern Detroit at the end of World War II, had lived in her home for more than fifty years at the time of the interview.[29] Lillie Shelby, whose husband was a veteran, qualified for V.A.-backed loans. The purchase of her home, built by the developer Practical Homebuilders, necessitated that the family have assets of $1,000 in the bank. The Shelbys paid a deposit of $250, and initially had a mortgage payment of only $49 a month. This later evolved into $60 a month.[30]

The project's geographic scope gave rise to a multiplicity of housing forms. Because the majority of interviews took place in the migrants' homes, I learned quite a bit about the diversity of options. One interview took place in a city office, one in the home where the woman worked as a domestic, and a few occurred in the homes of friends. One took place in a recently acquired condominium.

Two interviews took place in nursing homes, and one in the narrator's beauty salon. Yet the other interviews allowed me to see the migrants' homes. Sharp economic differences separated the narrators. Although all came from families who were motivated to migrate, at least in part, for higher wages, the families had quite different means when they began their migration. Often, a slight edge in one generation translated into considerable economic stability in the next. Migrants whose parents had more education, or owned land in the South, tended to do better themselves. The housing clustered in four types: apartments in low-income housing (high rises and/or housing projects), single-family homes of quite modest means (usually in segregated neighborhoods), single-family homes of more substance (often on the edges of segregated neighborhoods), and sizable middle-class and upper-middle-class homes in areas of mixed ethnicity and even predominantly white neighborhoods.

Those who had lived in public housing in the 1950s and 1960s spoke surprisingly well of the option. Of course, circumstances quickly changed. In the late twentieth century, public housing came to be associated with gangs and rampant drug use. Raising a family in such conditions proved dangerous. Better acquainted with the myriad of problems in the more modern projects, we forget the initial enthusiasm for them. In the 1960s, Ella Sims of Grand Rapids reveled in acquiring a public housing unit. The Sims family made their home in the project for seven years. They preferred the apartment to their single-family home, because the home needed a host of repairs. The city razed much of Sims's neighborhood, taking homes by eminent domain and building public housing in their stead. Sims grew distraught when the demolition stopped three blocks from her house; she would not be part of the automatic movement into public housing, but had to negotiate her way into the projects instead. Sims worked to bring more public housing units to Grand Rapids, sitting in planning meetings and advocating for change. Many of the homes available to African American residents simply fell below acceptable standards. Sims recalled the three-bedroom apartment she, her husband, and many children lived in for seven years as "wonderful." Sims explained: "It was like we had moved up to a mansion, you know. Right. And so, our house, it just pushed over, really. Oh, we bought one house and we wore it out. It was big and that's the thing about it—it was the years, is what did it. Because, you know, when you sat in the house, it didn't look so bad. But if anything was wrong, it was so major, you know, it just wasn't feasible to have it done."[31]

Sims's initial attitudes toward public housing are echoed by LaJoe Anderson Rivers in Alex Kotlowitz's book on poverty in Chicago, *There Are No Chil-*

dren Here, and Ruby Haynes, interviewed in the 1980s by journalist Nicholas Lemann, for *The Promised Land*. Anderson Rivers and her family celebrated their move into the West Side's Henry Horner Homes in the late 1950s. Kotlowitz writes:

On the first day at Horner, the Anderson family knew only hope and pride. The future seemed bright. The moment, particularly for the children, was nearly blissful. Leila Mae [LaJoe's mother] made doughnuts to celebrate and played Sam Cooke and Nat King Cole albums on her hi-fi through the evening. That night, in one of the back bedrooms, the sisters lay on their narrow cots and stared out the windows. Because there was no one yet living in the building and few streetlights, they could clearly see the moon and the stars. They had their very own window on the universe.[32]

Upon moving into Chicago's Robert Taylor Homes in 1962, Ruby Haynes experienced elation at the level of the new accommodations. Lemann relates:

It was a great day. There was a feeling of excitement and of festivity that went along with the inauguration of an impressive building, especially since the accommodations there were better than any of the tenants had ever had. Janitors were there to help everyone with their things. Workmen were grading the area around the building and planting grass. Everything was new and clean . . . As Ruby's son Larry, who was twelve years old at the time, says, "I thought it was the beautifullest place in the world."[33]

Whatever housing type they inhabited, however, all the migrants interviewed for this study exhibited care in decorating their homes. Solid, traditionally styled furniture was featured, and special keepsakes, including glass figurines, dainty decorative objects, and family pictures, often served as the focal points of the living rooms and dining rooms in which the interviews took place. These were welcoming homes, whatever the social class of their owners or occupants. Lillie Shelby offered a memory regarding the purchase of her home in Detroit and the acquisition of its furnishings. She and her husband supported eleven children. Shelby mused:

In between babies and things I worked here [in Detroit]. I worked out in Orchard Lake for a while. I couldn't tell you the different places I did it because if someone needed someone for a day, I couldn't turn them down because I had children. My husband worked for Great Lakes [Steel] and he got paid every two weeks and what I made in between I would get groceries with that and that was how we was able to take care of them and when these houses got built we were able to buy a house. I been right across the street since August of '49. I raised all of the kids here.

There was a man, he had a furniture store in Wyandotte, Mr. Walker Cadillac. So we got over there and all you had to do was show you worked at Great Lakes and he would let you have a certain amount of furniture. At that particular time and I still got the clipping somewhere over there now, he had a big old television screen and we didn't have no television. We bought that as the children's present—$775—and they even put that in the paper that a Negro had bought that $775 television. I still got it there. I said one day I am going to have a bar made out of it. You know, television on one side and record player on the other side. We put it in the corner and all the children sit down and look at the television.

Shelby spoke with pride of this acquisition, yet was quick to put the purchase in context. As Ogretta McNeil theorized earlier in the chapter, Shelby claimed that happiness came primarily from the couple's ability to care for their family, rather than from any extravagance. Shelby concluded, "We survived it and we're doing good. I'm just satisfied. I am right here in my little house and happy. The house next to me, it kept getting vacant and getting vacant and I was finally able to buy it. So I got a daughter living in it—right next door to me—so I'm happy. As they say, 'I'm not nigger rich, but I am living.'"[34]

Establishing a life in the North would not constitute an unmitigated joy. The migration story would not play out like a Hollywood film with a happy ending, with all problems ultimately solved. The trouble with the North became apparent to many families right at the time of arrival. Some migrants were greeted soon thereafter by rioters. Black rioters took to the street to protest urban conditions, when the ballot box, the picket line, and other means of protest were ineffective in expressing the pent-up power of their rage. White rioters and police officers mixed into the melee. The predominantly white police forces seemed resistant to the black newcomers. Interracial violence plagued the mid-twentieth century city streets. Thousands of white families in these urban neighborhoods fled to the suburbs after a riot. Even the long-established black communities exhibited scorn for their country cousins, and did not embrace them as their own initially. Around the edges of the hard-won migration, daunting problems showed through. The move would not solve all the problems of the migrant family. Migration was just another step in the march towards equality.

Bernita Howard's attitudes towards her move to Detroit in the summer of 1943 were tempered by the 1943 riot. The disruption began when fighting between white and black park visitors broke out in the city's Belle Isle. The tensions moved across the water and into the city. Howard felt that she had to make the migration regardless of the violence in Detroit, but certainly this event worried her. She stated, "The riot was in '43 and I came here right after the riot. When I got ready to come, the people who I was working for said that they just had a riot where you are going."[35] Minnie Chatman also moved to Detroit around the time of the 1943 riots, but this provided little dissuasion. Chatman's husband had fully committed to the move, and she abided by his wishes. Chatman reported that he insisted, "We was never going back there [to the South], and he didn't go back there."[36]

Annie Benning, ninety-one years old at the time of the interview, had moved into her well-appointed brick home in Detroit in 1960. Her husband, a GM auto mechanic, made a comfortable living, and Benning was able to stay at home as a full-time homemaker. The riot of 1967 shook Benning's comfortable existence. The disruption waged on just a few blocks from her home. Benning exclaimed: "They had one [a riot] right down there on Fort Road and way up almost to Jefferson. There was a riot . . . we didn't see none of it but what we heard it [sic] on the air. The next morning we [went] outside and it was tore up. I was nervous because you didn't know which way they was going to turn again. Breaking in, tearing down, setting a fire and all that."[37]

When Barack Obama worked as a community organizer in Chicago in the 1970s, the sense of dismay that had settled in African American neighborhoods was apparent to him. The physical scars of former riots showed clearly on the city, and African American Chicagoans wondered where hope would come from. Obama writes:

The area had never fully recovered from this racial upheaval. The stores and the banks had left with their white customers, causing main thoroughfares to decompose. City services had declined. Still, when the blacks who'd lived in their homes for ten or fifteen years looked back on the way things had turned out, they did so with some measure of satisfaction. On the strength of two incomes, they had paid off house notes and car notes, maybe college educations for the sons and daughters whose graduation pictures filled every mantelpiece. They had kept their homes up and kept their children off the streets; they had formed block clubs to make sure that others did too.

It was when they spoke of the future that a certain disquiet entered their voices. They would mention a cousin or a sibling who came by every so often asking for money; or an adult child, unemployed, who still lived at home. Even the success of those children who'd made it through college and into the white-collar world harbored within it an element of loss—the better these children did, the more likely they were to move away. In their place, younger, less stable families moved in, the second wave of migrants from poorer neighborhoods, newcomers who couldn't always afford to keep up with their mortgage payments or invest in periodic maintenance. Car thefts were up, the leafy parks were empty. People began to spend more time inside; they invested in wrought iron doors; they wondered if they could afford to sell at a loss and retire to a warmer climate, perhaps move back to the South.[38]

By the 1970s, when Barack Obama acquainted himself with the streets of Chicago, the dream some African American families had glimpsed in earlier decades looked as if it was not going to come to fruition. Granted, middle-class and wealthy African American families headed out to the suburbs in unprecedented numbers. Yet they left behind a great many families. These families now had no well-to-do neighbors to emulate. The projects, once a better alternative to substandard, privately owned housing, failed to withstand the test of time. As factories relocated to the South, the jobs that had once drawn people to the northern cities dried up. Empty lots remained where homes had been set ablaze during riots. Gangs transformed the corridors of public housing complexes into fearsome places. In the project where LaJoe Anderson Rivers once dreamed of a better life, she and her family encountered a high level of crime. Author Alex Kotlowitz states, "In the summer of 1987, six thousand people lived at Horner, four thousand of them children. They would quickly tell you that they dared not venture out at night. At Horner, for every one thousand residents there were approximately forty violent crimes reported, a rate nearly twice Chicago's average."[39]

Thus the major urban riots of the 1930s–1960s and the more minor upheavals that followed left visible and invisible scars upon the cities and urban dwellers. The later riots quelled the hopes of the migrants, who felt that in their new homes, things might, at long last, change. The financial, legal, and other gains made by this generation would not sweep up every family in their wake. For those left to live in the segregated areas of the city, life could still be difficult.

Negotiating the Public Sphere and the Workplace

Migrants never knew quite what would happen when they entered the public world of the northern city. Florence Allison left Livingston, Alabama, for Detroit in 1947, where she found a job sewing dining room upholstery. Yet she quickly discovered the social limitations of her new city. At the department store, the clerks made their disapproval of her patronage clear. Allison remembered, "I went to Winkelman's. And they wanted to know what white woman sent me there. I told them no one sent me."[40]

Simone Landry of Detroit spoke openly about the boundaries between the white and black communities of the North. Although the region did not have a system of legal boundaries the equivalent of the South's Jim Crow, the North had its own form of de jure and de facto Jim Crow. Many newcomers did not have access to housing outside of segregated neighborhoods. Their children continued to attend segregated schools. Blacks were paid lower salaries than whites. Northern blacks thought carefully about what areas of the city they entered and what businesses they patronized. As a busy mother of three girls, Landry had less need to enter into the edges of the white world than some others. She delineated:

> There were certain places that you didn't go. If they don't hire black people then you don't go in there—they referred to it as colored people at the time. I do remember that whatever the rate of pay was, we got less than what others got and stuff like that. But there again, I wasn't worried. There were some places you went and some places you didn't. I just have been fortunate, that's all. I was young and I didn't do a lot of going anyway because I was not single.[41]

Thelma Lane compared Pittsburgh favorably with her birthplace of Montgomery, Alabama, but still encountered limitations. She lamented, "In Pittsburgh, you had more privileges but you also found some places that they didn't want Negroes in—some of the little old restaurants and things. They didn't want to cater to Negroes or to the blacks."[42]

FAITH RICHMOND
Boston (Dorchester), Massachusetts

Although I did not happen to ask Richmond a formal question regarding Boston racism, she recounted two incidents early on in the interview, referring to them as

"my two times." The housing incident, recorded above, and this refusal of employ-
ment, discussed below, fastened themselves tightly to Richmond's memory.

The next thing, I got a job typing. Well, I thought I had the job. I passed the test for S.S. Pierce Company, they hired me. The employment office person took me upstairs to where I was going to work and to meet the supervisor. The supervisor told him right in front of me, "I will never have a nigger in here." Yes, she did, right in front of me. So, the man said, "I have hired her." She said, "I don't care what you did, she is not coming up here to work." So, he said, "You have a person going out on maternity." She said, "I don't care what I told you, she is not coming here to work. I don't have niggers working in this department." So he brought me downstairs and said how sorry he was, but that didn't solve anything. That was my two times.[43]

WILLIE JEAN CLARK LEWIS
Southfield, Michigan

Willie Jean Clark Lewis credits affirmative action programs of the 1960s and 1970s
for her ability to gain admittance to the management ranks at the Ford Motor
Company. She felt the pressure of being one of the few black employees at her level
of administration. One boss even called her derogatory names; Lewis did not pro-
vide details on why this occurred, although I did ask her directly. She may have
misheard the question, or she may not have wanted to expand on the story. Born in
Flat Lick, Kentucky, in 1941, Lewis came to Detroit as a child. Her father, who did
not know anyone in the area before heading to Michigan, located employment and
sent for his family. Lewis was a highly personable woman whose energetic attitude
belied her years. I interviewed her in her daughter's expansive home in Southfield,
Michigan, a town that lies sandwiched between largely African American Detroit
and the city's predominantly white northern suburbs. Southfield is the first inde-
pendent suburb across the infamous Detroit boundary, Eight Mile Road. By cross-
ing it, one changes worlds. Southfield, easily accessible from the area's crisscrossing
highways, features tidy suburban streets of uniform middle- and upper-middle-
class homes, as well as a scattering of office parks and an occasional high-rise office
building. In 2006, Southfield's population of 75,053 was composed of 30.1 percent
white residents, 65.8 percent African Americans, 1 percent Hispanics, or Latinos,
and others.[44] On the day I interviewed Lewis, a shiny Jaguar automobile was
parked in the curved driveway outside her daughter's beautiful home. I would learn
that Lewis's husband had founded his own business, Lewis Metal Stamping, which
Lewis's daughter continued to run after his death. The cordial family welcomed stu-

dent Elizabeth Cote and me and ushered us into a large living room with soaring vaulted ceilings. We interviewed Lewis, her mother, Lillian Clark, and daughter, Jacquie Lewis Kemp, in turn. The day felt somewhat celebratory, a special time set aside to recall memories and think about intertwining lives. It proved especially informative to interview across three generations. Lewis opened up about her career in business administration.

I was born in 1941 in Flat Lick, Kentucky. It's the southeast corner of Kentucky, not too far from the Tennessee border. It's rural. Momma was a housewife and Dad worked on the railroad. My father came up, and then us. I came here to Detroit when I was two. So I didn't really live down there, but we went back every year on vacation for two weeks. It was very different, because down there, especially when I was a teenager, they didn't allow black people to sit at counters or enter places. Forgetting that, I would go in and sit down and people from behind the counter would say, "You're not from around here, are you?" So it was very different than up here.

In high school, I worked co-op with Blue Cross. I was a file clerk. I thought it was good. I enjoyed it. I attended high school and I went on to university. I studied business at Wayne State University. That's where I met my husband. Well, I knew my husband before and then we got married. I didn't finish the degree then. I returned to school at fifty, my kids were all gone and I went back to school. I earned my degree in 1991.

I married and we moved to another home in Inkster, Michigan. I was a homemaker and then we moved to Ypsilanti and back to Westland. I then worked at Ford Motor Company, 1963 until 1999. At first, I was just a secretary. Not just a secretary, because that's an important job. Then I was an analyst in human resources. I liked that one. For a long time I was the only black person. We were all mostly in the clerical positions. The analysts and the supervisors and the managers were all white. I think my pay was comparable for what I was doing at the time. Now I would get promotions and they always took care of me, but there were a number of black people that applied for positions and didn't get them.

I did feel like a trailblazer. I felt that I had to work extra hard and I felt that I had to do the best job I could so they would hire another black person. I didn't get a lot of pressure, but I thought I was qualified to do the job anyway and that was good, but I really felt that I was part of the impression [regarding black workers] that I was going to make on my boss.

One thing that one of my bosses told me that I have never forgotten is that you determine your career. We determine the direction of our jobs. That's stuck with me. That's more true today than it was back then when I started working. Women can go to school for various careers and go to positions to utilize those careers.

They moved me along because I helped their numbers. I think I did a good job. I worked hard and tried to do the best job I could do. I never really had a problem. I had a boss one time that said "nigger" but that was the most he said to me. I felt that sometimes I could do the job better than they could because I had to teach them how to do their job, but I didn't let it bother me that much. I did my best. The young people coming in don't have the knowledge of how to start up a group project and know what all has to be done. So the older people that have been there have to train the young people or they don't get a lot done.

Northern racism often seemed at its most tangible in the workplace. Just securing a job proved to be a significant hurdle. Some migrants, like Richmond, were rejected openly due to their race. Some employers acted with racist intent but veiled their racism under references to "rules" or "tests." When the migrants aimed at jobs in the middle tier, administrators often invented reasons to reject their applications. The phone company infamously snubbed black women job seekers. Alverrine Parker applied for a position with the phone company in Grand Rapids in 1955, even taking the job placement test. Told she did not pass, Parker demanded to see her test. Parker thought the company would hire light-skinned African Americans. She related, "I think my color skin was too black. They were hiring by the color of the skin. The lighter the skin, the more, you know, the jobs were more available." Parker did not take her rejection quietly. The incident led her to migrate to California for a time, in search of a more open community. Parker said, "I always had a big mouth—didn't do any good, but I wanted them to know that I know what they did . . . That's one reason why I went to California."

From time to time, especially when relations at work were pressured due to increased work load, a conflict, or other issues, white northerners would bare their more intolerant sides. Southern migrants expressed little surprise over these revelations. Ruth Margaret Covington recalled a racially tainted remark billed as a compliment. Her boss at a clothing store, pleased with Covington's demeanor, stated that she "had no business being black." In other words, in comparison to all others of her race, the boss considered her unusually adept. Covington tried to take this remark in a complimentary way.[45] Addie Smith encountered racism among her fellow workers in the supply room at a Massachusetts hospital. She quit her job rather than deal with such treatment.

Smith explained, "So she [a co-worker] started a little problem, so, naturally the woman [supervisor] believed the white person over me. So I left. I said, 'I don't have to stay with this.' So I went to Fairlawn Hospital and I worked there twelve years."[46]

Leaving a position became a frequent response to an intolerable solution. Dealing with a myriad of slights on a continual basis, migrants learned to judge which fences could not be mended. They also lacked or believed they lacked sympathetic supervisors at the topmost levels of their workplaces. Rather than filing grievances or appealing suspect attitudes and behaviors to higher-ups, the women often simply quit. In domestic work, no higher authority existed than the man and woman of the house—thus there was no recourse when employers acted inappropriately. The more informal the job, the more informally the working relationships came to be ended. Historian Kim Phillips found quitting to be a common tactic for the African American male migrants to Cleveland she studied. Phillips writes, "When faced with limited job mobility, black men used the one recourse available to them—they quit, and did so at a rapid pace whenever better jobs or wages could be found."[47] Sociologist Pierrette Hondagneu-Sotelo came to a similar conclusion when documenting the lives of Latino immigrant workers in California. Hondagneu-Sotelo explains, "Many housecleaners find it expedient to just stop going to a problematic job. After finishing their cleaning on a Tuesday afternoon, they may quietly—or at least unbeknownst to the employers—decide never to return."[48] This tactic kept day worker Fannie Mae Kennedy from having to deal with unpleasant employers for too long. Even though she documented a variety of undesirable bosses in her stories, she chose to summarize her life's work as relatively pleasant—because she had the option of leaving the jobs. Kennedy concluded, "I never had any real bad experiences because if there was something going on that I really didn't like, I didn't go back."[49]

Even women in higher-ranking positions, such as Willie Jean Clark Lewis, bore witness to terrible prejudice on the job. Sometimes the malicious comments came from underlings and other times from supervisors. Thelma Lane remembered a heated argument with a white woman insubordinate at her workplace, the Department of Defense offices in Washington, D.C. Lane, even with her college education, could not insulate herself from workplace exchanges that bore the taint of racial prejudice. As in this instance, many whites did not bow to the authority of their black supervisors. The white woman insisted on capitalizing the word "white" but not "Negro." Lane explained that she had it backwards. Only Caucasian is capitalized, Lane tried to explain. Such incidents fueled Lane to keep a careful record of workplace goings-on. She admitted, "I kept a big log of all the things that happened, not to anyone else, but to me—who was promoted over me, when they were promoted, when I had my last promotion. . . ."[50]

For some women, the issues stemmed not from work colleagues, who tended to know the migrants on a personal level, but from customers, clients, students, or patients who were utilizing the migrant's services. Migrant Mary Edmonds, interviewed in 2001 for the Grand Rapids Public Library by Marg Ed Kwapil, became the first African American to teach music in the Grand Rapids public school system. Despite her college degrees and years of training, students initially questioned her skills, likely because of her race. Edmonds remembered, "Students questioned my ability when I was teaching music. My first conversation in class was with a little girl who told me that I just didn't direct like her former teacher, my other colleague. I asked her if she was ready for a demotion, since she could go back to ninth-grade choir. I'm teaching here and this is the way I direct [laughter]. Then I didn't have any more problems. I got along very well with the students."[51]

Jacqueline Dock of Detroit labored as a nurse's aide, a surgical instrument technician, and a babysitter during her adult work life. Dock admitted, "Well, being an aide, the main thing it taught me [was] humility. I didn't like a lot of people, but it taught me to listen to what people are saying to you and it taught me not to be selfish." Initially, most of her co-workers were white. Dock said, "I had a couple of problems with patients, but not with co-workers." Dock's job duties involved taking the patients' temperature and pulse, as well as helping them with personal hygiene. One patient's attitude was particularly objectionable. Dock notified the patient that she was laboring only for "extra" money. In making this statement, Dock defined herself for the onlooking patient and white nurse as a free agent and as a consumer, rather than as a lower-status worker trying only to get food on the table (and thus tied without choice to her job). Dock recalled:

When you come back around, this lady felt that I was inferior to her. From her talk and especially her mannerisms, I knew that she thought I was inferior to her. She told the nurse that I lacked in my job as an aide by doing her personal hygiene. So the nurse came to me and said what the lady had said. And I went in and said to the lady with the nurse and said, "You tell her in front of me that I did a bad job." Then she started to call me names. I said, "Well, you know that I have done what I am supposed to do." I said, "I am here because I am greedy. I am not here because I have to work."

Dock's patient was reassigned to another aide. In similar circumstances, Glennette Taylor of Grand Rapids, Michigan, worked at Butterworth Hospital in the nursing department for six years during the late fifties and early sixties. Taylor had her share of trying patients. Male patients openly confronted her regarding racial difference. In one case, Taylor transformed an uneasy relationship with a female patient into a friendship through unwavering kindness. Taylor opened up:

> I had an experience with a man. He cornered me outside of his daughter's room and he wanted to know how I felt about taking care of Caucasians. I said, "Well, you know, I haven't thought about that. I am assigned a patient and the color of your skin doesn't even enter my mind." I was telling him, "God loves Judy [the patient], and I am there to do my job, regardless." He was quite upset that I would take care of her. And, oh, I had a minister that had a heart attack. He didn't want my kind taking care of him. And the nurse in charge said that "if you are unhappy with our floor and our nurses, you have to ask the doctor to have you moved." But that was shocking.
>
> It is sad, but it's true. And I had an experience with a lady. She did not want me to touch her. Not at all, don't come near her. Nobody else would take care of her. So when her light came on, I would check her out and we became the best of friends. The meaner she was to me, the better I was to her, if I could be any better. [Later I was] downtown in front of Steketee's Department Store, I kept hearing someone saying, "Mrs. Taylor, Mrs. Taylor," and it was this lady. We embraced right there in front of Steketee's with people walking around. I said, "Now, Mrs. X, a number of months ago, no one would have believed this." The Lord did it.

Taylor concluded her thoughts on northern racism with this statement: "There [the South] you really know where you stand, and here it is not so blatant, but yet it is, if I am making any sense. It's still around but there are groups like our media that are working towards making things better. But yes, it still exists, and I think it always will. But it is up to the stronger ones to try and wipe it out, and we do the best we can and live with those that we can."[52]

In domestic work, negotiating relationships with employers required a deft hand. Work in a private home is complex on a variety of levels. The work is highly personal and employers divulge much more about their own lives to their workers than the employers know about their employees. Employers may feel uncomfortable with their role as boss, and may even deny it altogether.

Rather than speaking clearly to the employee regarding their needs, employers often speak indirectly or not at all. Many employers failed to acknowledge the special skills of domestic workers, and assumed everyone could clean a house or watch children with equal aptitude. These employers treated their employees with continual disdain.

Fannie Mae Kennedy, born in Louisiana in 1925, labored in a wide variety of jobs at the bottom of the pay scale, including domestic work. Interactions with employers ranged from surprisingly warm to highly uncomfortable. Her memories indicate that the seemingly small things—where a domestic sat while eating, or what food they were to eat—structured the quality of the employer/employee interaction. Kennedy matter-of-factly recalled her various employers:

> Doing day work here [in Detroit], the first person I worked for doing day work was a Jewish lady. My momma never did teach us about segregation, but some way or another I found out that we wasn't supposed to sit with the white folks and eat. So at lunchtime, she fixed my food. She and the children was sitting at the table, but I sit at the counter, and she said to me, she said, "Fannie, you don't have to sit at the counter." She said, "You come to the table and sit with us." And I thought that was the most nicest thing that I had ever heard from white people. From then on, I did [sit with them], you know.
>
> I worked for a lady once and it was lunchtime so she had boiled a lot of corn. And so I sit and I ate the sandwich she had and she said, "You don't eat corn? You don't want the corn?" I said, "No, I don't like it." She said, "Well, you the first Negro I ever seen that didn't like corn." I said, "Well, I don't," and we just sat there like that. Maybe it shouldn't have bothered me, but it did. So then I worked for some people doing day work in Taylor. Now this lady was real nice, but her husband used to say things to hurt you. You know what I mean, but I didn't feel it that much. So when I stopped doing day work then I worked for two people at the same time. I'd work at her house for half a day, and then go three streets over and work for this other lady for half of a day. Altogether it wasn't but ten dollars a day. So I got pregnant and after then I quit working for them.[53]

Ultimately, the African American women migrants characterized their encounters with the northern city as a mixed set of experiences. Most women were glad that they had migrated, yet they bore witness to the deep flaws of their new communities. Some considered, or even planned, relocations back to the South. The northern cities offered improvements over life in the South in terms of increased legal rights and fatter paychecks, but provided only ambiguous modifications to the day-to-day onslaught of racism. The migrants, for the most part, spoke of their decision to migrate as the best possible choice for the time, yet readily admitted to their homesickness for family in the South, and even the southern way of life. Some wondered what life would have held for them if they had stayed. Those who migrated near the end of the Second Great Migration felt that they had just missed significant positive changes in their home communities. Migrants like Mary Smith could not help but notice that her relatives in Georgia and Florida owned beautiful (and relatively affordable) homes, and held desirable jobs.

The women migrants worked hard to carve out a space for themselves in their new northern homes, holding themselves proudly despite the prejudice of those they encountered. The women often felt compelled to act to hone down the sharp edges of this discrimination; they accomplished this by showing even more kindness to clients or patients who were cruel, or by making a well-considered remark. The constant onslaught of racially charged moments proved challenging to negotiate. A tight grasp of religious doctrine, a belief that God would help out where and when He could, brought many through the hard moments. A moral steadiness provided a refuge of sorts, a steady perch above the fray of an uncomfortable workroom, unwelcoming department store, or harsh city street. And then there were the triumphs, more subtle perhaps than one might hope, yet emblazoned on the memory forever. Fannie Mae Kennedy found herself sitting at the table with her employer and her family, her humanity recognized in the all-too-often dehumanizing situation of domestic service. Glennette Taylor embraced her former recalcitrant patient in front of Steketee's Department Store in downtown Grand Rapids; with a little help from "on high" she felt she had worked through a difficult situation and discovered a pleasant outcome. Anniese Moten, in a similar vein, shared her personal moment of triumph—the time in which she had rushed to the bank to verify that she had in fact paid off her mortgage on her domestic's salary. Such are the well-earned moments of life.

Mrs. Thomas, the wife of a wholesale grocer, in the kitchen with an unidentified domestic worker. San Augustine, Texas, April 1943. Photograph by John Vachon for the Farm Security Administration. Library of Congress, American Memory Collection.

CHAPTER FIVE

The Work of a Domestic

I've been struggling here a long, long time. So I just thank the Lord as well as it is because I could be worse. But every time I think about how far I have come and how the Lord has brought me, I just get joy, unspeakable joy, thinking about how good God has been to me, you know.
—ANNIESE MOTEN, DETROIT, MICHIGAN[1]

ESTHER WOODS
Grand Rapids, Michigan

Esther Woods and I had this conversation on a warm June day. Esther owned a tranquil-looking beige clapboard home of two stories, situated on a corner lot with many thick shade trees. The neighborhood, at the northern border of the city, had transitioned over the second half of the twentieth century from an area of white families to a hub for the city's African American community. Many of the stately older homes had been subdivided into rental units, but their architecture still proved impressive. During the interview, we sat at Woods's highly ornate dining room table, just feet from the front door. Woods had a lovely dining room hutch, crafted of the same dark wood as the table, which held dainty china dishes laid out to best effect. In Woods's front parlor, visible through the open doorway, she had positioned two welcoming love seats and a collection of colored glass vases and candy dishes, a few of which had originally sat in my own great-grandmother's living room. Just off the dining room was a very small bedroom, inhabited off and on by Woods's niece, whom Woods had helped to raise. The home's first floor had a small powder room, decorated with brand-new gauzy white curtains, and an expansive kitchen featuring mid-twentieth-century appliances and countertops. The home was sparklingly clean.

Woods found herself working exclusively for the Jewish community of Grand Rapids. Some of her employers and their friends were active in liberal-minded volunteer organizations, such as the board of the Brough Community Association, the local affiliate of the Urban League.[2] Working exclusively for Jews, Woods developed a specialty service. She knew about the customary foods and rituals of the Jewish holidays, and could help in holiday preparations. She could make the traditional potato pancakes, known as latkes, and knew how to set out the unleavened bread, matzah, for Passover. In the small Jewish community, in which everyone seemed to know each other, almost all the community children who had run through these homes or attended one of the holiday parties had become acquainted with Woods. After knowing these families for more than fifty years, Woods still referred to many of the women by using a proper title, their husband's first name, and surname. I never heard her speak of any white employers by their first names. In another conversation, Woods confided in me that her formality sometimes caused comment. In one case, she referred to a little girl in her care as Miss —. The little girl took affront to such treatment, saying, "Esther, I'm not a 'Miss,' I am a little girl!" I noticed, however, that no one, including the little girl in the story, granted Esther the courtesy title of Mrs. Woods. Traditionally, such niceties remained the privilege of whites. Yet formal language also may have served a purpose for Woods. Her use of proper names long after such practices had generally fallen from fashion in this fairly casual city may have served to bolster Woods's professional boundaries, strengthening her veneer of detachment. The physical closeness between employee and employer in domestic work could prove uncomfortable; a high level of etiquette on the part of the employee could partly mediate the situation. In some ways, manners provided a mask, shielding the real woman from the family for which she labored. This form of speech also could carry an element of mockery, although this was not readily apparent in Woods's case. White scholar Susan Tucker recalled her own use of excessive formality when employed as an au pair in France. Tucker admits, "I also came quickly to realize that the deference I gave them had another quality that would more aptly be described as mocking. And I knew that I had learned to imitate, learned to act, learned to mock, at least in some ways, from black domestics. I heard in my words their voices."[3]

After the interview, we walked through Woods's garden, viewing the vegetables beginning to flower and the decorative perennials lining the sidewalk that flanked Woods's kitchen door. Every inch of the beds had been put to some sort of plan. Woods had placed green wire cages over her tomatoes the day before. The garden featured collard greens and cabbage, all staples Woods would use. She had invested a substantial part of her lifetime in establishing an order in this home.

I was born on a farm in Alabama—Cuba, Alabama, and I lived there until I was nineteen years old. [Woods was born in 1913.] I worked in York, Alabama, which was about eight miles from my home, before I ever left there the first time. But it is a small town—wasn't very much work there for me any longer, so I figured it was time for me to move on to something better. I lived in East Chicago, Indiana, for three years. And I went back home and stayed with my father for another two years, and then I came here. I came here in April of 1945. I was keeping house for my brother the first year that I was here, because he had my sister's children. She was in the state hospital, and he had her children. Frankly, that's why I came here, to help him with those kids. I wouldn't have stayed there [Cuba, Alabama], because there was nothing to do.

I said at one time I wasn't going to stay here [Grand Rapids] because I didn't like it. Then in October of 1946, I had surgery at St. Mary's Hospital, and the doctor dismissed me and said I could go to work. By then I started looking for work. But the type of work I wanted at the time—I wanted to go to a factory. And the doctor told me I shouldn't go into a factory because at that time, I would have blackout spells—I would black out on the job. And my stomach was very weak. And he told me, he says, "You look like a very healthy, strong person, but you're not." He says, "If you go into a factory, they're gonna put you on a machine, because then you might get killed or you might cause someone else to get killed." He says, "So, I wouldn't tell you to go to a factory at all."

So, then, I started looking for an electrical business because that's what I was equipped to use. I couldn't be a secretary or have a job like that because I didn't have the education for it. So I looked in the paper, and I found this ad there, and I went over to see the — [family] and I got hired the same day I went there. And then, February of 1947, I started work for Mr. and Mrs. Jerome Baer. And believe it or not, when I retired, I had worked for them for forty years. It didn't seem like I had been in Grand Rapids for forty years, but I had.

Mrs. Rosenbaum came by Mrs. B's one day and I met her there. And she wanted to know if I had any spare time, would I give her a day's work, which I did. So I started working for her—that was in '59. And from Mrs. Rosenbaum, I met Mrs. Sam Albert. She wanted some time. So I told her some weeks I didn't work every day at Mrs. B's. And when I had some extra time, that's how I started working at Rosenbaum's. As the Bs' kids grew up, then I would have more extra time. And from Mrs. Sam Albert, I went to Mrs. Sy Albert. And I worked for them for a while. In the meantime, after Mr. Rosenbaum's sister got married, she wanted me sometimes, so I had an extra half a day I would give her. And in the meantime, when I started working for Mrs. Carpenter, I met Mrs. Krissoff. And at the same time, I stopped working for Mrs. Sy Albert. And then I gave Mrs. Krissoff the time. I was working for her for a day and a half.

I would work there on Tuesdays, and I'd go there a half a day on Thursdays, and then in the afternoon I'd go to Mrs. Carpenter's. And in the meantime, when I was working for Mrs. Sam Albert, some days when I was supposed to go there, she would have me to go to her daughter's house, Mrs. Kravitz, instead of coming to her house to help her out. She had three children.

I cleaned the house, done the laundry, watch the kids. And along the way, every so often, I'd have a day off, I would go to Mrs. Sarah Albert. If I had some time off, I would go there and work for her. And take care of the kids. It was very nice working for all of them. They all were very nice, and Mrs. Sam Albert had taken me all over East Grand Rapids, I guess. When they were having parties together, you know, all of that stuff, which was nice. And all of the peoples were lovely—they were nice people to work for. And I did the best that I could to please them with my work.

And I'll tell you something funny. When I started working for each one of them, I says, "I'm going to do my best to give you a good day's work." I said, "But if it starts to thunder and lightning," I says, "I'm going to go somewhere I can get down close to the ground." And they laughed at me, and said, "Why, Esther?" I said, "I just can't work if it starts thundering and lightning like that." And they were all very nice people; there were never no misunderstandings about anything, and I did the very best that I could to do all of the little things, you know, that lots of people don't do when they doing their work, but I would. I have to laugh at Mrs. Krissoff. Sometimes as she tells me, she says, "Esther," she says, "all the little things that you do that no one else ever does," she says, "you do those things." Well, when I went in the bathroom, to clean the bathroom, I felt that everything in there should be clean. They had mugs—they each had a mug with their toothbrushes in there, and twice a week, I would clean those mugs with toothbrushes like I would clean their countertops, the mirrors, and everything else. I felt that they should be clean too—if there was a little drip of water from the toothbrushes, the little toothpaste lying there—and I would always wash them, twice a week.

I tried to think of all the things that needed to be done. I didn't want to leave anything undone; I didn't want them to have to come to me and say, "Oh, you didn't such-and-so," you know, I'd rather get everything done.

I think Mrs. Krissoff was the only one that was working [out of the house.] But they all kept their houses pretty neat. They kept their houses pretty neat, and they kept the clothes picked up pretty neat. Now some of the kids didn't. Course at Mrs.Baer's, she kept her house neat, but sometimes she'd tell Larry to clean his room, and you know where he used to put everything? He's got everything together and throw it up under the bed. And he knew I was going to be there from under the bed to put it away, so he would hide it above there from her so she didn't know where it was. And we'd laugh about it. She'd go in there, "Larry, your room clean?" He'd say, "Yes, ma'am, my room is all clean." I'd go in there, I'd look under the bed, and there's all everything was underneath the bed. But, that's plain human nature, too, for a child.

And working for the different people, there were never any misunderstandings about anything, or hurt feelings because everybody was nice to me and I tried to be nice to them. Because I felt that I had to work for a living. And I knew some people that were here for a while, [saying], "Oh, I don't want to work there, blah, blah, blah." And they give it up. So I thought to myself, why work here a little while, go somewhere else to work a little while, as long as you got to work and you get along with people, stay where you are. And that's what I did. And there was never no misunderstandings, or no nothing. I don't think I made any of them angry. Maybe I did, I can't say I didn't, I can't say I did. They never showed it, if they was ever angry about anything. Now there may have been times that maybe I would forget one little something. But it didn't bother me if they told me or showed it to me. Now I have met some people that I don't think I could work for.

But you can't just be completely perfect all the time with everything. But I tried. I did the best that I could, because I wanted to satisfy the people I was working for, and they all was nice to me, and at the time, common labor was very cheap. And the most of them would give me more than what common labor was.

I can't say anything [too positive] about the work. For the simple reason, we all know what housework consists of. And if you're gonna do the messy work, you know what you're supposed to do. So, just do it. And it's no use in saying, well, I'll do this, I'll leave that alone. I always had certain places I would start in the morning when I would get there. And then, as the people would leave and get out, then I would . . . Of course, I watched the soap operas, and I'd make sure I would be when the owners come home not to watch television. It wasn't an addiction to television. I wasn't watching it that much because it didn't affect my work. I didn't let nothing like that affect my work.

Now, I wouldn't tell anybody that I love to work, because I wouldn't be telling the truth. But I have always been the type of person that doesn't mind working for an honest living. Because I never wanted to beg; I never wanted to steal; I knew I had to work. And I told all of the people that I started working for, I says, "I'm going to tell you now," I says, "in working in your house," I says, "I might see something in here that I like, and I might ask you to give it to me. But if you don't want to get rid of it and you don't want to give it to me, you don't have to put it behind lock and key because I'm not going to steal it." And I know some of the people I've been in their houses and worked for them—I'm very sure that they left some money around to see if it would disappear. I'd pick that money up and dust under it, and put it right back down where it was.

In working for these families for forty years, Woods had supported herself financially. She came to Grand Rapids to attend to the children in her own family, but soon had to bring in an outside income. One niece continued to reside with her while she worked, and Woods did marry for a time. (See chapter six for more on this marriage.) Woods turned to the job advertisements in the newspaper, the most common way to locate a position. She readily revealed that domestic work—the work of her life—was not something she particularly enjoyed doing. Woods credited her doctor's warning against factory work for her choice of labor type. Factory positions were not bountiful for black women in Grand Rapids in 1947. Although World War II has been known as the era in which women gained access to higher-paying factory work, most of the faces of the much mythologized Rosie the Riveters were white. Nationwide, black women had begun to enter into industrial work in significant numbers only after the threatened march on Washington—spearheaded by A. Philip Randolph of the Brotherhood of Sleeping Car Porters—encouraged President Franklin D. Roosevelt's Executive Order 8802. This order, which established the Fair Employment Practices Commission (FEPC), mandated that the federal government and defense industries end discriminatory hiring on the basis of race, creed, color, or national origin. The act did not mention discrimination on the basis of sex. The government did not assiduously pursue violators of this order. Black women made some limited gains during the war, particularly in the maintenance crews at the factories, or in other of the less coveted factory positions. After the war ended in 1945, however, black women were among the first workers dismissed in favor of the returning soldiers. According to historian Jacqueline Jones, black women's share of the domestic labor market actually rose during the war, as white women headed for the factories. In 1944, African American women filled 60 percent of the jobs in private households, a gain of 13 percent over 1940. In Detroit, black women and their supporters, including the leftist minister

Rev. Charles A. Hill, took to the streets, decrying the women's exclusion from these lucrative positions.

Woods's doctor's warning may have been contrived; a friend of Woods's told me a similar story regarding her doctor's pronouncements on her health. I later wondered if the women shared a physician. Did the doctor or doctors have some other motive in preventing patients from seeking factory work—perhaps a fear of a domestic worker shortage or a disapproval of women laboring in factories? Woods valued being treated decently by her employers, and for the most part, she was. Clearly, boundaries existed between employer and employee, boundaries compounded by differences in social class, race, regional origin, and religion.[4]

Woods's interview highlights the process by which domestic workers met potential employers while on other jobs. In Woods's case, her employers formed a tight community, and with each needing only a day or so of work, she could spread out her services. The women even introduced Woods to their friends. For domestic workers laboring for a single family, meeting a potential new boss might mean ending the current working relationship altogether. The new employer would be seen to have "stolen" the employee from her former boss. Animosities could build between employers, each seeking the services of reputable employees.

Migrant women often termed work of this nature "day work." The term emphasized the fact that the worker did not live in with the family she worked for—a situation usually considered undesirable by the time of the Second Great Migration. "Day work" could be defined as a position that took as little as a few hours, or that encompassed the entire day, or that spread over multiple days per week. Day workers often gave their days to multiple employers. Some found one-time day work jobs at placement agencies. Yet the term had a wide variety of meanings. Many workers referred to their full-time, non-live-in jobs for a single employer as day work as well.

Jobs involving cleaning, particularly in domestic work in private homes, but also positions on the cleaning crews of hotels, trains, and offices, could be located relatively easily. The Grand Rapids Urban League reported in 1940, "It should be stated here that of the 287 families which came, almost a half had jobs in less than a week's time." They also concluded that the majority of migrants headed to Grand Rapids with the primary objective of securing work. Grand Rapids was not a waypoint on the migrant's journey, but rather the ultimate destination. The study concluded that 93 percent of African American women had jobs classified as being in the laboring or domestic services.[5] Alberta Hardy of Detroit, summing up her job search experience, described the event as being perfectly straightforward: "I just went there [a local hotel] and applied for a job and they hired me."[6] Some women even found themselves set up with employment before they considered themselves true migrants. Venturing to the North to visit, a woman fielding an offer of higher wages might just make the visit a long-term one. Ella Sims encountered such a situation during her visit to Grand Rapids in 1946. Such temptations offered themselves up more readily to male migrants, for men's positions tended to pay much more than would opportunities in the South. Men not only realized the regional pay differentiation but also gained access to entry-level industrial work. Industry offered the highest possible wages for blue-collar workers. Women also made noticeable financial gains, but they remained working in domestic and private service to a significant degree.

In limited instances, placement agencies connected female workers with potential employers. In addition to connecting women with jobs, the employment agencies provided the benefit of a reference. Employers preferred hiring women with known work histories. Minnie Chatman remembered bringing a reference from a family in Memphis with her to Detroit, but encountered no problems with her lack of local contacts.[7] Reliance on the placement agency was more frequent during the First Great Migration. Only a few of this study's respondents utilized an agency to find work. Avezinner Dean mentioned placement by an agency in her oral history. Lillie Shelby of Detroit also worked through an agency for years. The agency located employers seeking domestic servants, and then placed a call to Shelby. She would take a bus to the local mall, where her employers would pick her up in their cars.[8] The local branches of the Urban League also provided job placement services. A typewritten history of the Grand Rapids Urban League found in the organization's records stated, "The Urban League works primarily in the field of employment, creating new job opportunities, and in aiding newcomers to adjust to their new environment. It attempts to accomplish this goal through the technique of counseling, negotiation, direct approach, etc." The Detroit Urban League offered courses for urban newcomers, starting in 1916 with its Day Workers' Training School (renamed the Domestic Service Training School in 1920). The migrants came to disdain the courses that offered only cursory housework skills, preferring courses on more unusual skills. The Urban League hierarchy expressed a range of prejudices against the southern migrants, especially during the First Great Migration. League documents reveal the leadership's perception that the migrants dressed sloppily, had lax attitudes towards their work, and remained unable to operate modern appliances. Contrary to these misperceptions, the majority of migrants had no real difficulty with the work and quickly adapted to the few tasks that were unfamiliar. Jobs in housework could be located easily, and certification by the Urban League proved unnecessary. Women did take advantage of the placement service, especially in times when it was harder to find work, like the Great Depression. The Urban League also provided assistance in locating housing and obtaining childcare.[9]

Those that did not turn to the newspaper frequently found positions through friends. More often than not, a female network connected the women migrants with job openings. Simone Landry explained that jobs came through "association, you know, people that you talk with and they refer you to somebody and then you call."[10] Minnie Chatman of Detroit knew a woman who knew of a white woman in a neighboring town who sought a household employee. Chatman spoke warmly of her contact, saying, "She was just like a sister and we was real close." Chatman followed this position with a job caring for the family of a doctor in the legendary upper-class Detroit suburb of Grosse Isle. She worked for this family five days a week, arriving as the employers were heading out the door to work. Chatman cared for the family's home, oversaw the children, and even stayed overnight if they needed her. She later took on additional cleaning for the doctor's neighbors. Well after retirement, Chatman remained curious about the wealthy families and the spectacular, oversize houses on tree-shaded streets of Grosse Isle and Grosse Pointe. Chatman admitted to visiting the neighborhood in the years following her employment there. "Sometimes I just drive out that way and look," she confided.[11]

Bernita Howard recalled that, when she arrived in Pittsburgh, her cousin's wife procured a placement for her in a hotel. Howard cleaned thirteen rooms a day. She explained, "She had a sister working there and she introduced me to her and I got the job." Howard had never held this type of position before, but her co-workers quickly taught her the duties.[12] Mattie Bell Fritz took on her day work position at the urging of a friend. The friend located a good job for Fritz, who even formed a friendship with her employers. Fritz remembered the friend's casual query: "'I do day work, you wanna?'" Fritz continued, "I said, 'Yeah.' So I got this job on Grosse Isle. Her name was Mrs. Walker and she was a wonderful woman. I worked for her until she moved to California. I think I worked for her about four or five years. She moved to California and she sent for me twice to come out to visit her. She lived in [name of city unclear] and you didn't see blacks but they was so nice. Her neighbors and everybody was so nice to me."[13]

Liddie Williams of Chicago related her job search experience. Williams, sixty-four at the time of the interview, still worked as a housekeeper for a family. After a long-term career in the publication industry—she worked as a "jogger," assembling *Playboy* magazines—a friend passed along Williams's number to a potential employer. Williams negotiated the job with the husband of the couple she would come to work for. Negotiating with the husband was an unusual, but not entirely unheard of, situation. Williams said, "He called me and we talked and he say, 'I like the way you talk.' I say, 'I like the way we hit it off.' 'Well, how about coming out for an interview?' I forgot what day, I think it was on a Wednesday and I came for an interview. That's the way we hit it off. It's been almost fifteen years." For some time, Williams worked from nine to two, Monday, Wednesday, and Friday, then added Tuesday to her regimen as well. In some years, she juggled a Tuesday/Thursday family along with her primary employer.[14]

Employee/Employer Relationships

AVEZINNER DEAN
Detroit, Michigan

For Avezinner Dean, personal dignity and a place in the community were established through her career as a beautician. Dean also worked as a domestic during adolescence, and then again briefly in the Detroit area. She demanded that people treat her courteously; she would accept nothing less.

Dean was born in Mississippi in 1928. She attended a one-room school with, she insisted, one hundred and fifty other African American children. Her father co-owned a four-hundred-acre farm with a few of his siblings. Their grandfather had handed this impressive piece of land down to his children. Dean's father had people who labored for him as sharecroppers, which constituted a significant achievement and placed him in the upper echelon of black farming families. Dean moved between Mississippi, Alabama, and Tennessee. She lived in Michigan for a few years, returned to the South, and moved up again permanently at the end of World War II. As I conducted the interview, Dean's teenaged granddaughter Sarah went in and out of the room. Dean had helped to raise Sarah; Sarah's parents had high-level careers requiring extensive travel, and they relied on Dean at times for child care. Sarah occasionally stopped to speak to us, sharing her college plans and dreams of medical school. She attended the elite private boarding school Cranbrook just outside of Detroit. Her clearly expensive telescope sat in the middle of the Dean's tiny living room, an incongruous addition to the modest bungalow home.

Dean lived in a completely African American neighborhood in the southwest corner of Detroit. The neighborhood was made up of single-family homes, all of them bungalow style. Dean was known for sitting on the front porch of her home with her shotgun, just to make a certain kind of impression.

Dean recalled being sent out by a placement agency to work for a woman who was said not to hire African Americans. The white woman's unease became apparent immediately. Dean set up limits for the kind of speech she would allow in her presence, what kind of work she would do, and the kind of treatment she expected.

When I first came up here [to Detroit] I did work in a home for about a year. It was so strange. [On the first day] when I rang the doorbell and she came to the door . . . [she turned] so red. She looked at me and said, "You look too big [for the uniform]." I said, "I work in a T-shirt and jeans." She said, "Come in," and I said, "What do you want me to do." She went and called the bank where her husband owned the bank. She said [to me], "I am so nervous." They wanted me to wash [the floors] on my knees. I don't even get on my knees to pray. She said, "Just work in the kitchen; do what you can and do whatever you want. When you finish that I want the upstairs bathroom." I said, "Lady, how much do you think I can do in eight hours. You done give me two days' work." That floor was bigger than this whole house. I could have been there a week.

The next day she said, "I am going to leave this little girl [from across the street with you, along with the other children]." The children had hamburgers, potato chips, and something for lunch. She said, "Well, you can have the rest of the hamburger they didn't eat." I told her I didn't eat garbage. She said, "I am going to take my daughter to the barbershop and get her hair cut." I said, "I'll cut it for her." I said, "Show me how you want it cut." I cut the little girl's hair.

She looked so pretty and then she showed the lady across the street and she said, "Momma don't work niggers." I said, "Well, how do a nigger look, I never seen one." She looked at me. [She said,] "I was in a restaurant and they didn't serve niggers." I said, "I'm glad you don't. I don't eat them."

I said, "You go home. I don't have to bother with you." I said, "These kids didn't bother me and you come in and bother them and got them acting cuckoo. Now you go home." I said, "I don't care what your momma say, I am babysitting for [this family]. I wasn't hired to keep you." I made her go home, and, well, she sat there on the porch all day. When Mrs. came home she said, "What happened?" I said, "That little girl come over here and she was messing up for me to clean up the house and she put hell in your kids. I had had no trouble with your children until she come over here and I told her to go home. You didn't hire me to babysit for your neighbors. You asked me to watch the kids and do their rooms." I don't know what she said to the neighbor lady but the little girl never did come over [again] when I was there.

In the narrative above, Dean was sent by the agency into the home of a known racist, and the employer exhibited strange behavior from the first moment of Dean's employ. The white woman, exceedingly fearful, even called her husband, a successful banker, for some immediate advice. Dean refused to bend to the employer's demands that she wear a uniform or clean more of the home than was practically possible in the allotted time. Dean also chose to set out boundaries for the work. She would not care for a neighbor child who used racist language, even if it meant that the little girl, her mother presumably out for the day, had to sit on her doorstep and wait for reentry into her home. Dean established some limits in this seemingly untenable situation.

As in any type of work, domestic work presented a nearly endless variety of employer types. The migrants described a wide variety of employee/employer relationships. Some, like Mattie Bell Fritz, formed close bonds, even bonds bordering on friendship, with employers. Fritz characterized her employer as a "wonderful, wonderful lady." However, Fritz, as has been previously stated, referred to her employer as Mrs. Walker, even after visiting her in California for vacation.[15] Anniese Moten of Detroit, a career domestic worker, became a valued mentor to her employer. Moten recalled offering advice to this single mother. This woman trusted Moten's guidance in child development and in adult personal matters. Moten recalled:

> Before she [one employer] got married, she would bring her boyfriends in and she asked me, "Anniese, how you like him?" I said, "Let him go, you don't need him." "Oh, you don't like him, I like him pretty good." "Oh, no, that is not your husband." She said, "It ain't?" I said, "No." But she would, she would let him go. Then she would bring another one. She ask me, "How you like him; he is a preacher." I said, "Let him preach somewhere else, not here. No, I don't like him." So she met a senator from Toledo, and he came, so when he left she said, "Anniese, how did you like him?" I said, "Marry him." "Marry him?" "Because he is the one." She said, "You like him?" I said, "Ooh, I said anybody that take up time with your children and not put a lot of confusion in their head[s]." I say, "He's nice, he's real

nice." She said, "Oh, Anniese." So she married him and they had a little girl after I left.[16]

Scholar Mary Romero warns that employee/employer relationships ought to be carefully scrutinized. The employer's assertion that an employee was a dear friend or a family member often led to a lessening of worker rights. This claim bolstered the employer's inability to view his or her home as the employee's work site. Playwright Alice Childress famously revealed the farce surrounding the employer's claim that a domestic worker was truly "one of the family" in her work *Like One of the Family: Conversations from a Domestic's Life*. In Childress's story, the worker, Mildred, overhears her boss describe her as just "like one of the family," although Mildred eats in the kitchen. Romero surmises, "Domestics, particularly women of color, may be more vulnerable to employer's definition of their relationship as 'one of the family' because they seek respect, a rare quality in the employee-employer relationship."[17] Solid emotional connections did make domestic work more pleasant, but employee and employer could perhaps never be friends or family in the usual sense.

The migrant women frequently categorized the employer-employee relationship as "nice." Some of the narrators utilized the term "nice," a rather bland attribute, in part as a corrective to the mainstream historical narrative, which would paint the migrant women's lives, and particularly their employment, as unmitigated drudgery. Sociologist Judith Rollins made similar findings in her 1985 study of domestics and employers in Boston. Rollins writes, "To create a career that was 'real nice' is to create a self of worth. Socially safe because of the ingratiating persona it requires but psychologically fragile because of the discrepancies between reality and the women's versions of it, this is one possible way of coping with a life lived on the lowest strata of this society's class, race, and gender hierarchies."[18] Many of the narrators, entering into old age, hoped to describe their lives as meaningful and more fulfilling than the lives of some others. These women chose the term "nice" as a way to retell their stories in a favorable light. Certainly many of the stories highlighted the more humiliating aspects of household work, and the patronizing tone of employers. Some narrators used the term "nice" to describe their relationship with an employer, and subsequently told unsettling stories about the same employer. In these cases, "nice" might mean simply "better than it could have been."

Susan Tucker discovered a similar tendency to proclaim things were "nice" in her study of domestics in the South. In the interviews collected by Tucker, who is white, and her African American research assistant, social worker Mary

Yelling, many interviewees insisted that the overall tenor of their life was "nice." As in my own study, the label often seemed to contradict the stories the women recounted. Yet, the word had utility for the memoirist, who used the term to protest those who would characterize her as somehow inadequate. It is important that interviews conducted by both Tucker and Yelling utilize the term; it was not the racial difference between Tucker and her interviewee, or between myself and the women of my study, that encouraged the use of the word. Bonnie Thornton Dill, a sociologist who is African American, also encountered a widespread use of the term in her interviews with domestics. Characterization of the past as "nice" imparts a dignity to the personal history of the women workers. Tucker writes, "In most of the interviews, I found the general tendency to choose stories that show the 'good' in one's life over the 'bad.' To choose, if you will, the revised version." Later, Tucker adds, "Revision allowed the recollection of sadness and hurt feelings with dignity."[19] Thus, use of the label "nice" or other positive terms actually allowed for the admission of less than positive stories, because a claim for acceptability had been made.

Few of the women interviewed extolled the virtues of their employers. The employers might have been passable—even, as many insisted, better than average—but the majority of the women were not overly fond of the families they worked for. In recounting the stories of their lives, only a few of the women offered positive details about the employer's family. This silence on the part of the migrants would have no doubt surprised their former employers.

The setting of the work—private homes—magnified the more objectionable aspects of some employers' personalities. It is one thing to have a minor disagreement with an employer in an office or a public setting. It is quite another to have a disagreement in the homeowner's kitchen, or in the presence of the boss's children. The domestic worker, most often working alone in the home of another, faced isolation and an unbalanced power dynamic. If something went awry, she had little recourse other than leaving the job altogether.

Mattie Bell Fritz, who so cared for one of her employers, easily admitted that she had had some objectionable employers. Fritz recalled a particularly agonizing day. Clearly, this story figured centrally in her memories of domestic work. She had told this story to others in the past. Fritz recited:

> When I got off the bus there was another [African American] lady going and she said, "Are you new out this way?" And I said, "Yes, this is my first day out here." So when I went to their house, she said, "This is going to be your first and this is going to be your last day." And that's what she said but I don't know what she meant. So I went on.

First, she [the employer] told me she had a piano and she wanted the keys washed with milk. So I cleaned and then she had a chandelier and she wanted me to take each one of those crystals off and wash them. Then she wanted me, after I did that, to clean the stairway all the way down the same way.

So that evening the same lady, both of us walking to the Woodward [Avenue] streetcar, she say, "Are you coming back?" I said, "No, I am not!" But I could only handle that one day.[20]

Many African American women used domestic work to fill in between other, more sought after, employment opportunities. In fact, women of all races continue to use child care jobs in this occasional manner. Women of color linger longer in the field, and more undertake domestic labors for a lifetime. And the jobs held by women of color tend to contain a wider variety of duties than those held by white women. Black women's positions more often contained an element of housework than white women's jobs. When extra money was needed, the jobs were easily located. Many took on this work while young, as the flexibility of the work hours went well with young women's focus on schoolwork. Ogretta McNeil remembered that while attending Howard University in Washington, D.C., "I would do some house cleaning or some babysitting. Later, about my junior year, I got a babysitting job. Not anything. Just spending money." The funds complemented her parents' financial support and her partial scholarship.[21]

In the years when she was primarily concerned with raising her large family, Ella Sims sometimes joined family members at their domestic jobs for extra pay. Sims recalled, "My mother-in-law and her sister, they both worked for prominent families doing their work, and sometimes when they spring cleaned or they got hard up, I'd go help them with something." This money, the kind of income dismissed as "pin money" by uninformed cultural commentators, figured importantly in Sims's financial picture and added to her sense of self-reliance. She noted, "I always think about that, I was always so glad to have twenty or twenty-five dollars in my hand to stop at the store and spend every penny—little stuff I couldn't buy just on my husband's salary."[22] Simone Landry, who lived in Detroit, New York, and Chicago, performed both factory and domestic work. Landry stressed the transitory nature of her domestic work; she did not categorize herself as a domestic worker, although she did find employment in the field from time to time. Her husband earned enough to keep her out of the workforce for the most part, and Landry enjoyed both the status and the flexibility of his solid income. If she wanted to go out of town, she was not tied down by a job. Landry said, "I did some day work, but it was nothing that I had to rely on." She offered this description of her occasional foray into the field: "When I felt like doing something or somebody told me that such and such a person needs somebody, you know, 'Would you mind?' I would try it out . . . It's nothing I relied on."[23] Annie Benning worked as a domestic in Georgia, but never labored outside the home once she arrived in Michigan in 1948. Benning was one of the limited number of African American women to land factory work during the war. She recalled, "I did housework for a year, then I got a job working in Belkes Cotton Mill, and I worked there to 1948, and that's when I come to Michigan."[24] Fannie Mae Kennedy pointed out that domestic work offered both flexibility and a paycheck—two things she needed as a mother. She stated, "I started doing day work because, see, after then I had children, and I couldn't hold no job, but I could do day work every once in a while."[25]

Some women tried domestic work for a very short time, immediately coming to the conclusion that the work was not for them. Florence Allison of Livingston, Alabama, who worked for much of her life as a seamstress, undertook domestic work for just a single day. Allison forthrightly said that she did it for "one day and I didn't like it so I didn't do it." Allison explained, "Well, it was in Wyandotte [Michigan] and the lady had small children. She said I was the first black person that had ever come so I made sure that I would be the last one."[26] Barbara Purifoy-Seldon also worked as a domestic worker for just one day. She had graduated early from high school, and found herself with few marketable skills. She had to fill the winter and spring with some useful work. Purifoy-Seldon stated:

> So the gentleman across the street whose name was Mr. Dallas, he had
> a domestic business. He would take his children around to clean Jews'
> homes in the suburbs. He took me one day. I only went one day. I was the
> worst housekeeper. I did nothing right and the people asked him not to
> bring me again. I was only seventeen and I just couldn't understand why
> I was doing domestic work, but I had to earn some money, so I did it. But
> it was horrible. I was there all day and when they were eating I sat outside
> on the porch and there was a lot of things that I did not like. Then I would
> come in and I was supposed to clean the bathtub. They gave me a scour-
> ing towel and I had never used a scouring towel. They were very upset.
> They didn't like me at all.[27]

As many scholars have noted, black domestics served as a bridge between black and white worlds. African American females were often the sole non-whites ever to enter inside their employers' homes. The domestic laborers were some of the only African Americans with whom the employers were personally acquainted. But the domestic workers knew far more about their employers' intimate lives than the employers knew about the workers' lives. For personal safety, women migrants often created a boundary between themselves and their bosses. Few personal facts were divulged. Some workers feigned intimacy, revealing only inconsequential details, just to make conversation. Laboring in private homes, the workers knew a great deal about their employers. All too often, as seen earlier in the chapter, the women workers witnessed their employers' highly inappropriate behaviors. The employers exhibited bad behavior towards their employees, and they also revealed personal oddities in front of their employees because they were forgetful or dismissive of their presence. The migrants categorized the interactions between employee and employer on a range between "nice" and completely objectionable. Although whites often considered their household workers "one of the family," the workers rarely used such language to describe their work relationships. Not a single narrator told me that she considered her employers family; the most effusive simply labeled their employers as "friends," but clear divisions remained.

Domestic Work and Relations with Children

LOIS STEVENS
Worcester, Massachusetts

I contacted Lois Stevens after an article ran in the Worcester [Massachusetts] Telegram and Gazette *documenting her one hundredth birthday. Stevens was born in Greenville, Alabama, in 1902. We met in her nursing home apartment, where, although she had moved in only recently, she had already gathered a close group of friends due to her engaging personality. Three students working on a summer course on oral history methodology attended the interview. Lois had been sorting through her closet before we arrived; piles of discarded dresses lay on the bed.*

On a small bookshelf, I spotted a sepia-colored photograph of Stevens, wearing a soft smile. On the wall above the brown settee were framed color photos of a formally dressed woman with President Bill Clinton and Vice President Al Gore. We discovered during the interview that Stevens had served as the nanny for Denise Eisenberg Rich. Denise's parents, Emil and Gery Eisenberg, owned the Desco Shoe Corporation of New York and Webster, Massachusetts, and were co-owners of the Worcester company Jefferson Cable and Wire. The Eisenbergs, Jewish immigrants from Austria, had hired Stevens to care for their daughters, Monique and Denise. Denise Eisenberg Rich, who became a Grammy-winning songwriter, captured public attention for her generous donations to the Democratic Party and the William J. Clinton Presidential Library, as well as for President Clinton's subsequent pardon of Rich's former husband, the fugitive financier Marc Rich, on Clinton's last day in office.

I got a job with a family. They had a little girl, well, they had two girls, but one was older [Monique] and attending school in Europe. She [Denise, the younger girl] took to me and I took care of her. She came over for my party. She is living in this country now. She had been living in Europe. She lived there many years after she married, and now she is back in America.

The other girl went to school in Europe; this little one went to school here. She and I had a grand time. She is living in New York now.

The parents of the girl didn't have much to say. They were so glad to have someone to take care of things. I took care of the whole house. They had a shoe business, and they were very well liked. I guess they appreciated having me around there. The little girl had to travel to school and I would take her and pick her up. I had been invited to Thanksgiving dinner and her parents were someplace else, so my friend said, "Bring your little girl." Sure enough, I took her.

I stayed until the little girl got married. I didn't make the wedding; I wasn't feeling well. Her mother cried because I didn't get to the wedding. The child was so used to me, and naturally she didn't know what to think that I wasn't at her wedding. She lived in Europe; she married a fellow that was working in Europe. She came home after she had two children and said to me, she wished I lived over there, so her children could love me as she does. I said, "Honey, your children don't have to love me because you do. They might think you were nuts." Now, she is a grandmother.

They [the child's parents] felt safe that they could go as they please and their child was taken care of. We all took music lessons together. Piano. I had been at it longer so I could help her with her lessons. We had a good time. I remember when the older girl got married, and I didn't have much to do with the older one. I had the little one, and if someone invited me to dinner they would say, "Bring your little girl." And she would go. She went to church with me, she enjoyed these things. She got older and decided to get married and went to Europe. She always called me "her Lois."

Stevens's story illuminates the special bond that could form between children and domestic workers. Not having children of her own, Stevens may have relished the relationship with young Denise in a manner similar to that of a mother. Friends came to know Denise as Stevens's "little girl," and the child often spent holidays with her nanny rather than with her parents. Although Jewish, the child accompanied Stevens to church. The title "her Lois," used in reference to Stevens, reveals the close relationship between Denise and Lois, although the lack of a surname and title also indicates Stevens's role as a servant for the Eisenberg family.

Emma Jo Hustede, interviewed as a part of the "Oral Histories of Low Income and Minority Women" series by Fran Leeper Buss, spoke similarly about her relationship with a young child. Hustede was born in Texas to a sharecropping family, and her mother died when she was just three months old. Foster parents raised Hustede in Washington, D.C., where she received a high school education. She attended Howard University for about six months. Hustede told her interviewer of her nanny job during the 1930s in Roswell, New Mexico, saying, "It was my first experience of the working and making my own way." Hustede's first paid employment blossomed into real affection between her young charge and herself. She recalled, "I done everything for this child just like he was mine . . . I taught him how to read and write long before school . . . I just adored him." She left the work because she wanted to move to a city with a greater number of eligible men, and to leave the prejudice of the New Mexico town behind.[28]

Hustede, Moten, and others concerned themselves primarily with child care. For many domestic workers, child care responsibilities came with the job, but only as an ancillary assignment. Employers had hired women to clean, cook, and run the house; their primary assignment remained housework. Yet when these employers left the house, child care responsibilities transferred to the employees. Even when the employers were at home, some level of interaction with children was inevitable. The workers who were hired primarily as cleaners and cooks kept an eye on the children, but did not get involved in their games or concern themselves with their psychological or intellectual development in most cases. Mary White of Detroit explained that her domestic job entailed "everything. Washing, ironing, cleaning, washing walls and linens. Name it, I have done it." She only watched the family's children if the woman of the house stepped out while she happened to be cleaning.[29]

This tangential relationship to the children in part stemmed from the attitudes common to the era. In the period, mothers tended to play a more removed role than is common in twenty-first century parenting. By the postwar years, too, experts warned women not to overly mother their children, for fear of "momism." "Momism," a psychological weakness purportedly prevalent in the male children of overly domineering mothers, had played a role in the rejection of thousands of would-be military recruits during the World War II draft. Experts openly blamed coddling mothers for homosexuality, another trait deemed incompatible with military service. Historian Sara M. Evans writes, "In the middle-class world of consumerism and abundance, they [the experts] charged, women had lost a sense of duty and turned instead to emotionally devouring their children."[30] Public intellectuals such as writer Philip Wylie, joined by social scientists, attributed the weakened American character to the early imprinting of the mother's feminine character on their sons. Fearful of such an effect, mothers took a step back from their children, male and female, in the late 1940s and 1950s. According to the experts, mothers should be present—working moms were shunned—but they should remain emotionally at arm's length from their children.

In many cases, domestic workers had a fairly casual relationship with the children of their employers. If it was not necessary for mothers to overly involve themselves with their children's every emotion, then it certainly was not the concern of a hired assistant. If the parents happened to step out, the domestic worker simply took over as the adult eyes and ears in the home. For some laborers, the duties of domestic work included all tasks otherwise assigned to the woman of the house—everything from cooking to child care. Anniese Moten, whose position working for a single mother included doing laundry, vacuuming, closet arrangement, and child care, assumed the multitude of duties her employer would have undertaken had she been a stay-at-home mother. In rarer instances, however, the housekeeper was hired specifically as a companion for the children.

The no-frills lives of the migrant women often contributed to the women's honest, open style with children. Having little of value in their pockets, the women took great pride in their personal moral values and bore themselves with great dignity. Children, who see through pretense, understood this authenticity. Sociologist Bonnie Thornton Dill made a similar observation in her interviews with African American household workers. Dill concluded, "Because most young children readily return love that is freely given and are open and accepting of people without regard to status factors that have meaning for their parents, the workers probably felt that they were treated with greater equality and more genuine acceptance by the children of the household."[31] In some cases, the domestic workers could manage the children, even if the children's own parents could not. The spoiled attitudes of many of the middle- and upper-class children must have been galling to the hard-working domestic workers, many of whom had labored for pay since childhood. Minnie Chatman remembered her direct approach with the son of a client: "She had a son and he didn't want to get up and stayed in bed all day and didn't want nobody [to] clean up. When I went there I could talk to him and he would get up. 'Minnie, I know you going to come directly, you want to come in my room.' I say, 'Yes, but I want you out,' and he just went. I told [him] that he ought to be ashamed of himself. 'You just stay in bed and don't ever come down and help your mother do nothing.' And he began to talk to me."[32]

Special Work Skills

ANNIESE MOTEN
Detroit, Michigan

Anniese Moten and I met to work on this book during a warm June day. We sat in her formal dining room, a nearby fan keeping the room only partially cool. Moten's dining room and living room featured display shelves with glass collectibles. Moten raised her cousin's three boys as her own, and also took in other relatives and friends over the years, offering shelter to all she could. She financially supported herself and others, despite having to leave school at a very young age due to an automobile accident. She expressed a great joy in caring for her own home and the homes of the people she labored for over the years. Moten had particular talent for organizing home storage and caring for unruly children. She advocated corporal punishment for disobedient children. Her testimony regarding her organizational and managerial talents illustrates the fact that some domestic workers brought special skill sets to the work.

I love to keep the house. I like all of my drawers organized, you know, everything—my socks one place and everything is organized. I love that organizing! My cousin used to come over here and open my drawers and say, "Just look in, just look in." And they say, "How she do that?" And I just love it.

It's just a gift the Lord just give—and folding sheets. I fold sheets just like they do at the hospital, and I never have worked at the hospital. I worked for people and they say, "Anniese, how did you learn how to fold sheets?"

You know I got a paper with a sheet, it was showing you how to fold them. I tried to teach them. They would say instead, "I want you to come over and get my linen closet fixed up." I worked for white people and I would fix up their linen closets and they would say, "Oh, Anniese! That is just so nice, everything is just so nice." And I also keep their children, you know. And I tell them, now, "If I can't discipline these kids, I don't need to be here. Because they ain't going to run all over me and they ain't going to take over this house." And they would tell me, "Yeah, we want you to discipline them," you know.

Sometimes I would have to spank them, but they know that Anniese would get them, you know, and I would just look at them. One little boy, Chipper, he told me, he said, "Anniese, you won't have to whup me anymore." I said, "I won't?" "No," he said, "this is the last time because I am going to obey you and I going to do what you say." I said, "Okay, that's good," because, see, a lot of times they would be playing in the room with me, you know, and I have eyes and I told them, "Don't do that." And they would say, "How did you know that?" And I tell them, "The Lord I serve is able to teach me that you are doing something you ain't got no business [doing]." So one day, some little boys came up there and they were going [to] the back of my head, looking for eyes, and I said, "What is you looking for?" They say, "I don't know, Chipper say you got eyes in the back of your head," and I say, "Chipper don't know what he was talking about." I said, "The Lord I serve got eyes everywhere," and I said, "when they doing something wrong I know they doing wrong." Chipper say, "I don't mean no harm, I didn't mean no harm." I said, "I know you didn't, Chipper."

The family left and went overseas. I told the mother, I said, "Now if Chipper get to playing and he won't mind you, send him back to me and I put him in shape." Because he got to the place that he won't mind here and went to hiding his clothes and all of that and I said, "Chipper, if something else been missing, me and you going to have a fight." He said, "Anniese, I don't know where they at." I said, "Okay, you better know where they at, because your mother buys you expensive things and you know that they nice, because the other kids doesn't wear nice things, you don't want to wear them, you want to look like a bum." I said, "But you ain't going to look like no bum going out of here." He would wear them sweaters and hide it on the way, and then come back and get them and put them on and come on to the house.

Now, the one family I worked for, she had four kids. May God bless her. She said, "Anniese, these are your kids, now you raise them, you do what you have to do for them." They broke three picture windows out of the house before I got there. The neighbors didn't even allow those kids to come on their property. "Go back! Go back! Don't come over here, go back!" I says, "Now I wonder why they don't want them children to come on their property." They won't let them play with the kids. I said, "This is terrible," and one day we were going over to the grandmother's house. When we got over there, she had every door locked but the bathroom and the den and the kitchen. Every room was locked and I said, "I wonder what this is for." When we'd go places and when we drive up to a filling station, they say, "I want candy, I want a pop, I want this." I said, "Listen, now you be quiet." I said, "If they want to get you something, they will, if they don't, they won't." "But I want it, I want it." I said, "That's all right if you do want it." I said, "There is a whole lot of stuff I would love to have, but I don't have it." I got those kids where the man come to the car and he said, "Where are the children?" I said, "They're here." He said, "They ain't hollering. They ain't whooping and hollering." She [the female employer] said, "Them is Anniese's kids now, she straightened them out." And you know, before I left there they was inviting those kids to spend the night. I said, "No, my kids don't spend the night, because I am going to see them go to bed and all of that and they cannot spend the night with you." One lady next door, she begged me to work for her. She said, "If you just work for me, Anniese, and straighten my kids out like you have straightened them out, I would be happy." They had dogs and there was so much dog [excrement] downstairs and all that stuff that I had to get a hoe and scrape it up and wash it up and all of that. And the yard, ugh, you couldn't walk nowhere because it was so filthy. But when I left everything was clean. I worked for them about half of [a] year.

Then another lady, I went working for her, she moved to Toledo. [Anniese lived in with her and commuted back to Detroit on her days off.] Now them kids, she had three little boys, and they said, "Anniese, my momma ain't there. We can do this and that." I said, "No, you can't do that." I said, "You got to be nice." And one day the oldest of the boys says, "I going to run away." I said, "You are?" He says, "Yeah, I going to run away." I say, "Where you going?" He says, "I don't know, but I am going to run away because I am tired of staying here." I said, "Well, okay, I am going to pack you a lunch and I am going to pack you some clothes in a bag." I said, "If you not back here by eleven o'clock, you not getting back in here. I am going to call the police to pick you up." "You would call the police on me?" I said, "Yep, I call the police on you." So when the mother came, she said [to her son], "What's wrong with you?" "I am going to run away." I shook my head at her so she wouldn't say nothing, you know. She said, "Well, go on and run away, just help yourself and run away." "Oh, what did Anniese say about it?" Now she was one lady who really cooperated beautiful with me and kids. She said, "What did Anniese say about it?" "She said go on and run away, and she done fixed me lunch." "Well, I will fix you a sandwich too," [said the mother.] So he went and got his sleeping bag and went out into the yard and when it was getting dark, he didn't wait to no eleven o'clock.

It was ten and he was knocking on that door. I said, "Okay, you come on in here and put your lunch in the refrigerator." He put it in there and got his bath and he went to bed. I says, "Okay, now, you all done running away."

And the next little boy, he was crying. He says, "I don't want my brother to run away." I says, "Let him run." I says, "We can get another little boy and name him that. Let him run away, that's good," I said, "another little boy won't run away." But that boy come back in that house and we laughed and laughed. From then on she asked, "What did Anniese say about it?"

And I would come back [to Toledo from her home in Detroit], most of the time the baby would be chapped so bad. I said, "Why did you let him chap like this?" She said, "Oh, Anniese," she said, "I don't know, I have been trying to change him." I said, "At night you get up and go in there and change him and oil him down," and I said, "then put another diaper on him." I said, "He won't even wake up. You just turn him back over and he go on back to sleep." She said, "He will?" I said, "Yes." So she went to doing that, then he stopped chapping. But they just be raw when I get back. Oooh, that would hurt me so bad. Blue Seal Vaseline is the best thing for them, you know. So the kids was just wonderful. It just a gift the Lord give me to care for kids. I just love kids, but they have to obey. They really have to obey. So after all, the children, they come and before they go to bed, they have to hug and kiss me and every morning they would get up and tell me they enjoyed their sleep. "Anniese, I enjoyed my rest last night." I said, "That's good, that's wonderful. I am so glad you did."[33]

Moten brought a host of skills to her work. Hampered because of the limited schooling she had received, she nonetheless had little trouble finding paid work. She had an eye for arranging storage areas, including drawers and closets. Moten followed a set of directions on a printed diagram she had obtained to fold sheets in the most pleasing manner, and arranged her clients' linen closets for them. Today, closet organizing companies charge high fees for such services. In the late twentieth and early twenty-first centuries, organizing even became fodder for television programs. *Clean Sweep*, a show on TLC (The Learning Channel) that is dedicated to organizing, featured hour segments in which guests purged their homes of excess clutter and profited from the advice of a motivating expert. Celebrities like Oprah Winfrey have brought television cameras into their own closets to teach their audiences about how to make a pleasing and useful arrangement. Moten also had a deep understanding of children's psychology. She worked with children, especially wayward boys, deemed practically incorrigible by their parents. If necessary, she resorted to physical punishment. But she could usually talk a child out of his bad behavior.

The migrants remained divided on physical punishment. Some saw it as a means to get otherwise difficult children to behave. Mary White said straightforwardly, "Spare the rod and spoil the child. Some don't know the difference between discipline and abuse. Of course, you don't slap your child in the face, because nature had a better place. So use the behind and bring them up to have respect for people."[34] Annie Benning related a story in which just the threat of physical punishment worked to calm a child in her care. Benning worked as a cook for a postman and his family in Georgia, simultaneously making dinner and managing the children of the household. Benning remembered:

> I started cooking for them because they had a little girl. She was named Angie and they couldn't do nothing with that little child. But, honey, I just sit her down in the little chair and me and her be playing, and I tell her, "If you don't be good you know that your mother will whup you when she come home." I said, "She going to burn you up. Your mother will whup you good. You better be good." She'll sit down by me, and she really mind me. And they come in at night and they say, "Annie, what did you do to Angie? She's so quiet." I say, "I didn't do nothing, just sit down and talk to her. I told her y'all were going to whup her when you come in if she didn't be good." They said, "Well, you sure got her cooled down." Well, I never did have to hit her and they didn't have to whup after, because the other lady they had, I don't know what she did to her. I don't know if she whupped or what she did, but I didn't have to whup her or do nothing.[35]

Others felt that corporal punishment, real or threatened, imparted serious psychological damage. Dental hygiene professor Barbara Purifoy-Seldon took particular umbrage at the use of corporal punishment to encourage children to mind adults. She collected artifacts related to the American history of slavery and racism, including actual slave shackles and books featuring racist depictions of black characters. Purifoy-Seldon wanted African Americans never to forget the history of their people. Physical punishments figured in the containment of slaves. Purifoy-Seldon asserted, "I tell black folks that they should remember how the slave master used to hit and wanted to control that slave."[36]

To bear witness to the true meaning of these life stories, we ought to pay attention to the ways in which the women's narratives defy common preconceptions. Although domestic work has long been considered unskilled, the women told stories of how they learned their trade. They report that a high degree of training was necessary for most of their jobs. Looking back on their experiences, many domestic workers consider their southern training, particularly the apprenticeships served to their own mothers or other female relatives, as central to their acquisition of housework skills. (This theme was introduced in chapter two.) Lottie Lewis, born in 1908 in Dennison, Texas, remembered that her mother's careful teachings about the "thus and so" of housework led her to take great pride in her later work as a maid in a number of upscale Michigan hotels. She related with satisfaction that "it gave you a push to the air" when a guest recognized her handiwork with a tip.

Some women even served formal apprenticeships. For instance, Minnie Chatman's mother apprenticed her daughter to a white seamstress so that Minnie could earn a trade. Annie Nipson, interviewed for the Schlesinger Library's "Black Women Oral History Project," attended a domestic science school in North Carolina funded by the Vanderbilt family. Nipson's training led her to work in the Vanderbilts' Biltmore Estate, as well as for another very wealthy family. Nipson spoke in a positive tone about domestic work and her training, saying, "That [domestic work] was something that I could do, something I was interested in, and I worked very hard in this course. And now, after I was there, I don't remember just how long I was there, but it was a course there for, oh, a couple of years or something like that. And I finished that and got my little diploma. And then, from then on, I was able to get with a very rich class of people. That was a wonderful thing for all of us."[37]

Nipson provided her clients with specialized services, such as party planning, that garner high fees and a great deal of respect in today's marketplace. Nipson arranged flowers and centerpieces, planned menus, and created the festivities fitting the upper-class family she served in Asheville, North Carolina. Minnie Chatman revealed that her duties working for upper-class families in the Detroit suburbs included decorating, another highly respected job in contemporary urban areas. Chatman stated, "I used to cook for that lady, wash for her, clean her house, and do her draperies and decorate. It was just fun to me and they was so glad they found me."[38]

Both Nipson and Chatman worked for wealthy families; the status of one's employer affected the work. Domestic workers who labored for upper-middle-class or upper-class families stressed the family's social position. In many cases, the higher on the economic ladder the family was, the "higher" the caliber of the domestic work. Nipson and Chatman's narratives illustrate this point. The class status of the family, however, could not account for personalities, and inconsiderate bosses abounded at many income levels. Objectionable messes and backbreaking labor figured as part of domestic work for families of all income levels. Still, if the homes offered considerable creature comforts, employees might be more inclined to view them as favorable work sites. I interviewed Liddie Williams of Chicago in the home where she worked. The Gold Coast apartment, located on Lake Shore Drive just doors from the renowned Drake Hotel, featured huge picture windows framing breathtaking views of Lake Michigan. Colorful artwork dotted the walls, and the expansive gourmet kitchen offered cool granite surfaces inviting to the touch. Williams commented, "Like I told Lynne [Williams's employer], it's just like being on vacation. Vacation with pay. I enjoy it—I enjoy coming to work. You know, a lot of people hate going to work, but I enjoy it."[39]

The work of a full-time party planner or flower arranger differs vastly from that of a domestic worker who also undertakes these duties. Domestic workers usually tackle a wide-ranging set of tasks. While a domestic worker might bake dainty cakes or plan a menu on one day, she might also spend hours washing the family laundry, mopping the floors, cleaning the toilet bowl, and other more disagreeable activities. Annie Nipson, in working for the Vanderbilts, labored with blacks and whites on a staff of at least fifteen or twenty. Nipson labeled the work as "very pleasant at times," yet admitted, "sometimes it wasn't."[40]

Domestic Work and Personal Dignity

Whether or not the workers consistently found the work pleasant, almost all judged their own actions to be of value to society, and took pride in their labor. The women looked back on their lives and judged their labors of merit. They especially noted their personal dignity in the face of challenges. As scholar Susan Tucker argues in her work on southern domestics, it is important to acknowledge this pride in personal strength, while at the same time critiquing the tendency to stereotype all black women as strong. American mythology has long categorized African American women as exceedingly strong physically. The mythology was created in part to address the fact that black women's labors in the field and their difficult work in domestic situations took them out of the realm of what society deemed acceptable for white women. American society also cast African American mothers as the emotional linchpins of their families, in part to erase the guilt for the mistreatment of African American men, many of whom, unable to find decent paying work, could not provide as they wished for their families. It would be equally wrong, however, to ignore women's achievement in surviving such situations. Tucker writes, "Black urban domestics who knew of the value of their work to their families, as well as these perceptions the whites had of them, expressed a strong sense of pride in themselves. The sense of pride allowed them a different, but nonetheless related, self-image centered around strength. This self-image was projected both to whites and to blacks."[41]

In 1994, Elaine Moon published a collection of oral histories entitled *Untold Tales, Unsung Heroes: An Oral History of Detroit's African American Community, 1918–1967*. Many of the women and men interviewed for Moon's study took part in the First Great Migration, between 1914 and 1930. Ernestine E. Wright is one of the few domestic workers whose story is part of the collection. Wright left Eudora, Kansas, for Detroit in 1929, just the time at which many African American women demanded to be allowed to live away from their jobs. Wright, a devoted member of Detroit's Second Baptist Church, recalled that as a live-in worker, she never had a chance to attend church, even if she had been promised Sundays off. She explained, "So I'd have to wait until they got up and had their breakfast, and wash up the dishes and make the beds, and tidy up the bathroom, and then I would get off [if there was time]."[42] Wright expressed little satisfaction in housework. For her, the church proved to be the central inspiration of her life. Wright said, "I love the Second Baptist Church because their vespers meant so much to me through the years when my husband was sick. I have known times when I didn't have my meal for the next day, but I didn't cry." Wright's church extended her a loan of eighty dollars and later refused to take repayment. Wright never forgot this kindness.[43]

Not all migrants took so little pleasure in their work. A number of the women in this study found the work highly satisfying, an assertion that should be acknowledged, and not dismissively critiqued by the contemporary paradigm that seemingly only allows Americans to value work also highly valued by the marketplace. Domestic workers understood the necessity of housework—the cleaning of dishes, the sweeping and mopping of floors, the preparation of food, and the care of children. These were not tasks that could be overlooked. While many families handled these chores without outside assistance, the chores had to be completed. Due to illness, job responsibilities, and other concerns, some employers could not completely care for themselves. Even the able-bodied and relatively unencumbered benefited by some assistance with household labor. Surely some domestics labored for employers who were truly lazy, and the class differential that often, but not always, stood between employer and employee complicates even a partially positive critique of this labor. Yet the work of caring for families and households was necessary and honorable, whether done by members of the household or by those assisting them with that work. If the basic tasks of the household were not achieved, nothing else could be accomplished. Those who worked outside the home relied on a smoothly functioning household. The domestic labors made possible every other occupation or pastime pursued by household members.

Most migrant women did not characterize domestic work as pleasant, and they did not describe the duties as ones they would have chosen freely. The marketplace greatly circumscribed the work opportunities open to black women during the twentieth century. Yet many still did not utterly disparage the work. Among the women interviewed who engaged in domestic work, three distinct patterns emerged. First, some of the domestic laborers, although cognizant of the underlying inequities that brought them into the field of domestic work, expressed a degree of satisfaction with the work. A second group, comprising the majority of domestic workers interviewed, characterized the work as undesirable, yet stressed their control over some aspects of the work. These women carefully negotiated their way through the job market, at times choosing domestic work as the best possible option. This group divulged that they would have vastly preferred finding other types of employment or having the ability to work solely in their own homes. Yet they also valued having some degree of choice about the work they took, or having the wherewithal to shape their lives in response to that work. Such choices included deciding what employers to consent to work for or what types of work to perform, determining the hours worked, ascertaining when to enter and exit the workforce, or even choosing the kind of tone to use in addressing an employer. The third group consisted of the women with the fewest options. They found themselves hampered by educational limitations, intense financial hardship, and societal prejudice, and thus their choices only concerned nonwork activities. Their choices consisted of such things as deciding to devote oneself to the local church, participating in other community activities, or taking solace in God through prayer.

When asked what words of wisdom she would like to pass on to younger women, Fannie Mae Kennedy offered her analysis of domestic work. Kennedy argued:

It's nothing wrong with being a day worker. You learn a lot about people and you are also helping when you are doing day work. Day work is nothing like it used to be. Did you see my knee? That's from day work. You used to have to crawl on your knees and scrub. Now I finally got it [the callused skin] off of this one, but I guess I was on this one more than the other because that will not come off. That is my skin. I don't feel bad about it. I did what I could because of my education. I was afraid to branch out and say, "I'll do this and I'll do that" when I knew that I didn't have the education. So I stuck with what I knew and I couldn't go through enough people telling about me, because I can clean a house, honey.[44]

Scholars often render quick judgments of domestic work, deeming it inherently degrading and far less preferable than factory work. Some of the twentieth and twenty-first century unease with domestic work stems from the racial difference commonly found between employers and employees. Clearly, white women tend to be the employers and women of color the employees. In the twentieth century, legions of African American women labored in the homes of white families; by the twenty-first century, Latino women filled many of the country's domestic positions, especially in the southwestern and western United States. The clamor for household help rose as more white, American-born women entered the paid workforce. Onlookers continue to question the morality of having the work of former stay-at-home mothers done by paid employees. The hackles of these critics rise further if the woman laboring in the home is nonwhite. Compellingly, few wonder about the morality of employing a young, white babysitter. A former household employee myself, I earned spending money in college and graduate school by doing dishes, changing diapers, chasing young children, and picking up errant toys in comfortable living rooms. Granted, as mentioned earlier in the text, employers typically assign fewer household cleaning responsibilities to white babysitters, while the domestic workers of the second half of the twentieth century found such duties to be their primary responsibilities. I myself was never explicitly asked to clean. I felt, however, that it was my duty to clean the entire kitchen if I fed the children dinner, or to straighten the play area while the children napped. I never vacuumed. Sociologist Pierrette Hondagneu-Sotelo comments on this disjuncture: "Racial inequality increases the likelihood that employers will require the same employee both to care for children and take full charge of housekeeping. While white American nannies are generally not expected to do housecleaning work, Latinas regularly are."[45] So were African American domestic workers. Yet it is primarily the poor treatment by employers that makes a position degrading and unpleasant; household work is not inherently lowly, but rather crucial, needed work.

The distaste Americans currently hold for housework is socially constructed and particular to the period. In colonial America, especially in frontier situations, much of the work done in homes was well regarded. Certainly colonial Americans understood that all of the work done in frontier settings was necessary for human survival. With industrialization, the nature of what was done in the home began to alter, along with popular perceptions of housework. Housewives began to purchase goods that had formerly been manufactured in the home, the women's roles transforming from that of producers to that of consumers. At this point, popular culture began to show signs of disregard for household work. The perception of the field continued to diminish to the point that in the late twentieth century, some did not even consider housework to be "work" at all. As Pierrette Hondagneu-Sotelo explains, much of the tension between current employers of domestic workers and the workers themselves stems from the employers' refusal to acknowledge, even to themselves, that their homes function as work sites. Hondagneu-Sotelo argues, "Parents hire nanny/housekeepers to do work involving intimate care, yet may fundamentally resist the idea that these services require monetary compensation." So housework has transformed itself from well-regarded work to a somewhat hidden, shameful exercise.[46] Oddly enough, this characterization increasingly began to manifest itself at the same time that the mania for organization and cleaning showed up in popular culture. Americans ought to be organized and clean, but only if the work is "fun," almost like a hobby. The hours of backbreaking labor involved in caring for a home and a family cannot be featured on a reality television show.

Many studies concentrate only on domestic workers in private homes. But the same women often alternated between service work in private settings and service work in semiprivate or public settings. In their overview of black women and work, Sharon Harley, Francille Rusan Wilson, and Shirley Wilson Logan note that after World War II "black domestics were much less likely than before the depression to live in, and more worked as janitors and charwomen in offices, factories, and schools."[47] Annie Evelyn Collins of Detroit detailed, "I came here [from Kentucky] in 1950 and basically I was a housekeeper and in 1952 I started working cleaning a dentist's office for a couple of years. After that, in 1965, I went to Sears. I was there twenty years in the maintenance department."[48]

In both domestic work in private homes and domestic positions in other settings, workers encountered few opportunities for advancement. In factory work, workers commonly could avail themselves of a promotion system. In household work, a worker could not negotiate an entirely new position. The workers held only dim hope of a pay raise. No workers on cleaning crews in trains, office buildings, and hotels knew anyone who had climbed the corporate ranks from the humble origins of the bottom rung. Ella Sims of Grand Rapids expanded on this theme, drawing here from her experience as a maid at the upscale Pantlind Hotel:

> On occasion, I don't mind it. Well, it was all right. I didn't know anything about any work, so I didn't have anything to compare it to. I'd never

been in a hotel in my life, really, it was nice, nice things, and I liked it. And I liked to work, and so, it was all right. But I knew, even then, that it wouldn't be anything; I wouldn't be there five years from now—like some of the people, you know, that work there, you know. And even then, I knew something else—that the nice jobs the white folks had. You see, that's the contrast, too, you know, you're not gonna be a supervisor, you know, you're not gonna be this, you're not gonna be that. So, I just knew then that it wasn't anything I cared to do.[49]

Domestic work ought not to be considered inherently lowly and degrading work. In all private homes, significant labor takes place. All public facilities also must be cleaned. Weighty questions come in regarding who performs that work, why they undertake the work, under what conditions they labor, and for what pay. Is it ethical to hire a person outside of a household to perform domestic work under any circumstances? How much does paying a decent wage ease the issues inherent in the transaction? Inez Smith, who grew up in Mississippi, wondered about the practice of hiring domestics. Smith's mother shunned paid domestic labor, greatly preferring the work involved with running her restaurant. As described in chapter two, Smith worked as a domestic growing up, helping out her aunts on their jobs. She believed domestic work required learned skills, and regarded the work in a better light than her mother. Smith recalled her mother's brief foray into domestic work after an extended illness:

When she began to feel a bit better she would go and clean, but she didn't like that. She was always against it. She would rather help my aunt run that café. We would make four times the money [at the café]. I don't know if they even gave her four dollars a day at that time, which was really ridiculous. Women would go and take care of white families and raise kids and at the end of the day, the pay was three dollars a day. It was just crazy. I think that is one thing that sometimes I think about [that] is the one thing that upsets me. I said, you know, I don't know how anybody could have somebody do that—run your whole household, look after your kids and you hand them three dollars at the end of the day. I always had a problem with that in the South, and I had an aunt who did do it all of her life, but you know, that was her business.[50]

Domestic work performed during the middle part of the twentieth century differs in part from that done during recent years. In the 1950s, 1960s, and 1970s, many white families could afford to live solely on the male family member's income. Many African American domestics were employed by a stay-at-home mom and her husband. In the twenty-first century, most American families require two incomes to live comfortably. In many cases, two incomes are necessary just to subsist. In many families, there is more housework to be done than the free hours available to the adult family members could allow for. Hiring help remains an option. Many of the domestic workers interviewed for this study preferred working for a two-worker family, but not all. In such a situation, no one hovered around while the woman worked. Yet some domestics preferred not working for employed mothers, as cleaning an empty house could prove lonely.

Some workers regarded the hiring of household help a luxury for stay-at-home mothers. These women could be very demanding employers of household help. As Mary Romero points out, full-time homemakers often based much of their self-image on the house, children, and outsiders' views of the family's home life.[51] Working mothers tended to be less worried about obtaining status through the home, and thus were more accepting of imperfect employees. Significant status issues, however, remained. And working mothers developed jealousies when strong ties formed between home child care workers and children.

Pierriette Hondagenu-Sotelo concluded, after studying Latina domestic workers at the end of the twentieth century, that despite the great inequities facing those laboring in housework and in-home child care, the job type did provide a sought-after starting point for immigrants. Many of the problems now present in the work may have remedies. Hondagenu-Sotelo posits, "Because domestic employment in the United States will continue (absent a major restructuring of our society) to be not only one of the best sources of employment for many Latina and Caribbean immigrant women but also a necessity for many of the families who employ them, I advocated the upgrading, not the abolition of the occupation."[52]

If employers and others recognized the number of skills necessary for household work, its status as an occupation could rise. Categorized as women's work, the labor of the household has long been considered something women were born knowing how to perform. Housewives and household workers know differently. Many women remember the training their mothers imparted in the kitchen—small girls stood on a box while their mothers made soup or taught the lessons of a proper pie crust. Mothers insisted their daughters iron baskets of laundry again if not done properly. As women's work, too, the labor has never been properly recognized for its role in undergirding the rest of the economy, nor has it been assigned a fair wage.

As the work week of midgrade and executive employees lengthens, the time they can devote to housework dwindles. Salaried employees find themselves working seventy hours a week and longer; hourly employees encounter mandatory overtime, and some find it necessary to hold multiple jobs. In many families, elderly relatives have shouldered day-to-day housework and child care responsibilities. Yet in other cases, elderly relatives have put off retirement due to insufficient retirement funds and cannot be called upon for household work. The nuclearization of our households and the migratory nature of the workforce have removed many families from the geographical proximity of their relatives. The continued assignment of the bulk of housework to women family members proves problematic, and seems incongruous with the gains women have made in the workforce. Employers still assume men have household support at home, and often give little regard to men's requests for flextime or alternative hours. Traditionally, work sites employing high numbers of women have offered greater flexibility, but, in many cases, the options still fail to allow women to attend to all household needs. Adult men assume more household duties than their male predecessors, but women still complete more hours of housework than their male partners. Many American families seek to pay for assistance with household work. Some consider the immorality of hiring others to complete household work lessened when employees share the racial heritage of the hiring households. This attitude could promote racist hiring practices. And even when the worker and employer share the same racial background, employers often fail to grant employees the proper respect. Louise Rafkin's memoir, *Other People's Dirt*, and Emma McLaughlin and Nicola Kraus's autobiographical novel, *The Nanny Diaries*, expose the struggles of these well-educated, white household workers. For instance, Louise Rafkin's employer berated her for leaving two Cheerios in the sink of her summer home.[53]

Hiring outside of one's race or working for employers of another race offers an opportunity for firsthand reflection on the racial inequities of American society. A greater percentage of white families than minority families earn the extra income necessary to pay for domestic workers. A greater percentage of minority workers are reduced to seeking jobs that offer only a low remittance. Employers of household workers fail to even follow legal guidelines governing the work, including those laws governing minimum wages, overtime, social security payments, and workman's compensation. If a host of problems were addressed, however, the work could begin to rise in status and slowly evolve into a more tolerable labor option.

White domestic worker Louise Rafkin claims, "I myself like cleaning, though other people can't understand it, and it is often hard to explain why I like an activity other people find unbearable."⁵⁴ It *is* hard for most people to understand. Nothing in Rafkin's cheeky but honest memoir points to anything but truthfulness in her claim. However, not a single African American domestic worker interviewed for this book described her work in such a positive way. Rafkin has the benefits of her identity as a white woman and a college graduate to bolster her unusual attitudes. But the oral histories studied here reveal a more favorable characterization of the work than often was made publically heretofore. Women testified to their considerable skills at housework, and expressed pride in these talents. The household laborers developed warm relationships with some employers, and felt empowered—at least eventually—to quit working for employers who acted in unacceptable ways. Domestic workers did not claim to "like" the work, but neither did they characterize it as unimportant. While the pay was small, it helped to sustain the worker's own family and, when deposited faithfully in the bank for years on end, succeeded in paying the mortgage.

Young couple sitting on the steps of home, holding a baby, 1952. Library of Congress, Prints and Photographs Division.

CHAPTER SIX

Family Aspects

I appreciate the people that helped me because, you know, you can't do it all by yourself.
—BESSIE LEE STAFFORD, WACO, TEXAS[1]

It's the women who keep everything together. They take care of everybody and I've learned so much from them. They are just great warriors.
—ZENARA COVINGTON, DAUGHTER OF MIGRANT RUTH MARGARET COVINGTON, DETROIT, MICHIGAN

Caring for Children and Other Family

ADDIE SMITH
Worcester, Massachusetts

Addie Smith and I were introduced through a mutual acquaintance, Shirley Wright, then executive director of the Office of Human Rights for the city of Worcester, Massachusetts. We met in Wright's office in Worcester's city hall, an impressive edifice built in an Italianate style. Despite the official surroundings, Smith seemed at ease and launched into her story. She proved to be an apt storyteller, crafting a nuanced vision of her past.

Addie Smith's life story illustrates the kinds of limited agency wielded by the respondents in shaping their migration. Although there are misogynistic and racialized power structures at play in Smith's story that must be fully acknowledged, her words also urge a recognition of her ability to negotiate a life that met her needs. Smith made the hard choices necessary for financial survival. Her history forces a philosophical debate: to what extent are "choices" made under the great inequities of American society really choices at all? If the word "choice" is defined as deciding between limited options rather than picking from an endless array of options, then the word serves as a better descriptor. Too often "free will" has been interpreted as "unlimited choice," yet even kings or despots have various types of boundaries that impinge on their actions. To lose the ability to employ the word "choice" at all leaves scholars stranded in the second stage of women's studies, the stage where victimization of women is acknowledged and addressed. The third stage, the stage academics struggle to operate in today, seeks to transcend victimhood and to examine women's lives through the prisms of their own experience. When scholars employ gender as a category of analysis, their scholarship can yield unexpected results. These unexpected findings can radically alter operating paradigms, transforming contemporary understanding of American history.

Contemporary examinations of the twenty-first century work lives of white middle- and upper-class women take place within both academic scholarship and more mainstream publications. Both types of works tend to reject the use of the word "choice" in their analyses. The women studied do not head into the workforce simply on a whim, the commentators point out, but for a host of financial and personal issues that make working outside the home a necessity. (Whether or not these women consciously structure their concept of work around the idea of necessity is the subject of debate, however.) The current tenor of the discussion on contemporary working women ought not to lessen our ability to address the working women of the 1940–1970 period. Conceiving of African American migrant women as actors in their own lives—as they themselves vociferously attest that they were—rather than passive victims of societal restrictions proves essential in the reconsideration of this particular labor history. Documenting the women's choices, although they are, of course, choices made under staggering limitations, assigns recognition to the women's own readings of their lives. When relating their life histories, Addie Smith and her contemporaries fashion dark dramas with hopeful endings, rather than unremitting melodramas or tragedies.

Smith's most gut-wrenching choice involved her decision to provide for her children by leaving them in North Carolina when she came to Massachusetts. Relying on family for child care was a learned survival mechanism. Smith's mother had also placed her children in the care of their grandmother. Smith's mother did not migrate to another region, however, and only lived in a neighboring town. Like many migrant women of the time, Addie Smith believed that putting her children in the care of her mother, in the known, albeit severely flawed, society of the South, was in the children's best interest. Where could the children safely have played in the concrete jungles of the urban North? How could her small paycheck have stretched to cover food, clothing, and shelter for her family in the expensive setting of the city? These questions, however, were moot; Smith worked as a live-in domestic and companion—she had no option of having her children live with her.

The millions of mothers currently traveling the globe in search of adequate pay share Smith's dilemma. In order to support their families financially, millions of women leave their children behind, and often do not see them again for years. Rhacel Salazar Parreñas exposes the circumstances facing Filipina women who emigrate in search of higher-paying positions. In recent decades, the Phillippines has become increasingly dependent on the remittances sent to families from workers abroad. Studies place the number of Filipinos directly reliant on such payments as high as 34 to 54 percent of the total population. Parreñas writes, "Indeed, the transnational family has become a norm in the Philippines, where according to representatives of local non-governmental organizations in Manila, there are approximately 9 million Filipino children under the age of eighteen who are growing up without the physical presence of at least one migrant parent in the country."[2]

Smith's narrative illuminates the plight of all women workers. On a global level, we have yet to solve the issue of child care for working women. In this study, the history of working women from the twentieth century allows for insight regarding the plight of women and children in contemporary situations. Additionally, it proves compelling to consider the situation of twenty-first century elite white women, ostensibly the women with the most options, and those furthest away from Smith's reality. Twenty-first century middle-class and upper-middle-class white women face significant daily issues juggling work and family. The weightiest issue still proves to be child care. High levels of education and a lack of racial discrimination do not dissolve all of the pressure on working mothers. And, ironically, while we are reticent to utilize the word "choice" when discussing the lives of African American women workers in the mid-twentieth century, the popular paradigm regarding white elite women workers of recent decades overstresses the concept of choice. Modern working women themselves have gotten so accustomed to talking of their life "choices" that it is difficult for them see beyond such rhetoric. For these women, as well as for those who critique them, less emphasis on personal choice and a clear realization of the American societal pressures on working women, and families generally, would be an important corrective. Clearly, these women have far more freedom to act than the African American women workers of the twentieth century. Yet they are much more constrained by the lingering sexism of the workplace than is usually admitted. These women, raised and educated to be workers, find the complications of life multiplied if they bear children. According to social commentator and New York Times columnist Judith Warner, "Like the women of the pre-feminist 1960s, most women today almost never stop to think that perhaps the choices they've been offered aren't really choices to begin with." Of high importance here are Warner's words "they've been offered."[3] If women are waiting to be offered an array of choices, presumably by a society controlled by financially secure white males, the freedom of all women appears even more circumscribed.

We ought to afford dignity to the lives of all women, listening to the ways in which women fashioned their life courses the best they could. At the same time as we honor the personal successes in women's lives, historians and policy makers must come to understand how all women's lives—across class and across race— have been deeply impacted by cultural misogyny. In her oral memoir, Addie Smith, age seventy-nine at the time of the interview, explains how she came to move from North Carolina to Worcester, Massachusetts. She decided financial stability was very important to her family and worth significant change. Smith presents her story as that of a successful, yet difficult, life. Through hard choices, Smith financially cared for the needs of her five children and her mother, all on her own.

I was born in Claremont, North Carolina, on August 15, 1924. I was the second child; my sister is four years older than I am. My mother was a homemaker. My father was a brickmaker. My father died when I was about three years old. I do remember him, but I was just three when he died.

My mother took my sister and I to my grandmother's. My grandmother had fifteen kids, so we stayed there, and my mother went to another town and got a job working in the home for some wealthy white people. And we stayed with my grandmother and she took care of things. Mother'd come home on the weekend and visit with us, and then she'd go back on Sunday evening, and we all week went to school, worked in the garden, and picked cotton, and just whatever happened on the farm. We were just there to do it.

I was about twelve years old when I left my grandmother's and I went to where my mother was working in that town that she was living, which was Hickory, North Carolina. My mother married this man and I didn't like him. And when my mother was away, he would, you know, try to, you know, mess over with me. And I told my mother and my mother got after him. So he left her and went back to live with his family. And so, my mother said, "Okay, you got to pull together here."

I went to Brookford Mill, that's the shop where they make socks and things, and we run these looms and things, until I got, I don't know, something in the building there. I must've got pneumonia, and I got highly congested, so I came out. So I came out of there and went to work for Richard Baker Hospital, and I trained in Central Supply as a technician. And I worked there for fourteen years, at the same job. You're setting up the instruments and the trays that they do surgery with. And you'd have to know how to set up, say, major basic sets, cut-down sets—whatever set they used in surgery, you'd have to know how to set that up.

I really liked the work [as a hospital technician]. And then this man from Worcester had a business, batting for furniture. He also had a business there in Hickory [North Carolina], and he had an apartment there, and he needed somebody [to clean], too. I worked at the hospital, and Saturday I'd clean his apartment. I guess I had two weeks vacation [from the hospital], and he said to me that Saturday, "Addie, what are you doing this weekend?" I said, "Why?" You know, just like that—this is a man from up north asking me what I'm doing; I'm cleaning his house. He said, "My wife is sick; she has multiple sclerosis. She's in a wheelchair." I said, "And?" He said, "Well, my housekeeper got sick and she had to go into the hospital." And he said, "Can you go for the weekend?" I said, "Go? Where?" He said, "To Massachusetts." I said, "Go to Massachusetts? What are you talking about?" He said, "You're on vacation, aren't you?" I said, "Yeah." He said, "Can you go up there for the two weeks that you have off and help my wife out until my housekeeper gets better, then you can go back to work." I said, "Mr. Solly, I gotta talk to my mother," and I said, "I got five kids and a mother, and I'm working and I'm supporting. My mother takes care of my kids while I work every day." He said, "Whatever you got to do, do it, and tell me how much it costs."

I knew him because I'd worked for him and he'd been down in North Carolina, so I didn't mind helping out for two weeks. But when she [the housekeeper] passed, he called me from North Carolina and he said, "I want you to stay." I said, "Man, I got family!" He says, "I'll be home tonight." He caught a flight, came home. "Pick me up at Logan Airport." So I had to pick him up at Logan Airport. He came home and he told me what he would give me to stay there. "Now, I'm gonna be home," he says, "for two weeks. You go home." I had my plane ticket, everything. "You go home, and you get your business straightened out." I said, "Man, I got bills and things, what do you think?" This is a Jewish man, he's loaded. "Get everything straightened out, put it on paper, and bring it to me."

So I got things together and talked to my mother. "Well, if that's what you want to do," she said. "You know, but these kids are here." And of course, my kids were all upset—they didn't want me to go. The youngest was eight. Mother was at the age where she could stay out of work. And she took care of things very good, and whenever I got back to Worcester, I gave him [the bills]. He says, "I take care of this." My mother sent me all the receipts and everything—he took care of everything.

I went up for two weeks in 1960 in July, and I'm still here. The housekeeper died, and Mrs. Solly liked me and he did too, and I took care of things.
I had to see that she had food, and a bath, and got dressed, and all that. I
mean, it was not a hard job; it was just being there. And I'm just there every
day, you know, with her.[4]

Addie Smith's life merits the acknowledgment of her agency. Faced with limitations, she took advantage of her best financial option for herself and her family. Smith stressed that her boss, whom she nicknamed Mr. Solly, offered her a
financial security her other job could not provide. The boss's complete assumption of the payment of her family's bills encouraged Smith to migrate north,
even if it meant living apart from her family. Interestingly, Smith's acceptance of
a negative stereotype—that Jews are well off—led her to trust in her employer's
financial abilities. She left her job as a hospital technician, considered higher
status than domestic work, although she did resume hospital work in later years.
Smith's labor for the Worcester, Massachusetts, family would be subsumed under a medical heading today, perhaps "in-home care," but at the time caring for
invalids often fell into the category of domestic work. Smith performed other
domestic duties in addition to personal care.

In 1960, Smith left five children in the care of her mother and accepted a
permanent job in Massachusetts. She chose not to present the situation with
a lament; she did what she felt was best for her family. Her children were well
cared for by a trusted caretaker. Smith never mentioned co-parenting with her
children's father, who served in the military. The financial responsibilities for
the children rested on her alone. Smith remarried four years after arriving in
Worcester; she and her second husband had met at church. The couple spent
fourteen years together—Smith's second husband died in 1978 from medical
complications due to leukemia and pancreatic cancer. As discussed in the introduction to this book, author Mary Catherine Bateson poses a provocative question in her study *Composing a Life*. After studying a number of women, all of
them leaders in their fields yet survivors of daunting challenges, she asks, "At
what point does desperate improvisation become significant achievement?"[5]
Smith's ability to negotiate the difficult terrain of the work world in order to
benefit her family qualifies as a significant achievement. While women like
Smith structured their life choices within severe restrictions, they were still
consciously composing a life.

Creamy McKinney of Worcester employed positive language to describe
the period in which she and her children had to separate and live in different
regions of the country. McKinney gave birth to her first child while staying with

her sister in New York City, and later married the child's father, her first husband. The couple had four children together. McKinney obtained a live-in position with a Jewish family in upstate New York. There she performed housework and cared for the family's two children. During this time, McKinney's mother cared for the children in Alabama. When McKinney retrieved the children, her mother despaired. The grandmother had enjoyed the constant contact with the children. McKinney felt that bringing her children to the Alabama countryside was not overly difficult for her or the children; the country setting offered a healthy place for them to grow up. McKinney argued, "It was such a nice place in the country, and my kids loved it. They loved it. And, so, they still love it out there; they love the country."[6]

Mary Smith of Boston, who made reference to two marriages, assumed sole economic responsibility for her family. Smith had three children, one with the first husband and two with the second. Her mother raised the children in Georgia for many years, while Smith resided in Boston. Smith's first child was born in 1959, and she moved to Boston in 1962. Smith, like McKinney, presented this aspect of her life in straightforward terms. Smith says only, "When I came here, I left them with my mother." One year, she allowed the children to visit during the summer months; another year, they traveled to Boston for Christmas. Smith found the visits disruptive to her carefully guarded routine. After the children visited Boston, it took her months to put her house and her life back together again. Smith clearly considered working and separating from the children physically preferable to the alternative of applying for government assistance. She also provided a model of hard work for her children. Smith stated, "But, you know, I could have went, got here [Boston] and got me a job . . . and a place, and went back and got them, and come back and got on welfare like a lot of people did, but that wasn't for me because I wanted them to know it's no free ride." Smith spoke with pride about purchasing her first car in 1967 and buying her home in 1968. Although she acknowledged her achievements, Smith also presented her financial independence as typical for the era. Single mothers have to provide for their children. "It's more women in the workplace than mens now," she explained. "As you know, it's no dad to bring home the bacon." After the death of her father in 1976, Smith moved her mother and her children to Boston. She expressed no regrets about her choices. Instead, she said, "You know, it was nice. If I had to do it over again, I would do the same."[7]

Some of the migrant women had a view of the level of bonding necessary between parent and child that differed from what is now in vogue. Few expressed an extreme level of angst about whether or not they had spent enough quality time (a more modern concept to begin with) with their children; if finances faltered, locating paying jobs proved the foremost worry. The relative quiet on this topic can be attributed in part to the respondents' more advanced age. The women's children had reached adulthood, and the migrants had already successfully shepherded their families through the highly demanding early years. Except for the women who ran in-home day care centers, the care of crying babies, wiggly toddlers, and constantly inquisitive school-age children did not figure centrally in the migrants' current list of everyday worries.

The care of their children ranked foremost in the women's concerns during their early adult lives. The women spent as much time with their children as possible. While work proved necessary, the women missed their children. Women structured their jobs so as to allow for the best possible parenting. Domestic work and cosmetology beckoned due to their flexible hours, although remuneration was low. Alverrine Parker, following the advice of her physician, drove a school bus. Parker had the summers off, and of course did not work late hours. For one year, her young son rode along for her afternoon route, safely ensconced in a special seat. Parker remembered, "He was four years old when I took him with me, so that way he haven't had to have a babysitter. So then I got him into Head Start I think—they didn't want us to go into there, either, because my husband was working, I was working." In time, Parker related, her son "knew my route better than I did. Yeah, he did." When he went to Head Start, the separation from her son proved painful for Parker. "Oh, I cried when I went back to work," Parker admitted. "I know it's difficult." Parker dreamed of an America where all work sites offered on-site day care, so that parents could easily visit their children.[8]

Like many women, Gussie Nash of Grand Rapids only returned to work when her children were all old enough to attend school.[9] Beatrice Jackson, who ultimately worked as a beautician, secured a position near home, so she could be close to her children. Bernita Howard had to hire a babysitter for her young son while she went to waitress at the veterans' hospital in Detroit. Howard noted, "I would have to get somebody to take care of him. That's one of the things I hate because I couldn't spend so much time with him." And Howard, like almost all women, worried about the quality of care her son received. She noted the difficulty of child care work, and felt lucky that she was able to employ the relative of a close friend on many occasions. Yet not all of the babysitters were as trusted. Howard explained, "Some people weren't good and would let him do what you didn't want." All of the migrants spoke of hiring African American child care workers; the migrants often worked for whites, but they were not in a position to hire whites as workers in their own homes. Child care workers often moved on to other positions. Howard went on, "Sometimes, when I would get somebody good, they didn't stay long."[10] If a migrant lived with her husband, and the husband had secured a sufficient salary, the wife often left the work force. The women's abandonment of paid work often came at their husbands' urging, as a stay-at-home wife allowed for a certain societal cachet. (The husbands' attitudes will be explored at length further on in this chapter.)

Family members constituted the most trusted child care providers, according to working mothers. Mattie Bell Fritz's cousin-in-law, Frankie, who had no children of her own, always cared for Fritz's children during the years she worked on the cleaning crew for the UAW offices. Lillian Gill of Grand Rapids, born on a farm near Tupelo, Mississippi, sent for her father and stepmother after the untimely death of her young husband. She returned to work, while her parents watched over the children.[11] Willie Jean Clark Lewis found her job in human resources at Ford possible only with the live-in assistance of her mother-in-law. Even with the help, the family needed to be highly organized to function successfully. Every family member took on a share of the work. Lewis explained, "We had our jobs around the house and my children had their jobs around the house." Her mother-in-law "monitored the home and chores. I did laundry and things like that."[12]

Ogretta McNeil, who earned a Ph.D. in psychology at Clark University and secured a faculty position at Holy Cross College, utilized the services of day care provider Essie Smith, who operated the Happy Day Child Care center in McNeil's new home town, Worcester, Massachusetts. Smith even accepted McNeil's children before they were toilet trained, usually against the rules. Smith also picked up McNeil's children in the morning, and brought them home at night. McNeil admitted, "You can't do it [work full-time] and not be completely crazy unless you have that." She attributed her children's independence to this early schooling experience. McNeil spoke eloquently about the benefits of a strong community. "I think it's about having that community around you, guiding and supporting you and caring about you," she said. And McNeil, like many migrants, also saw the pieces of her life coming together—education, friends, employment—as a sign of God's intervention in her life. McNeil asserted, "You can't say all of this is just by chance. Somebody else planned all this because it just couldn't happen by accident."[13] Dotty Goldsberry, a psychiatrist who earned her medical degree at Howard University, settled in Worcester, Massachusetts, with her husband, also a physician. Goldsberry, a migrant from Oklahoma, benefited from her husband's family's multigenerational residence in Worcester. Goldsberry, like McNeil, placed her children with Essie Smith. Goldsberry relied on the additional help of a host of babysitters, as well as the help of her mother-in-law.[14]

In the challenging circumstances of the regional migration, families contracted and expanded to meet personal needs. If children needed adult guidance, they could be informally (or legally) adopted by other family members, stepparents, or friends. The kinship networks created by necessity both complicated and simplified the women's lives. The women often provided care for more children than they had given birth to—a factor that no doubt added stress to their lives, although in many cases bringing joy as well. The women also took comfort in the fact that their own children and extended family benefited from this community of care. Such support proved necessary in a nation where employers of African Americans typically paid rock- bottom wages. And even the few legal safety nets available, such as the Fair Labor Standards Act of 1938, contained loopholes exempting categories of labor in which high numbers of blacks found employment. The personal stories also reveal a high degree of sickness and untimely deaths within these families. Family members often could not afford necessary health care. Usual illness rates in the African American communities were expanded due to exposure to high levels of toxic chemicals in dangerous occupations and environmentally unsound neighborhoods.

Zenara Covington, daughter of migrant Ruth Margaret Covington of Alabama, added her insights about the commitment to caring for extended family. Covington spoke vehemently about the strength and courage of African American women. She proclaimed, "We really have a lot of extended family within African American culture—that's part of it. Mom's two rules—there's always food and there's always love regardless of the bloodline and that alone tells you then in order for that to happen there's got to be a strong base. Somebody is taking care of business by being there and who will listen and who will take time in spite of whatever else they are trying to maintain."[15]

Liddie Williams of Chicago expanded her family to include her stepson, saying warmly, "He just like mine."[16] Ella Sims brought an adopted daughter into her large family—this child would be her only girl.[17] Glennette Taylor of Grand Rapids revealed the elaborate planning inherent in juggling paid labor and the care of her own children and that of a cousin. Taylor said, "I did that [patient care at a hospital] while I was attending the school of cosmetology, but after that, I needed to leave because I had taken on other kids in the family and we couldn't afford sitters and I had to get hours opposite of his [her husband's job at an auto plating firm] so someone would be there all the time." Even with this child care plan, Taylor remembered times when her cosmetology work extended past the usual hours and the children had to be left unattended.[18]

The women also cared for their grandchildren. Daughters entered the work force and needed assistance with their children. Some grown children also struggled with health issues and could not care for their own children alone. Avezinner Dean said, "My daughter got very ill and I moved the beauty shop in the basement to raise her children. She married and worked. I kept my grands." But Dean's caretaking extended even further. Although seventy-four at the time of the interview, Dean cooked and provided hair care to other senior citizens in her church, Southwest Baptist Church of Detroit. Dean said of these volunteer efforts, "I help all of the old people in the neighborhood and cook for the holidays. There are about four in the block back this way. When they got retired a lot of them is ill. Now about six or eight of them. Bring them downstairs [to her basement beauty shop] and mostly I cook."[19]

Anniese Moten assisted in the parenting of her stepchildren and the children of her cousin. Moten found benefits in these investments in care, because as she aged the young cousins she helped raise began providing emotional support for her. Moten admitted, "I don't know what I would do if it wasn't for them." For Moten, caretaking drew on religious motivation. Her difficult life passage was feasible only with the constant solace of church, prayer, and tightly held faith. In addition to her role as a substitute parent, Moten opened her house to others in financial need. She took in family members and friends, finding them shelter wherever she could in her two-bedroom home. At times, friends slept in her dining room. "I have taken care of a lot of peoples and then charged them nothing. We just all bunked in here," she said. "Let this house be God's house, and just called 'the house by the road,'" she preached, giving her home the title it was known by to others. With considerable emphasis, Moten continued, "'The house by the road,' if you want to stay somewhere, go there to [she gives her address], 'the house by the road' and she will take you in."[20]

Women migrants, like many other women, also devoted significant labor to caring for their aging spouses and other ill family members. Rosa Young of Grand Rapids spoke with a quiet sadness about the years spent nursing her husband, who suffered from Alzheimer's disease. For three years, she served as his primary caregiver; his condition demanded round-the-clock surveillance. Young lamented, "Three years, and I had to sometimes change him like a baby." Ultimately, as her husband was big and difficult to control physically, Young placed him in a nursing home. Her fifty-two-year marriage ended when, after suffering a cracked hip and an operation, her husband quit eating. The death of Young's daughter compounded the sorrow. Young described these painful losses by saying, "You don't get over it; you just get through it."[21] Lilly Shelby, eighty-two at the time of her interview, cared for her ailing husband and her son, who both suffered from strokes, and she also assumed the care for her grandchildren while her daughters worked.[22]

At the time of the interview, many of the migrants were themselves suffering from age-related diseases. Fannie Mae Kennedy revealed that illness had slowed her down, saying, "I had a stroke. I don't do nothing but wipe up in the middle of the floor at my house." Mary White had had a stroke during her usual walk between her Detroit home and the nearby Southwest Baptist Church. Mattie Bell Fritz faced a host of medical concerns, including the ravages of two kinds of arthritis. Fritz admitted, "I have to take Ensure, the iron pills, all kinds of pills. Living off of the pills." Fritz could no longer drive. She bemoaned her lack of freedom. She sighed, "I like to go to the store and just look around, but they don't let me do that . . . I missed all of the Christmas sales."[23] As Kennedy's and Fritz's words disclose, the migrant women found it difficult to slow their lives down to accommodate the physical limitations of aging.

Attitudes of Husbands Regarding Wives' Paid Labor

ELLA SIMS

Grand Rapids, Michigan

Ella Sims did not work during the years of her first marriage, which began at age seventeen. Following the sudden death of her first husband, her subsequent move to Michigan, and a second marriage, Sims left the work force again for many years. For the most part, Sims remained out of the work force between the ages of twenty-six and forty-five, devoting herself to raising her children. Occasionally she cleaned houses alongside female family members, just to have a little spending money of her own. Yet for her husband, Clive Sims, Ella's full-time presence in the home carried much importance. Clive Sims's community standing and his self-image related to his ability to financially support his family.

And then, after I started working at the C&O [Railroad]—because, you see, I wasn't at the C&O over four or five months before I met my husband. And I think the last thing I would've been thinking about was marrying again—you see what I mean? But then, after we were going together for a year, we got married. And so, because in all, I worked for about four years for the C&O. I remember there I had Clive, Jr., and then I was pregnant with Tommy. Now, they are just eighteen months apart. And I remember he was begging me not to go back to work. Now, he was from those who thought that a wife should stay home. I can remember like yesterday, the thing he said that made me agree to stay home. He said, "Oh, I know how come you won't quit." And I said, "Why?" He said, "You don't think I can take care of you. I know that's the truth!" I said, "It's not that—but I just know, you know, we could do better, we could pay for this, we could both afford a house." That's how come I went back to work. See, when I had the first baby [Clive, Jr.], I wasn't going back to work, but we wanted to buy a house.

His mother just worked in all private families, and he would only let me go back to work if his mother stayed home and kept Clive, Jr. And so I went back to work for us to put together enough for a house. And so by then, I was already pregnant with Tommy. And, I mean, I was still working when I was six or seven months pregnant with him.

I must've worked up until six weeks before he was born. But then there was the issue of going back. And so, that's when we cussed and had this argument. So I never went back after Tommy. So, after that, after Tommy was born, I never went to work again until I was forty-five, and my last child was five. Yeah, so all that time I stayed home, I was a stay-at-home mom.[24]

With the advent of American industrialization in the late 1700s and early 1800s, and the growing perception of a separation of the workplace and the home, full-time motherhood gained a widespread symbolic value, and served as an important indicator of family financial solvency. Despite the pressures of this ideology, a significant percentage of working-class Caucasian families could not manage on the earnings of one adult worker. In the years after the repeal of slavery, many African American families attempted to live up to this ideal of motherhood, envisioning it as a key statement about their freedom as a people. Yet many could not attain this goal. Stay-at-home mothers proved to have continued symbolic value on into the twentieth century, with each subsequent period ascribing its own particular, yet no less culturally resonant, meanings to the role. As white families fled the urban core for the beckoning new suburban developments after World War II, full-time mothers served as linchpins for the ideal of the thriving American white family. Black families, although not able to follow the movement out of the inner city, could at least attempt to don the mantle of respectability acquired through this cult of motherhood. The concept resonated more with black men than black women, many of whom appreciated the power inherent in having one's own money. Many women migrants spoke about their resistance to their husband's efforts to keep them at home. Ella Sims loved and respected her husband, but they fought bitterly when he requested that she leave the workforce. He felt that her presence on the railroad cleaning crew publically mocked his money-making abilities. She had three children at home (one was from her first marriage), and he felt her place was with them. Sims did not submit readily to her husband's demands, yet she did ultimately decide to stay out of the workforce.

For the women establishing families in heavily industrialized cities during the 1940s and 1950s, stay-at-home mothering became a more realistic goal due to the relative stability of their husbands' work. Industrial positions, typically in the maintenance, foundry, painting, and other highly dangerous work sectors, supplied African American men with more stable incomes than their fathers, who had often worked hardscrabble farms to make ends meet. According to Ruth Margaret Covington, whose own husband found a position with DeSoto in Detroit, "most men always do okay [financially]."[25] Michigan resident Alberta Hardy related that while she worked as a hotel maid as a young woman, she was able to leave the workforce in later years. Hardy's husband worked for Great Lakes Steel for thirty-five years. Hardy had no children, yet her role at home was no less prized.[26] Migrants who settled in the Midwest spoke of their husbands' commitment to full-time mothering far more often than migrants to New England. The interviews conducted in Texas for the Baylor University Institute for Oral History, although conducted with African American women of the same age range as those interviewed directly for this study, made only fleeting references to such cultural views on mothering. In the midwestern families, only the relatively high-paying positions of the husbands made living up to this ideal remotely feasible.

At the same time, families were severely disrupted, both financially and emotionally, by the high death rates of these male workers. In addition to the environmental challenges of many of the lines of work open to the men, health care options for African American men (not to mention for African American women and children) lagged far behind national standards. Many of the migrant women recalled losing spouses at an extremely early age. Ella Sims's first husband died just years into their marriage due to an infection which could have been easily cleared up with greater access to the latest medical treatment. Creamy McKinney lost her husband when he was just thirty-nine.[27] Annie Evelyn Collins's husband became ill when she entered her thirties. She obtained a job on the all-black maintenance crew at a Sears department store, thus providing for her family.[28] Florence Allison said forthrightly, "Well, one thing is, I learned how to manage a household because I lost my husband twenty-two years ago and I had to go on."[29]

Anniese Moten recalled her husband's disapproval of her work outside the home, despite the fact that she had no children of her own. Moten's phrasing suggests that her husband's subsequent abandonment carried the positive side effect of increased freedom. "He wanted me to stay home," Moten explained, "so I told [him], I said, 'Well, I love to work, I like to get out and work.' But after he see fit to leave me and stay with somebody else. I had to get out then and got me a job and go to work. But the Lord has been good, good, good to me down through the years. He has made a way, and I tell you, I just like Him for His goodness and His mercy."[30]

Simone Landry referred often to her mixed emotions over her husband's edict against paid work. While she characterized her husband's ability to provide for the family as "fortunate," the repetition of her positive attitudes towards paid work reveal tensions surrounding her husband's cultural views. At one point in the interview, Landry stated, "I worked if I felt like doing something, if not, fine. It would have been nice [to work], but he felt that I should have been home with the children. 'You stay here and take care of these children, and I take care of you'—that was the way he felt. I was fortunate, I think." Later on in the interview, Landry offered, "I would say that I was fortunate, because I didn't suffer as much as a lot who were not blessed to have someone they could count on for survival. I mean, like even when we lived in Chicago—he said, 'You don't have to go to work.' I didn't mind working and I would stay home."[31]

Even for women whose husbands clearly provided a stable income, the thought of outside work constantly came up. Lillian Clark considered full-time motherhood a fulfilling job, and did not wish to enter the marketplace as a paid laborer. Clark's husband worked at Uniroyal Tire and as a minister serving a congregation in Ontario, Canada. Yet female friends brought up the possibility of employment to her. Clark noted, "A lot of people have said to me and still said today that I needed to work, now why I don't know, but I found it [housewifery] to be a fulfilling thing." Clark put serious effort into her role as the minister's wife, attending church every Sunday and serving on the Sunday school committee and other church-related activities. She maintained that her role as full-time wife and mother allowed for her husband's success in the workforce. Clark detailed:

I didn't ever work. He didn't know how to cook, how to wash, how to do the ironing, nothing and whatever. He didn't want me to work. When he was getting ready to go to work in the morning, he had to have his breakfast, but he was going to work, but he didn't want me to go out to work.

He had to be at the plant at seven o'clock in the morning. He had to start work at seven. So I had to get his biscuits going.

It wasn't too bad. You know, if you like what you are doing, it's not hard. And I liked what I was doing. I stayed home all day with the children and would have his dinner ready. Then after dinner he would relax for a bit.[32]

Employers also considered males the unequivocal heads of their households. Sandra Gantt of Detroit, whose mother was a domestic, recalled that gains in civil rights encouraged the management of Chrysler Financial Corporation to consider her for a promotion. Although the job offer was buoyed by affirmative action, the company placed a sexist contingency on Gantt's acceptance. Gantt stated, "As a result of this [the national civil rights movement], I was asked to be in management. I never forgot when they offered me the job, they told me [to] go home that night and ask my husband if it's all right."[33]

Many husbands strongly disapproved of their wives working in private homes. Not only did women in domestic service appear to publicly demonstrate their husbands' limited earning power, but they often faced real danger in the homes of whites. Lessons regarding the dangers of working in private homes had been learned in slavery. House slaves faced threats from lustful white males and vengeful, jealous white women. House slaves were easily in reach for physical punishments and open to a wide variety of general mistreatment. Twentieth-century domestic work carried both a real threat and a type of stigma. Domestic workers labored in proximity to people outside of their community, and performed this work in secluded private spaces, where crimes against them could occur unseen. Very real worries regarding domestic work haunted black families in the North and the South. Eunice Brown Johnson of Texas recalled her husband's grave disapproval of domestic work. Ultimately, however, she accepted a job opportunity in the field. A white woman named Mrs. Brown asked her if she would come and cook for them. Johnson could not immediately consent. "So I told her I didn't know. I'd have to let her know later," Johnson admitted. She explained, "So my husband didn't want me to work." She only hinted at his reasoning, implying that it was far from acceptable to speak of such matters in the public record of an interview. Johnson's interviewer was white, and perhaps Johnson felt she would be speaking out of turn if she detailed her husband's fears of white employers. One can read between the lines, however. Most likely Mr. Johnson feared there would be affronts to her personal dignity, and perhaps even her physical safety, in a white man's home. Johnson wanted to accept the work, and she coaxed her husband to relent. She related, "So, but I went ahead and I just told him, I said, 'I can always quit.' But I worked for her, and we got along just fine. Mrs. Brown was a good, good person."[34]

Vivienne Malone-Mayes's mother did not permit her daughter to work in private homes. Malone-Mayes told her interviewer, historian Rebecca Sharpless, "All middle-class blacks and any blacks that could afford it kept their kids, as a rule, as far away from white people as they could to keep them from two things—from being hurt." Malone-Mayes recalled that when she was an adolescent, her friend's mother, a teacher, augmented her salary by laboring for a white family on the weekends. Malone-Mayes's friend accompanied her mother and earned a small wage, and Malone-Mayes grew jealous. Malone-Mayes's mother, also a teacher, scoffed at her daughter's desire. When a white woman asked Malone-Mayes to babysit—a request commonly made to young, black females, regardless of their financial status—Malone-Mayes's mother laid out her objections more explicitly. Malone-Mayes recounted, "And she began to explain that we could not ever go into any white people's home to work." She continued, "And so she began to tell us how that you never knew what day the woman might not be there, then the man could return home unexpectedly, and that you would be in a compromising position. And that was why you could not work in service. You could not work in a white home, and you forgot it." As she matured, her mother allowed Malone-Mayes to accept a job in a pharmacy; this work was more acceptable, due to its public nature.[35]

Relationships with Husbands

The migrants' relationships with men, including husbands, brothers, sons, and fathers, were tempered by the daily stresses faced by these men. While African American men had more success in securing paid work in the industrial sector than women, their jobs often proved dangerous or objectionable. African American men died at younger ages than African American women. All too often, alcohol, the pool room, or other unhealthy pastimes appeared to be the only outlet from grinding work. Ogretta McNeil, who herself had a notable career as a professor and community leader, spoke directly about the trouble her brother faced migrating to Washington, D.C., "with the changes that he had to go through coming from that environment to another. You know, the pool room was there and all kinds of lures for him, and you can't lock the kid in the house."[36]

Some migrants recalled the love affairs between themselves and their husbands. Creamy McKinney gushed about the care-taking abilities of her second husband. The two shared memorable trips around the United States and even traveled to Mexico. Many years older than herself, McKinney's husband resided in a nursing home at the time of the interview. McKinney visited him every day after she finished her work in her hair salon. She said of their marriage, "When we first got married [in the 1980s], I didn't have nothing to do. He did all the cooking and the cleaning and he did all the housework. I didn't have to do anything, but come to work. Then, he would come down here [to the salon], he would do the laundry, he would do floors and stuff for me, and [he] had food on the table when I got home."[37] Minnie Chatman expressed warm memories of her husband's care for her, especially his cooking. Chatman said enthusiastically, "I like for him to cook me ham and fried pineapple. He could make me a fixing and they would be so good."[38] Others expressed dissatisfaction with their mates. Avezinner Dean lamented, "I let the first one [husband] go and married him [her second husband]. This one had a different education. The other one was a fool and was overbearing."[39] Due to the high level of societal discrimination against black men, some fared poorly on both economic and emotional levels.

A few of the migrants, including Annie Benning, Alberta Hardy, Anniese Moten, Barbara Purifoy-Seldon, Lois Stevens, and Esther Woods, had no children. Moten and Woods had rocky marriages that may have precluded children. Annie Benning had had to raise her younger siblings. Stevens never married, and Purifoy-Seldon married later in life. Purifoy-Seldon remained the only narrator who prolonged marriage for career goals. She acquired graduate degrees in dental hygiene and education, and only married at age forty-five. She divulged, "In my acquisition of knowledge and skills, sometimes you put marriage on hold. I don't have any children either." Purifoy-Seldon served as associate professor of dental hygiene at the University of Detroit Mercy, and also had served as Assistant Dean for Special Projects at the university. An army veteran, she was the president of the Southfield, Michigan, Veterans' Organization and had been appointed by Governor John Engler to the Michigan Board of Dentistry. Purifoy-Seldon spoke poignantly about trying to merge marriage and this type of fast-paced career. Her statements recalled negative stereotypes about the views of black men towards educated women, but seem to genuinely reflect her own lived experience: "I think marriage is difficult, [it is difficult] to find somebody, especially when black women really want so much out of life. Black men think if I get out of high school and get in a factory I will be able to do just fine. So then the black women are going to college. There is a big gap there in knowledge and understanding. Education broadens you and lead[s] you right out. So sometimes guys are threatened by a lady's education."

Purifoy-Seldon met her future husband in graduate school. The marriage ceremony provided her with an opportunity to connect a moment in her individual history with African American history as a whole. The couple sanctified their commitment by jumping over a broom. The observation of this ritual solidified a connection with African American couples in the past. In slavery, marital unions were illegal, and jumping the broom sanctified a moment not recognized by law. Purifoy-Seldon related, "You probably hear a lot about jumping the broom. It's part of our history. We don't want to forget. A lot of people just wish we would forget about all of that stuff . . . You ask a Jewish person to forget the Holocaust? He is going to tell you you are crazy. They sure would like for us to forget, but I don't think we should."[40]

As explored in the section concerning attitudes towards paid work, black families often maintained quite traditional roles for men and women. For the migrants coming from rural areas, the norms had been established on the farm. Men often took charge of the crops and animals. Women typically reigned over the kitchen, and usually the vegetable garden, but only assisted with the farm's major crops during certain busy seasons. If they pursued paid labor, women took on jobs suitable for women, like domestic work, laundry, or the sale of eggs or baked goods. Family members rarely transgressed gender roles. Rubie Wilburn Evans remembered her father and grandfather cooking simple meals for the family in the kitchen, an uncommon household contribution for men with wives. However, the men never prepared the biscuits for the family; biscuits remained solely the domain of the women. Evans's parents reversed roles in other ways as well; her mother was a better cotton picker than her father. When the harvest time came, Evans's father busied himself with weighing the cotton rather than picking it. These variations in Evans's family system evoked her comments years later; she had no doubt forgotten many details of her early life, but not these uncommon characteristics.[41]

A significant number of the women migrants made only passing reference to their husbands during the interviews. A few failed to mention the marriage at all. These acts of omission mirrored those found in interviews conducted by other scholars. In my own oral history work, I try to privilege the narrator's storytelling. Normally, I would not interject if a woman failed to mention a marriage in her recounting. The migrants knew I wanted to know about their lives, their work, and the migration experience. The mothers who were interviewed always mentioned their children, but they sometimes remained quiet regarding boyfriends and husbands. In some cases, the absence of an explanation regarding a spouse helped to instill the narrative with a positive tone. A number of marriages ended badly, and the women did not want the stories of these relationships recorded for posterity.

Sociologist Bonnie Thornton Dill made a similar discovery in her interviews with domestics in the 1970s. In an interview with Dill, migrant Lena Hudson spoke for some time with no mention of her husband whatsoever. When she finally did speak of him, Hudson admitted to a tumultuous relationship. Hudson revealed that Wilber Hudson was "not a family man. Sometimes I knew where he was, and sometimes I didn't."[42] Hudson's unstable marriage was not entirely uncommon.

I knew that my friend Esther Woods had married earlier in life—and Woods was aware of my knowledge. On one occasion, in which we were meeting for a social gathering, she chatted with me openly about memories of her husband. Woods wryly commented on his lack of attention to the home. He left the cleaning solely to her, she complained, as husbands were wont to do. Yet in the "official" story of Woods's life, as presented in her recorded oral history, she made no mention of her husband at all. The omission reveals interesting aspects of the oral history process. If the interviewer refrains from leading the narrator, as I attempt to do, is the interviewer complicit in a sanitation of the past, or is the interviewer simply honoring the narrator's intention? Can the interviewer speak openly about the omission in his or her scholarly work, as I am doing here? Personally, I have decided that, during the interview process, my role centers on assisting the narrators in delivering the testimony they feel comfortable with. Yet, as a historian, I must speak openly and honestly about my insights into the created document.

In an incident during the 1960s, Woods's husband physically attacked her. Someone, perhaps Woods herself, phoned in a complaint to the Grand Rapids police. When the policeman arrived to subdue the violent outburst, Woods's husband killed him. After the conviction, Woods and her husband divorced. This dreadful piece of her life was excluded from Woods's life narrative. Why did she not relate this story? Perhaps she considered it too ghastly to include. Conceivably, Woods wanted to cast her life as a more tranquil one. She may have felt that this incident had no place of importance in her own self-conception, and thus she chose not to discuss it during the oral history. Or perhaps she did not imbue the incident with the importance of history, an event worth recording for posterity. The absence of the story in her oral narrative proves highly compelling. Woods knew that I knew of the story, yet she deftly skirted the issue throughout our interview. In creating the official memoir of her life, she omitted her marriage and its dramatic and deadly conclusion. I cannot know that she made the omission consciously, and the omission proves compelling whether or not Woods made it deliberately. Had I prompted her, even towards the end of our recorded discussion, I would have gravely disrupted Woods's storyline. I can only prove that she entirely omitted her marriage from the oral history if I also refrained from bringing up the topic. If I had mentioned it, I would not have known if she herself would have included it, perhaps revealing it right at the end of our recorded interview. By discussing her husband with me in other venues, Woods acknowledged my own more intimate view of her life. She knew I knew, but the story was not for the consumption of others. Nor perhaps was it a story she frequently told herself. It may simply have been too painful.

Remaining silent regarding a spouse was not unique to Woods or Hudson. Women with far less acrimonious relationships failed to highlight the marital relationship in their interviews. Narrators providing their life stories for the Baylor University's Family Life and Community History Project interviewers often devoted little time to their husbands. Harriet Caulfield Smith first mentioned her husband on the forty-fourth page of her fifty-five page-transcribed interview. Bessie Lee Stafford similarly made no mention of her husband until well into the interview. When asked to provide an oral memoir of their lives, the women included their children and their extended family, yet some, surprisingly, included little commentary on their spouses.

Perhaps the omission in my own interviews can be attributed to the interviews' focus on the themes of work and migration. Children did figure centrally in women's work; their care took up much of a mother's day. In postwar America, typical husbands did not intimately involve themselves with the day-to-day concerns of child raising, and the men were not working alongside their wives in the home. Rather, these men were busy with their own occupations for the majority of the day. While housewives certainly did care for their husbands' welfare, children occupied the bulk of their labor. The sheer volume of child care, and the interrelatedness between motherhood and labor—both paid and unpaid—may account for the greater emphasis on children than husbands in these interviews. The worlds of men and women were also vastly different. Vivienne Malone-Mayes, interviewed in 1987 by the Baylor University Institute for Oral History, remembered the separateness of her parents' leisure activities. Her father relaxed with friends in the Mecca Drug Store, and her mother devoted time to her sorority and playing bridge. Their lives intersected less than one might imagine, especially on a public level. Malone-Mayes argued, "In fact, even to this day, black people very seldom associate as a couple."[43]

Little mention was made in most interviews of courtship, marriage ceremonies, or romantic moments. Migrant women met good men and loved them, but their life stories did not revolve around white dresses, long veils, and dramatic walks down the aisle. There was no "happily ever after" for migrant women. Nor was a fairy-tale ending ever expected. Black men could lose their jobs at any time, and, due to high levels of discrimination in hiring, the men could not depend on finding another job easily. Black workers were almost always the "last hired, the first fired." The scramble to survive remained a central concern for many migrant families. The migrant women relied on their own skills, education, and work ethic to care for themselves and their families. If their husbands could shoulder most of the families' economic burden, their financial prowess might be celebrated, but it was rarely expected. Migrant women trusted first and foremost in themselves. Although there were a few women interviewed for this study—including Annie Benning and Lillian Clark—who married and subsequently never worked outside the home for pay, most married women could not leave the workforce. And many who did leave paid work for a time did so at the behest of their husbands, as a fulfillment of his wishes rather than their own. Working outside the home was an ingrained practice, in addition to being a necessity, for many women. Vivienne Malone-Mayes, the first African American professor hired at Baylor University, was the daughter of a schoolteacher and a businessman. Malone-Mayes commented on the high numbers of African American female workers in the Southwest:

> I don't know anyone [female] who didn't work. I don't know any—if people didn't work it was either because they didn't have any education or they couldn't find a job but they were looking for one. I don't—I grew up in an environment—in fact, my mother always told me that black women had to work and grow up. And so the main thing was to get prepared to work where you could make a decent wage. This is why it was so important to get an education. But I don't remember anyone not working. I don't remember a black woman sitting at home just being a housewife. Now, I imagine some were . . .[44]

Zenara Covington, the successful daughter of a migrant, called the women of her mother's generation "great warriors." Artist Willie Cole, moved by his mother's and grandmother's work as domestics, fashions iron scorch marks into shields. Forced by circumstance to balance both jobs for hire and work at home, the women did what they had to do, and did it well. They accepted great responsibility. Parenting, no doubt the weightiest of all responsibilities, proved much more complicated given the limited economic opportunities in the South during the period. Like immigrant fathers who journeyed alone to America in the late nineteenth and early twentieth centuries seeking work, many mothers felt compelled to assign the physical care of their children to others in order to care for them financially. They often left the region in search of higher wages. This sacrifice perhaps resonates even more strongly because the migrants were mothers, and motherhood has a symbolic and emotional value that is difficult or impossible to substitute for. Yet when families rely on mothers for economic support, especially when they are the sole economic support, such sacrifices can be considered logical choices. As the oral histories attest, black families adopted multifaceted survival strategies to best cope with an inequitable system. Individuals were willing to relocate, often at great distances and more than once, to find suitable work. Families attempted to compensate for inadequate pay by forming strong networks of care. Women took in the children of family members, raising younger siblings, cousins, and even the children of friends, when the other adults faced illness or death. They took comfort in the knowledge that their children could also benefit from these safety nets, should the need arise.

Brookford Cotton Mill, Brookford, North Carolina, near Hickory. Migrant Addie Smith, of North Carolina and Worcester, Massachusetts, labored in this mill. Courtesy of the North Carolina Collection, University of North Carolina Library at Chapel Hill.

CHAPTER SEVEN

Experiences with Other Types of Employment

When I start to feel sorry for myself, I think about other people who have had much harder times than I. I have been a Christian since I was thirteen, and, I'm telling you, God had brought me a mighty long way. I tell people, don't turn back, but look back, and see from where you have come. You can make it.
—MARY WHITE, DETROIT, MICHIGAN[1]

JERLIENE "CREAMY" MCKINNEY
Worcester, Massachusetts

Creamy McKinney and I spoke in her beauty salon, a large space decorated with advertisements for beauty products. We met early in the morning, before McKinney's customers would start trickling into the shop. The shop was located in an inner courtyard of Plumley Village, the 430-unit, Section 8 complex in which McKinney resided. The apartments stood at the eastern edge of Worcester's downtown, and the interstate highway entrance ramps and overpasses circled the buildings, bringing with them a hum of traffic. The high density of the sixteen-building village assured McKinney of a steady customer base. McKinney, born in Cullman, Alabama, a small town just over one hundred miles from Tuscaloosa, had been a domestic worker in New York City, New York State, and Massachusetts before settling into cosmetology. She had managed her own salon business for twenty-seven years at the time of the interview.

I was growing up, I went to a school called Cullman High School, from kindergarten to the tenth and eleventh grade. I left Alabama at the early age of, ah, seventeen, eighteen. I went to New York; I spent—I don't know—it was about six or seven years in New York. I got married, had four kids, and came to

Massachusetts here. And I started to work in a coat factory down here on Main Street. Then I got a job at Jefferson Wire and Cable. I went to Jefferson Wire and Cable for about six, seven years. I worked there. Then I went to hairdressing school. Beals Beauty Institute. Seven months—I went full-time. I only missed three days, and I made that up [laughing]. And I graduate, I went to Rob Roy's hairdressing school for different courses. I went to Rob Roy's beauty salon; my first job was there. From there I worked five or six years with Rob Roy. I left there; I came here with Miss Lucille. I got a job here, and I worked with her for about four or five years, maybe, three or four years. And when she passed away, I [have] taken over the business. And I've been working here—oh, so now I've been in the hairdresser business about thirty-one, almost thirty-two years.

I started when my kids were small; I raised all my kids. And my husband died at the age of thirty-nine. Seven, eight, or nine years, then I remarried. And then I've just been working. Just working alive. I go to Second Baptist Church; I'm a member there. All my kids are a member of Second Baptist. And, I run the Pastor Aid at the Second Baptist too.

I always wanted to be a hairdresser. My mom used to do hair when I was small. In the country, they used to do hair out in the yard. They used the to-bacco can; they made a little fire outside, and they'd take the chair and stuff. And they'd put the combs in the can, in the tobacco cans, and I used to carry the comb to her, back and forth. When the comb got hot, I would take it to her. It was exciting. People would come up on Saturday, and sometimes Sunday afternoon, and they would pay her. She did all the hair as a little girl; washed and braid, and combed my hair. Press it and curl it, and when she press your hair, it would stay till you wash it. It would stay straight till you wash it. I don't know how they learned how to press and curl, but she was doing it as I was growing up. Pressing and curling people's hair. They would come in, and sometimes we had to do housework while she pressed and curled.

So, I went to hairdressing school, and I've just been a hairdresser for many years. Now, I'm getting ready to retire. It's killing my legs. And everybody's saying, "Creamy, don't retire. Not yet." They don't want me to give it up, but I says, "Its after four o'clock, I'm done." I have so many customers. Whew. [In a day] twenty, thirty, sometimes forty. And my daughter, Jennifer. My grand-daughter Keisha—she helps me. And my sister Karen does the shampoos. My granddaughter Keisha does shampoos. And I do shampoos. Jennifer does shampoos. So we work. We work good together.

I worked with Lucille Harriet for about two or three years. And while I was going to hairdressing school, she died. But she wanted me to take it over. And she knew she was getting ready to retire. But then she died before she retired. So, she had spoken the offers for me to take the place over, anyway. So, after she passed, the kids closed it down and everything. So they called me in and said, "Creamy, give it a shot." And I've been here ever since. Back in the seventies, I started to work. I've been here for many years in this village. I should own it [laughing].

I worked for Rob Roy's [salon] too, in Shrewsbury [Massachusetts]. I worked for them five years and a half. I worked for Jefferson Wire and Cable. I did factory work. Doing coats and housecoats, robes, and stuff like that. I worked for a laundry company for a while. I worked for a laundry company pressing sleeves and things of different clothes, and stuff like that. I worked at Austin Restaurant, repairing and shopping for the restaurant. A waitress. And a cook. It was near the bus stop in Queens. And, [now] I works at Mercadante Memorial Funeral Parlor, too. Yeah, dead people's hair. That's what I do. I go down and do their hair and makeup. They need me and they call me, and I go right down and do their hair. Black peoples mostly. I do their hair, by request. When I retire, I hope to continues working with Mercandante's.[2]

Most studies of domestic work focus on women who worked in the field almost exclusively. But scholars ought to widen their view of the work to include the numbers of women who took up domestic work along with other types of employment. High percentages of African American women were engaged in domestic work at any given point in the twentieth century. Yet, the chance that *any* given black woman had done domestic work during her lifetime was even higher, as is demonstrated in the oral histories. The flexibility of the work and the ease in finding a position meant that women used it as a first job after their migration, an occasional way to make money while primarily concerned with raising their own families, or a way to earn supplemental income after retirement. Many women had worked in the homes of white families in the South, commencing paid work when still adolescents. Some women, particularly migrants to the Midwest whose husbands earned a steady, substantial income, left domestic work behind in the South. Others did not have the opportunity to forgo paid labor. Many women found jobs that were, in effect, domestic chores done in a public setting, such as cleaning for an office or store, waitressing, or working as a hospital aide or technician. Women often considered these public jobs of higher status than household labor, and the level of pay and the relative safety of working in public did bear out this attitude. However, a number of the actual tasks involved in the service sector remained similar to those of domestic labor. A significant number of women also entered factories—some gained access during World War II, although deep discrimination remained in industrial hiring during the war. More African American women entered factory work in the 1950s and beyond, as the wages for industrial labor declined and white workers increasingly moved out of the field. Thus black women finally gained access to coveted jobs in the industrial sector just as the social capital and actual pay rates for these positions declined. In this period, too, the industrial jobs the migrants had followed northward began to move to the South, where pay rates were lower and unionism was not yet entrenched.

Many women found employment as both domestic workers and cosmetologists during their work lives. Cosmetology shared the flexibility of domestic work; hours could revolve around other responsibilities to some extent. Cosmetology offered work sites solidly within the African American community, an added benefit. Most, but not all, of the cosmetologists worked in salons serving primarily African American clients. These salons were safer spaces than white families' kitchens. The separation of salons by race was standard practice, but was not a necessity. Hair stylist Avezinner Dean of Detroit pointed out that she had trained to serve both black and white clients; many whites doubted her ability to cut "white" hair, an assumption she highly resented.[3] Increasingly, cosmetology schools stressed that graduates were ready to serve a variety of clients. In practice, however, salons have remained quite segregated.

Although historian Julie Kirk Blackwelder informs readers that salons were "one of the few institutions as segregated as the church," her study of southern beauty establishments also lauds the businesses as centers of pre–urban renewal black civic culture. Blackwelder urges a rereading of the shops. They ought to be considered examples of black entrepreneurship, rather than institutions out to prey on women's insecurities.[4] Fierce debate has always churned around cosmetology services aimed at African American women, for beauty practitioners have historically pushed beauty aids that whitened skin and straightened hair. A'Lelia Bundles, descendent of the famous beauty entrepreneur Madame C. J. Walker, presses for a reconsideration of her ancestor, whose company, Bundles insists, did not tout such products during her lifetime.[5] As one of the few careers available to black women trying to go into business on their own, the field deserves recognition as a means of financial independence for women. Criticisms of cosmetology's traditional deference to white versions of beauty ought to be noted, but need not stultify any mention of women's business achievements within the field.

Detroit resident Avezinner Dean testified to the flexibility of cosmetology for migrants; she worked in the beauty industry in a number of cities. Dean also invested time and resources in expanding her knowledge of the field over time. For women who may not have had the opportunity to complete their formal schooling, beauty school remained an option. Obtaining added credentials in the field offered a way to advance in pay and status, increase one's skill set, and add to one's self-image. Dean attended beauty schools in both the South and the North. She said, "I wanted to be a hairdresser. I worked in Alabama and had a shop. I had a shop in Mississippi. I moved to Michigan and I worked in Inkster, and moved back to Alabama and stayed seven years, and I went to Nashville and got another diploma and I wanted to bob hair and I didn't know how to bob. Then I moved back to Michigan in '55."[6]

Cosmetology offered a social workplace. Working primarily for black clients, African American cosmetologists insulated themselves from the interracial conflict so common to domestics and many other service workers. In serving mostly female clients, cosmetologists reduced their risk of sexual exploitation. The work called for a personal interaction between client and beautician; satisfied customers returned again and again, and the client and cosmetologist developed a rapport. Cosmetologists often worked alongside other women, while domestic workers often labored alone. Glennette Taylor of Grand Rapids worked as a hair stylist for about eighteen years. Taylor served both male and female clients in a local shop, until her work tenure ended due to a diagnosis of diabetes. Taylor enjoyed the sociability of the job. She observed, "The other cosmetologists were nice to work with and so were the barbers. They were all nice to work with and I met some interesting people."[7] During her years raising small children, Beatrice Jackson selected a career in the beauty industry. She said, "I wasn't so good at it, but I liked the people."[8]

Mary White opened her salon, Mary and Lee's Beauty Salon of Detroit, at a key moment in her life. Friends expressed incredulity when White, forty-five years old at the time, commenced studying beauty at night in 1955. But the choice proved fortuitous. White explained, "After that, my husband got sick. Six months later he died. So in a way I was lucky to have opened my salon when I did. Otherwise, I would not have been in the position to start a business and care for a household." White kept the business open for many years, out of financial necessity. She noted, "I really didn't have much choice. It was better than doing domestic work, going from place to place." White favored cosmetology over all the other forms of employment she had tried, including domestic work, factory work, and office work. Her father had inspired her interest in the field. He had become a barber at a time in which no formal training was open to African Americans—rather he learned by watching others. White felt she always made the best of her lot. She acknowledged, "I have always just adjusted to circumstances. Whatever I had to do, I enjoyed doing it."[9]

Cosmetology contained an entrepreneurial aspect that migrants like White used to full effect. A few migrants interviewed for the book also opened other types of businesses. Establishing one's own business remained a way to make a living when relatively few establishments hired blacks as employees. Bernita Howard agreed to run a bakery started by her husband, who had worked as a baker in the South. The Howards opened the bakery on the strength of a small bank loan, and then used Mr. Howard's paychecks from his work as a baker at the veterans' hospital to fund their start-up costs. Howard proved so competent at the management that she permanently assumed the major responsibility for the bakery. Her husband retained his other job. The business first supplied a few stores with their wares, and then expanded to serve more stores than Howard could handle comfortably. Howard mused that it was a "lot of work and when I just started, I really loved it. At that time, no black had a bakery and so it was kind of hard. We made fried pies. I would make them in the morning and afternoon and then I would get in my car and take them to the stores in the afternoon." Eventually Howard added cakes to the bakery's repertoire as well.[10]

Faith Richmond launched her own travel business in Boston; she arranged group tours around the United States, as well as to Panama, Paris, Greece, Africa, and Turkey. Richmond laughed, "It makes me happy and keeps me quite busy. I mean *busy*." The business did not provide her with substantial savings, as some of her friends suspected. Rather each trip financed her launch of another and kept Richmond personally fulfilled. She sighed, admitting, "If I had more education or had someone to really work with me I would have been a little bit further." Yet later Richmond praised her own achievements, saying, "This is the amazing thing of my life, knowing I did this with a high school education."[11]

Factory work remained preferable to domestic work for many women migrants, although not all. Annie Benning, who lived in both Alabama and Georgia, worked in cotton mills (later converted to war materials) in the South and also labored as a cook for a private family. She much preferred her mill work, as the set hours gave her some time to fulfill her domestic responsibilities to her extended family. Benning, who had no children of her own, nonetheless had many household duties. In response to the question of whether she preferred working in the mills to cleaning, Benning stated, "Oh yeah, Lord, yeah, Lord, because I had them eight hours—I made them and went on home and took care of my house because my husband was in the service and my mother when she died—she had some young children, and I raised them two girls and two boys."[12] Although Rosa Young of Grand Rapids initially did not like her work at the General Motors factory, in time she found the work quite interesting. Young made the "lace-around" for car seats, as well as the upholstered car doors and headrest. In the 1970s, Young made a little over four dollars an hour in her position, as well as benefits. Due to the development of back problems, she took an early retirement.[13]

Many of the factory experiences took place during World War II, when the majority of the interviewees were in their primary work years. However, as previously stated, black women's opportunities to enter into factories were far more limited than white women's. Although the percentage of employed African American women doing domestic work fell from 59.5 percent in 1940 to 44.6 percent in 1944, the proportion of African Americans working in the field rose, as white women increasingly fled from paid household work. While the percentage of black women in industry rose from 6.5 percent to 18 percent during the war, the women were at the very bottom of the industrial hierarchy, most often relegated to custodial work, objectionable tasks, and/or the most dangerous jobs within the plants.

Even as America claimed to be zealously searching out potential labor sources, racist hiring practices persisted. Some plants sent out recruiters to encourage the migration of more southern whites rather than resort to hiring the black workers already living in their cities. Managers claimed that hiring black women was impossible, because white employees would refuse to work side-by-side with them or share lavatory facilities, locker rooms, and dining halls. Northern whites were not keen to share work space with black workers, and many white industrial workers were recent migrants from the South, acclimated to strict legal segregation. Managers who wished not to hire blacks also overplayed their employees' inability to work with African Americans. If integrated workplaces had offered the only route to industrial employment, surely the majority of white workers would have had to acquiesce.

Black industrial workers staged a number of wildcat strikes between 1943 and 1944. One of the main areas of contention for the strikers was the treatment of black women workers and the discriminatory hiring practices. Six hundred male workers left their jobs in protest of the conditions faced by black women at the Chrysler Highland Park facility in March 1943. At this plant, trained women found themselves in the most dangerous, strenuous work, or assigned to the custodial team. Rev. Charles A. Hill, the chairman of the committee Jobs for Negro Women, launched a public crusade on behalf of African American women looking for industrial positions. On April 11, 1943, activists demonstrated in Detroit's Cadillac Square, protesting the dire situation in workplaces around the city. The black-owned newspaper the *Michigan Chronicle* reported, "In this arsenal of democracy, the Negro worker is being forced to fight in order to make his contribution to the war effort. Our women are jobless which [*sic*] production is menaced by a shortage of labor." Karen Tucker Anderson concluded that in Detroit, nonwhite women held only 1,000 of the 96,000 jobs occupied by women in major war industries by February 1943. Unfortunately,

few concrete gains were realized by the efforts of Rev. Charles A. Hill's committee and other activists. At the end of the war, black women found it hard
to hold on to their very modest gains in industry. In 1950, there were 782,520
black women employed in domestic work—40 percent of all working black
women.[14]

A few women interviewed for this study obtained industrial jobs during
the war, but none did so in the factories most infamous for discriminatory hiring practices. Minnie Chatman made bunk beds for soldiers in a factory in the
South.[15] Annie Benning produced rubber for automobile tires and much-needed
nylon. She earned about a dollar an hour, with double for overtime.[16] Simone
Landry of Detroit worked for Federal Motor Works while her husband was in
the service during World War II. Landry, who also performed day work, said, "I
liked working in the factory [better] because you made more money, you know,
and then the hours were more regular."[17] Mary White of Detroit shied away from
factories like Ford, which had a reputation of refusing to hire black women. A
neighbor provided White with a tip on a factory job involving inspecting airplane springs and related activities. At her particular plant, White's race did not
prove an insurmountable obstacle.[18]

Other migrants located factory jobs in the decades after the war, when hiring practices evolved. Faith Richmond worked for B. F. Goodrich in Massachusetts in the 1950s. She was assigned to the cutting machine. Then Richmond
took a factory position making athletic shoes, and she enjoyed the time with
her workmates. "I was the lead person," she related. "Why they put me there
I don't know. I would play around. I would do a lot, then I would talk. It was
fun."[19] Rebecca Strom, who came to Boston to work as a domestic, later took a
variety of more preferable factory jobs, including making chocolate in a factory in South Boston.[20] As previously mentioned, Liddie Williams of Chicago
worked as a "jogger," assembling *Playboy* magazines for approximately twenty
years. Williams was unique in ending her working days, rather than beginning
them, as a domestic worker. She categorized the factory work as "pretty good"
because the workers there "made pretty good money." Williams described the
work, saying, "The machine was a press and we had pages to put in and it moves
along the line and all of the pages folded. You got to watch your pages." The job
ended when the company, like so many in the Midwest, moved south to Tennessee. Williams found factory work more physically demanding than her subsequent domestic labor. "When I was working factory work," Williams related,
"I had to pick up those heavy books. So many girls, they have to have surgery
on their shoulders and on their wrists, and my wrists hurt so bad when I was
working there and it's a funny thing—they don't hurt now."[21]

Maggie Langham Washington had a wide variety of jobs, including industrial work. Washington was born in Texas and later migrated to Chicago. As a young girl, she labored at home, assisting her mother as she washed and ironed the laundry of others. Washington sometimes missed school to work, and she resented her mother for involving her so deeply in the strenuous labor. A kind schoolteacher, sensing Washington's hunger, as well as her pride, invented a small job for the student. Each day the teacher paid Washington five cents to fetch her lunch box, and Washington used the money to purchase her own school lunch. At Texas's Paul Quinn College, she earned her tuition by washing and ironing for thirty-two male classmates each week (each was allowed to have five dress shirts) and cleaning a college office. She became a cosmetologist, and then moved to Chicago, where she labored as a bartender and as a factory worker. The industrial work gave her a broader understanding of how commerce and manufacturing functioned. At the Continental Canning Company, Washington fashioned the half-pint, pint, and quart containers used to package ice cream, and also produced matchboxes. She said, "That was when I really realized how interdependent we are, because I always had an idea that people that made the matches made the boxes to put them in, you know. But that's what the company did. Made containers." Washington fled from Chicago, where she lived for eight years, when her doctor insisted she have a necessary surgery. (She somehow felt she could avoid surgery if she returned to Texas.) She postponed the surgery for many years, finally relenting when overcome by the pain. Washington spent time in the military, completed a teaching degree from a four-year college, and moved to Midland, Texas. There, she labored as a household domestic worker, a hotel maid, and a substitute teacher. Eventually Washington took up full-time teaching in Midland and Dallas. Because she was the first black teacher to integrate the schools in Midland, the white teachers snubbed her.[22]

Cleaning in public settings occupied many migrant women. Such jobs offered higher wages than household work, as well as the attributes of steady employment, work colleagues, and, if the women were lucky, some benefits. Work in a public setting contained fewer threats of sexual harassment than jobs in private homes, although women were never immune to this danger. The drawbacks of such positions included the lack of flexibility, the low wages in comparison to those of others working at the same setting, and the nature of the job tasks. The repetitive movements could result in injury, and many of the products used in cleaning proved toxic, although this was not largely understood at the time. A great many women performed this type of labor in their younger years. Each day, the newly married Alberta Hardy single-handedly cleaned sixteen hotel rooms, constituting the entire first floor of the hotel. She described her labors: "I just fix the rug, made the beds, and cleaned up and that's all. They [also] house [*sic*] a man housekeeper . . . the heavy work—he did that." She stated that the hotel patrons kept their rooms relatively neat, and she remembered the work itself in a generally positive way.[23] Ella Sims cleaned coaches for the C&O Railroad until she got pregnant with her third child. At its leanest, the C&O cleaning crew consisted of twelve people. They would wait for the train to come into the station, and immediately enter and begin cleaning. The crew washed the train windows, cleaned the bathrooms, and pulled out the seat cushions to dislodge the dirt hidden there. The teams, divided into two groups, started at each end and met in the middle of the train.[24]

Many other migrants related their experiences cleaning in public settings. Thelma Lane's mother, who worked at a hospital, located a job for her daughter, then a junior in high school. The position involved cleaning the apartments of the hospital nurses, who lived in dormitories adjacent to the hospital. "I used to go up there and run the sweeper and dust," remembered Lane. For other women, such work comprised their lifetime employment. As explored in chapter five, Annie Evelyn Collins, born in 1930, cleaned for a dentist's office, and later worked for the maintenance department at a Sears department store in Detroit. She retired from the latter position in 1983. Collins appreciated the higher wages at the Sears job, but noted that all the employees in her department were black. She said of white women, "They don't like cleaning."[25] Mattie Bell Fritz of Detroit labored part-time in a dress shop. She described the work: "We just take the clothes off and put them on the shelves, clean, keep the clothes and things clean, and keep the dust from building." Following this position, Fritz cleaned the UAW offices for eight years, from five p.m. until ten p.m. Her colleagues consisted of both white and black employees, and she found them cordial. Fritz retired when she was beset with arthritis. If she had persisted two more years she would have earned an increased benefit package, but her health precluded it.[26]

Many women found employment in positions that, while not labeled domestic work, included some similar duties. The jobs were not considered high status by society at large, and most often paid low salaries. Respondents for this study seemed to regard such positions as socially preferable to domestic work. In the second half of the twentieth century, jobs in service industries such as nursing homes, commercial laundries, fast food restaurants, and day care centers proliferated. Northern cities substantially deindustrialized, lessening the chance that factory work could be found, and much of the service work that had once taken place inside homes (especially cooking, laundry, and child care) moved to public spaces. The move did not substantially alter the structure of the

work. Many of the migrants were on the leading edge of this trend towards public service work. Sociologist Patricia Hill Collins observes that in contemporary
America, black women continue to transition away from domestic work and
enter into fields that bear striking resemblance to black women's former roles in
private homes. Collins writes:

> The work performed by employed poor Black women resembles duties
> long associated with domestic service. During prior eras, domestic service
> was confined to private households. In contrast, contemporary cooking,
> cleaning, nursing, and child care have been routinized and decentralized
> in an array of fast food restaurants, cleaning services, day-care centers,
> and service establishments. Black women perform similar work, but in
> different settings. The location may have changed, but the work has not.[27]

Many women worked in commercial laundries, a field dominated by African American women in many cities. In the South, the migrants' mothers, like
Maggie Langham Washington's, had often earned extra money for the household by washing the laundry of other families. Some women had gathered laundry from families and washed it at their own homes, while others had done the
laundry at the employers' homes. Their daughters now labored in commercial
laundries in northern, urban settings, undertaking the notoriously difficult
work. Workers had to lift irons and contend with dangerous machinery such as
presses; additionally, laundries were extremely hot, and the pace could be backbreaking. Lillie Shelby,who worked in a laundry for two years in Detroit, remembered, "That was fast work. You had to be fast to be able to do that because there
was somebody else doing something. If they were body pressing and you were
sleeving, the collar and the yoke, you got to keep your hand going, so it was fast
work."[28]

Migrants undertook work that resembled domestic labor in a wide variety
of settings. Sometimes the women were the only workers in the setting undertaking work of that nature. Ruth Margaret Covington worked in a drugstore as
a young mother in the 1950s. Her job consisted of waiting on customers and
dusting the store products.[29] During high school, Mary White, born in 1910,
began working in a Detroit decorating shop as a Jane-of-all trades, and she
remained at the shop for eleven years. White did "a little of everything. Answer-
ing the phone, cleaning, and everything else. Rearranging the furniture."[30] Fannie Mae Kennedy of Detroit, born in 1925, headed up the salad bar at a restaurant for seventeen years and four months. She singly-handedly replaced two
women who had left the restaurant to return to school. She had been working

at the restaurant, Chicago Road House, as a dishwasher for six months, when the promotion took place. "They always worked the hell out of me," Kennedy lamented. At first, the tasks required bewildered her. "Like I said, I was from the country," Kennedy said, "and I didn't know nothing about these chef salad[s] and shrimp cocktails." Her pay, four dollars an hour at the time of retirement, was higher than that of day work, yet she never considered it adequate. She also seemed to be working longer hours and getting paid less than her colleagues. Yet she considered the position preferable to all others she had held. Kennedy said of the job, "I met a lot of people and I learned a lot of things." She and her fellow restaurant workers still gathered once a year to reminisce. Kennedy looked back on her life with some regret, for she wished she had had a better education. She mused, "I never thought about it [school] then. Now for the last ten years it has been on my mind. I really want to go to school and I had said I was going last year and I had the stroke. There was a lot of time between there that I could have went but I didn't because I have five children."[31]

Operating a home day care center interestingly brought one of the duties of the private household worker—child care—into the worker's *own* house. Two of the Boston respondents, Mary Smith and Rebecca Strom, both former domestic workers, were operating day care centers in their homes at the time of the interviews. Smith had worked previously as a domestic, a hospital dietary aide, a key-punch operator, and a staff member at Harvard University. Needing a change of pace, Smith turned to child care. She cared for six children, the maximum allowable by law at any one time. Smith laughed, "Yeah, day care would be a challenge, and believe me . . . the younger they are, the louder they are!"[32] Rebecca Strom found that the demeanor of contemporary children differed from that of those in the past. As a child, she would wash the dishes or attend to chores if her parents asked. Children today might balk at a request to help out. The modern children, according to Strom, appeared outspoken and did not listen to their elders. Her charges arrived at 6:45 a.m. and left by 4:30 p. m. Strom commented, "It's a long day to have them. After you do it for so long you find a way to keep them from killing each other, and from getting hurt. That's what I have been hoping, that I never have to call a parent and say, 'Come, something happened.' So far, I have been lucky."[33]

Migrant women also found employment in a variety of hospital jobs—from surgical instrument technician to patient aide. Although some of the duties resembled work done in private homes, the mission of the hospital and the public nature of the work brought added respectability. In the hospital a rigid protocol remained in place, and tiny mistakes could have grave consequences. Although some patients balked at being tended to by black hospital workers, others expressed clear appreciation for their assistance. Glennette Taylor of Grand Rapids stressed, "It's hard work, and yet, the hours have been long, but no matter how hard your day has been at the end of the day it is always a consolation knowing that you have helped someone."[34] Jacqueline Dock of Detroit acquired cosmetology certification at the urging of her mother, but never used this skill in the workplace. Rather, Dock worked as an aide in the hospital, and then secured a job as a surgical instrument technician. Dock provided a detailed description of her position, which was to "make sure that the instruments were sharp and that they were all there and then wrap them in packages and then send them back to medical supplies so they could be sterilized. You had to know everything about the instruments. I did that for about twelve and [a] half years."[35] Alverrine Parker, born in Mississippi, held a wide variety of jobs, including working as a trimmer for Catalina Bathing Suits in Los Angeles, serving as an aide in a nursing home in Grand Rapids, working ten years at the Calvinator factory making refrigerator motors, and driving a bus for the local schools. Parker located the nursing home job quickly. She said, "So I think I wasn't home [from California] even a week, I started to work for them—a nurse's aide. And oh, but I was looking for something better—more money. I think she wasn't even paying a dollar an hour there then [in 1959]." Parker knew this rate was too low. She continued, "You know, what the funny thing [was], well, I told her about minimum wages. She said she would pay me but not to tell the rest of them, and I didn't like that." Parker confided, "[Of] course there were all black girls working there, and she [knew], I guess, maybe they had families, a lot of them had children and all, and they usually work [for] what they knew they could get." Parker summed up all of her jobs, saying, "Never really liked any of them, but it was a living. Because then I didn't know about grants-in-aid and all that stuff to go to school—we didn't have it."[36]

As is still the case for people of underprivileged economic status, the armed services beckoned the migrant women with its training and opportunities. Barbara Purifoy-Seldon of Detroit joined the United States Army on a program called the "buddy system"—she was allowed to join up with a friend. She reminisced, "In the buddy plan, two ladies could go together if they were willing to stay three years and the army recruiter said that we would see the world and that we will get an education. We saw wonderful pictures and a wonderful film. These army [recruits] had wonderful formal dresses and they were also so perfect and my friend and I thought that was just the best thing." Purifoy-Seldon initially planned to pursue dental hygiene studies once she had enlisted—a specialty she studied after she was discharged. Yet after singing and dancing for a contest, she found herself assigned to the special services entertainment unit instead. The performing proved to be welcome training for the formerly reserved young woman.[37] Lois Stevens served for two years in the army, joining on a whim after two neighbors signed on. Stevens, one hundred years old at the time of the interview, said of her early job, "You had to know what your duties were. I was a driver in the army. I had to work nights and the boys were very nice to me. The cook always had something nice for me to eat."[38]

Maggie Langham Washington, who had already graduated from junior college, joined the WACs (Women's Army Corps—initially known as the Women's Army Auxiliary Corps and abbreviated accordingly) in an impulsive moment. She was having a spat with the administration at Paul Quinn College, where she had worked as a temporary librarian. She quit and joined the WACs. Washington expressed outrage at the fact that, even as a member of her nation's armed services, she had to eat in restaurant kitchens rather than in their main dining rooms. Eating establishments from Texas to Washington, D.C., refused to feed the group of fourteen black female soldiers and their white female escort in public. Nor could the travelers sit in the main car of the train. When they arrived in Washington, D.C., two young WACs, one white and one black, set off sightseeing together, but they were told, according to Washington, to leave town—mixed-race socializing was not allowed. Later, en route to Germany on the USS *George Goethels*, an officer's wife slighted Washington, and the incident stayed in Washington's memory for life. The woman confided to Washington how pleased she was to see WACs on board, because they always cared for the officers' children while at sea. Washington bridled at this presumption, asking the woman if she had inquired as to the availability of the white WACs on the upper deck of the ship. Washington said she would only take care of her own children. And, as she indeed had none of her own, she told the woman, she would not be doing any child care. The officer's wife did not understand Washington's remark, and Washington worried she would be court-martialed for her refusal. A meeting was called by the ship's captain. Washington spoke laughingly about being placed in the ship's jail, but her sarcastic tone makes it a bit hard to ascertain the actual punishment, if any, for her refusal.

Washington had already gotten in some trouble by breaking curfew, so she may have been punished just for her previous infraction. She said, laughing, "And they couldn't do anything for me [for refusing the officer's wife] but put me in jail, because I had already been busted. I am sure I was the only recruit that crossed the Atlantic [in the brig] but then the trip was very pleasant."[39]

Local schools also provided some employment opportunities for migrant women, both in teaching positions and a myriad of other duties. Teaching was among the most obvious occupations for any woman, white or black, who had graduated from college in the mid-twentieth century. Many historically black colleges offered an education major and the teaching certificates needed for employment. Women with less extensive education coveted jobs with the school system as well. The jobs often included time off in the summers (crucial for women with children) and they imparted a certain social status. Gussie Nash worked in a factory making baby clothes, and later found a position as an aide at a local hospital, carrying trays and setting things up for the patients. In the 1970s, Nash worked with parents of school-age children in Grand Rapids; she took the parents to nutrition classes and other important parenting skills workshops. She later assisted disabled children in the school district. When we talked about her career, Nash firmly advocated for higher wages for women.[40]

African American women had a difficult time securing teaching jobs in many northern cities. Prior to 1940, three African American women with teaching degrees from Western State Teachers College (a predecessor to Western Michigan University) were turned away by the Grand Rapids School Board. The Grand Rapids Urban League commented, "This is a most unfortunate circumstance for Grand Rapids, for not only is it losing its best minds and potential leaders, but it is losing the very examples which it needs for the younger generation which must have some concrete evidence of what it can strive for in the community."[41] Indeed, teachers in southern segregated schools served as revered community leaders. Northern schools, many facing de facto segregation due to neighborhood boundaries, if not outright de jure segregation due to city ordinances, nonetheless were not major employers of black teachers. Thelma Lane, born in Alabama in 1920, moved repeatedly between Alabama and Pennsylvania. She earned her high school diploma in Pittsburgh and graduated from Alabama State Teachers College. Following graduation, Lane taught in Troy, Alabama. After she married, she and her husband moved to Virginia, where she taught in an all-white school. Lane remembered making fifty-four dollars a month teaching in Alabama, and about a thousand dollars a year in Virginia. Male teachers earned higher salaries than female teachers, a practice Lane fervently lobbied against. Following her years in teaching, Lane had an extended career as a clerical worker for the Department of Defense in Washington, D.C.[42]

Migrants found job openings in other assorted fields. Minnie Chatman, who had undergone an apprenticeship with a seamstress, opened her own tailoring shop for a time on Beaubien Street in Detroit. Even as a youth, Chatman could create a pattern for any design she saw, using newspaper or flour paper.[43] Government jobs increasingly opened to black women in the second half of the twentieth century. These jobs attracted a significant number of college-educated black women. The United States Post Office offered steady and respectable entry-level work for migrants. Ruth Margaret Covington stated, "I carried mail and sorted it and drove the truck." Covington later worked as a property management clerk at the Veterans Administration. Beatrice Jackson of Detroit, a college graduate, also worked for the government as a staff person; she worked for Detroit's city hall.[44]

Some migrants acquired college degrees, and a few even attended graduate school. Migrant families emphasized education, and the women were readied to take advantage of any opportunity open to them. Ogretta McNeil arrived in Worcester from Washington, D.C., to attend graduate school in psychology in 1956. Born in Georgia, McNeil had pursued an undergraduate degree at Howard University. Her parents had attended normal schools, institutions of higher education consisting of both high school and college studies. Normal schools primarily offered degree programs in teaching. McNeil's parents attended a segregated normal school serving only black students. Neither parent worked in positions that drew directly on this education, but the advanced study did place them in the upper echelon of educated African Americans at the time. McNeil always believed that her parents had not attended college; she later came to understand that the normal school they attended was a type of college. As normal schools offered a range of services, from high school remediation to bachelor's degrees, it is often difficult to tell what attendance at such an institution means by today's education standards. As a teenager, McNeil had little understanding of how one might apply to college, but when a friend readied her own application, McNeil decided to apply as well. She taught for twenty-seven years in the psychology department of Holy Cross College in Worcester, Massachusetts, and also served on the board for the five-college system of the University of Massachusetts. After retirement, McNeil was elected (and reelected) to a seat on the Worcester School Committee.[45]

Ella Sims, mother of a large family, defied all odds in her journey from being the child of sharecroppers in rural Mississippi to being a member of the board of trustees of Aquinas College in Grand Rapids, Michigan. Sims's turning point came through her church work and broader community activism. She explained, "I think that the church is one of the best workshops in the world for leadership. I didn't realize that then, but you're doing some mighty things if you're involved and it reaches out and then, by that time I was president of the PTA, [I] got involved in housing in that area." Sims volunteered for a local empowerment program that evolved into an Office of Economic Opportunity

(OEO) branch project called Kent-Cap. She became a paid employee of the OEO from 1965 until 1974. Sims said, "My husband said when I went to work that I just started getting a little pay for something I'd been doing for years for free." In 1974, she became vice president of the executive board of Kent-Cap. Her program offered, among other services, training for those seeking jobs as cashiers and assistance for young pregnant women. Sims came to head up the urban agents for the OEO in Grand Rapids. She traveled extensively, made speeches about the Grand Rapids poverty program, trained others in the community, and kept statistics. Aquinas College administrators learned of Sims through her community work, and asked her to serve on its board of trustees. She later directed programs for minority students at the college. Ostensibly, the program director position called for someone with a master's degree. Sims's extensive background as a community leader encouraged the college to overlook her lack of a college degree. After accepting the role, Sims earned both a bachelor's and a master's degree.[46]

Dotty Goldsberry was raised in Langston, Oklahoma, where her father taught at Langston University. Goldsberry attended Langston herself, and developed an interest in medicine. She gained admittance to the Oklahoma School of Medicine, but worried about being the first black woman to attend the institution, racial restrictions on enrollment recently having been removed. She instead enrolled in the medical school at Howard University, where she met her future husband. Goldsberry created a life centered around her four children, her fruitful career, and community service. She remembered:

> Well, I graduated from medical school and then I went to do an internship at the Howard University Hospital, just a general rotating. And I also thought I wanted to be a pediatrician, and I got married the day after I graduated from medical school so then I got pregnant my internship year, so I thought, "Oh gee," so I actually took off a good part of the following year, and the next year I thought, "I'll just do a year in psychiatry," and it was primarily a daytime residency. So I spent a year at Saint Elizabeth's Hospital. It's a huge psychiatric hospital in Washington. It was really fascinating that year. And so I was going to go back to pediatrics and it turned out I never did, I stayed in psychiatry. Then we moved to . . . we moved to Worcester [Massachusetts] and I was still torn whether to go to pediatrics so I decided I may as well finish my psychiatric residence. So then I did the residency—the next two years—at the Worcester State Hospital. And then I moved into child psychiatry.[47]

Volunteer Work and Leisure Time

Studies that chronicle the urban life of African American women, and particularly middle-class women, most often devote considerable space to the examination of volunteer or club work. Frequently forced to accept paid positions that did not take full advantage of their many talents, black women looked elsewhere for fulfillment. And those who did not work outside the home craved some public role. Barred from the majority of the organizations populated by white women, black women were instrumental in creating their own social and volunteer societies. Organizations offered women a chance for the sociability and prestige often lacking at their jobs. Women who did not need to labor for pay had even more time to devote to volunteer organizations. Opportunities to volunteer centered around the churches. Almost every migrant interviewed for this book had formed a steady relationship with a church in their new city. In addition to the regular church services, the women took part in Sunday school leadership and a host of other church committees. Without their hard work and deep devotion, northern churches would not have been the bedrocks of community that they were. Women also formed community through many other organizations, including groups like the National Council of Negro Women (NCNW) and the National Association for the Advancement of Colored People (NAACP).

By and large, the women interviewed for this study were not active members of the NCNW, which filled most of its ranks with nonworking women. However, a number of the interviewees spoke of taking on leadership within the NAACP and local church organizations. Lillie Shelby attended NAACP meetings. Fannie Mae Kennedy of Detroit was a member of the board of directors of the local NAACP. She also attended the National Baptist Convention and sang second soprano in the 150-person Wolverine State Choir. Kennedy said of the NAACP, "Now I like it there. You learn a lot about what's going on in your communities, you know, and things like that." She spoke unblushingly about her singing talents. Using the third person, Kennedy said of herself, "She sings like a mockingbird. Everybody knows that about Mrs. Kennedy. All of the churches—they love to hear her sing."[48]

For many, the desire to expand oneself beyond home and school manifested itself at an early age. Young black women could take part in activities only if they remained of a highly respectable nature. Daughters were watched assiduously, yet still encouraged to pursue their talents. Lonnie Graves of Satin, Texas, remembered his sister's piano lessons. As the family did not own a piano, Graves's sister would walk to a home about three-fourths of a mile away each day for practice. Due to their mother's great protectiveness, Graves accompanied his sister on the walks as a chaperone.[49] It could be very dangerous for a young, unaccompanied black woman on the streets alone. Other women remembered practicing their piano skills by hammering out the tunes on a piece of cardboard on which keys had been drawn, in lieu of a real piano.[50] Music served as a wonderful way to expand boundaries, but many rules still applied. It was fine to exhibit musical talent at school or at church functions. Women could sing or play piano for the church on a regular basis. However, a life on the commercial stage brought women into dangerous surroundings, and thus work in the performing arts was highly discouraged.

Part of the lure of both the First and the Second Great Migration certainly stemmed from the large northern cities' wide variety of entertainment offerings. Alberta Hardy remembered that in her younger days she "used to go to ball games and to shows."[51] Facilities were segregated, even in the North, although restrictions relaxed with time. Rebecca Strom had limited free time when she first arrived in Boston because she was a live-in child care worker. On her days off, she met friends to go shopping and hang out, and then returned to her employer. She felt the Boston social life to be fairly staid. There appeared to be few young black men. Boston was not a major destination of the Great Migration, due to persistent rumors of regional racism. Yet a network of African American friends slowly developed. Strom remembered, "Every weekend and every other Sunday we would be invited to someone's home for dinner, that's how we got to meet other people." Strom met her future husband in this manner. He was the brother of Strom's girlfriend.[52] For older and married women, home-based pursuits, like decorating, crocheting, and quilting, occupied considerable free time. Anniese Moten busied herself with crochet work. Rosa Young completed a nine-hundred-piece block quilt, all done by hand. Young, who had worked as an upholsterer for G.M., said, "Sewing is really what I like to do."[53]

Studies in domestic labor tend to present all domestic workers as career laborers in the field. Yet oral memoirs testify to the fact that domestic work served as a convenient, although low-paid, fill-in position between other employment opportunities. Many migrants alternated between domestic work, factory work, and jobs in the service industry. The relative flexibility of domestic work also made it a good fit with motherhood. The intersection of racism, misogyny, and class prejudice relegated many migrants to entry-level positions, and many workplaces excluded them altogether. The World War II factory mobilization, one of the reasons for the Second Great Migration, resulted in many more industrial jobs for black men than black women. Rosie the Riveter was usually white. African American women migrated to make a new home, sometimes at the side of their husbands, to flee the threat of violence and the legal restrictions of the pre–civil rights South, and to take advantage of the higher wages in non-industrial employment. The higher wages alone made the decision to migrate quite clear for most women. With educational access, some black women pursued high-status careers in such fields as business, academia, law, and medicine. These pioneers marked the trail for the next generation of African American women, who would enter in even greater numbers into higher education degree programs and stable careers.

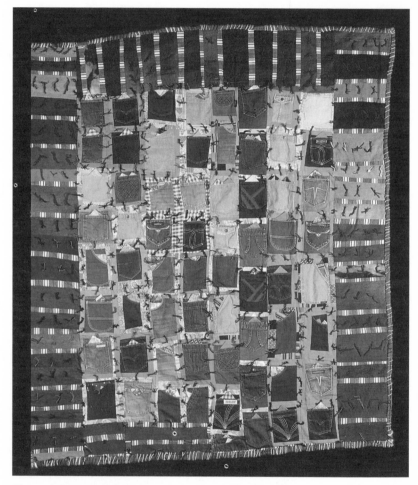

"Blue Jean Pockets," quilt made by Essie Robinson (born 1918), 1990, Detroit, Michigan. Courtesy of the Michigan State University Museum.

CHAPTER EIGHT

Reflections on the Migration and a Life of Work

The little people are forgotten, and they really make up the world, don't they? They make up America, they make up America.
—ERNESTINE G. ANDERSON[1]

A Changing South

In some respects, many migrants never fully left the South. The migrants remained southerners at heart, despite the harsh realities they had endured under Jim Crow. Warm childhood memories persisted, as well as southern cultural practices. But southern ties were not solely a matter of memory or cultural legacy; migrants actively maintained connections with their home region through regular visits. The ties proved so well established that many of the migrants' children returned to the South to raise their families. The post–civil rights movement South, with its burgeoning economy and invitingly warm weather, attracted African American young adults just as it did other young people.

Gussie Nash of Grand Rapids noted that she still returned to Arkansas each year to visit an aunt. Because of the out-migration of blacks and whites from the South, and the in-migration of millions of newcomers looking to secure work in the late twentieth century, Nash considered the contemporary South vastly different from the region of her childhood.[2] Migrants Creamy McKinney and Annie Benning also stressed that their visits to the South remained frequent. Alberta Hardy of Detroit recalled her initial loneliness at arriving in Detroit: "I was away from everybody, but I finally got used to it." Hardy's parents remained in Mississippi, and eventually relocated to St. Louis. Hardy's repeated visits to her parents in Mississippi strengthened family ties.[3] For Lillian Clark, return visits to Kentucky became a yearly ritual. Clark explained, "Every year we went back except in '59. We went back every year. We was going on the train and then we got a car. We would then drive every year."[4]

Just as children of immigrants identify with their parents' country of origin, the migrants' children had a nuanced understanding of the American South. Zenara Covington, daughter of a migrant, attested to ties with Alabama, which she visited every two to three years.[5] Migrant Liddie Williams traveled to Mississippi multiple times each year. Williams's sustained connection with her former home inspired her daughter to attend college in Mississippi and then settle there permanently. Williams's daughter enjoyed living in the South. Williams explained, "She says Chicago is too fast." Yet Williams noted that the South also experienced its share of gang violence and drug-related crimes.[6]

Mary Smith's interview revealed tensions surrounding her decision to leave Georgia and settle permanently in Boston in 1962. She had previously lived in both New York and Miami, so regional moves were clearly part of her response to the challenges of the job market. Smith noticed a positive change in the South about two years after she made her final migration. She revealed that she probably would not have moved to Boston if she had lingered in the South for just a while longer. While Smith expressed pride in her ability to purchase "two and a half" homes while working for Harvard University, as well as five new cars, she noted that her sisters and nephews owned beautiful homes in the South. Due to the extremely high cost of housing in Boston, Smith's investment dollar did not stretch as far as it would have in Georgia.[7]

Addie Smith of Worcester, who entrusted her five children to her mother's care when she migrated from North Carolina, was eventually joined in Massachusetts by some of her children. Her daughter Belinda had come to live near her mother. Belinda suffered from liver failure, and died far too young. One of Smith's sons still resided in North Carolina, and another son, in Louisiana at the time, planned to move back to North Carolina as well. Smith related that they would build an addition on the family home and then she would try to join them there.[8]

Jacqueline Dock left Climax, Georgia, for Detroit in April 1942. She found racist attitudes in her new city. Dock recounted difficulties in shopping, as well as in the workplace. She summarized her thoughts, saying, "Back in the forties, the difference was that there were places you couldn't go in the South, but now I would rather live in the South than in the North." Dock returned to Georgia every year to visit family and friends. In her interview in 2003, she pondered

Detroit's instability, saying, "Detroit needs strong leadership—to the church, to the police department, to the mayor's office, to the governor. Everywhere! It has to move to have strong leadership." She felt the daily injustices of life in Detroit keenly. Prejudice against African Americans remained palpable in many settings. Dock confided:

> Sometimes when you are going to the stores and you are not dressed the way they think you should be, they will look at you. If you go and you are going to buy jewelry especially, they are think[ing] I am looking at it to rob them. Or they show me cubic zirconium. "No, I don't want that. I want to look at this." I said, "Lady, do you know what, I have a charge card with nobody's name on it but mine. Nobody can use it but me. I can come in here and buy $13,500 with this card and it will be approved. I am not in here begging and I am not in here for stealing, I want to see what I asked for." You see, that because I am black, she thinks I can't afford it, you know what I am saying? They are like that.[9]

According to Glennette Taylor, Grand Rapids, Michigan, had changed for the worse. Grand Rapids transformed from a city boasting of a thriving industrial economy to a city with few opportunities for those in the working and lower middle class. Taylor watched as relatives with high school diplomas struggled to find work. A few decades earlier, a high school graduate felt certain of earning a living wage in the city. Taylor recounted, "It [Grand Rapids] has changed. There are a lot more changes that need to take place. I don't know if you are aware of the plants closing and the laying off here. There is quite a bit of change." Taylor blamed the loss of factory jobs on the global economy. She stated, "They keep taking it overseas or where they can get cheaper labor and it doesn't help us."[10]

Some of the boundaries between southern whites and blacks, stringently maintained by those in power for generations, began to break down in the late twentieth century. Barbara Purifoy-Seldon of Detroit related that her white Purifoy relatives urged the family to come together at a family reunion. Purifoy-Seldon, for whom African American history is a subject best confronted head-on, matter-of-factly referred to Purifoy as her "slave name." She did not mention attending the reunion.[11] This newfound sense of family across color lines usually resonated more strongly with white southerners, who may have wanted to release some of the guilt associated with the actions of their ancestors, than for mixed-race (legally and culturally most often categorized as simply African American) family members. The latter may not have found it as healthy to explore these family ties, although a few did attempt to claim this extended family as well.

Children of Migrants

JACQUIE LEWIS KEMP
Southfield, Michigan

Jacquie Lewis Kemp and I met in her home in Southfield, Michigan. The house was an expansive home of an inviting, contemporary architectural style typical of the Detroit suburbs. The great room where Kemp and I talked featured a sliding glass door providing views of a sunny backyard. The room, painted in neutral tones, had vaulted ceilings, and the stairway to the second floor opened onto the room, so that someone could look down into the room from the second floor. Kemp's walls were dotted with family photographs, including pictures of her son and a framed photograph of a magazine cover that featured her late father's image. We spoke during a series of interviews. I also interviewed Kemp's grandmother, a minister's wife from Flat Lick, Kentucky, and Kemp's mother, also from Flat Lick, who had worked in the Human Resources Department at Ford. Kemp exemplified the spirit of the migrant children, who were schooled by watching the struggles of the generations before them. Kemp, a highly educated woman, had succeeded in business despite a struggle with illness. As a working mother, she also faced a number of challenges in attempting to care for her child and attend to her business responsibilities.

I was born in Wayne, Michigan—March 30, 1962. I went to grade school in Westland and my parents didn't want me to go to middle school there. The middle school was rough. The neighbor was moving and building a new house and he said, "You should see mine." So they went and really liked it. He talked them into buying the acres next door. They had ten acres. In 1974, we moved.

My dad worked for General Motors and then he left and went to work for Ford Motor Company. She [Kemp's mother] worked for Ford. My [paternal] grandmother stayed with us and took care of us. Now my son spends time at my grandmother and grandfather's house.

[I attended] Lincoln High School. It was southeast of Ann Arbor. I went to the University of Michigan. My bachelor's is in communication and political science and my master's is in public policy. I finished in five years. I had an internship in Lansing. I worked for the Department of Commerce. I thought about working in politics, but my dad, when I was in high school, started his own business. So, um, I started thinking more and more about it. I had two cousins who went to U. of M. I talk to my son now and say you don't have to go there. Look here, look there, go here, go there, and he says, "Why?" I keep thinking—I only applied to one school. That was dumb.

It was a metal stamping business [Lewis Metal Stamping] in Highland Park. So I went there the Monday after graduation [in 1985]. I was his production control manager. I talked with the customers about their orders and, at that time, they implemented a new system and I wrote a computer program to help because it was taking too long with the new system. And they are still using it. After working there for two years, my dad said to come home and save my money to buy a house. So I did that. I moved home and then things got crazy at work, so I said, "Dad, I am going crazy, let me try my degree." He said, "Okay, go ahead," and I worked for the U.S. General Accounting Office for one year. It used to be in Detroit. They had one office in Detroit.

It [the new work] was interesting. It was different. It was so slow. I was up to here [Kemp points to her neck] before, but this was so slow. I didn't feel like I was impacting anything. Before, if I didn't ship parts, they couldn't build cars, but here it was just slow and I felt like I did better with hands on where I could get things done. I came back.

I worked there and then my dad died suddenly in 1991. When I was seven years old I was diagnosed diabetic. It was actually a good age. Taking the shot was like nothing, you just do it. It wasn't a big deal like when you are a teenager. My parents, both of them, always said, you can do whatever you want as long as you work hard. Work hard. Today, I still believe it. Every little hurdle, you just work around it. In November 2000, my kidneys failed as a result of my diabetes. I started dialysis in May and I didn't let anyone know—only my immediate family. I would carry the tube and put it under my desk. I had a separate door for the stuff. I would close the door and put the phone [on hold] and they would think I was on a personal call for a half hour and then I would do my exchange. A couple of times I would do it on the way to a meeting. I had to be there. I decided at the end of 2001, two weeks before the kidney transplant—my brother gave me his left kidney—I decided it was too much. I had a pancreas transplant in May. Because my immune system is so bad, I got West Nile disease in September. I am trying to figure out what I am going to do now.

I had a lady who took care of children in her home until he [Kemp's son] went to school and then I had a nanny for a while because my mom was still working. She was a live-in and I wanted somebody who really loved him and [would] play with him. But you can't do that with people. There were a couple of times when I was really jealous. There is a big dilemma now. Do you stay home with your kids or do you work and want to be able to afford the things you want? We travel and want to provide and afford things. With middle school, I am finding that he really needs me more now than when he was little. If I can work when he is in school, but be done in order to pick him up, that would be best.[12]

Like her mother and grandmother, both migrants from the South, Kemp has persevered against adversity. She watched as her mother struggled in the workplace without a degree (Willie Jean Clark Lewis did eventually finish her undergraduate work), and Kemp knew that she would attend college directly after high school. The granddaughter of a minister, she understood the power of education. Her grandmother, Lillian Clark, had set an example by graduating first in her class in high school. Kemp took over her father's business when he died in 1991, becoming president and CEO of Lewis Metal Stamping. Kemp also served on the Board of Visitors for Oakland University's School of Business Administration. Research conducted in 2007 showed Lewis Metal Stamping's thirty-four-thousand-square-foot building and various kinds of equipment up for sale, no doubt a victim of Detroit's precipitous downturn. In that year, Michigan had the highest unemployment rate in the nation.

The migrants' families ranged in size. A number of the respondents for this study had no children at all. Some of the women never married; others may have desired children but found themselves unable to reproduce. Some women had their hands full raising other family members—whether it be nieces and nephews, cousins, or very young siblings—and this duty precluded bearing additional children. The majority of migrants had the midsized families common to those living in urban settings in the second half of the twentieth century. Between 1880 and 1940, African American birth rates fell at a faster rate than that of whites. African American women, who had 7.5 births per woman in 1880, had just 3 per woman in 1940.[13] A few of the women in this study had large families—up to eleven children. Some migrants had thirty or forty grandchildren.

The migrants may have been the first generation in their families to employ active family planning techniques. A few women felt they did not get the guidance they needed from their mothers in this regard. Ruth Margaret Covington's mother never talked to her about sex, and she felt unsure about the processes involved even at the time of her marriage.[14] Although many birth control methods were illegal or inaccessible through regular shops, migrants gained advice from other women on how to limit family size. Annie Mae Prosper Hunt, born in 1909, had been told that having many children benefited a woman's health. She knew nothing about diaphragms, and, having been pregnant thirteen times, wished someone had explained them to her. She did know women who took bluing or quinine to induce abortions, but this often resulted in their death, and Hunt would not take such a drastic step. Hunt termed abortions "throwing away babies." Mary White had seven children while she was between the ages of twenty and twenty-eight, and then she put a stop to childbearing. She confided, "No birth control or anything at that time. But after the age of twenty-eight, I didn't have any more."[15] Olivia Watson Mitchell's doctor sterilized her, although she was not completely briefed on the procedure ahead of time. She repeatedly discussed the fact that she had had only two children; clearly, the sterilization unsettled her. The history of the forced sterilization of nonwhite women is a frightening aspect of American public policy, although it is unclear exactly why Mitchell's doctor felt compelled to perform the procedure. Mitchell stated with some ambivalence, "So, I guess if I hadn't have been stopped I'd a had twenty kids. So I'm glad I was stopped."[16]

African American migrants from the South have long faced discrimination based on myths regarding their family structure. In 1932, E. Franklin Frazier asserted that "deviant" family structures were carried north with southern black migrants, upsetting the underpinnings of black communities like that of Chicago. Frazier argued that the southern families proved more volatile than those of northern-born blacks. Other writers have penned arguments in the same vein. Daniel Patrick Moynihan's 1965 report, "The Negro Family: A Case for National Action," drawing extensively from Frazier's work, brought national attention to the plight of the black family. Slavery, of course, strained family ties for African Americans. Yet Frazier and Moynihan argued that familial instability transcended slavery. According to these authors and others, this family form existed in the South during the Reconstruction period and early twentieth century and was exported to the North during the First and Second Great Migrations. Nicholas Lemann's 1991 study of the Second Great Migration introduced a new generation of readers to the "tangled pathology" argument regarding the black family. Yet newer research weakens these assertions. Most convincingly, sociologist Steward E. Tolnay uses data from the Integrated Public Use Microdata Series (IPUMS) from the Social History Research Laboratory at the University of Minnesota to conclude that "northern urbanites with 'southern origins' actually exhibited more traditional family patterns—more children living with two parents, more ever-married women living with their spouses, and fewer never-married mothers" than the northern-born black population. While Tolnay notes that "there is little question that the family life of African Americans in northern cities has undergone a profound transformation during this century," the numbers clearly indicate that the changes in family pattern occurred *in* the northern setting—affecting both families of southern origin and families of northern origin—and the transformation of family was not a southern transplant. In fact, migrants had a "migrant advantage," actually having slightly more stable families than the native-born blacks. In 1940, Tolnay found that 74 percent of the children of northern origin parents living in northern and western central cities resided with two parents. In the same year, 76.4 percent of the children of southern origin parents living in these same cities lived in two-parent households. The rates of children living with two parents declined precipitously over the next fifty years, yet a slight southern advantage remained. Using the data for 1990, Tolnay discovered only 31.5 percent of African American children of northern origin parents and 37.7 percent of African American children with southern origin parents living with two parents.[17]

Tolnay's findings refute a long-standing mythology of a pathologically strained family structure among southern migrants. In my own set of respondents, while not a statistically random sampling, there were no never-married mothers. Some women bore children before marrying, and a significant number no longer lived with a spouse. This again fits with Tolnay, who finds "the percentage of all ever-married women living with their spouses fell from 71.4% to 46.7% between 1960 and 1990." Many of the women interviewed for this study had become widows in midlife, never to marry again. Very few of the elderly women still resided with their husbands, who had a shorter life expectancy than their wives. A large number of the respondents had divorced or separated from their husbands at early ages, and many of the men played a limited role in their children's lives. Note too that the women of this study had largely defied the odds, some living decades beyond their life expectancy. Thus the women in *Making a Way out of No Way*, interviewed between 2000 and 2007, represented a dwindling subset of Americans. Fewer and fewer Second Great Migration migrants remained, especially those who had made the migration as adults during the 1940s and 1950s.

Tolnay's study points to an interesting supposition—if southern migrants had lower education levels than northern blacks, yet still had more stable families, higher rates of workplace participation, higher overall incomes, lower rates of unemployment, lower levels of poverty, and lower rates of reliance on welfare, might not personal attitudes have factored into their relative success? Perhaps there was some degree of selective migration, such that only those best suited for taking on the northern work left the South. Presumably the southern migrants would tend to be younger, able-bodied people in the prime of their work life. Yet these differences might not explain the southerners' success. Indeed, personal attitudes might have had a statistical effect. The attitudes could include the inclination to accept difficult work and even the consolation of religious faith. Tolnay proposes, "Perhaps it [southern success in the North] was because their economic opportunities in the North compared favorably with their recollections of the southern labor market with its lower wages and more powerful racial discrimination." Or, Tolnay suggests, "they had not yet had time to become permanently discouraged by the obstacles they faced in the urban marketplace."[18]

Through the example of their tenacious parents, the children of migrants learned the value of hard work. Due to positive changes in the hiring practices within American companies, this generation proved statistically more able to locate jobs that would secure them a place in the middle class. However, the children of migrants also faced daunting health challenges, due in part to the environmental concerns facing many black neighborhoods and the physical dangers resulting from criminal activity. A few of the narrators' children had themselves tangled with the law.

Like mothers the world over, migrant mothers struggled alongside their children during life crises, and rejoiced with them when their dreams came true. Mattie Bell Fritz's son lived across the street from her own home, and she worried about him. Fritz used the unobstructed view from her living room picture window to keep an eye on his comings and goings. During one of my visits to her home, she peered out at him, expressing general dismay. Ella Sims lamented the fact that one of her grandsons had had ten children with multiple women. She also remembered the troubled time she had with her son "when he killed that man, went to prison—first he went to a mental institution."[19]

A number of the migrants' children died untimely deaths. Mary White had survived all but three of her seven children. Simone Landry lost two of her three daughters. Faith Richmond of Boston, mother of seven, nursed one child during an extended illness. The son, one of Richmond's two gay children, received unwavering support from his mother. Richmond recalled, "Sam came back home in 1988. I took care of him until he passed. I put him in a hospice the last few weeks. He would keep you laughing. What a funny boy." Sam's death occurred in 1991; Richmond's son John died in 1992.

Some of Richmond's other children have had more successful trajectories. One daughter had her master's degree and directed an intercultural program in a midwestern city. Another graduated from culinary arts school and moved to Georgia.[20]

Ruth Margaret Covington of Detroit had shepherded three children through college. As a divorcée, Covington shouldered the majority of the parental responsibilities. Her son, who had attended Shaw University and Marquette University, pursued a career in asbestos management. A daughter, Deborah, who resided in Texas, attended Wayne County Community College and became a housewife; a second daughter, Zenara, earned degrees from both the University of Michigan and Pennsylvania State University. Zenara Covington, a speech pathologist, had worked for Wayne State University. She subsequently launched her own catering business.[21] Ogretta McNeil also had highly successful children. One son, an ordained minister, lived in New York City, where he directed a peace organization, while another son worked as a professional photographer in Oakland, California.[22] Alverrine Parker, mother of two, expressed pride over her children's college graduations and incredulity over the previous generation's ability to raise large families. Parker stated, "God is really good to us. And He's really brought the black race from a long way. Yeah, He did. But [what] we had to go through with raising your families and children. I looked to see what my dad had made with seven kids—I don't know how he did it." Parker's oldest son, a mechanical engineer, had worked for Goodyear and Ford; her younger son, a businessman, also worked as a barber.[23]

Advice from the Migrants to a Younger Generation

Prior to the interviews, I wrote a list of questions as a guide. After a few interviews, I typically reviewed the questions before each session, and kept the typed questions hidden away in my book bag. If the question list had been visible to the narrators, it may have discouraged them from taking the conversation in their own directions. I took a few notes during the interview, writing down follow-up questions while talking with the narrator so that I would not forget to cover them. With fairly unobtrusive recording equipment, the interview proceeded in a casual manner, much like a conversation. As is now the practice of many oral historians, I allowed the narrator to lead the story as much as possible. I found that, although venturing down an unexpected conversational path, the narrator and I most often covered all of the topics outlined on my guide. Given the one-to-two-hour space of an interview, the narrators found plenty of time to discuss the major storylines of their lives. I would begin by saying something to the effect of "tell me about your life and the work you did, and let's start at the beginning." A few inadvertent themes emerged from this methodology. The last question I often asked—"Is there anything else you would like us to know?" or, sometimes, "Is there anything else you think people should understand about women and work?"—offered a serious moment of reflection for the narrators, an invitation for them to speak directly to a younger generation concerning life lessons. The women gave the gift of their stories in order to instruct younger people about the American past and provide guidance. The narrators' roles as teachers were enhanced by the fact that students often accompanied me to the interview sessions, in a few instances asking questions near the end of the exchange.

The advice offered contained repeated themes. A number of women wanted to discuss gender roles. While almost all of the migrants had worked outside of their homes for pay as adults, these respondents still valued a division between male and female spheres. Each of the married women deferred to her husband's authority to some extent, or at least regarded her husband as the head of the household during the marriage. Rosa Young, born in the mid-1920s, considered it acceptable if a woman worked "a little" outside of the house, as long as her husband maintained a position as the prime breadwinner and ultimate household authority. Young herself held a host of jobs, many of them factory positions. "I think the women should stay feminine," she offered, "the feminine role, you know. And, uh, it's all right to work, but then [not] still try to take over the man's role."[24] Florence Allison concurred that some boundaries ought to be maintained, insisting, "I don't think women should be a truck driver. To me, that's a man job."[25] Texan Annie Mae Prosper Hunt offered an extended discussion of feminism in her interviews with author and activist Ruthe Winegarten. Despite Hunt's pride in raising her children by herself, she strongly believed in differentiated roles for men and women. She insisted, "But I don't want no equal rights. I don't want to be no man."[26]

As this book concerned labor and the Second Great Migration, a number of respondents chose to conclude with a discussion of general advice for workers. Rebecca Strom of Boston counseled, "Just find the thing you like and hang on there with it. Some jobs it's not really the job, but the people you work with. If you can get past those obstacles, you could be happy anywhere."[27] In a similar vein, Creamy McKinney suggested that women should "be on time, do their work, the best they can do, and be kind to your customers, your people. Always be kind, speak, say hello, and just be friendly, you know?"[28] Much of the advice drew on Christian religious beliefs, which figured centrally in most migrants' lives and attitudes. Ruth Margaret Covington concluded, "Do the best you can and do it as you would do to the glory of God. Always help whenever you can and take time out for people, because you never know how life is going to end." Jacqueline Dock offered, "Do unto others as you would do unto yourself." For believer Minnie Chatman, too, the most important teachings stemmed from the Bible. "If you look in the Bible, it will tell you, do unto others as you would have done unto," Chatman stated passionately. "And if you do that, I believe He will bless you because He has blessed me and I feel so good about it, and I just be happy and I can talk until it makes you cry sometimes." Addie Smith, born in North Carolina in 1924, included memories of injustice and practical advice in her statement:

> Anything you go into, say, you go into a private home to work, I think you should be honest and do your job well, and be fair. And I think you should be straightforward with the person you're working for and they should be the same with you. You should be treated humanly, you know. Some people don't do that because down South, they hardly do things like that, you know. You wanna come in the back door or do this—I don't know what they do now. But back then, I used to see people when they go to work, they had to go in the back, because as a child, I followed a lot of different things that were, you know, not right.[29]

Another line of commentary included admonitions aimed directly at a younger, black audience. Aspects of recent trends rattled the aging migrants, who felt they might lead to negative repercussions for the black community. Alverrine Parker of Grand Rapids bemoaned the fashion trend of low-riding pants, fearing that it revealed a disassociation between the young men who adopted the style and the larger American community. Parker felt the young men simply did not care about negative attitudes towards the style choice, and perhaps had little regard for their own future. Parker also expressed incredulity at continued racist statements made by those in power, and specifically referenced Senator Trent Lott's 2002 praise for Strom Thurmond's 1948 campaign for president on a segregationist platform. Parker also posited that blacks felt differently from how white Americans did regarding the violence of the terrorist acts of 9-11. Many African Americans had witnessed other violent acts, or had heard tales about how violence born of cultural hatred had impacted the lives of family members. Violence was perhaps less surprising to these Americans than to others. Black history, both that of lived experience and that learned through study and family stories, added a number of complex layers to many African Americans' processing of the events of 9-11.[30]

Conclusion

"My life is not dull and is not exciting; it's just a life."[31]

"That's about my life. I just worked. I didn't want no problems with nobody. I think people have to like me because I was honest."[32]

"I think . . . we have God in our hearts, and if we didn't, I don't know how we would've made it. I really don't."[33]

"The journey has been a good one."[34]

The women interviewed for this study were not overly surprised to have a request for a formal interview. One of the women had fielded such a request before. Others had books of African American history lining their coffee tables and bookshelves. Living through the civil rights movement, the women had long ago learned the importance of African American history, and the transformative aspect of adding new voices to the pages of our national story. Yet many summarized their lives humbly. Annie Evelyn Collins characterized her life story by saying, "It's just a life," and Avezinner Dean concluded, "I just worked." They could not conclude their oral histories with one meaningful anecdote or an overarching tale of triumph. Social historians search out the usual story, the typical person, in order to get a sense of an age or a movement. The women featured here, who migrated north during the Second Great Migration, did not earn great fame, and their lives were filled with hours devoted to paid and unpaid labor. Sociologist Patricia Hill Collins points out, "In the context of Black family studies that either castigate or glorify them, the theme of how hard Black women *work* is often overlooked."[35] Scholars have heretofore devoted inadequate space to the black migrant women's lived reality. These courageous women expressed agency in creating their lives, choosing the best options for themselves and their families.

African Americans rarely use the term "American Dream." The phrase calls to mind immigration by choice, yet the ancestors of the vast majority of African Americans living in the United States in the twentieth century had traveled to this country on slave ships. Malcolm X provocatively declared, "I don't see any American Dream; I see an American nightmare." His remarks stood in stark contrast to those of Martin Luther King, who, while unblinkingly acknowledging

American imperfections, did speak of a great dream of racial integration in the decades to come. In the same 1964 speech, "The Bullet or the Ballot," Malcolm X argued that he and other blacks, overtly relegated to the edges of society, were not even really Americans.[36] In America, if one's lived experience does not presently represent the American Dream, one at least wants to have the freedom to pursue it. Kept even from joining the race, some African Americans, including Malcolm X, critiqued the whole package of the American promise. Was it real? Could it be sustained? Based on whose labor and at whose expense had prosperity for millions come to fruition?

Black female migrants would never associate the experiences of their ancestors with the American Dream. Indeed, these male and female ancestors, many born into slavery, had lived a true American nightmare. For the migrants themselves, life stood somewhere between dream and nightmare. The migrants experienced racially motivated violence and lived with the threat of physical reprisal during much of their lives. The neat streets of small single-family homes they settled into in Detroit or the multicolored, tightly arranged rows of three deckers they claimed in Dorchester remained preferable to the Jim Crow South for most migrants, yet violence still factored into daily existence in the northern cities. Neighbors rioted in the streets, the migrants repeatedly clashed with white urban residents, and black city dwellers feared indiscriminate police officers, quick to resort to force. Migrants frequently found the doors of employers and landlords shut to their inquiries. Yet they took advantage of the few doorways they were allowed to pass through, making the most of every opportunity, whatever its size. The women migrants crafted lives of great meaning—successful lives—and provided their children even broader access to American opportunities.

Migrants like Lillian Clark enjoyed making quilts in their spare time. For Clark, the quilts represented a great achievement, and were a testament to her housewifery skills. She exclaimed, "I got one that was begun in 1936 and I gave it to my daughter. This is hers [pointing to an elaborate quilt]. I made this one. The names on it are embroidered on the quilt. We did a lot of that. We did everything that you were supposed to do at home."[37] In the late 1990s, the Charles H. Wright Museum of African American History in Detroit launched an impressive exhibit showcasing modern quilts made by African American women. The myriad of quilts, from the popular crazy quilt to patterns that drew on designs devised during slavery, dazzled in their complexity and the sheer determination they required. The artists used a broad array of fabrics, from the newest synthetic fibers to scraps handed down by family members over generations. Rubie Wilburn Evans, growing up in the Gholson community of central Texas, remembered her mother piecing elaborate quilts of simple cotton. "They were usually made of cotton scraps. And they were fancy. Different, stars and first one thing and then the other," Evans related. Her mother also made "britches quilts" for Evans's brothers; these heavy quilts were made of the boys' worn and outgrown pants.[38] Ultimately, the cloth chosen did not much matter. A seamstress could use even the oldest or most careworn piece of cotton and produce a stunning coverlet, for it was the artist's sewing skill and the overall design of the piece that truly affected the end result. In a manner of speaking, the same could also be said of the African American women's lives. Supplied with only scraps from the scrap bag, the women had very little raw material with which to work. Yet the end product, of their own careful devising, proved impressive.

"I'm glad that you want to write on black women, though, because we have been working all our lives and raising our children," commented Alverrine Parker. Parker asserted that African American women had stories worth compiling and analyzing. In the midst of the seemingly endless work that is women's lot, few have the opportunity for extended reflection, let alone the time to record their insights for posterity.[39] Working with the women whose stories fill this book proved to be one of the great honors of my life. More than any other research study I have yet embarked on, this work proved personally and professionally satisfying. I hope that I have sufficiently captured the wisdom imparted by these women, true teachers, who have generously shared their life stories.

Like the women who rallied in the 1943 protests of the racist hiring practices at Detroit's industrial plants, the women interviewed for this study maintained a clear vision of the discriminatory practices rampant in America. While the northern cities did not have quite as extensive a variety of legal racial restrictions as the South, discrimination flourished, and, in fact, seemed more poignant to many migrants than the southern variety. If such deep cultural fissures existed in the North, where did hope reside? The northern cities were the ultimate destination for the migrants; they had no new places to go in trying to seek out true democracy. The women had spent their lives moving. First their families had moved within the South, in search of better farms, looking perhaps for a setting where the white landowner more fairly shared profits with his sharecroppers or kept the books more carefully at the plantation store. Then the migrants tried various southern cities, drawn by urban life and economic opportunity. Mostly relegated to low-paying service jobs in southern urban settings, they ventured north, in search of higher wages, a lessened threat of violence, and a chance to hold one's head up a little higher. No one really thought they would find Nirvana in the North. But it would have been nice for the North to have been a bit more hospitable than it turned out to be.

Black women migrants headed north for a variety of reasons. Many accompanied husbands or fathers as the men sought placement in the northern factories. Some set off unaccompanied by men. Women migrants knew they had limited hope of finding their own industrial jobs in the 1940s, although they pursued them. When the women finally broke into industrial work in the 1950s and 1960s, such jobs did not offer a clear route to a stable life as they once had. Many of the families were just making do. Were the women content with the fact that their male family members had access to better paying, yet initially racially restricted, industrial jobs? Contentment was not an emotion expressed by the migrants in these interviews. They were pleased with the increased options for the men in their lives, but the negative attitudes towards black women, so apparent in hiring practices, grated terribly. Women living in cities with greater options for black men seemed to have more stable marriages, although the oral history sample size and lack of randomization cannot offer definitive answers regarding this point.

The migrant women moved north because they had a number of problems to solve and they had learned to address problems by moving. The decision to move proved agonizing, even when millions of other African Americans were also moving northward. The move had many elements that are compelling to view from the women's viewpoint. The Second Great Migration is by no means a male-oriented story, although it has been portrayed that way.

Unfortunately, the migration did not provide a remedy to all of these families' difficulties. Nor were the migrants utterly convinced that they had made the right decision. The migrants' children moved "back" South, to a region some of them had known only through visits. A few migrants themselves planned permanent moves to the South.

Memoirist M. J. Andersen, who relocated to the East Coast, writes of a longing for her former South Dakota world. She extends the lessons of her tale to more Americans. Anderson posits, "The great tragedy of our era was uprooting and separation. But the American variety of this experience largely goes unnoted. Our brand of exile is assumed to be voluntary; our separation from family and place is believed to be freely chosen."[40] Home proves to be a wily concept for Americans. Many of us must relocate for economic reasons, but we couch these moves in the language of choice, which belittles the imperative behind them. Moving, especially across regions, proves emotionally unsettling. And the feeling of dislocation does not abate quickly, but rather persists for decades. Thus the migrants offered detailed memories of their childhood homes. They recalled each variety of plant in their mothers' kitchen gardens. Then, too, with the exception of Native Americans, all people in the United States are living in a state of continental diaspora. (Native Americans, of course, have faced relocation within their home continent.) The African diaspora, with the complication of slavery, has bequeathed a tangled legacy to the descendants of slaves. Relatively few African Americans have found relief by moving to Africa.[41] For African American migrants, different varieties of American regional racism complicated the unsettled feelings of displacement. Where then is home, where the promised land? At the dawn of Reconstruction, African Americans set out searching for a place where they could count on being treated equitably. The search continued during the First and Second Great Migrations. Most African Americans are yet to find complete social and economic justice.

The problems of working women still prove vexing. African American women made great strides in the job market during the last decades of the twentieth century. Many obtained college degrees and moved into management positions in business and civil service. Although most black women left domestic work behind, too many still were relegated to low-paying service jobs in settings like hospitals, day cares, and retail sales, performing low-status tasks with little chance for advancement. It remained difficult to combine work and care for family. In the early twenty-first century, the United States remained one of the few industrialized nations not to offer paid maternity leave to working mothers. The Family and Medical Leave Act, authorized by President Bill Clinton in 1993, did not go far enough, offering only unpaid leave to employees who gave birth to or adopted a child, needed to provide care for a relative, or were themselves ill. And to qualify for this benefit, employees were required to work for a job site with at least fifty other employees, and the employee had to have worked in the position for a full year before receiving benefits. As seen in the oral histories, migrant women often made great sacrifices in order to provide for their children or other relatives under their care. The migrants undertook this work without even the limited legal assistance of the 1993 Family and Medical Leave Act. A good many of them worked for cash wages, and were thus not eligible for social security based on their own labor or workers' compensation payments. Caretaking responsibilities remained whether or not the federal government provided a safety net for caregivers.

It is truly important to expand our historical lexicon to include voices like those of the migrants. Their story is the story of America—the quest for a better life, the pursuit of freedom, the perseverance of hope despite all odds. Although the migrants did not live the American Dream, they never gave up on it, and this makes them truly Americans. In history courses across the United States, the First and Second Great Migration are accorded brief mention, and, at times, overlooked altogether. Yet the migration transformed life in northern cities, and by extension, American life and culture as a whole. We need to take care to guard against any further loss of the artifacts and documents related to the African American past. Because the history had been disregarded, important documents were misplaced, and our potential understanding of African American history is degraded. Unfortunately, those who hold personal memories of the Second Great Migration are now slipping from the earth, and we have fewer stories to collect. My thoughts go frequently to the women who trusted their stories to me, yet who will never see this book in publication. For Esther Woods and others, the book remains a crucial legacy. Sociologist Sudhir Alladi Venkatesh argues for the importance of the human voice in attesting to the histories of marginalized peoples:

> Archives exist, but rarely do they capture the nuances of an American group whose life has been so selectively represented and so consistently expunged from full, meaningful participation in the national record. Indeed, any formally available source of information can never document a history defined by contest, resistance, and at times evasion of a public gaze. It is the human voice that must be carefully heard; it is personal and collective memory that must be tilled with rigor and then matched against the formal record.[42]

The women migrants made a way out of no way. Even when the way proved elusive, they forged on. By sharing their stories, they gave others a weighty gift. We must listen, treasuring the tales, rejoicing in the women's personal fortitude, and working towards the elimination of systematic prejudice within American society. The women expressed agency in creating meaningful lives out of the limited opportunities available. Comforted by deep religious beliefs, a strong upbringing, and the continued support of extended family and close friends, the women not only survived, but did so with considerable grace and dignity.

The author's early exposure to housework. Photograph by Madelon Krissoff.

Acknowledgments

Any study that relies on oral history entails collaboration. Scores of people volunteered their time to this project, and a number also joined on as paid research assistants. I am enormously grateful to the forty women who shared their life stories with me. They are: Florence Allison, Annie Benning, Minnie Chatman, Lillian Clark, Annie Collins, Ruth Margaret Covington, Zenara Covington, Avezinner Dean, Jacqueline Dock, Mattie Bell Fritz, Sandra Gantt, Dotty Goldsberry, Alberta Hardy, Bernita Howard, Beatrice Jackson, Jacquie Lewis Kemp, Fannie Mae Kennedy, Thelma Lane, Lottie Lewis, Willie Jean Clark Lewis, Simone Landry, Creamy McKinney, Ogretta McNeil, Anniese Moten, Gussie Nash, Alverrine Parker, Barbara Purifoy-Seldon, Faith Richmond, Lillie Shelby, Ella Sims, Inez Smith, Addie Smith, Mary Smith, Lois Stevens, Rebecca Strom, Glenette Taylor, Liddie Williams, Mary White, Esther Woods, and Rosa Young. In signing their "Deed of Gift," one of the two release forms required by the guidelines of the Oral History Association, the women truly provided me and all of the book's readers with a gift. They shared their wisdom and their stories, understanding the historical importance of their memories. Unfortunately, a number of the women have passed away during the eight years it took me to prepare this work. I am thankful that I had the chance to record the interviews and add them to the historical record. The memories of these women broaden our understanding of the Second Great Migration in countless ways.

Generous grants from Worcester State College, the Bentley Historical Library at the University of Michigan, the Schlesinger Library at Harvard University, and the Institute for Oral History at Baylor University aided the work. Worcester State College's minigrant program provided the project with multiple grants, funding trips to the Midwest, oral history equipment purchases, and transcription services. Bentley Historical Library awarded me the Bordin/Gillette Researcher Travel Fellowship for 2000–2001. I traveled to Ann Arbor and used the library's collections to better understand the reaction of the Detroit and Grand Rapids branches of the Urban League to the migration, as well as the role played by Rev. Charles Hill.[1] Bentley's William Wallach proved very supportive of the endeavor. At Baylor University, where I was the 2007–2008 Research Fellow in Oral History, discussions on oral history with Lois Myers, Elinor Mazé, and Stephen Sloan enriched my understanding of oral history. Lois Myers located oral history transcripts in the processing stages for my perusal. She also connected me with key secondary sources. Oral histories collected by Lois Myers and Rebecca Sharpless, who had left Baylor for the faculty at Texas Christian University, added to my understanding of African American life in the Southwest. Ellen Brown of the Texas Collection assisted me with accessing the collections of archived oral memoirs. Becky Shulda welcomed me warmly to Waco, and helped me locate housing and all other necessities. The library staffs at Worcester State College, the Grand Rapids Public Library, the Schlesinger Library of Women's History at Harvard University, the Walter E. Reuther Library at Wayne State University, and the Detroit Public Library all helped me procure key primary and secondary sources. Thank you to Nancy Cott and Kathryn Allamong Jacob at the Schlesinger Library and William Wallach at the Bentley Historical Library for their interest in acquiring my recordings and transcripts for their collections.

My students Elizabeth Cote, Audrey Kemp, Patricia Burke, Joan Goss, and Anna Gazos assisted with transcription. Cote, Kemp, Burke, and Goss accompanied me on some of the interviews, and occasionally interjected questions of their own, in order to learn the craft of interviewing and to obtain a clearer understanding of the interview for the benefit of their transcription. Using the interview guide, Elizabeth Cote also interviewed additional narrators on her own. Cote began working on the project during the summer of her freshman year of college, and completed her work as an interview assistant and transcriptionist during law school. It has been an honor to have played a part in her educational journey. Audrey Kemp and Anna Gazos also went on to graduate school, and I know their empathy and devotion will lead them to make a great impact on the world. Anna Gazos played a special role, for she also helped me to care for my children. Anna listened with a smile and offered comments as I would summarize the day's writing progress to her. I appreciate her quiet grace, her keen insights, and her rapport with my sons. Thank you to the extraordinary Marilyn Mullen, David and Peter's preschool teacher, for extending an offer to help me with the children during the final phase of the book.

Personal introductions to interviewees came from Elizabeth Cote and her mother, banker Kay Jones (Detroit), my dear friend Esther Woods (Grand

Rapids), my family friends Estelle Leven (Grand Rapids) and Lynne Golomb (Chicago), Worcester city administrator Shirley Wright, Professor Ogretta McNeil of Holy Cross College in Worcester, and Worcester State College students Patricia Burke (Worcester/Boston) and Aiwa Lewis (Boston). These introductions were crucial in this work.

For many years, my colleagues at Worcester State College, including but not limited to Steve Corey, Maureen Power, Tuck Amory, Julie Frechette, Annalise Fonza, Catherine Wilcox-Titus, Kristin Waters, Karen Woods Weierman, and Charlotte Haller have listened to me discuss the evolution of this project, offering their support and insights. Charlotte Haller and Steve Corey read drafts. Department administrator Linda Sweeney assisted me with photocopies of my notes and manuscript drafts. Thank you to all the students who encouraged my research and discussed the migrations with me in class. Panelists and commentators at a number of conferences provided key observations. Janis Appier, Sarah Stage, Richard Pierce, Bruce Stave, Leslie Brown, and Susan Tucker proved particularly helpful. Eileen Boris and Donna Gabaccia offered their support of the project. Steve and Amy Miller and Chico and Daniella Trevisan offered me housing during my research.

University Press of Mississippi editor-in-chief Craig Gill impressed me with his approach to the book from the outset. The anonymous reader provided outstanding insights on both the initial chapter drafts and the complete manuscript, which helped me polish the book. The copy editor, Carol Cox, brought her prodigious talents to the work, and I am grateful for the care she took with the text.

My family of origin, Madelon, Joel, Jonathan, and Sarah Krissoff have gone above and beyond in offering emotional support. My mother served as the book's very first reader. My grandparents, Abe and Sylvia Krissoff, spoke with me about the Second Great Migration and memories of Esther Woods. My husband, Chris Boehm, has discussed ideas with me, read chapter drafts, solved emergency technological issues, and obligingly watched our children single-handedly as I headed off for various interviews and far-flung libraries. He has been there every step of the way, and I look forward to making our continued journey hand-in-hand. My children, David and Peter Krissoff Boehm, have put up with their mom's project "about the ladies" with grace. Their unstoppable inquisitiveness and delight in the whole world has been a continued inspiration.

Finally, I wish to acknowledge the profound contribution made to this book by Esther Woods. She was a mentor, beloved elder, and respected friend, and her life was the inspiration for this work.

Notes

1. Approximately one and a half million additional people had made the transition during the First Great Migration, 1914–1930. Millions of white southerners also journeyed north in the twentieth century. Note that the numbers are rough estimates, given the mobility of the migrants.

2. See works including Joel Grossman, *Land of Hope: Chicago, Black Southerners, and the Great Migration* (Chicago: University of Chicago Press, 1989); Joe William Trotter, Jr., ed., *The Great Migration in Historical Perspective: New Dimensions of Race, Class, and Gender* (Bloomington: Indiana University Press, 1991); Joe William Trotter, Jr., *Black Milwaukee: The Making of an Industrial Proletariat, 1915–1945* (Urbana: University of Illinois Press, 1985); Peter Gottlieb, *Making Their Own Way: Southern Blacks' Migration to Pittsburgh, 1916–1930* (Urbana: University of Illinois Press, 1987). Exceptions are mostly written by women and written in recent years. See notably Kimberley L. Phillips, *AlabamaNorth: African-American Migrants, Community, and Working-Class Activism in Cleveland, 1915–45* (Urbana: University of Illinois Press, 1999); Katherine J. Curtis White, "Women in the Great Migration," *Social Science History* 29 (Fall 2005): 413–455; Katherine J. Curtis White, Kyle Crowder, Stewart E. Tolnay, and Robert M. Adelman, "Race, Gender, and Marriage: Destination Selection During the Great Migration," *Demography* 42 (May 2005): 215–241; Elizabeth Clark-Lewis, *Living In, Living Out: African American Domestics and the Great Migration* (New York: Kodnasha America, 1991); Gertrude Lemke-Santangelo, *Abiding Courage: African American Migrant Women and the East Bay Community* (Chapel Hill: University of North Carolina Press, 1996).

3. Betty Friedan, *The Feminine Mystique* (New York: Norton, 1983). In her later years, Friedan recognized the limits that access to work had in curing American sexism. Friedan characterized the work/family balance as the new "problem that had no name." See Simeon Moss, "Life Is More than Work," *Cornell News*, February 23, 2001, accessed at www.news.cornell.edu.

4. Patricia Hill Collins, *Black Feminist Thought: Knowledge, Consciousness, and the Politics of Empowerment,* 2nd ed. (New York: Routledge, 2000), 18.

5. The pogroms involved physical attacks, often condoned or even aided by government officials and police, that resulted in deaths, rapes, and pillaging within Jewish neighborhoods. Most Russian Jews were forbidden from living in major cities and prohibited from farming, so they tended to live in villages and make a living where they could from small business.

6. For more discussion of the term "agency," see philosophical discussions such as Robert Kane, "Free Agency and the Crisis of Nature," *Journal of Consciousness Studies* 12 (2005): 46–53. In history, see works on slavery including Eugene D. Genovese, *Roll, Jordan, Roll: The World the Slaves Made* (New York: Vintage Books, 1972).

7. See Peter Gottlieb, "Rethinking the Great Migration: The Perspective from Pittsburgh," in Joe W. Trotter, Jr., ed., *The Great Migration in Historical Perspective*, 77.

8. See "Spelman's Independent Scholars," http://www.spelman.edu/academics/enrichment/independent/index.shtml.

9. "Housework," performed by Carol Channing and written by Sheldon Harnick, *Free to Be . . . You and Me*, Artista Records, 1972 (record) and 1983 (compact disc).

10. Darlene Clark Hine, "International Trends in Women's History and Feminism: Black Women's History, White Women's History: The Juncture of Race and Class," *Journal of Women's History* (Fall 1992): 4, 125–133.

11. For more on the construction of racial categories, see the PBS film *African American Lives*, 2005.

12. Minnie Chatman, interview with Lisa Krissoff Boehm and Elizabeth Cote, Detroit, Michigan, October 19, 2001.

13. See Luisa Passerini, *Fascism in Popular Memory: The Cultural Experience of the Turin Working Class* (New York: Cambridge University Press, 1987), 8.

14. One narrator may have been surprised to greet a white interviewer at the door of her home. I believe the other narrators understood that I was white before the meetings. In the neighborhood of Detroit where this narrator resided, just seeing a white person walking down the street could evoke comment. One could safely assume most of the day's interactions would be of an intraracial nature.

15. Some Jews consider it improper to ask another to work in their place on the Sabbath. In the shtetl villages of Eastern Europe, some families used a hired hand known colloquially and, I feel, disrespectfully as a "Sabbath goy" to light the fire when this was forbidden on the Sabbath. Jews could, if they wished, offer similar services to Christians on their Sabbath. And Jews could provide services such as money lending, forbidden by Christianity at times, but not expressly forbidden to religious Jews by their faith.

On a personal note, I was briefly hired as a cook to work with the wife of a rabbi. She was to teach me her recipes, and I would work in her stead on the Sabbath. Having never practiced the Sabbath as a day of complete rest, I was thrilled to have the work. I also wanted to learn the special recipes. But I was promptly fired when my religion was discovered. The rabbi's wife would not hire a Jewish cook as a Sabbath breaker, even a nonobservant one.

16. Mary Catherine Bateson, *Composing a Life* (New York: Plume, 1990), 10.

17. Harold S. Kushner, foreword, in Victor Frankl, *Man's Search for Meaning* (Boston: Beacon Press, 2006), x.

18. Robert Ross refers to the philosophical discussion surrounding the existence of "choice under constraint" in his work. In this case, sweatshop workers choose to work for unfair wages rather than starve. Such choice cannot really be said to be a true choice, but

a choice under extreme constraint. See Robert Ross, *Slaves to Fashion: Poverty and Abuse in the New Sweatshops* (Ann Arbor: University of Michigan Press, 2004), 324–325. Many scholars would argue that all of our choices are mitigated by constraints, although the levels of impediment are heavier as one proceeds downward on the rungs of class.

CHAPTER ONE. MEMORIES OF THE SOUTHERN CHILDHOOD

1. Elizabeth Clark-Lewis, *Living In, Living Out: African American Domestics and the Great Migration* (New York: Kodnasha America, 1994), 198.

2. Judith Rollins, *Between Women: Domestics and Their Employers* (Philadelphia: Temple University Press, 1985), 16, 24.

3. Evelyn Nakano Glenn, *Issei, Nisei, War Bride: Three Generations of Japanese American Women in Domestic Service* (Philadelphia: Temple University Press, 1986), x.

4. For this reason, a number of the interviews done for this study will be archived at the Bentley Historical Library at the University of Michigan and the Schlesinger Library at Harvard University.

5. Sherna Berger Gluck, "What's So Special About Women: Women's Oral History," in David Dunaway and Willa Baum, eds., *Oral History: An Interdisciplinary Anthology* (Nashville: American Association for State and Local History, 1984), as quoted in Rebecca Sharpless, "The History of Oral History," Thomas L. Charlton, Lois E. Myers, and Rebecca Sharpless, eds., *The History of Oral History: Foundations and Methodology* (Lanham, MD: AltaMira Press, 2007), 18.

6. Rick Halpern, "Oral History and Labor History: A Historiographical Assessment After Twenty-Five Years," *Journal of American History*, 85, no. 2 (September 1998): 603, 605.

7. See Tera W. Hunter, *To 'Joy My Freedom: Southern Black Women's Lives and Labors After the Civil War* (Cambridge, MA: Harvard University Press, 1997); David Katzman, *Seven Days a Week: Women and Domestic Service in Industrializing America* (New York: Oxford University Press, 1978); Pierrette Hondagneu-Sotelo, *Doméstica: Immigrant Workers Cleaning and Caring in the Shadows of Affluence* (Berkeley: University of California Press, 2001); Susan Tucker, *Telling Memories Among Southern Women: Domestic Workers and Their Employers in the Segregated South* (Baton Rouge: Louisiana State University Press, 1988); Clark-Lewis, *Living In, Living Out: African American Domestics and the Great Migration*; Gertrude Lemke-Santangelo, *Abiding Courage: African American Migrant Women and the East Bay Community* (Chapel Hill: University of North Carolina Press, 1996).

8. In 2006, for the annual meeting of the Organization of American Historians in Washington, D.C., I organized a panel to look at recent scholarship on women migrants. Some of the cutting-edge research includes the papers by Leslie Brown (Washington University of St. Louis), "'The Most Striking Phenomenon of the Urban Negro Population': African American Women and an Even Greater Migration" and Janis Appier (University of Tennessee), "'Daughters of the Road': Public Identities versus Private Memories of Female Transients During the Great Depression," presented for this panel. My own paper was entitled "Oral Histories with African American Female Migrants: The Issues of Agency and Identity." See Joanne Meyerowitz, *Women Adrift: Independent Wage Earners in Chicago, 1880–1930* (Chicago: University of Chicago Press, 1988).

9. Labor histories of women accord the battles scant space, and traditional labor histories overlook the distinctly female story of the activism. Unfortunately, the work of Robert Korstad and Nelson Lichtenstein, "Opportunities Found and Lost: Labor, Radicals, and the Early Civil Rights Movement," an important reminder of the often-forgotten 1940s civil rights protests, does not consider the way in which Michigan-based activism was solidly oriented towards a fight for *women's* rights. Even the critical work of historian Karen Tucker Anderson can create a false impression. Anderson adds a missing page to the understanding of labor history with her work on the black women who gained access to industrial plants across the nation during World War II. Anderson's focus on black women in war work necessarily concentrates her work on a minority of black women. In Detroit, according to Anderson's own figures, nonwhite women held only one thousand of the ninety-six thousand jobs occupied by women in major war industries by February 1943. Robert Korstad and Nelson Lichtenstein, "Opportunities Found and Lost: Labor, Radicals, and the Early Civil Rights Movement," *Journal of American History* 75, no. 3 (December 1988): 786–811; Karen Tucker Anderson, "Last Hired, First Fired: Black Women Workers During World War II," *Journal of American History* 69, no. 1 (June 1982): 82–97.

10. Not all historians of migration break the Great Migration in two. It makes sense to me to refer to the years 1914–1930 as the First Great Migration (in which 1.5 million migrants moved north) and 1940–1970 as the Second Great Migration (in which 5 million migrants moved north). The years of the Great Depression considerably slowed northern movement in many cities. The First Great Migration was fueled in the early years by the industrialization due to World War I, while the Second Great Migration began as American industry responded to the beginning of World War II in Europe.

11. For more on his ideas on memory, see John Bodnar, *Remaking America: Public Memory, Commemoration, and Patriotism in the Twentieth Century* (Princeton: Princeton University Press, 1993). The act of commemoration, as studied by Bodnar and others, provides an interesting way in which to study memory. There are many different types of memory. One type, referred to as autobiographical memory by sociologist Barbara Misztal, is discussed in this study. See Barbara Misztal, *Theories of Social Remembering* (Philadelphia: Open University Press, 2003), 10–14; Barbara Misztal, "Memory and Democracy," *American Behavioral Scientist* 48, no. 10 (June 2005): 1336; James Fentress and Chris Wickham, *Social Memory: New Perspectives on the Past* (Cambridge: Blackwell, 1992), 46, 89.

12. Note that while this work is necessary, it obviously does not need to be performed by black female workers. The multitude of reasons why household laborers are performing work that might be done by family members is a burgeoning field within feminist labor studies.

13. Anniese Moten, interview with Lisa Krissoff Boehm and Elizabeth Cote, Detroit, Michigan, June 22, 2000.

14. Inez Smith, interview with Lisa Krissoff Boehm, Grand Rapids, Michigan, January 4, 2003. A "truck patch" typically refers to a vegetable garden, especially one in which vegetables are grown for sale in the market.

15. Note that the distinction between tenant farming and sharecropping is not hard and fast. In different regions, and at different times, definitions varied. Rebecca Sharpless defines tenant farmers as those who provided their own farming materials and sharecroppers as those who received seed, farm tools, farm animals, or other needed farm supplies (referred to as the "furnish") from the landowner. See Rebecca Sharpless, *Fertile Ground, Narrow Choices: Women on Texas Cotton Farms, 1900–1940* (Chapel Hill: University of North Carolina

Press, 1999), 7. Tenant farmers, Sharpless details, often gave a third of their corn crop and a fourth of their cotton crop to the landowner—thus "farming on the thirds and fourths." Sharecroppers often split the crop, and were referred to as "halvers."

16. Nicholas Lemann, *The Promised Land: The Great Black Migration and How It Changed America* (New York: Vintage Books, 1992), 5–6.

17. Liddie Williams, interview with Lisa Krissoff Boehm, Chicago, Illinois, November 16, 2001.

18. Rosetta "Rosa" Lewis Young, interview with Lisa Krissoff Boehm, Grand Rapids, Michigan, January 4, 2003.

19. Rebecca Strom, interview with Lisa Krissoff Boehm, Patricia Burke, and Audrey Kemp, Dorchester, Massachusetts, November 12, 2002.

20. Annie Benning, interview with Lisa Krissoff Boehm and Elizabeth Cote, Detroit, Michigan, June 26, 2002.

21. Rosetta "Rosa" Lewis Young, interview with Lisa Krissoff Boehm, Grand Rapids, Michigan, January 4, 2003.

22. Esther Woods, interview with Lisa Krissoff Boehm, Grand Rapids, Michigan, June 10, 2000.

23. Oral memoirs of Maggie Langham Washington, interview with Doni Van Ryswyk, Waco, Texas, March 10, 1988, Texas Teachers Project, Baylor University Institute for Oral History, 3, 4, 6, 10.

24. Ruth Margaret Covington, interview with Elizabeth Cote, Detroit, Michigan, September 12, 2002.

25. Anniese Moten, interview with Lisa Krissoff Boehm and Elizabeth Cote, Detroit, Michigan, June 22, 2000.

26. Alverrine Parker, interview with Lisa Krissoff Boehm, Grand Rapids, Michigan, December 28, 2002.

27. Addie Smith, interview with Lisa Krissoff Boehm, Worcester, Massachusetts, July 8, 2002.

28. Ruthe Winegarten, ed., *I Am Annie Mae: An Extraordinary Woman in Her Own Words: The Personal Story of a Black Texas Woman* (Austin: Rosegarden Press, 1983), xv, 54.

29. Rosetta "Rosa" Lewis Young, interview with Lisa Krissoff Boehm, Grand Rapids, Michigan, January 4, 2003. Young said of those years, "It was fun times, you know, with the kids."

30. Oral memoirs of Ruth Weatherly Manning, interview with Rebecca Sharpless, April 25, 1987, Family Life and Community History Project, Baylor University Institute for Oral History, 22.

31. Thad Sitton and James H. Conrad, *Freedom Colonies: Independent Black Texans in the Time of Jim Crow* (Austin: University of Texas Press, 2005), 2, 7.

32. Minnie Chatman, interview with Lisa Krissoff Boehm and Elizabeth Cote, Detroit, Michigan, October 19, 2001.

33. Annie Evelyn Collins, interview with Elizabeth Cote, Detroit, Michigan, January 11, 2003.

34. Sharecroppers usually lived on the land and worked a set piece of the land as their own, with a fee or a portion of the crops going to the landowner. Other workers performed farm tasks for a daily salary. It is unclear here if Dean is referring to day laborers who worked on her family farm as sharecroppers or if she is saying that there were two types of workers,

sharecroppers and day laborers, working the land. Avezinner Dean, interview with Lisa Krissoff Boehm and Elizabeth Cote, Detroit, Michigan, June 25, 2002.

35. Avezinner Dean, interview with Lisa Krissoff Boehm and Elizabeth Cote, Detroit, Michigan, June 25, 2002. African American schools often ended in eleventh grade in this period.

36. For an interesting and accessible discussion of this subject, see *African American Lives*, PBS Films, 2006.

37. Thelma Lane, interview with Elizabeth Cote, Detroit, Michigan, December 27, 2002.

38. Ogretta McNeil, interview with Lisa Krissoff Boehm, Worcester, Massachusetts, January 6, 2003.

39. Fannie Mae Kennedy, interview with Elizabeth Cote, Detroit, Michigan, July 31, 2002.

40. Anniese Moten, interview with Lisa Krissoff Boehm and Elizabeth Cote, Detroit, Michigan, June 22, 2000.

41. Liddie Williams, interview with Lisa Krissoff Boehm, Chicago, Illinois, November 16, 2001.

42. Bernita Howard (pseudonym), interview with Lisa Krissoff Boehm and Elizabeth Cote, Detroit, Michigan, July 9, 2003.

43. Annie Benning, interview with Lisa Krissoff Boehm and Elizabeth Cote, Detroit, Michigan, June 26, 2002.

44. Lillian Clark, interview with Lisa Krissoff Boehm and Elizabeth Cote, Southfield, Michigan, January 2, 2003. For more on African American clubwomen in Detroit, see Victoria W. Wolcott, *Remaking Respectability: African American Women in Interwar Detroit* (Chapel Hill: University of North Carolina Press, 2001).

45. Esther Woods, interview with Lisa Krissoff Boehm, Grand Rapids, Michigan, June 10, 2000.

46. Barbara Purifoy-Seldon, interview with Lisa Krissoff Boehm and Elizabeth Cote, Southfield, Michigan, January 2, 2003.

47. Lillie Shelby (pseudonym), interview with Elizabeth Cote, Detroit, Michigan, July 31, 2002.

48. Rebecca Strom, interview with Lisa Krissoff Boehm, Audrey Kemp, and Patricia Burke, Dorchester, Massachusetts, November 12, 2002.

49. Ella Sims, interview with Lisa Krissoff Boehm, Grand Rapids, Michigan, July 2, 2002.

50. Solomon Burke, "Detroit City" in *Home in Your Heart: The Best of Solomon Burke*, Atlantic Records, 1992.

CHAPTER TWO. GUIDING INFLUENCES AND THE YOUNGER YEARS

1. Maya Angelou, *I Know Why the Caged Bird Sings* (New York: Bantam, 1993), 120–121.

2. Jacqueline Dock (pseudonym), interview with Elizabeth Cote, Detroit, Michigan, January 11, 2003.

3. Lillian Clark, interview with Lisa Krissoff Boehm and Elizabeth Cote, Southfield, Michigan, January 2, 2003.

4. bell hooks, *Bone Black: Memories of Girlhood* (New York: Henry Holt, 1996), 137.

5. Esther Woods, interview with Lisa Krissoff Boehm, Grand Rapids, Michigan, June 10, 2000.

6. Jerliene "Creamy" McKinney, interview with Lisa Krissoff Boehm, Worcester, Massachusetts, January 9, 2003.

7. Liddie Williams, interview with Lisa Krissoff Boehm, Chicago, Illinois, November 16, 2001.

8. Rebecca Strom, interview with Lisa Krissoff Boehm, Audrey Kemp, and Patricia Burke, Dorchester, Massachusetts, November 12, 2002. It is unclear whether the town of Cahaba was still legally in existence during Strom's childhood. If not, she still employed the term to describe her neighborhood.

9. Annie Benning, interview with Lisa Krissoff Boehm and Elizabeth Cote, Detroit, Michigan, June 26, 2002.

10. Addie Smith, interview with Lisa Krissoff Boehm, Worcester, Massachusetts, July 8, 2002.

11. Minnie Chatman, interview with Lisa Krissoff Boehm and Elizabeth Cote, Detroit, Michigan, October 19, 2001.

12. Oral history memoir of Shirley Ann Watson Graves, interview with Anne Radford Phillips, April 4, 1992, Family Life and Community History Project, Baylor University Institute for Oral History, 6–12.

13. Lois B. Stevens, interview with Lisa Krissoff Boehm, Audrey Kemp, Joan Goss, and Patricia Burke, Worcester, Massachusetts, August 22, 2002. Stevens lived 102 years, passing away on November 8, 2004, at her old age home, Christopher House, where we interviewed her.

14. Alberta Hardy, interview with Lisa Krissoff Boehm and Elizabeth Cote, June 25, 2002.

15. Inez Smith, interview with Lisa Krissoff Boehm, Grand Rapids, Michigan, January 4, 2003.

16. Annie Evelyn Collins, interview with Elizabeth Cote, Detroit, Michigan, January 11, 2003.

17. Thelma Lane, interview with Elizabeth Cote, Detroit, Michigan, December 27, 2002.

18. Faith Richmond (pseudonym), interview with Lisa Krissoff Boehm and Patricia Burke, Dorchester, Massachusetts, October 3, 2002. Franklin Delano Roosevelt is most often connected with a sanatorium in Warm Springs, Georgia.   '

19. Ogretta McNeil, interview with Lisa Krissoff Boehm, Worcester, Massachusetts, January 6, 2003.

20. Addie Smith, interview with Lisa Krissoff Boehm, Worcester, Massachusetts, July 8, 2002.

21. Alverrine Parker, interview with Lisa Krissoff Boehm, Grand Rapids, Michigan, December 28, 2002. Perhaps an overly idealized vision of the older generation was not the best; those who found no fault with their parents grew easily impatient with their children's generation, a generation facing far different challenges and roadblocks. See Kim Lacy Rogers, *Life and Death in the Delta: African American Narratives of Violence, Resilience, and Social Change* (New York: Palgrave Macmillan, 2006), 42.

22. Liddie Williams, interview with Lisa Krissoff Boehm, Chicago, Illinois, November 16, 2001.

23. Avezinner Dean, interview with Lisa Krissoff Boehm and Elizabeth Cote, Detroit, Michigan, June 25, 2002.

24. Rosetta "Rosa" Lewis Young, interview with Lisa Krissoff Boehm, Grand Rapids, Michigan, January 4, 2003.

25. Barbara Purifoy-Seldon, interview with Lisa Krissoff Boehm and Elizabeth Cote, Southfield, Michigan, January 2, 2003.

26. Lillie Shelby (pseudonym), interview with Elizabeth Cote, Detroit, Michigan, July 31, 2002.

27. Oral memoirs of Ophelia Mae Mayberry Hall, interview with Rebecca Sharpless, Gatesville, Texas, May 26, 1986, Family Life and Community History Project, Baylor University Institute for Oral History, 15.

28. Katherine Aldin, "Koko Taylor: Down in the Bottom of that Chitlin' Bucket," *Living Blues* (July/August 1993): 11; Ella Sims, interview with Jane Idema and Bunny Voss, Grand Rapids, Michigan, Greater Grand Rapids Women's History Council Oral Interviews, Grand Rapids Public Library, 6–7.

29. Oral memoirs of Ophelia Mae Mayberry Hall, interview with Rebecca Sharpless, Gatesville, Texas, May 26, 1986, Family Life and Community History Project, Baylor University Institute for Oral History, 29.

30. Lillian Gill, interview with Margaret Voss, June 6, 1997, Grand Rapids, Michigan, Greater Grand Rapids Women's History Council Oral Interviews, Grand Rapids Public Library.

31. Jerliene "Creamy" McKinney, interview with Lisa Krissoff Boehm, Worcester, Massachusetts, January 9, 2003.

32. Liddie Williams, interview with Lisa Krissoff Boehm, Chicago, Illinois, November 16, 2001.

33. See oral memoirs of Vivienne Lucille Malone-Mayes, interview by Rebecca Sharpless, August 4, 1987, Waco, Texas, Baylor University Project, Baylor University Institute for Oral History, 84.

34. Lois E. Myers and Rebecca Sharpless, "'Of the Least and the Most'; The African American Rural Church," in R. Douglas Hurt, ed., *African American Life in the Rural South, 1900–1950* (Columbia: University of Missouri Press, 2003), 55–59.

35. Minnie Chatman, interview with Lisa Krissoff Boehm and Elizabeth Cote, Detroit, Michigan, October 19, 2001.

36. Ruth Margaret Covington, interview with Elizabeth Cote, Detroit, Michigan, September 12, 2002.

37. Anniese Moten, interview with Lisa Krissoff Boehm and Elizabeth Cote, Detroit, Michigan, June 22, 2000.

38. Oral memoirs of Ruth Weatherly Manning, interview with Rebecca Sharpless, April 25, 1987, Family Life and Community History Project, Baylor University Institute for Oral History, 7.

39. Oral memoirs of Maggie Langham Washington, interview with Doni Van Ryswyk, Waco, Texas, March 10, 1988, Texas Teachers Project, Baylor University Institute for Oral History, 13, 15, 24.

40. Bernita Howard (pseudonym), interview with Lisa Krissoff Boehm and Elizabeth Cote, Detroit, Michigan, July 9, 2003.

41. Minnie Chatman, interview with Lisa Krissoff Boehm and Elizabeth Cote, Detroit, Michigan, October 19, 2001.

42. See Susan Tucker, *Telling Memories Among Southern Women: Domestic Workers and Their Employers in the Segregated South* (Baton Rouge: Louisiana State University Press,

1988); Faith Richmond (pseudonym), interview with Lisa Krissoff Boehm and Pat Burke, Boston, Massachusetts, October 3, 2002.

43. Tucker, *Telling Memories Among Southern Women*, 18.

44. Avezinner Dean, interview with Lisa Krissoff Boehm and Elizabeth Cote, Detroit, Michigan, June 25, 2002.

45. Gussie Nash, interview with Lisa Krissoff Boehm, Grand Rapids, Michigan, June 28, 2002.

46. Glennette Taylor (pseudonym), interview with Lisa Krissoff Boehm, Grand Rapids, Michigan, July 27, 2002.

47. Jerliene "Creamy" McKinney, interview with Lisa Krissoff Boehm, Worcester, Massachusetts, January 9, 2003.

48. Lynn May Rivas, "Invisible Labors: Caring for the Independent Person," in Barbara Ehrenreich and Arlie Russell Hochschild, eds., *Global Woman: Nannies, Maids, and Sex Workers in the New Economy* (New York: Metropolitan Books, 2002), 76.

49. Oral history memoirs of Vivienne Malone-Mayes, interview with Rebecca Sharpless, August 4, 1987, Waco Texas, Baylor University Project, Baylor University Institute for Oral History, Texas Collection, Carroll Library, 103; Beatrice Jackson, interview with Lisa Krissoff Boehm and Elizabeth Cote, Detroit, Michigan, June 25, 2002.

50. Fannie Mae Kennedy, interview with Elizabeth Cote, Detroit, Michigan, July 31, 2002.

51. Ruth Margaret Covington, interview with Elizabeth Cote, Detroit, Michigan, September 12, 2002. Covington reported that she did not iron too much anymore.

52. Alverrine Parker, interview with Lisa Krissoff Boehm, Grand Rapids, Michigan, December 28, 2002.

53. Jacqueline Dock (pseudonym), interview with Elizabeth Cote, Detroit, Michigan, January 11, 2003.

54. Inez Smith, interview with Lisa Krissoff Boehm, Grand Rapids, Michigan, January 4, 2003.

55. Oral memoirs of Harriet Caulfield Smith, interview with Thomas L. Charlton, November 22, 1977, Waco, Texas, Waco and McLennan County Project, Baylor University Program for Oral History, 5.

56. Oral history memoirs of Harriet Caulfield Smith, interview with Thomas L. Charlton, November 22, 1977, Waco, Texas, Waco and McLennan County Project, Baylor University Program for Oral History, Texas Collection, Carroll Library, 35.

57. Oral memoirs of Maggie Langham Washington, interview with Marla Luffer, Waco, Texas, April 18, 1988, Texas Teachers Project, Baylor University Institute for Oral History, 49

58. James N. Gregory, *The Southern Diaspora: How the Great Migrations of Black and White Southerners Transformed America* (Chapel Hill: University of North Carolina Press, 2005), 106–107.

59. Barbara Purifoy-Seldon, interview with Lisa Krissoff Boehm and Elizabeth Cote, Southfield, Michigan, January 2, 2003.

60. Ella Sims, interview with Lisa Krissoff Boehm, Grand Rapids, Michigan, July 2, 2002.

61. Oral memoirs of Harriet Caulfield Smith, interview with Thomas L. Charlton, November 22, 1977, Waco, Texas, Waco and McLennan County Project, Baylor University Program for Oral History, 8, 12–14, 37.

62. Lois B. Stevens, interview with Lisa Krissoff Boehm, Audrey Kemp, Joan Goss, and Patricia Burke, Worcester, Massachusetts, August 22, 2002; Bill Maxwell, "Black Boarding Schools Provide Haven of Discipline, Learning," *St. Petersburg Times*, March 30, 2003, accessed at www.sptimes.com; Peter Applebome, "Boarding Schools for Blacks Are Having a Resurgence in Popularity," *New York Times*, September 21, 1994, accessed at www.nytimes .com.

63. Thelma Lane, interview with Elizabeth Cote, Detroit, Michigan, December 27, 2002.

64. Alverrine Parker, interview with Lisa Krissoff Boehm, Grand Rapids, Michigan, December 28, 2002.

65. Anniese Moten, interview with Lisa Krissoff Boehm and Elizabeth Cote, Detroit, Michigan, June 22, 2000.

66. Alberta Hardy, interview with Lisa Krissoff Boehm and Elizabeth Cote, June 25, 2002.

67. Jerliene "Creamy" McKinney, interview with Lisa Krissoff Boehm, Worcester, Massachusetts, January 9, 2003.

68. Ogretta McNeil, interview with Lisa Krissoff Boehm, Worcester, Massachusetts, January 6, 2003.

69. Mary White, interview with Lisa Krissoff Boehm and Elizabeth Cote, Detroit, Michigan, June 25, 2002.

70. Anne Moody, *Coming of Age in Mississippi* (New York: Dell, 1968), 43, 45.

CHAPTER THREE. THE MOVE NORTH

1. Robert Sklar, "Reinforcing Black-Jewish Bonds," *Detroit Jewish News*, as quoted in the "10 Minutes of Torah," *Union for Reform Judaism*, August 25, 2006.

2. Alverrine Parker, interview with Lisa Krissoff Boehm, Grand Rapids, Michigan, December 28, 2002.

3. Addie Smith, interview with Lisa Krissoff Boehm, Worcester, Massachusetts, July 8, 2002.

4. Ogretta McNeil, interview with Lisa Krissoff Boehm, Worcester, Massachusetts, January 6, 2003.

5. Alverrine Parker, interview with Lisa Krissoff Boehm, Grand Rapids, Michigan, December 28, 2002.

6. Addie Smith, interview with Lisa Krissoff Boehm, Worcester, Massachusetts, July 8, 2002.

7. Rosetta "Rosa" Lewis Young, interview with Lisa Krissoff Boehm, Grand Rapids, Michigan, January 4, 2003.

8. Faith Richmond (pseudonym), interview with Lisa Krissoff Boehm and Patricia Burke, Boston, Massachusetts, October 3, 2002.

9. Kim Lacy Rogers, *Life and Death in the Delta: African American Narratives of Violence, Resilience, and Social Change* (New York: Palgrave Macmillan, 2006), 24; William D. Carrigan, *The Making of a Lynching Culture: Violence and Vigilantism in Central Texas, 1836–1916* (Urbana: University of Illinois Press, 2004), 4, 133; James H. Madison, *A Lynching in the Heartland: Race and Memory in America* (New York: Palgrave Macmillan, 2003), 13–16.

10. Patsy Cravens, *Leavin' a Testimony: Portraits from Rural Texas* (Austin: University of Texas Press, 2006), 35–36.

11. Carrigan, *The Making of a Lynching Culture*, 1–2; Patricia Bernstein, *The First Waco Horror: The Lynching of Jesse Washington and the Rise of the NAACP* (Austin: University of Texas Press, 2005), 108–110.

12. Rogers, *Life and Death in the Delta*, 44; Bernstein, *The First Waco Horror*, 202; oral memoirs of Carrie Skipwith Mayfield, interview with Valerie Malone-Mayes, December 22, 1989, Waco, Texas, Waco and McLennan County Project, Baylor University Institute for Oral History, Carroll Library, Texas Collection, 15. See also Carrigan, *The Making of a Lynching Culture*, and J. B. Smith, "The Waco Horror: Grisly 1916 Lynching Still Overshadows City, *Waco Tribune Herald* Archive, March 6, 2005.

13. Lillie Shelby (pseudonym), interview with Elizabeth Cote, Detroit, Michigan, July 31, 2002.

14. Annie Evelyn Collins, interview with Elizabeth Cote, Detroit, Michigan, January 11, 2003.

15. Ruth Margaret Covington, interview with Elizabeth Cote, Detroit, Michigan, September 12, 2002.

16. Thelma Lane, interview with Elizabeth Cote, Detroit, Michigan, December 27, 2002.

17. Ogretta McNeil, interview with Lisa Krissoff Boehm, Worcester, Massachusetts, January 6, 2003.

18. Gussie Nash, interview with Lisa Krissoff Boehm, Grand Rapids, Michigan, June 28, 2002.

19. Avezinner Dean, interview with Lisa Krissoff Boehm and Elizabeth Cote, Detroit, Michigan, June 25, 2002.

20. Ella Sims's father sent his children to board with relatives in Helena, Arkansas, to attend school, there being no high school for black children in their Mississippi town.

21. Ella Sims, interview with Lisa Krissoff Boehm, Grand Rapids, Michigan, July 2, 2002.

22. Darlene Clark Hine, "Black Migration to the Urban Midwest: The Gender Dimension, 1915–1945," in Joe William Trotter, Jr., ed., *The Great Migration in Historical Perspective: New Dimensions of Race, Class, and Gender* (Bloomington: Indiana University Press, 1991), 129.

23. Peter Gottlieb, "Rethinking the Great Migration: A Perspective from Pittsburgh," in Trotter, Jr., ed., *The Great Migration in Historical Perspective*, 71.

24. See Davison M. Douglas, *Jim Crow Moves North: The Battle over Northern School Segregation, 1865–1954* (New York: Cambridge University Press, 2005).

25. SueEllen Hoy, *Good Hearts: Catholic Sisters in Chicago's Past* (Urbana: University of Illinois Press, 2006), 12, 20, 30–31.

26. Florence Allison, interview with Elizabeth Cote, Detroit, Michigan, July 31, 2002.

27. Annie Benning, interview with Lisa Krissoff Boehm and Elizabeth Cote, Detroit, Michigan, June 26, 2002.

28. Katherine Aldin, "Koko Taylor: Down in the Bottom of that Chitlin' Bucket," *Living Blues* (July/August 1993), 13.

29. Faith Richmond (pseudonym), interview with Lisa Krissoff Boehm and Patricia Burke, Boston, Massachusetts, October 3, 2002.

30. Lillian Clark, interview with Lisa Krissoff Boehm and Elizabeth Cote, Southfield, Michigan, January 2, 2003.

31. Minnie Chatman, interview with Lisa Krissoff Boehm and Elizabeth Cote, Detroit, Michigan, October 19, 2001.

32. Mattie Bell Fritz, interview with Lisa Krissoff Boehm and Elizabeth Cote, Detroit, Michigan, August 4, 2001.

33. Liddie Williams, interview with Lisa Krissoff Boehm, Chicago, Illinois, November 16, 2001.

34. Rosetta "Rosa" Lewis Young, interview with Lisa Krissoff Boehm, Grand Rapids, Michigan, January 4, 2003.

35. Ruth Margaret Covington, interview with Elizabeth Cote, Detroit, Michigan, September 12, 2002.

36. Glennette Taylor (pseudonym), interview with Lisa Krissoff Boehm, Grand Rapids, Michigan, July 27, 2002.

37. Esther Woods, interview with Lisa Krissoff Boehm, Grand Rapids, Michigan, June 10, 2000. Statistics for York, Alabama, in 2005 found median household income in this town of less than three thousand people to be close to nineteen thousand dollars. The town was 78.3 percent African American. See www.citydata.com.

38. Barbara Misztal, *Theories of Social Remembering* (Philadelphia: Open University Press, 2003), 76.

39. Barbara Purifoy-Seldon, interview with Lisa Krissoff Boehm and Elizabeth Cote, Southfield, Michigan, January 2, 2003. This memory of holes in the floor of a car strikes a chord with me. I remember well an aging Dodge Colt my husband and I had in our early years together where one literally could watch the street pass beneath one's feet. We placed tin foil on the floor to shield passengers from this charming view. The sister's memory of walking to Michigan with her feet through holes sounds like a child's understanding of these gaping holes' purpose.

40. Bernita Howard (pseudonym), interview with Lisa Krissoff Boehm and Elizabeth Cote, Detroit, Michigan, July 9, 2003.

41. Annie Evelyn Collins, interview with Elizabeth Cote, Detroit, Michigan, January 11, 2003.

42. Mary Smith, interview with Lisa Krissoff Boehm, Audrey Kemp, and Patricia Burke, Boston, Massachusetts, October 12, 2002.

43. Elizabeth Clark-Lewis, *Living In, Living Out: African American Domestics and the Great Migration* (New York: Kodansha American, 1994), 124–146.

44. For more on Freedom House, see www.freedomhouse.com.

45. Rebecca Strom, interview with Lisa Krissoff Boehm, Audrey Kemp, and Patricia Burke, November 12, 2002.

46. Chad Berry, *Southern Migrants, Northern Exiles* (Urbana: University of Illinois Press, 2000), 21.

47. Avezinner Dean, interview with Lisa Krissoff Boehm and Elizabeth Cote, Detroit, Michigan, June 25, 2002.

48. Beatrice Jackson, interview with Lisa Krissoff Boehm and Elizabeth Cote, June 23, 2002.

49. Jerliene "Creamy" McKinney, interview with Lisa Krissoff Boehm, Worcester, Massachusetts, January 9, 2003.

50. Gussie Nash, interview with Lisa Krissoff Boehm, Grand Rapids, Michigan, June 28, 2002.

51. Oral history memoir of Olivia Watson Mitchell, interview with Deborah Jane Hoskins, November 11, 1992, Burton, Texas, Family Life and Community History Project, Baylor University Institute for Oral History, 2, 30.

52. June Cross, *Secret Daughter: A Mixed-Race Daughter and the Mother Who Gave Her Away* (New York: Viking, 2006).

53. Roderick J. Harrison, "The Great Migration South," *New Crisis* (July/August 2001): 20; William H. Frey, *The New Great Migration: Black Americans' Return to the South, 1965–2000*, Center on Urban and Metropolitan Policy, Brookings Institution, May 2004.

CHAPTER FOUR. ENCOUNTERING THE CITY

1. Barbara Purifoy-Seldon, interview with Lisa Krissoff Boehm and Elizabeth Cote, Southfield, Michigan, January 2, 2003.

2. Faith Richmond (pseudonym), interview with Lisa Krissoff Boehm and Patricia Burke, Dorchester, Massachusetts, October 3, 2002.

3. Census 2000 Demographic Profile Highlights, accessed at www.census.gov.

4. Mary Smith, interview with Lisa Krissoff Boehm, Audrey Kemp, and Patricia Burke, Dorchester, Massachusetts, October 12, 2002.

5. Gretchen Lemke-Santangelo, *Abiding Courage: African American Migrant Women and the East Bay Community* (Chapel Hill: University of North Carolina Press, 1996), 37.

6. Gwendolyn M. Parker, *Trespassing: My Sojourn in the Halls of Privilege* (New York: Mariner Books, 1997), 30.

7. Richard Wright, *Black Boy (American Hunger): A Record of Childhood and Youth* (New York: HarperPerennial, 1993), 307.

8. Lillie Shelby (pseudonym), interview with Elizabeth Cote, Detroit, Michigan, July 31, 2002.

9. Elizabeth Hutton Turner, *Jacob Lawrence, The Migration Series* (Washington, D.C.: The Rappahannock Press and the Phillips Collection, 1993), 52–128.

10. Addie Smith, interview with Lisa Krissoff Boehm, Worcester, Massachusetts, July 14, 2002.

11. Avezinner Dean, interview with Lisa Krissoff Boehm and Elizabeth Cote, Detroit, Michigan, June 25, 2002.

12. Lois Stevens, interview with Lisa Krissoff Boehm, Audrey Kemp, Joan Goss, and Patricia Burke, Worcester, Massachusetts, August 22, 2002.

13. Addie Smith, interview with Lisa Krissoff Boehm, Worcester, Massachusetts, July 14, 2002.

14. See Ronald Takaki, *A Different Mirror: A History of Multicultural America* (Boston: Little, Brown, and Company, 1993), 51–78.

15. Alverrine Parker, interview with Lisa Krissoff Boehm, Grand Rapids, Michigan, December 28, 2002.

16. Ogretta McNeil, interview with Lisa Krissoff Boehm, Worcester, Massachusetts, January 6, 2003. For more on racist and segregationist practices in northern public education, see Davison M. Douglas, *Jim Crow Moves North: The Battle Over Northern School Desegregation, 1865–1954* (New York: Cambridge University Press, 2005).

17. Anniese Moten, interview with Lisa Krissoff Boehm and Elizabeth Cote, Detroit, Michigan, June 22, 2000.

18. Faith Richmond (pseudonym), interview with Lisa Krissoff Boehm and Patricia Burke, Dorchester, Massachusetts, October 3, 2002. The name Quentin Richmond is also a pseudonym.

19. See Kevin Boyle, *Arc of Justice: A Saga of Race, Civil Rights, and Murder in the Jazz Age* (New York: Henry Holt, 2004.)

20. June Manning Thomas, *Redevelopment and Race: Planning a Finer City in Postwar Detroit* (Baltimore: Johns Hopkins University Press, 1997), 7.

21. Ogretta McNeil, interview with Lisa Krissoff Boehm, Worcester, Massachusetts, January 6, 2003.

22. Arnold R. Hirsch, *Making the Second Ghetto: Race and Housing in Chicago, 1940–1960* (Cambridge, U.K.: Cambridge University Press, 1990), 20.

23. Dr. Warren M. Banner, Director of Research and Community Projects, "A Review of the Progress and Activities of the Brough Community Association, September 10–24, 1945," 20, in "Grand Rapids Urban League Studies" file, Grand Rapids Urban League Papers, Box 4, and "Statement of Robert C. Weaver," 2, "General File 1940," Detroit Urban League Papers, Box 4, Bentley Historical Library, University of Michigan, Ann Arbor.

24. Thomas Sugrue, *The Origins of the Urban Crisis: Race and Inequality in Postwar Detroit* (Princeton: Princeton University Press, 1996), 33, 37, 40.

25. "The Negro Population of Grand Rapids, Michigan: 1940. A Social Study Conducted for the Interracial Committee of the Council of Social Agencies," National Urban League, Department of Research, 52, in "Grand Rapids Urban League Studies" file, Grand Rapids Urban League Papers, Box 4, Bentley Historical Library, University of Michigan, Ann Arbor.

26. Anniese Moten, interview with Lisa Krissoff Boehm and Elizabeth Cote, Detroit, Michigan, June 22, 2000.

27. Willie Jean Clark Lewis, interview with Lisa Krissoff Boehm and Elizabeth Cote, Southfield, Michigan, January 2, 2003.

28. Avezinner Dean, interview with Lisa Krissoff Boehm and Elizabeth Cote, Detroit, Michigan, June 25, 2002.

29. Alberta Hardy, interview with Lisa Krissoff Boehm and Elizabeth Cote, Detroit, Michigan, June 25, 2002.

30. Lillie Shelby (pseudonym), interview with Elizabeth Cote, Detroit, Michigan, July 31, 2002.

31. Ella Sims, interview with Lisa Krissoff Boehm, Grand Rapids, Michigan, July 2, 2002.

32. Alex Kotlowitz, *There Are No Children Here: The Story of Two Boys Growing Up in the Other America* (New York: Anchor Books, 1991), 24.

33. Nicholas Lemann, *The Promised Land* (New York: Vintage Books, 1992), 107.

34. Lillie Shelby (pseudonym), interview with Elizabeth Cote, Detroit, Michigan, July 31, 2002.

35. Bernita Howard (pseudonym), interview with Lisa Krissoff Boehm and Elizabeth Cote, Detroit, Michigan, July 9, 2003.

36. Minnie Chatman, interview with Lisa Krissoff Boehm and Elizabeth Cote, Detroit, Michigan, October 19, 2001.

37. Annie Benning, interview with Lisa Krissoff Boehm and Elizabeth Cote, Detroit, Michigan, June 26, 2002.

38. Barack Obama, *Dreams from My Father: A Story of Race and Inheritance* (New York: Three Rivers Press, 1995, 2004), 156–157.

39. Kotlowitz, *There Are No Children Here*, 25–26.

40. Florence Allison, interview with Elizabeth Cote, Detroit, Michigan, July 31, 2002.

41. Simone Landry (pseudonym), interview with Lisa Krissoff Boehm and Elizabeth Cote, Detroit, Michigan, June 26, 2002.

42. Thelma Lane, interview with Elizabeth Cote, Detroit, Michigan, December 27, 2002.

43. Faith Richmond (pseudonym), interview with Lisa Krissoff Boehm and Patricia Burke, Dorchester, Massachusetts, October 3, 2002.

44. 2006 American Community Survey, accessed at www.factfinder.census.gov.

45. Ruth Margaret Covington, interview with Elizabeth Cote, Detroit, Michigan, September 12, 2002.

46. Addie Smith, interview with Lisa Krissoff Boehm, Worcester, Massachusetts, July 14, 2002.

47. Kimberley L. Phillips, *AlabamaNorth: African-American Migrants, Community, and Working-Class Activism in Cleveland, 1915–45* (Urbana: University of Illinois Press, 1999), 67–68.

48. Pierrette Hondagneu-Sotelo, *Doméstica: Immigrant Workers Cleaning and Caring in the Shadows of Affluence* (Berkeley: University of California Press, 2001), 128.

49. Fannie Mae Kennedy, interview with Elizabeth Cote, Detroit, Michigan, July 31, 2002.

50. Thelma Lane, interview with Elizabeth Cote, Detroit, Michigan, December 27, 2002.

51. Mary Edmonds, interview with Marg Ed Kwapil, Grand Rapids, Michigan, August 29, 2001, 5, Greater Grand Rapids Women's Oral History Council. Collection of the Grand Rapids Public Library.

52. Glennette Taylor, interview with Lisa Krissoff Boehm, Grand Rapids, Michigan, June 27, 2002.

53. Fannie Mae Kennedy, interview with Elizabeth Cote, Detroit, Michigan, July 31, 2002.

CHAPTER FIVE. THE WORK OF A DOMESTIC

1. Anniese Moten, interview with Lisa Krissoff Boehm and Elizabeth Cote, Detroit, Michigan, June 22, 2000.

2. Corporate Records and Minutes of the Brough Community Association, 1, Grand Rapids Urban League Papers, Box 1, Bentley Historical Library, Ann Arbor, Michigan.

3. Susan Tucker, *Telling Memories Among Southern Women: Domestic Workers and Their Employers in the Segregated South* (Baton Rouge: Louisiana State University Press, 1988), 72.

4. Esther Woods, interview with Lisa Krissoff Boehm, Grand Rapids, Michigan, June 10, 2000; Jacqueline Jones, *Labor of Love, Labor of Sorrow: Black Women, Work, and the Family from Slavery to the Present* (New York: Vintage Books, 1985), 237; Paula Giddings, *When and Where I Enter: The Impact of Black Women on Race and Sex in America* (New York: Amistad/Harper Collins, 1984), 235. See Lisa Krissoff Boehm, "Reverend Charles A. Hill: Leftist Religious-Based Activism in an Urban Context," presented at the annual conference of the New England American Studies Association, Hartford, Connecticut, April 2003.

5. "The Negro Population of Grand Rapids, Michigan: 1940. A Social Study Conducted for the Interracial Committee of the Council of Social Agencies," National Urban League,

Department of Research, 5, 13, in "Grand Rapids Urban League Studies" file, Grand Rapids Urban League Papers, Box 4, Bentley Historical Library, University of Michigan, Ann Arbor.

6. Alberta Hardy, interview with Lisa Krissoff Boehm and Elizabeth Cote, Detroit, Michigan, June 25, 2002.

7. Minnie Chatman, interview with Lisa Krissoff Boehm and Elizabeth Cote, Detroit, Michigan, October 19, 2001.

8. Lillie Shelby (pseudonym), interview with Elizabeth Cote, Detroit, Michigan, July 31, 2002.

9. "The Urban League," 2, typewritten history, no date, and Jennora Brown, "Report of Work, St. Phillips Center, Beginning July 15, 1942," handwritten report, 3, located in "Grand Rapids Urban League Early History" file, Grand Rapids Urban League Records, Box 1, 1941–1986, Bentley Historical Library, University of Michigan, Ann Arbor, Michigan; Victoria W. Wolcott, *Remaking Respectability: African American Women in Interwar Detroit* (Chapel Hill: University of North Carolina Press, 2001), 84.

10. Simone Landry (pseudonym), interview with Lisa Krissoff Boehm and Elizabeth Cote, Detroit, Michigan, June 26, 2002.

11. Minnie Chatman, interview with Lisa Krissoff Boehm and Elizabeth Cote, Detroit, Michigan, October 19, 2001.

12. Bernita Howard (pseudonym), interview with Lisa Krissoff Boehm and Elizabeth Cote, July 9, 2003.

13. Mattie Bell Fritz, interview with Lisa Krissoff Boehm and Elizabeth Cote, Detroit, Michigan, August 4, 2001.

14. Liddie Williams, interview with Lisa Krissoff Boehm, Chicago, Illinois, November 16, 2001.

15. Mattie Bell Fritz, interview with Lisa Krissoff Boehm and Elizabeth Cote, Detroit, Michigan, August 4, 2001.

16. Anniese Moten, interview with Lisa Krissoff Boehm and Elizabeth Cote, Detroit, Michigan, June 22, 2000.

17. Mary Romero, *Maid in the U.S.A.*, 10th Anniversary Edition (New York: Routledge, 2002), 153–155.

18. Judith Rollins, *Between Women: Domestics and Their Employers* (Philadelphia: Temple University Press, 1985), 138.

19. Tucker, *Telling Memories Among Southern Women*, 4; Bonnie Thornton Dill, *Across the Boundaries of Race and Class: An Exploration of Work and Family Among Black Female Domestics* (New York: Garland, 1994), 44.

20. Mattie Bell Fritz, interview with Lisa Krissoff Boehm and Elizabeth Cote, Detroit, Michigan, August 4, 2001.

21. Ogretta McNeil, interview with Lisa Krissoff Boehm, Worcester, Massachusetts, January 6, 2003.

22. Ella Sims, interview with Lisa Krissoff Boehm, Grand Rapids, Michigan, July 2, 2002.

23. Simone Landry (pseudonym), interview with Lisa Krissoff Boehm and Elizabeth Cote, Detroit, Michigan, June 26, 2002.

24. Annie Benning, interview with Lisa Krissoff Boehm and Elizabeth Cote, Detroit, Michigan, June 26, 2002.

25. Fannie Mae Kennedy, interview with Elizabeth Cote, Detroit, Michigan, July 31, 2002.

26. Florence Allison, interview with Elizabeth Cote, Detroit, Michigan, July 31, 2002.

27. Barbara Purifoy-Seldon, interview with Lisa Krissoff Boehm and Elizabeth Cote, Southfield, Michigan, January 2, 2003.

28. Emma Jo Hustede (pseudonym), interview by Fran Leeper Buss, "Oral Histories of Low Income and Minority Women" series, transcript, 1979, 1–25, Archives of Labor and Urban Affairs, Wayne State University.

29. Mary White, interview with Lisa Krissoff Boehm and Elizabeth Cote, Detroit, Michigan, June 2002.

30. Sara M. Evans, *Born for Liberty: A History of Women in America* (New York: Free Press, 1997), 235.

31. Dill, *Across the Boundaries of Race and Class*, 136.

32. Minnie Chatman, interview with Lisa Krissoff Boehm and Elizabeth Cote, Detroit, Michigan, October 19, 2001.

33. Anniese Moten, interview with Lisa Krissoff Boehm and Elizabeth Cote, Detroit, Michigan, June 22, 2000.

34. Mary White, interview with Lisa Krissoff Boehm and Elizabeth Cote, Detroit, Michigan, June 25, 2002.

35. Annie Benning, interview with Lisa Krissoff Boehm and Elizabeth Cote, Detroit, Michigan, June 26, 2003.

36. Barbara Purifoy-Seldon, interview with Lisa Krissoff Boehm and Elizabeth Cote, Southfield, Michigan, January 2, 2003.

37. Lottie Lewis (pseudonym), interview with Lisa Krissoff Boehm, Grand Rapids, Michigan, June 3, 2000; Annie M. Nipson, September 15 and September 16, 1978, in Ruth Edmonds Hill, ed., *Black Women Oral History Project*, vol. 8 (Westport, CT: Meckler Press, 1991), 208. Permission granted by Schlesinger Library, Radcliffe Institute for Advanced Study, Harvard University.

38. Minnie Chatman, interview with Lisa Krissoff Boehm and Elizabeth Cote, Detroit, Michigan, October 19, 2001.

39. Liddie Williams, interview with Lisa Krissoff Boehm, Chicago, Illinois, November 16, 2001. Texan Vivienne Lucille Malone-Mayes attested, "And the status in those days was if you—the richer your family you worked for, the more status you had in the black community." See oral memoirs of Vivienne Lucille Malone-Mayes, interview with Rebecca Sharpless, Waco, Texas, August 4, 1987, Baylor University Project, Baylor University Institute for Oral History, Texas Collection, Carroll Library.

40. Annie M. Nipson, September 15 and September 16, 1978, in Hill, ed., *Black Women Oral History Project*, vol. 8, 208. Permission granted by Schlesinger Library, Radcliffe Institute for Advanced Study, Harvard University.

41. Tucker, *Telling Memories Among Southern Women*, 109.

42. Elaine Latzman Moon, *Untold Tales, Unsung Heroes: An Oral History of Detroit's African American Community* (Detroit: Wayne State University Press, 1994), 113.

43. Ibid., 94.

44. Fannie Mae Kennedy, interview by Elizabeth Cote, Detroit, Michigan, July 31, 2002.

45. Pierrette Hondagneu-Sotelo, *Doméstica: Immigrant Workers Cleaning and Caring in the Shadows of Affluence* (Berkeley: University of California, 2001), 148.

46. Ibid., 120.

47. Sharon Harley, Francille Rusan Wilson, and Shirley Wilson Logan, "Introduction: Historical Overview of Black Women and Work," in Sharon Harley and The Black Women

and Work Collective, eds., *Sister Circle: Black Women and Work* (New Brunswick: Rutgers University Press, 2000), 7.

48. Annie Evelyn Collins, interview with Elizabeth Cote, Detroit, Michigan, January 11, 2003.

49. Ella Sims, interview with Lisa Krissoff Boehm, Grand Rapids, Michigan, July 2, 2002.

50. Inez Smith, interview with Lisa Krissoff Boehm, Grand Rapids, Michigan, January 4, 2003.

51. Romero, *Maid in the U.S.A.*, 133.

52. Hondagneu-Sotelo, *Doméstica*, 210.

53. Louise Rafkin, *Other People's Dirt: A Housecleaner's Curious Adventures* (New York: Plume, 1999), 86–87; Emma McLaughlin and Nicola Kraus, *The Nanny Diaries* (New York: St. Martins, 2002).

54. Rafkin, *Other People's Dirt*, 157.

CHAPTER SIX. FAMILY ASPECTS

1. Oral memoirs of Bessie Lee Barnes Stafford, interview with Rebecca Sharpless, Family Life and Community History Project, Institute for Oral History, Baylor University, 21.

2. Rhacel Salazar Parreñas, *Children of Global Migration: Transnational Families and Gendered Woes* (Stanford: Stanford University Press, 2005), 12, 18.

3. Judith Warner, *Perfect Madness: Motherhood in the Age of Anxiety* (New York: Riverhead Books, 2005), 55.

4. Addie Smith, interview with Lisa Krissoff Boehm, Worcester, Massachusetts, July 8, 2002. Cotton batting is typically used for furniture upholstery.

5. Mary Catherine Bateson, *Composing a Life* (New York: Plume, 1990), 10.

6. Jerliene "Creamy" McKinney, interview with Lisa Krissoff Boehm, Worcester, Massachusetts, January 9, 2003.

7. Mary Smith, interview with Lisa Krissoff Boehm, Audrey Kemp, and Patricia Burke, Dorchester, Massachusetts, October 12, 2002.

8. Alverrine Smith Parker, interview with Lisa Krissoff Boehm, Grand Rapids, Michigan, December 28, 2002.

9. Gussie Nash, interview with Lisa Krissoff Boehm, Grand Rapids, Michigan, June 28, 2002.

10. Bernita Howard (pseudonym), interview with Lisa Krissoff Boehm and Elizabeth Cote, Detroit, Michigan, July 9, 2003.

11. Lillian Gill, interview with Margaret Voss, Grand Rapids, Michigan, June 6, 1997, Greater Grand Rapids Women's History Council Oral History Project, Grand Rapids Public Library.

12. Willie Jean Clark Lewis, interview with Lisa Krissoff Boehm and Elizabeth Cote, Southfield, Michigan, January 2, 2003.

13. Ogretta McNeil, interview with Lisa Krissoff Boehm, Worcester, Massachusetts, January 6, 2003.

14. Dorista "Dotty" Goldsberry, interview with Lisa Krissoff Boehm, Worcester, Massachusetts, April 26, 2007.

15. Zenara Covington, interview with Elizabeth Cote, Detroit, Michigan, October 28, 2002.

16. Liddie Williams, interview with Lisa Krissoff Boehm, Chicago, Illinois, November 16, 2001.

17. Ella Sims, interview with Lisa Krissoff Boehm, Grand Rapids, Michigan, July 2, 2002.

18. Glennette Taylor (pseudonym), interview with Lisa Krissoff Boehm, Grand Rapids, Michigan, June 27, 2002.

19. Avezinner Dean, interview with Lisa Krissoff Boehm and Elizabeth Cote, Detroit, Michigan, June 25, 2002.

20. Anniese Moten, interview with Lisa Krissoff Boehm and Elizabeth Cote, Detroit, Michigan, June 22, 2000.

21. Rosetta "Rosa" Lewis Young, interview with Lisa Krissoff Boehm, Grand Rapids, Michigan, January 4, 2003.

22. Lillie Shelby (pseudonym), interview with Elizabeth Cote, Detroit, Michigan, July 31, 2002.

23. Fannie Mae Kennedy, interview with Elizabeth Cote, Detroit, Michigan, July 31, 2002; Mary White, interview with Lisa Krissoff Boehm and Elizabeth Cote, Detroit, Michigan, June 25, 2002; Mattie Bell Fritz, interview with Lisa Krissoff Boehm and Elizabeth Cote, Detroit, Michigan, August 4, 2001.

24. Ella Sims, interview with Lisa Krissoff Boehm, Grand Rapids, Michigan, July 2, 2002.

25. Ruth Margaret Covington, interview with Elizabeth Cote, Detroit, Michigan, September 12, 2002.

26. Alberta Hardy, interview with Lisa Krissoff Boehm and Elizabeth Cote, Detroit, Michigan, June 25, 2002.

27. Jerliene "Creamy" McKinney, interview with Lisa Krissoff Boehm, Worcester, Massachusetts, January 9, 2003.

28. Annie Evelyn Collins, interview with Elizabeth Cote, Detroit, Michigan, January 11, 2003.

29. Florence Allison, interview with Elizabeth Cote, Detroit, Michigan, July 31, 2002.

30. Anniese Moten, interview with Lisa Krissoff Boehm and Elizabeth Cote, Detroit, Michigan, June 22, 2000.

31. Simone Landry (pseudonym), interview with Lisa Krissoff Boehm and Elizabeth Cote, Detroit, Michigan, June 26, 2002.

32. Lillian Clark, interview with Lisa Krissoff Boehm and Elizabeth Cote, Southfield, Michigan, January 11, 2003.

33. Sandra J. Gantt, interview with Elizabeth Cote, Detroit, Michigan, July 31, 2002.

34. Oral memoirs of Eunice Brown Johnson, interview with Rebecca Sharpless, April 14, 1987, Gatesville, Texas, Family Life and Community History Project, Institute for Oral History, Baylor University, Carroll Library, Texas Collection, 41.

35. Oral memoirs of Vivienne Lucille Malone-Mayes, interview by Rebecca Sharpless, Waco, Texas, August 4, 1987, Baylor University Project, Baylor University Institute for Oral History, Carroll Library, Texas Collection, 102–103.

36. Ogretta McNeil, interview with Lisa Krissoff Boehm, Worcester, Massachusetts, January 6, 2003.

37. Jerliene "Creamy" McKinney, interview with Lisa Krissoff Boehm, Worcester, Massachusetts, January 9, 2003.

38. Minnie Chatman, interview with Lisa Krissoff Boehm and Elizabeth Cote, Detroit, Michigan, October 19, 2001.

39. Avezinner Dean, interview with Lisa Krissoff Boehm and Elizabeth Cote, Detroit, Michigan, June 25, 2002.

40. Barbara Purifoy-Seldon, interview with Lisa Krissoff Boehm and Elizabeth Cote, Southfield, Michigan, January 2, 2003.

41. Oral history memoir of Rubie Wilburn Evans, interview with Rebecca Sharpless, August 3, 1990, Waco, Texas, Family Life and Community History Project, Baylor University Institute for Oral History, 26, 38.

42. Bonnie Thornton Dill, *Across the Boundaries of Race and Class: An Exploration of Work and Family Among Black Female Domestics* (New York: Garland, 1994), 49.

43. Oral memoirs of Vivienne Lucille Malone-Mayes, interview by Rebecca Sharpless, Waco, Texas, August 4, 1987, Baylor University Project, Baylor University Institute for Oral History, Carroll Library, Texas Collection, 92.

44. Oral memoirs of Vivienne Lucille Malone-Mayes, interview by Rebecca Sharpless, Waco, Texas, August 4, 1987, Baylor University Project, Baylor University Institute for Oral History, Carroll Library, Texas Collection, 84.

CHAPTER SEVEN. EXPERIENCES WITH OTHER TYPES OF EMPLOYMENT

1. Mary White, interview with Lisa Krissoff Boehm and Elizabeth Cote, Detroit, Michigan, June 25, 2002.

2. Jerliene "Creamy" McKinney, interview with Lisa Krissoff Boehm, Worcester, Massachusetts, January 9, 2003.

3. Avezinner Dean, interview with Lisa Krissoff Boehm and Elizabeth Cote, Detroit, Michigan, June 25, 2002.

4. Julia Kirk Blackwelder, *Styling Jim Crow: African American Beauty Training During Segregation* (College Station: Texas A&M University Press, 2003), 140; Sherrie Tucker, review of *Styling Jim Crow: African American Beauty Training During Segregation* by Julia Kirk Blackwelder, *The Journal of American History* (September 2004): 673.

5. A'Lelia Bundles, *On Her Own Ground: The Life and Times of Madam C. J. Walker* (New York: Scribner, 2001), 20.

6. Avezinner Dean, interview with Lisa Krissoff Boehm and Elizabeth Cote, Detroit, Michigan, June 25, 2002.

7. Glennette Taylor (pseudonym), interview with Lisa Krissoff Boehm, Grand Rapids, Michigan, June 27, 2002.

8. Beatrice Jackson, interview with Lisa Krissoff Boehm and Elizabeth Cote, Detroit, Michigan, June 25, 2002.

9. Mary White, interview with Lisa Krissoff Boehm and Elizabeth Cote, Detroit, Michigan, June 25, 2002.

10. Bernita Howard (pseudonym), interview with Lisa Krissoff Boehm and Elizabeth Cote, Detroit, Michigan, July 9, 2003.

11. Faith Richmond (pseudonym), interview with Lisa Krissoff Boehm and Patricia Burke, Dorchester, Massachusetts, October 3, 2002.

12. Annie Benning, interview with Lisa Krissoff Boehm and Elizabeth Cote, Detroit, Michigan, June 26, 2002.

13. Rosetta "Rosa" Lewis Young, interview with Lisa Krissoff Boehm, Grand Rapids, Michigan, January 4, 2003.

14. Robert W. Thomas, *Life for Us Is What We Make It: Building Black Community in Detroit, 1915–1945* (Bloomington: Indiana University Press, 1992), 244–246; Karen Tucker Anderson, "Last Hired, First Fired: Black Women Workers During World War II," *Journal of American History* 69, no. 1 (June 1982): 82–97; "Biographical Sketch," in "Booster, 1931–1961" file, Box 1, Charles A. Hill Family Papers, Bentley Historical Library, University of Michigan, Ann Arbor.

15. Minnie Chatman, interview with Lisa Krissoff Boehm and Elizabeth Cote, Detroit, Michigan, October 19, 2001.

16. Annie Benning, interview with Lisa Krissoff Boehm and Elizabeth Cote, Detroit, Michigan, June 26, 2002.

17. Simone Landry (pseudonym), interview with Lisa Krissoff Boehm and Elizabeth Cote, Detroit, Michigan, June 26, 2002.

18. Mary White, interview with Lisa Krissoff Boehm and Elizabeth Cote, Detroit, Michigan, June 25, 2002.

19. Faith Richmond (pseudonym), interview with Lisa Krissoff Boehm and Patricia Burke, Dorchester, Massachusetts, October 3, 2002.

20. Rebecca Strom, interview with Lisa Krissoff Boehm, Audrey Kemp, and Patricia Burke, Dorchester, Massachusetts, October 12, 2002.

21. Liddie Williams, interview with Lisa Krissoff Boehm, Chicago, Illinois, November 16, 2001.

22. Oral memoirs of Maggie Langham Washington, interview with Marla Luffer, March 7, 1988, April 18, 1988, March 9, 1989, March 13, 1989, Waco, Texas, Texas Teachers Project, Baylor University Institute for Oral History, Texas Collection, Carroll Library (April 18, 1988, interview) 71, 76, 87, 99.

23. Alberta Hardy, interview with Lisa Krissoff Boehm and Elizabeth Cote, Detroit, Michigan, June 25, 2002.

24. Ella Sims, interview with Lisa Krissoff Boehm, Grand Rapids, Michigan, July 2, 2002.

25. Annie Evelyn Collins, interview with Elizabeth Cote, Detroit, Michigan, January 11, 2003.

26. Mattie Bell Fritz, interview with Lisa Krissoff Boehm and Elizabeth Cote, Detroit, Michigan, August 4, 2001.

27. Patricia Hill Collins, *Black Feminist Thought: Knowledge, Consciousness, and the Politics of Empowerment* (New York: Routledge, 2000), 46, 62.

28. Lillie Shelby (pseudonym), interview with Elizabeth Cote, Detroit, Michigan, July 31, 2002.

29. Ruth Margaret Covington, interview with Elizabeth Cote, Detroit, Michigan, September 12, 2002.

30. Mary White, interview with Lisa Krissoff Boehm and Elizabeth Cote, Detroit, Michigan, June 25, 2002.

31. Fannie Mae Kennedy, interview with Elizabeth Cote, Detroit, Michigan, July 31, 2002.

32. Mary Smith, interview with Lisa Krissoff Boehm, Audrey Kemp, and Patricia Burke, Dorchester, Massachusetts, October 12, 2002.

33. Rebecca Strom, interview with Lisa Krissoff Boehm, Audrey Kemp, and Patricia Burke, Dorchester, Massachusetts, October 12, 2002.

34. Glennette Taylor (pseudonym), interview with Lisa Krissoff Boehm, Grand Rapids, Michigan, June 27, 2002.

35. Jacqeline Dock (pseudonym), interview with Elizabeth Cote, Detroit, Michigan, January 11, 2003.

36. Alverrine Smith Parker, interview with Lisa Krissoff Boehm, Grand Rapids, Michigan, December 28, 2002.

37. Barbara Purifoy-Seldon, interview with Lisa Krissoff Boehm and Elizabeth Cote, Southfield, Michigan, January 2, 2003.

38. Lois Stevens, interview with Lisa Krissoff Boehm, Audrey Kemp, Joan Goss, and Patricia Burke, Worcester, Massachusetts, August 22, 2002.

39. Oral memoirs of Maggie Langham Washington, interview with Marla Luffer, March 7, 1988, and April 18, 1988, Waco, Texas, Texas Teachers Project, Baylor University Institute for Oral History, Texas Collection, Carroll Library (March interview), 110, and (April interview), 52–53. Also accessed tape of March 7, 1988, interview.

40. Gussie Nash, interview with Lisa Krissoff Boehm, Grand Rapids, Michigan, June 28, 2002.

41. "The Negro Population of Grand Rapids, Michigan: 1940. A Social Study Conducted for the Interracial Committee of the Council of Social Agencies," National Urban League, Department of Research, 26, in "Grand Rapids Urban League Studies" file, Grand Rapids Urban League Papers, Box 4, Bentley Historical Library, University of Michigan, Ann Arbor.

42. Thelma Lane, interview with Elizabeth Cote, Detroit, Michigan, December 27, 2002.

43. Minnie Chatman, interview with Lisa Krissoff Boehm and Elizabeth Cote, Detroit, Michigan, October 19, 2001.

44. Ruth Margaret Covington, interview with Elizabeth Cote, Detroit, Michigan, September 12, 2002; Beatrice Jackson, interview with Lisa Krissoff Boehm and Elizabeth Cote, Detroit, Michigan, June 25, 2002.

45. Ogretta McNeil, interview with Lisa Krissoff Boehm, Worcester, Massachusetts, January 6, 2003; Pamela Reponen, "Where Are They Now?," Holy Cross Magazine, vol. 34, no. 1 (Winter 2000).

46. Ella Sims, interview with Jane Idema and Bunny Voss, Grand Rapids, Michigan, May 1994, Greater Grand Rapids Women's History Council Oral Interviews, Grand Rapids Public Library Collections; Ella Sims, interview with Lisa Krissoff Boehm, Grand Rapids, Michigan, July 2, 2002.

47. Dorista "Dotty" Goldsberry, interview with Lisa Krissoff Boehm, Worcester, Massachuestts, April 26, 2007.

48. Lillie Shelby (pseudonym), interview with Elizabeth Cote, Detroit, Michigan, July 31, 2002; Fannie Mae Kennedy, interview with Elizabeth Cote, Detroit, Michigan, July 31, 2002.

49. Oral memoir of Lonnie Graves, interview with Anne Radford Phillips, October 10, 1991, Satin, Texas, Family Life and Community History Project, Baylor University Institute for Oral History, 41.

50. See oral history memoir of Ernestine G. Anderson, interview with Lois E. Myers, February 17, 1999, Riesel, Texas, Religion and Culture Project, Baylor University Institute for Oral History, 6.

51. Alberta Hardy, interview with Lisa Krissoff Boehm and Elizabeth Cote, Detroit, Michigan, June 25, 2002.

52. Rebecca Strom, interview with Lisa Krissoff Boehm, Audrey Kemp, and Patricia Burke, Dorchester, Massachusetts, October 12, 2002.

53. Anniese Moten, interview with Lisa Krissoff Boehm and Elizabeth Cote, Detroit, Michigan, June 22, 2000; Rosetta " Rosa" Lewis Young, interview with Lisa Krissoff Boehm, Grand Rapids, Michigan, January 4, 2003.

CHAPTER EIGHT. REFLECTIONS ON THE MIGRATION AND A LIFE OF WORK

1. Oral history memoir of Ernestine G. Anderson, interview with Lois E. Myers, March 30, 1999, Riesel, Texas, Religion and Culture Project, Baylor University Institute for Oral History, 118.

2. Gussie Nash, interview with Lisa Krissoff Boehm, Grand Rapids, Michigan, June 28, 2002.

3. Jerliene "Creamy" McKinney, interview with Lisa Krissoff Boehm, Worcester, Massachusetts, January 9, 2003; Annie Benning, interview with Lisa Krissoff Boehm and Elizabeth Cote, Detroit, Michigan, June 26, 2002; Alberta Hardy, interview with Lisa Krissoff Boehm and Elizabeth Cote, Detroit, Michigan, June 25, 2002.

4. Lillian Clark, interview with Lisa Krissoff Boehm and Elizabeth Cote, Southfield, Michigan, January 2, 2003.

5. Zenara Covington, interview with Elizabeth Cote, Detroit, Michigan, October 28, 2002.

6. Liddie Williams, interview with Lisa Krissoff Boehm, Chicago, Illinois, November 16, 2001. See Stewart E. Tolnay, "The African American 'Great Migration' and Beyond," *Annual Review of Sociology* 29 (August 2003): 209–232, and William W. Falk, Lany Hunt, and Matthew O. Hunt, "Return Migrations of African-Americans to the South: Reclaiming a Land of Promise, Going Home, or Both," *Rural Sociology* 69 (December 2004): 490–509.

7. Mary Smith, interview with Lisa Krissoff Boehm, Audrey Kemp, and Patricia Burke, Dorchester, Massachusetts, October 12, 2002.

8. Addie Smith, interview with Lisa Krissoff Boehm, Worcester, Massachusetts, July 14, 2002.

9. Jacqueline Dock (pseudonym), interview with Elizabeth Cote, Detroit, Michigan, January 11, 2003.

10. Glennette Taylor (pseudonym), interview with Lisa Krissoff Boehm, Grand Rapids, Michigan, June 27, 2002.

11. Barbara Purifoy-Seldon, interview with Lisa Krissoff Boehm and Elizabeth Cote, Southfield, Michigan, January 2, 2003.

12. Jacquie Lewis Kemp, interview with Lisa Krissoff Boehm and Elizabeth Cote, Southfield, Michigan, January 2, 2003.

13. White women's rates fell from 4.4 children per woman to 2.1 in the same period. See Andrea Tone, *Devices and Desires: A History of Contraceptives in America* (New York: Hill and Wang, 2002), 85.

14. Ruth Margaret Covington, interview with Elizabeth Cote, Detroit, Michigan, September 12, 2002.

15. Ruthe Winegarten, ed., *I Am Annie Mae: An Extraordinary Woman in Her Own Words: The Personal Story of a Black Texas Woman* (Austin: Rosegarden Press, 1983), 59, 65; Mary White, interview with Lisa Krissoff Boehm and Elizabeth Cote, Detroit, Michigan, June 25, 2002.

16. Oral history memoir of Olivia Watson Mitchell, interview with Deborah Jane Hoskins, November 11, 1992, Burton, Texas, Family Life and Community History Project, Baylor University Institute for Oral History, 40.

17. Daniel P. Moynihan, "The Negro Family: The Case for National Action," Office of Policy Planning and Research, United States Department of Labor, March 1965, accessed at http://www.dol.gov/oasam/programs/history/webid-meynihan.htm; Stewart E. Tolnay, "The Great Migration and Changes in the Northern Black Family, 1940–1990," *Social Forces* 75 (4) (June 1997): 1213, 1218–1220, 1223, 1232.

18. Tolnay, "The Great Migration and Changes in the Northern Black Family, 1940–1990," 1226, 1232–1233.

19. Ella Sims, interview with Lisa Krissoff Boehm, Grand Rapids, Michigan, July 2, 2002.

20. Mary White, interview with Lisa Krissoff Boehm and Elizabeth Cote, Detroit, Michigan, June 25, 2002; Simone Landry (pseudonym), interview with Lisa Krissoff Boehm and Elizabeth Cote, Detroit, Michigan, June 26, 2002; Faith Richmond (pseudonym), interview with Lisa Krissoff Boehm and Patricia Burke, Dorchester, Massachusetts, October 3, 2002.

21. Ruth Margaret Covington, interview with Elizabeth Cote, Detroit, Michigan, September 12, 2002; Zenara Covington, interview with Elizabeth Cote, Detroit, Michigan, October 28, 2002.

22. Ogretta McNeil, interview with Lisa Krissoff Boehm, Worcester, Massachusetts, January 6, 2003.

23. Alverrine Smith Parker, interview with Lisa Krissoff Boehm, Grand Rapids, Michigan, December 28, 2002.

24. Rosetta "Rosa" Lewis Young, interview with Lisa Krissoff Boehm, Grand Rapids, Michigan, January 4, 2003.

25. Florence Allison, interview with Elizabeth Cote, Detroit, Michigan, July 31, 2002.

26. Winegarten, ed., *I Am Annie Mae*, 113.

27. Rebecca Strom, interview with Lisa Krissoff Boehm, Audrey Kemp, and Patricia Burke, Dorchester, Massachusetts, October 12, 2002.

28. Jerliene "Creamy" McKinney, interview with Lisa Krissoff Boehm, Worcester, Massachusetts, January 9, 2003.

29. Ruth Margaret Covington, interview with Elizabeth Cote, Detroit, Michigan, September 12, 2002; Jacqueline Dock (pseudonym), interview with Elizabeth Cote, Detroit, Michigan, January 11, 2003; Minnie Chatman, interview with Lisa Krissoff Boehm and Elizabeth Cote, Detroit, Michigan, October 19, 2001; Addie Smith, interview with Lisa Krissoff Boehm, Worcester, Massachusetts, July 14, 2002.

30. Alverrine Parker, interview with Lisa Krissoff Boehm, Grand Rapids, Michigan, December 28, 2002.

31. Annie Evelyn Collins, interview with Elizabeth Cote, Detroit, Michigan, January 11, 2003.

32. Avezinner Dean, interview with Lisa Krissoff Boehm and Elizabeth Cote, Detroit, Michigan, June 25, 2002.

33. Alverrine Parker, interview with Lisa Krissoff Boehm, Grand Rapids, Michigan, December 28, 2002.

34. Ogretta McNeil, interview with Lisa Krissoff Boehm, Worcester, Massachusetts, January 6, 2003.

35. Patricia Hill Collins, *Black Feminist Thought: Knowledge, Consciousness, and the Politics of Empowerment* (New York: Routledge, 2000), 46.

36. Malcolm X, "The Bullet or the Ballot," April 1964, Cleveland, Ohio. Quotation can be found on the Web site http://www.hartford-hwp.com/archives/45a/index-bda.html, which utilized the book *Malcolm X Speaks* (pp. 23–44), George Breitman, ed., published in 1965 by Grove Weidenfeld, New York, NY.

37. Lillian Clark, interview with Lisa Krissoff Boehm and Elizabeth Cote, Southfield, Michigan, January 2, 2003.

38. Oral history memoir of Rubie Wilburn Evans, interview with Rebecca Sharpless, August 3, 1990, Waco, Texas, Family Life and Community History Project, Baylor University Institute for Oral History, 25.

39. Alverrine Parker, interview with Lisa Krissoff Boehm, Grand Rapids, Michigan, December 28, 2002.

40. M. J. Andersen, *Portable Prairie: Confessions of an Unsettled Midwesterner* (New York: Thomas Dunne Books/St. Martin's Griffin, 2006), 202.

41. See Marita Golden, *Migrations of the Heart: An Autobiography* (New York: Anchor Books, 2005). Golden moved to Africa with her husband, searching for an ancestral home that could offer a comfortable, modern lifestyle as well. After years of difficulties, she returned to the United States. Golden's mother, a domestic worker, and her family experiences drew her to interesting conclusions on migration, home, and U.S. race relations.

42. Sudhir Alladi Venkatesh, *American Project: The Rise and Fall of a Modern Ghetto* (Cambridge, MA: Harvard University Press, 2000), 11.

ACKNOWLEDGMENTS

1. See Lisa Krissoff Boehm, "Reverend Charles A. Hill: Leftist Religious-Based Activism in an Urban Context," presented at the New England American Studies Association meeting, Hartford, Connecticut, April 2003.

Bibliography

Primary Sources

ORIGINAL ORAL HISTORIES

Allison, Florence, interview with Elizabeth Cote, Detroit, Michigan, July 31, 2002.

Benning, Annie, interview with Lisa Krissoff Boehm and Elizabeth Cote, Detroit, Michigan, June 26, 2002.

Chatman, Minnie, interview with Lisa Krissoff Boehm and Elizabeth Cote, Detroit, Michigan, October 19, 2001.

Clark, Lillian, interview with Lisa Krissoff Boehm and Elizabeth Cote, Southfield, Michigan, January 2, 2003.

Collins, Annie Evelyn, interview with Elizabeth Cote, Detroit, Michigan, January 11, 2003.

Covington, Ruth Margaret, interview with Elizabeth Cote, Detroit, Michigan, September 12, 2002.

Covington, Zenara, interview with Elizabeth Cote, Detroit, Michigan, October 28, 2002.

Dean, Avezinner, interview with Lisa Krissoff Boehm and Elizabeth Cote, Detroit, Michigan, June 25, 2002.

Dock, Jacqueline (pseudonym), interview with Elizabeth Cote, Detroit, Michigan, January 11, 2003.

Fritz, Mattie Bell, interview with Lisa Krissoff Boehm and Elizabeth Cote, Detroit, Michigan, August 4, 2001.

Gantt, Sandra, interview with Elizabeth Cote, Detroit, Michigan, July 31, 2002.

Goldsberry, Dr. Dorista "Dotty," interview with Lisa Krissoff Boehm, Worcester, Massachusetts, April 26, 2007.

Hardy, Alberta, interview with Lisa Krissoff Boehm and Elizabeth Cote, Detroit, Michigan, June 25, 2002.

Howard, Bernita (pseudonym), interview with Lisa Krissoff Boehm and Elizabeth Cote, Detroit, Michigan, July 9, 2003.

Jackson, Beatrice, interview with Lisa Krissoff Boehm and Elizabeth Cote, Detroit, Michigan, June 25, 2002.

Kemp, Jacquie Lewis, interview with Lisa Krissoff Boehm and Elizabeth Cote, Southfield, Michigan, January 3, 2003.

Kennedy, Fannie Mae, interview with Elizabeth Cote, Detroit, Michigan, July 31, 2002.

Landry, Simone (pseudonym), interview with Lisa Krissoff Boehm and Elizabeth Cote, Detroit, Michigan, June 26, 2002.

Lane, Thelma, interview with Elizabeth Cote, Detroit, Michigan, December 27, 2002.

Lewis, Lottie (pseudonym), interview with Lisa Krissoff Boehm, Grand Rapids, Michigan, June 10, 2000.

Lewis, Willie Jean Clark, interview with Lisa Krissoff Boehm and Elizabeth Cote, Southfield, Michigan, January 2, 2003.

McKinney, Jerliene "Creamy," interview with Lisa Krissoff Boehm, Worcester, Massachusetts, January 9, 2003.

McNeil, Ogretta, interview with Lisa Krissoff Boehm, Worcester, Massachusetts, January 6, 2003.

Moten, Anniese, interview with Lisa Krissoff Boehm and Elizabeth Cote, Detroit, Michigan, June 22, 2000.

Nash, Gussie, interview with Lisa Krissoff Boehm, Grand Rapids, Michigan, June 28, 2002.

Parker, Alverrine Smith, interview with Lisa Krissoff Boehm, Grand Rapids, Michigan, December 28, 2002.

Purifoy-Seldon, Barbara, interview with Lisa Krissoff Boehm and Elizabeth Cote, Southfield, Michigan, January 2, 2003.

Richmond, Faith (pseudonym), interview with Lisa Krissoff Boehm and Patricia Burke, Dorchester, Massachusetts, October 3, 2002.

Shelby, Lillie (pseudonym), interview with Elizabeth Cote, Detroit, Michigan, July 31, 2002.

Sims, Ella, interview with Lisa Krissoff Boehm, Grand Rapids, Michigan, July 2, 2002.

Smith, Addie, interview with Lisa Krissoff Boehm, Worcester, Massachusetts, July 14, 2002.

Smith, Inez Crockett, interview with Lisa Krissoff Boehm, Grand Rapids, Michigan, January 4, 2003.

Smith, Mary, interview with Lisa Krissoff Boehm, Audrey Kemp, and Patricia Burke, Dorchester, Massachusetts, October 12, 2002.

Stevens, Lois, interview with Lisa Krissoff Boehm, Audrey Kemp, Joan Goss, and Patricia Burke, Worcester, Massachusetts, August 22, 2002.

Strom, Rebecca, interview with Lisa Krissoff Boehm, Audrey Kemp, and Patricia Burke, Dorchester, Massachusetts, October 12, 2002.

Taylor, Glennette (pseudonym), interview with Lisa Krissoff Boehm, Grand Rapids, Michigan, June 27, 2002.

White, Mary, interview with Lisa Krissoff Boehm and Elizabeth Cote, Detroit, Michigan, June 25, 2002.

Williams, Liddie, interview with Lisa Krissoff Boehm, Chicago, Illinois, November 16, 2001.

Woods, Esther Ward, interview with Lisa Krissoff Boehm, Grand Rapids, Michigan, June 10, 2000.

Young, Rosetta "Rosa" Lewis, interview with Lisa Krissoff Boehm, Grand Rapids, Michigan, January 4, 2003.

MANUSCRIPT COLLECTIONS

Archives of Labor and Urban Affairs, Wayne State University, Detroit, Michigan
  Fran Leeper Buss Collection, Oral Histories with Low Income and Minority Women

Baylor University, Institute for Oral History, Waco, Texas
  Texas Collection of Oral Histories
    Baylor University Project
    Family Life and Community History Project
    Religion and Culture Project
    Texas Teachers Project
    Waco and McClennan County Project

Bentley Historical Library, University of Michigan, Ann Arbor, Michigan
  Grand Rapids Urban League Papers
  Detroit Urban League Papers
  Reverend Charles A. Hill Family Papers

Burton Historical Collections, Detroit Public Library, Detroit, Michigan
  Michigan Chronicle

Grand Rapids Public Library, Grand Rapids, Michigan
  Grand Rapids Women's History Council, Oral History Collection

Schlesinger Library for the History of Women, Radcliffe College, Harvard University,
Cambridge, Massachusetts
  Black Women Oral History Project

OTHER PRIMARY SOURCES

Alcott, Louisa May. *An-Old Fashioned Thanksgiving and Other Stories*. New York: Penguin
  Classics, 1995.
———. *Work*. New York: Penguin Classics, 1994.
Aldin, Katherine. "Koko Taylor: Down in the Bottom of that Chitlin' Bucket." *Living Blues*
  (July–August 1993): 10–21.
Andersen, M. J. *Portable Prairie: Confessions of an Unsettled Midwesterner*. New York:
  Thomas Dunne Books/St. Martin's Griffin, 2006.
Angelou, Maya. *I Know Why the Caged Bird Sings*. New York: Bantam Books, 1993.
Burke, Solomon. *Home in Your Heart: The Best of Solomon Burke*. Atlantic Records, 1992.
Cross, June. *Secret Daughter: A Mixed-Race Daughter and the Mother Who Gave Her Away*.
  New York: Viking, 2006.
Frankl, Victor. *Man's Search for Meaning*. Boston: Beacon Press, 2006.
Gilman, Charlotte Perkins. *The Living Charlotte Perkins Gilman*. Madison: University of
  Wisconsin Press, 1935.

Golden, Marita. *Migrations of the Heart: An Autobiography*. New York: Anchor Books, 2005.

Hansberry, Lorraine. *To Be Young, Gifted, and Black: An Informal Autobiography*. New York: Signet, 1970.

Holiday, Billie, with William Dufty. *Lady Sings the Blues*. New York: Penguin, 1992.

hooks, bell. *Bone Black: Memories of Girlhood*. New York: Henry Holt, 1996.

Moody, Anne. *Coming of Age in Mississippi*. New York: Dell, 1968.

Moon, Elaine Latzman. *Untold Tales, Unsung Heroes: An Oral History of Detroit's African American Community, 1918–1967*. Detroit: Wayne State University Press, 1994.

Murray, Pauli. *The Autobiography of a Black Activist, Feminist, Lawyer, Priest, and Poet*. Knoxville: University of Tennessee Press, 1987.

Obama, Barack. *Dreams from My Father: A Story of Race and Inheritance*. New York: Three Rivers Press, 2004.

Parker, Gwendolyn M. *Trespassing: My Sojourn in the Halls of Privilege*. New York: Mariner Books, 1997.

Walker, Melissa. *Country Women Cope with Hard Times: A Collection of Oral Histories*. Columbia: University of South Carolina Press, 2004.

Wright, Richard. *Black Boy (American Hunger): A Record of Childhood and Youth*. New York: HarperPerennial, 1993.

UNPUBLISHED PAPERS

Anderson, Erin. "'Whose Name's on the Awning?': Women Diner Owners at Annie's Clark Brunch." Unpublished graduate seminar paper, November 30, 2006.

Appier, Janis. "Daughters of the Road: Public Identities versus Private Memories of Female Transients During the Great Depression." Presented at the Organization of American Historians Conference, Washington, D.C., April 2006.

Brown, Leslie. "The Most Striking Phenomenon of the Urban Negro Population." Presented at the Organization of American Historians Conference, Washington, D.C., April 2006.

Boehm, Lisa Krissoff. "Reverend Charles A. Hill: Leftist Religious-Based Activism in an Urban Context." Presented at the annual conference of the New England American Studies Association, Hartford, Connecticut, April 2003.

Fonza, Annalise. "Roll Call in the House: Politics and Gender in the Massachusetts House of Representatives." Presented at the annual conference of the Oral History Association, Oakland, California, October 26, 2007.

Secondary Sources

African American Lives. PBS Films, 2006.

Alexander, J. Trent. "The Great Migration in Comparative Perspective: Interpreting the Urban Origins of Southern Black Migrants to Depression-Era Pittsburgh." *Social Science History* 22, no. 3 (Fall 1998): 349–376.

Anderson, Bridget. *Doing the Dirty Work?: The Global Politics of Domestic Labour*. London: Zed Books, 2000.

Anderson, Elijah. *Streetwise: Race, Class and Change in an Urban Community*. Chicago: University of Chicago Press, 1990.

Anderson, Karen Tucker. "Last Hired, First Fired: Black Women Workers During World War II." *Journal of American History* 69, no. 1 (June 1982): 82–97.

Applebome, Peter. "Boarding Schools for Blacks Are Having a Resurgence in Popularity." *New York Times*, September 21, 1994, accessed at www.nytimes.com.

Aptheker, Bettina. *Woman's Legacy: Essays on Race, Sex, and Class in American History*. Amherst: University of Massachusetts Press, 1982.

Avila, Eric. *Popular Culture in the Age of White Flight: Fear and Fantasy in Suburban Los Angeles*. Berkeley: University of California Press, 2004.

Babson, Steve, with Ron Alpern, Dave Elsila, and John Reville. *Working Detroit*. Detroit: Wayne State University Press, 1986.

Bateson, Mary Catherine. *Composing a Life*. New York: Plume, 1989.

———. *Full Circles, Overlapping Lives: Culture and Generation in Transition*. New York: Ballantine Books, 2000.

Baum, Willa. *Transcribing and Editing Oral History*. Nashville: American Association for State and Local History, 1991.

Bazelton, Emily. "A Question of Resilience." *New York Times*, April 30, 2006.

Berlin, Ira, Marc Favreau, and Steven F. Miller. *Remembering Slavery: African Americans Talk About Their Personal Experiences of Slavery and Emancipation*. New York: The New Press, 1998.

Berry, Chad. *Southern Migrants, Northern Exiles*. Urbana: University of Illinois Press, 2000.

Blackwelder, Julia Kirk. *Styling Jim Crow: African American Beauty Training During Segregation*. College Station: Texas A&M Press, 2003.

Blewett, Mary H. *The Last Generation: Work and Life in the Textile Mills of Lowell, Massachusetts, 1910–1960*. Amherst: University of Massachusetts Press, 1990.

Bodnar, John. *Remaking America: Public Memory, Commemoration, and Patriotism in the Twentieth Century*. Princeton: Princeton University Press, 1993.

Bontemps, Arna, and Jack Conroy. *Anyplace But Here*. Columbia: University of Missouri Press, 1966.

Boyle, Kevin. *Arc of Justice: A Saga of Race, Civil Rights, and Murder in the Jazz Age*. New York: Henry Holt, 2004.

Bundles, A'Lelia. *On Her Own Ground: The Life and Times of Madam C. J. Walker*. New York: Scribner, 2001.

Cahill, Susan, ed. *Writing Women's Lives: An Anthology of Autobiographical Narratives by Twentieth Century American Women Writers*. New York: Harper Perennial, 1994.

Callahan, John F. *The Collected Essays of Ralph Ellison*. New York: The Modern Library, 2003.

Carrigan, William D. *The Making of a Lynching Culture: Violence and Vigilantism in Central Texas, 1836–1916*. Urbana: University of Illinois Press, 2004.

Chafe, William H., Raymond Gavin, and Robert Korstad, eds. *Remembering Jim Crow: African Americans Tell About Life in the Segregated South*. New York: The New Press, 2001.

Chang, Grace. *Disposable Domestics: Immigrant Women Workers in the Global Economy*. Cambridge, MA: South End Press, 2000.

Clark-Lewis, Elizabeth. *Living In, Living Out: African American Domestics and the Great Migration*. New York: Kodnasha America, 1994.

Cohen, Lizabeth. *A Consumers' Republic: The Politics of Mass Consumption in Postwar America*. New York: Vintage Books, 2003.

Collins, Patricia Hill. *Black Feminist Thought: Knowledge, Consciousness, and the Politics of Empowerment*. New York: Routledge, 2000.

Crawford-Tichawonna, Nicole. "Spelman Oral History Project Preserves Black Women's Wisdom." *The Crisis* (March–April 2005): 5–6.

Cravens, Patsy. *Leavin' a Testimony: Portraits from Rural Texas*. Austin: University of Texas Press, 2006.

Dill, Bonnie Thornton. *Across the Boundaries of Race and Class: An Exploration of Work and Family Among Black Female Domestic Workers*. New York: Garland, 1994.

Dodson, Howard, and Sylviane A. Dioue. *In Motion: The African-American Migration Experience*. Washington, D.C.: National Geographic, 2004.

Douglas, Davison M. *Jim Crow Moves North: The Battle Over Northern School Desegregation, 1865–1954*. New York: Cambridge University Press, 2005.

Dunaway, David K., and Willa K. Baum, eds. *Oral History: An Interdisciplinary Anthology*. Walnut Creek, CA: AltaMira Press, 1996.

Ehrenreich, Barbara, and Arlie Russell Hochschild, eds. *Global Woman: Nannies, Maids, and Sex Workers in the New Economy*. New York: Metropolitan Books, 2002.

Evans, Sara M. *Born for Liberty: A History of Women in America*. New York: Free Press, 1997.

Falk, William W., Lany Hunt, and Matthew O. Hunt. "Return Migrations of African-Americans to the South: Reclaiming a Land of Promise, Going Home, or Both." *Rural Sociology* 69 (December 2004): 490–509.

Faulkner, Audrey Olsen. *When I Was Comin' Up: An Oral History of Aged Blacks*. Hamden, CT: Archon Books, 1982.

Fentress, James, and Chris Wickham. *Social Memory: New Perspectives on the Past*. Cambridge: Blackwell, 1992.

Frey, William H. *The New Great Migration: Black Americans' Return to the South, 1965–2000*. Center on Urban and Metropolitan Policy, Brookings Institution, May 2004.

Friedan, Betty. *The Feminine Mystique*. New York: Norton, 1983.

Frisch, Michael. *A Shared Authority: Essays on the Craft and Meaning of Oral and Public History*. Albany: State University of New York Press, 1990.

Genovese, Eugene D. *Roll, Jordan, Roll: The World the Slaves Made*. New York: Vintage Books, 1972.

Giddings, Paula. *When and Where I Enter: The Impact of Black Women on Race and Sex in America*. New York: Amistad, 1984.

Gilligan, Carol. *In a Different Voice: Psychological Theory and Women's Development*. Cambridge: Harvard University Press, 1993.

Glenn, Evelyn Nakano. *Issei, Nisei, War Bride: Three Generations of Japanese American Women in Domestic Service*. Philadelphia: Temple University Press, 1986.

Gluck, Sherna Berger. *Rosie the Riveter Revisited: Women, the War, and Social Change*. New York: Penguin, 1988.

———. *Women's Words: The Feminist Practice of Oral History*. New York: Routledge, 1991.

"Go South, Young Man." *Atlantic*, September 2004, vol. 294, 42–48.

"*Goin' to Chicago*." California Newsreel, video, 1994.

Golden, Marita. *Long Distance Life*. New York: Doubleday, 1989.

Goodwin, Doris Kearns. *No Ordinary Time: Franklin and Eleanor Roosevelt: The Home Front in World War II*. New York: Touchstone, 1994.

Gottlieb, Peter. *Making Their Own Way: Southern Blacks' Migration to Pittsburgh, 1916–1930*. Urbana: University of Illinois Press, 1987.

Gregory, James N. *The Southern Diaspora: How the Great Migrations of Black and White Southerners Transformed America*. Chapel Hill: University of North Carolina Press, 2005.

Grele, Ronald J. *Envelopes of Sound: The Art of Oral History*. 2nd ed. Chicago: Precedent Publishing, 1995.

Grossman, James R. *Land of Hope: Chicago, Black Southerners, and the Great Migration*. Chicago: University of Chicago Press, 1989.

Grover, Kathryn. *Make a Way Somehow: African-American Life in a Northern Community*. Syracuse: Syracuse University Press, 1994.

Halpern, Rick. "Oral History and Labor History: A Historiographical Assessment After Twenty-Five Years." *Journal of American History*, vol. 85, no. 2 (September 1998): 596–610.

Hamburger, Robert, and Susan Fowler-Gallagher. *A Stranger in the House*. New York: MacMillan, 1978.

Hareven, Tamara, and Randolph Langenbach. *Amoskeag: Life and Work in an American Factory City*. New York: Pantheon, 1978.

Harley, Sharon, and The Black Women and Work Collaborative, eds. *Sister Circle: Black Women and Work*. New Brunswick: Rutgers University Press, 2002.

Harnick, Sheldon. "Housework," from *Free to Be . . . You and Me*. Artista Records, Incorporated, 1983.

Harrison, Alferdteen, ed. *Black Exodus: The Great Migration from the American South*. Jackson: University Press of Mississippi, 1991.

Harrison, Roderick J. "The Great Migration South." *New Crisis* 108 (July–August 2001): 20–21.

Higginbotham, Elizabeth, and Mary Romero, eds. *Women and Work: Exploring Race, Ethnicity, and Class*. Vol. 6. Thousand Oaks, CA: Sage, 1997.

Hine, Darlene Clark. "International Trends in Women's History and Feminism: Black Women's History, White Women's History: The Juncture of Race and Class." *Journal of Women's History* 4 (Fall 1992): 125–133.

———. *Hine Sight: Black Women and the Reconstruction of American History*. Bloomington: Indiana University Press, 1994.

Hine, Darlene Clark, and Kathleen Thompson. *A Shining Thread of Hope: The History of Black Women in America*. New York: Broadway Books, 1998.

Hirsch, Arnold R. *Making the Second Ghetto: Race and Housing in Chicago, 1840–1960*. Cambridge, U.K.: Cambridge University Press, 1990.

Hochschild, Arlie Russell. *Commercialization of Intimate Life: Notes From Home and Work*. Berkeley: University of California Press, 2003.

———. *The Managed Heart: Commercialization of Human Feeling*. Berkeley: University of California Press, 1983.

Hondagneu-Sotelo, Pierrette. *Doméstica: Immigrant Workers Cleaning and Caring in the Shadows of Affluence*. Berkeley: University of California Press, 2001.

hooks, bell. *Where We Stand: Class Matters*. New York: Routledge, 2000.

Hoy, SueEllen. *Good Hearts: Catholic Sisters in Chicago's Past*. Urbana: University of Illinois Press, 2006.

Hunter, Tera. *To 'Joy My Freedom: Southern Black Women's Lives and Labors After the Civil War*. Cambridge, MA: Harvard University Press, 1997.

Hurt, R. Douglas, ed. *African American Life in the Rural South, 1900–1950*. Columbia: University of Missouri Press, 2003.

Hyman, Rick, and Ronda Hyman. *My Texas Family: An Uncommon Journey to Prosperity*. Charleston, SC: Tempus, 2000.

Jelks, Randal Maurice. *African Americans in the Furniture City: The Struggle for Civil Rights in Grand Rapids*. Urbana: University of Illinois Press, 2006.

Jones, Charisse, and Kumea Shorter-Gooden. *Shifting: The Double Lives of Black Women in America. Based on the African American Women's Voices Project*. New York: First Perennial, 2004.

Jones, Jacqueline. *American Work: Four Centuries of Black and White Labor*. New York: W.W. Norton, 1998.

———. *The Dispossessed: America's Underclasses from the Civil War to the Present*. New York: Basic Books, 1992.

———. *Labor of Love, Labor of Sorrow: Black Women, Work, and Family from Slavery to the Present*. New York: Vintage Books, 1985.

Kane, Robert. "Free Agency and the Laws of Nature." *Journal of Consciousness Studies* 12 (2005): 46–53.

Katzman, David. *Seven Days a Week: Women and Domestic Service in Industrializing America*. New York: Oxford University Press, 1978.

Kessler-Harris, Alice. *Out to Work: A History of Wage-Earning Women in the United States*. New York: Oxford University Press, 1982.

———. *A Woman's Wage: Historical Meanings and Social Consequences*. Lexington: University Press of Kentucky, 1990.

K'Meyer, Tracey E., and A. Glenn Crothers. "'If I See Some of This Writing, I'm Going to Shoot You': Reluctant Narrators, Taboo Topics and the Ethical Dilemmas of the Oral Historian." *Journal of Oral History*, 34, no. 1 (Winter–Spring 2007): 71–94.

Korstad, Robert, and Nelson Lichtenstein. "Opportunities Found and Lost: Labor, Radicals, and the Early Civil Rights Movement." *Journal of American History* 75, no. 3 (December 1988): 786–811.

Kotlowitz, Alex. *There Are No Children Here: The Story of Two Boys Growing Up in the Other America*. New York: Anchor Books, 1991.

LaLee's Kin: The Legacy of Cotton. HBO Documentaries, American Undercover Series, 2001.

Lamb, Wally, ed. *Couldn't Keep It to Myself: Testimonials from Our Imprisoned Sisters/ Wally Lamb and the Women of York Correctional Institution*. New York: Reganbooks, 2003.

Lanman, Barry A., and Laura M. Wendling, eds. *Preparing the Next Generation of Oral Historians: An Anthology of Oral History Education*. Lanham, MD: AltaMira Press, 2006.

LeGoff, Jacques. *History and Memory*. Translated by Steven Randall and Elizabeth Claman. New York: Columbia University Press, 1992.

Lemann, Nicholas. *The Promised Land: The Great Black Migration and How It Changed America*. New York: Vintage Books, 1992.

Lemke-Santangelo, Gertrude. *Abiding Courage: African American Migrant Women and the East Bay Community*. Chapel Hill: University of North Carolina Press, 1996.

Madison, James H. *A Lynching in the Heartland: Race and Memory in America.* New York: Palgrave Macmillan, 2003.

Marks, Carole. *Farewell—We're Good and Gone: The Great Black Migration.* Bloomington: Indiana University Press, 1989.

Maxwell, Bill. "Black Boarding Schools Provide Haven of Discipline, Learning." *St. Petersburg Times,* March 30, 2003, accessed at www.sptimes.com.

McLaughlin, Emma, and Nicola Kraus. *The Nanny Diaries.* New York: St. Martin's Press, 2002.

Meier, August, and Elliott Rudwick. *Black Detroit and the Rise of the UAW.* New York: Oxford University Press, 1979.

Meyerowitz, Joanne. *Women Adrift: Independent Wage Earners in Chicago, 1880–1930.* Chicago: University of Chicago Press, 1988.

Misztal, Barbara. "Memory and Democracy." *American Behavioral Scientist* 48 (June 2005): 1320–1338.

———. *Theories of Social Remembering.* Philadelphia: Open University Press, 2003.

Moss, Simeon. "Life Is More than Work." *Cornell News,* February 23, 2001, accessed at www .news.cornell.edu.

Moynihan, Daniel. "The Negro Family: The Case for National Action." Office of Policy Planning and Research, United States Department of Labor, March 1965, accessed at http://www.dol.gov/oasam/programs/history/webid-meynihan.htm.

National Research Council. *A Common Destiny: Blacks and American Society.* Washington, D.C.: National Academy Press, 1989.

Palmer, Phyllis. *Domesticity and Dirt: Housewives and Domestic Servants in the United States.* Philadelphia: Temple University Press, 1989.

Parreñas, Rhacel Salazar. *Children of Global Migration: Transnational Families and Gendered Woes.* Stanford: Stanford University Press, 2005.

———. *Servants of Globalization: Women, Migration, and Domestic Work.* Palo Alto: Stanford University Press, 2001.

Passerini, Luisa. *Fascism in Popular Memory: The Cultural Experience of the Turin Working Class.* New York: Cambridge University Press, 1987.

Petry, Ann. *The Street.* Boston: Houghton Mifflin, 1974.

Phillips, Kimberley L. *AlabamaNorth: African-American Migrants, Community, and Working-Class Activism in Cleveland, 1915–45.* Urbana: University of Illinois Press, 1999.

Portelli, Alessandro. *The Death of Luigi Trastulli and Other Stories: Form and Meaning in Oral History.* Albany: State University of New York Press, 1990.

Pruitt, Bernadette. "The African American Experience in Slavery and Freedom: Black Urban History Revisited." *Journal of Urban History* 33, no. 6 (September 2007): 1033–1047.

Raboteau, Albert J. *Canaan Land: A Religious History of African Americans.* New York: Oxford University Press, 1999.

Radford, Dr. Garry H., Sr. *African American Heritage in Waco, Texas: Life Stories of Those Who Believed They Could Overcome Impediments.* Austin: Eakin Press, 2000.

Rafkin, Louise. *Other People's Dirt: A Housecleaner's Curious Adventure.* New York: Plume, 1998.

Reponen, Pamela. "Where Are They Now?" *Holy Cross Magazine,* vol. 34, no. 1 (Winter 2000).

Ritchie, Donald A. *Doing Oral History*. New York: Twayne, 1995.

Rogers, Kim Lacy. *Life and Death in the Delta: African American Narratives of Violence, Resilience, and Social Change*. New York: Palgrave Macmillan, 2006.

Rollins, Judith. *Between Women: Domestics and Their Employers*. Philadelphia: Temple University Press, 1985.

Romero, Mary. *Maid in the U.S.A.* 10th anniversary edition. New York: Routledge, 2002.

Rosen, Ellen Israel. *Bitter Choices: Blue Collar Women In and Out of Work*. Chicago: University of Chicago Press, 1987.

Ross, Robert. *Slaves to Fashion: Poverty and Abuse in the New Sweatshops*. University of Michigan Press, 2004.

Sharpless, Rebecca. *Fertile Ground, Narrow Choices: Women on Texas Cotton Farms, 1900–1940*. Chapel Hill: University of North Carolina Press, 1999.

Sitton, Thad, and James H. Conrad. *Freedom Colonies: Independent Black Texans in the Time of Jim Crow*. Austin: University of Texas Press, 2005.

Sitton, Thad, and Dan K. Utley. *From Can See to Can't: Texas Cotton Farmers on the Southern Prairies*. Austin: University of Texas Press, 1997.

Sklar, Robert. "Reinforcing Black-Jewish Bonds." *Detroit Jewish News*, as quoted in the "10 Minutes of Torah," *Union for Reform Judaism*, August 25, 2006.

Smith, J. B. "The Waco Horror: Grisly 1916 Lynching Still Overshadows City." *Waco Tribune Herald* Archive, March 6, 2005.

Smith, Lillian. *Killers of the Dream*. New York: W. W. Norton, 1949.

Smith, Sidonie. *A Poetics of Women's Autobiography: Marginality and the Fictions of Self-Representation*. Bloomington: Indiana University Press, 1987.

Sommer, Barbara W., and Mary Kay Quinlan. *The Oral History Manual*. Walnut Creek, CA: AltaMira Press, 2002.

Sugrue, Thomas. *The Origins of the Urban Crisis: Race and Inequality in Postwar Detroit*. Princeton: Princeton University Press, 1996.

Sutherland, Daniel. *Americans and Their Servants: Domestic Service in the United States from 1800 to 1920*. Baton Rouge: Louisiana State University Press, 1981.

Takaki, Ronald. *A Different Mirror: A History of Multicultural America*. Boston: Little, Brown, and Company, 1993.

Terkel, Studs. *Coming of Age: Growing Up in the Twentieth Century*. New York: The New Press, 1995.

Thomas, June Manning. *Redevelopment and Race: Planning a Finer City in Postwar Detroit*. Baltimore: Johns Hopkins University Press, 1997.

Thomas, Richard W. *Life for Us Is What We Make It: Building Black Community in Detroit, 1915–1945*. Bloomington: Indiana University Press, 1992.

Thompson, Heather Ann. *Whose Detroit? Politics, Labor, and Race in a Modern American City*. Ithaca: Cornell University Press, 2001.

Thomson, Alistair. "Fifty Years On: An International Perspective on Oral History." *Journal of American History* 85, no. 2 (September 1998): 581–595.

Tolnay, Stewart E. "The African American 'Great Migration' and Beyond." *Annual Review of Sociology* 29 (August 2003): 209–232.

———. "The Great Migration and Changes in the Northern Black Family, 1940–1990." *Social Forces* 75 (June 1997): 1213–1238.

Tolnay, Stewart E., Katherine Curtis White, Kyle D. Crowder, and Robert M. Adelman. "Distances Traveled During the 'Great Migration': An Analysis of Racial Differences Among Male Migrants." *Social Science History* 29 (Winter 2005): 523–548.

Tone, Andrea. *Devices and Desires: A History of Contraceptives in America.* New York: Hill and Wang, 2002.

Tonkin, Elizabeth. *Narrating Our Pasts: The Social Construction of Oral History.* Cambridge Studies in Oral and Literate Culture. Cambridge: Cambridge University Press, 1992.

Trent, Alexander J. "The Great Migration in Comparative Perspective: Interpreting the Urban Origins of Southern Black Migrants to Depression-Era Pittsburgh." *Social Science History* 22 (Fall 1998): 349–376.

Trotter, Joe William, Jr. *Black Milwaukee: The Making of an Industrial Proletariat, 1915–1945.* Urbana: University of Illinois Press, 1985.

Trotter, Joe William, Jr., ed. *The Great Migration in Historical Perspective: New Dimensions of Race, Class, and Gender.* Bloomington: Indiana University Press, 1991.

Trotter, Joe W., Jr., Earl Lewis, and Tera W. Hunter. *The African American Urban Experience.* New York: Palgrave Macmillan, 2004.

Tucker, Sherrie. Review of *Styling Jim Crow: African American Beauty Training During Segregation* by Julia Kirk Blackwelder. *Journal of American History* (September 2004): 673.

Tucker, Susan. *Telling Memories Among Southern Women: Domestic Workers and Their Employers in the Segregated South.* Baton Rouge: Louisiana State University Press, 1988.

Turner, Elizabeth Hutton. *Jacob Lawrence, The Migration Series.* Washington, D.C.: The Rappahannock Press and the Phillips Collection, 1993.

Ulrich, Laurel Thatcher. *A Midwife's Tale: The Life of Martha Ballard. Based on Her Diary.* New York: Alfred A. Knopf, 1990.

Venkatesth, Sudhir Alladi. *American Project: The Rise and Fall of a Modern Ghetto.* Cambridge, MA: Harvard University Press, 2000.

———. *Off the Books: The Underground Economy of the Urban Poor.* Cambridge, MA: Harvard University Press, 2006.

Walker, Melissa. *All We Knew Was to Farm: Rural Women in the Upcountry South, 1919–1914.* Baltimore: Johns Hopkins Press, 2000.

———. *Southern Farmers and Their Stories: Memory and Meaning in Oral History.* Lexington: University Press of Kentucky, 2006.

West, Dorothy. *The Living Is Easy.* New York: The Feminist Press, 1996.

White, Deborah Gray. *Ar'n't I a Woman?: Female Slaves in the Plantation South.* New York: W. W. Norton and Company, 1985.

White, Hayden. *The Content of Form: Narrative Discourse and Historical Representation.* Baltimore: Johns Hopkins University Press, 1987.

White, Katherine J. Curtis. "Women in the Great Migration." *Social Science History* 29 (Fall 2005): 413–455.

White, Katherine J. Curtis, Kyle Crowder, Stewart E. Tolnay, and Robert M. Adelman. "Race, Gender, and Marriage: Destination Selection During the Great Migration." *Demography* 42 (May 2005): 215–241.

Widick, B. J. *Detroit: City of Race and Class Violence.* Detroit: Wayne State University Press, 1989.

Wilson, Francille Rusan. *The Segregated Scholars: Black Social Scientists and the Creation of Black Labor Studies, 1890–1950.* Charlottesville: University of Virginia, 2006.

Winegarten, Ruthe. *I Am Annie Mae: An Extraordinary Woman in Her Own Words*. Austin: Rosegarden Press, 1983.

Wolcott, Victoria W. *Remaking Respectability: African American Women in Interwar Detroit*. Chapel Hill: University of North Carolina Press, 2001.

Woodford, Frank B., and Arthur M. Woodford. *All Our Yesterdays: A Brief History of Detroit*. Detroit: Wayne State University Press, 1969.

Woodson, Carter G. *A Century of Negro Migration*. Mineola, NY: Dover Publications, 2002.

Yow, Valerie Raleigh. *Recording Oral History: A Guide for the Humanities and Social Sciences*. Walnut Creek, CA: AltaMira Press, 2005.

Index